Chris Amaris, MCSE
Alec Minty, MCSE

Edited by
Rand Morimoto

Microsoft®

SQL Server 2005

Management and Administration

SAMS | 800 East 96th Street, Indianapolis, Indiana 46240 USA

ISBN-13: 978-0-672-32956-2
ISBN-10: 0-672-32956-5

Mistry, Ross.
  SQL server 2005 management and administration / Ross Mistry, Chris Amaris, Alec Minty ; edited by Rand Morimoto.
    p. cm.
  ISBN 0-672-32956-5
  1. SQL server. 2. Database management. 3. Client/server computing. I. Amaris, Chris. II. Minty, Alec. III. Morimoto, Rand. IV. Title.
QA76.9.D3M57885 2007
005.75'85—dc22

                                   2007035788

Printed in the United States of America

First Printing: October 2007

Trademarks

All terms mentioned in this book that are known to be trademarks or service marks have been appropriately capitalized. Sams Publishing cannot attest to the accuracy of this information. Use of a term in this book should not be regarded as affecting the validity of any trademark or service mark.

Warning and Disclaimer

Every effort has been made to make this book as complete and as accurate as possible, but no warranty or fitness is implied. The information provided is on an "as is" basis. The authors and the publisher shall have neither liability nor responsibility to any person or entity with respect to any loss or damages arising from the information contained in this book.

Bulk Sales

Sams Publishing offers excellent discounts on this book when ordered in quantity for bulk purchases or special sales. For more information, please contact

    U.S. Corporate and Government Sales
    1-800-382-3419
    corpsales@pearsontechgroup.com

For sales outside of the U.S., please contact

    International Sales
    international@pearsoned.com

Editor-in-Chief
Karen Gettman

Acquisitions Editor
Neil Rowe

Development Editor
Mark Renfrow

Managing Editor
Gina Kanouse

Project Editor
Betsy Harris

Copy Editors
Chuck Hutchinson
Barbara Hacha

Indexer
Heather McNeill

Proofreader
Kathy Bidwell

Technical Editors
Todd Meister
J. Boyd Nolan

Publishing Coordinator
Cindy Teeters

Multimedia Coordinator
Dan Scherf

Book Designer
Gary Adair

Compositor
Nonie Ratcliff

Contributing Writers
Robert Jue, MCSE

Shirmattie Seenarine

Michael Noel, MS-MVP, MCSE

Contents at a Glance

> **Note**
>
> The following parts are located online. Go to www.informit.com/title/
> 9780672329562 to register your book and access these files.

Contents

Part II Managing SQL Server 2005

Note

The following parts are located online. Go to www.informit.com/title/
9780672329562 to register your book and access these files.

Part IV SQL Server 2005 Overview

Part V Disaster Recovery and High Availability

About the Authors

Ross Mistry, MCTS, MCDBA, MCSE Ross Mistry has spent more than nine years in the computer industry and is a seasoned veteran in the Silicon Valley. As a Principal Consultant and Partner with Convergent Computing (CCO), located in the San Francisco Bay area, he has had the opportunity to work with the SQL Server product for two to three years before versions release to the public. His primary focus is implementing and maintaining SQL Server in large enterprise environments with a global presence. He also focuses on Active Directory, Exchange, Operations Manager, and specializes in SQL Server High Availability. He has a strong understanding of how these technologies integrate with one another.

Ross has held several roles with Sams Publishing, including lead author, contributing writer, and technical editor. His works include *SQL Server 2005 Unleashed*, *SQL Server 2005: Changing the Paradigm*, *Exchange Server 2007 Unleashed*, *SharePoint 2007 Unleashed*, *SharePoint 2003 Unleashed*, and *ISA Server 2004 Unleashed*. Ross has also written numerous whitepapers and keynote seminars on SQL Server, in which he leverages best practices based on his experiences in the industry.

Chris Amaris, MCSE, CISSP Chris Amaris is the Chief Technology Officer and cofounder of Convergent Computing. He has more than 20 years' experience consulting for Fortune 500 companies, leading companies in the technology selection, design, planning, and implementation of complex Information Technology projects. Chris has worked with Microsoft SQL since version 4.2 on OS/2. He specializes in database management, messaging, security, performance tuning, systems management, and migration. A Certified Information Systems Security Professional (CISSP) with an Information System Security Architecture Professional (ISSAP) concentration, Certified Homeland Security (CHS III), Windows 2003 MCSE, Novell CNE, Banyan CBE, and a Certified Project Manager, Chris is also an author, writer, and technical editor for a number of IT books, including *Network Security for Government and Corporate Executives*, *Windows Server 2003 Unleashed*, *Exchange Server 2007 Unleashed*, and *Microsoft Operations Manager 2005 Unleashed*. Chris presents on Messaging, Operations Management, Security, and Information Technology topics worldwide.

Alec Minty, MCSE   Alec Minty is a Senior Consultant with Convergent Computing located in the San Francisco Bay area. He has more than 10 years' industry experience with extensive knowledge designing and implementing enterprise class solutions for a diverse array of organizations. Alec has been an early adopter of database technologies, operations management, systems management, and security technologies. He specializes in designing, implementing, migrating, and supporting complex infrastructures for a variety of large utility, telecommunications, and engineering organizations. Alec's experience spans the business and technology areas; he has in-depth experience in the deployment, migration, and integration of key business technologies such as SQL Server, Windows, Exchange, Active Directory, ISA, and Identity Management. Alec is coauthor of *MOM 2005 Unleashed* and is a contributing author on *Exchange Server 2007 Unleashed* and *ISA 2004 Unleashed,* all published by Sams Publishing.

Dedication

I dedicate this book to my wife, Sherry. I want to thank you for not only contributing to this book, but for your continuous love, patience, support, and understanding. We have come a long way since we met, and I am very grateful and value everything you do. I also dedicate this book to my children, Kyanna and Kaden, who inspire me to always achieve my best. And to my parents, Aban and Keki, thank you both for instilling good values, work ethics, and for always encouraging higher education.
—Ross Mistry, MCTS, MCDBA, MCSE

I dedicate this book to my wife, Sophia, whose love and support I cherish. And to my children, Michelle, Megan, Zoe, Zachary, and Ian, for whom all the long hours of writing is worthwhile. I also dedicate this book to my mother, Mary Jane Amaris, who always encouraged and supported me in my quest for knowledge.
—Chris Amaris, MCSE, CISSP

I dedicate this book to my beautiful wife, Sonia, whose patience knows no limits. And to my father David, who always believed in me.
—Alec Minty, MCSE

Acknowledgments

Ross Mistry, MCTS, MCDBA, MCSE I would like to provide special thanks to Rand Morimoto for your ongoing leadership and mentoring since I joined CCO. I have truly grown under your wing.

To my wife, thanks again for contributing and helping me on this book. I know it was not easy being pregnant, working, writing, and taking care of the family in my absence. Thanks for your extreme patience and cooperation during this time. I am sure Chapter 1 will be a constant reminder of the day we rushed to the hospital for the birth of our son, Kaden.

Thanks to both Alec Minty and Chris Amaris for taking on the coauthor role. I appreciate your involvement and commitment to turning the content around in a very short time frame. I could not have taken on this endeavor without your efforts.

Finally, I can't forget the team at Sams Publishing; thanks again for providing me with an opportunity to be involved in another best-selling title.

Chris Amaris, MCSE, CISSP I would like to thank Ross Mistry for leading the development of this book and for providing endless guidance, even while going through the exhausting joy of having his second child during the project. And I would like to thank Rand Morimoto for keeping the whole project on track, without which we would have never gotten off the ground.

And I want to thank my wife, Sophia, for her support during the long hours of writing. And especially to my children for keeping up with their schoolwork and getting excellent grades, even when I could not help them with their homework because of looming chapter deadlines.

Alec Minty, MCSE I would like to thank Rand Morimoto for all the opportunities and leadership. I would also like to thank Ross Mistry and Chris Amaris for being great people and a pleasure to work with on this project.

We Want to Hear from You!

As the reader of this book, *you* are our most important critic and commentator. We value your opinion and want to know what we're doing right, what we could do better, what areas you'd like to see us publish in, and any other words of wisdom you're willing to pass our way.

As a Senior Acquisitions Editor for Sams Publishing, I welcome your comments. You can email or write me directly to let me know what you did or didn't like about this book—as well as what we can do to make our books better.

Please note that I cannot help you with technical problems related to the topic of this book. We do have a User Services group, however, where I will forward specific technical questions related to the book.

When you write, please be sure to include this book's title and author as well as your name, email address, and phone number. I will carefully review your comments and share them with the author and editors who worked on the book.

Email: feedback@samspublishing.com

Mail: Neil Rowe
            Senior Acquisitions Editor
            Sams Publishing
            800 East 96th Street
            Indianapolis, IN 46240 USA

Reader Services

Visit our website and register this book at www.informit.com/title/ 9780672329562 for convenient access to any updates, downloads, or errata that might be available for this book.

Introduction

What Is in This Book?

SQL Server 2005 is Microsoft's product for providing data management and analysis solutions for the enterprise. SQL Server 2005 is a trusted database platform that provides organizations a competitive advantage by allowing them to obtain faster results and make better business decisions. This is all achievable via a new management studio, deep integration with Visual Studio, and a comprehensive business intelligence platform. The product is modular and broken down into the following technologies: database engine, Analysis Services, Integration Services, replication, Reporting Services, Notification Services, service broker, and full-text search.

Because SQL Server has been released for almost two years, organizations are well versed in designing, installing, and implementing SQL Server 2005. However, database administrators are currently facing new challenges, such as how to manage, administer, and monitor their new SQL Server infrastructure based on industry best practices. This book improves the experience these professionals have working with SQL Server.

In addition, this book provides detailed guidance on management, administration, and monitoring. These areas remain challenges to database administrators who have SQL Server already deployed. Because this book assumes the reader has experience with installing SQL Server 2005, it goes far beyond the basic installation and setup information found in hundreds of other resources. Instead, it focuses on day-to-day administration, best practices, and industry case scenarios. All topics and examples covered in this book are based on the new features and functionality included with SQL Server 2005 Service Pack 2.

The topic of SQL Server 2005 administration and management is huge, and the size of this book reflects the size of the topic. To help orient you within the book, the following sections describe the various parts and chapters in the book. This book is focused on the administration and management of SQL Server 2005. Apropos to that, the content of the book does not cover the topics of planning, design and installation of the SQL Server 2005 platform. These are broad and deep topics, with books such as *Microsoft SQL Server 2005 Unleashed* (Sams Publishing, ISBN: 0672328240) dedicated to those topics alone.

However, to facilitate running the steps given throughout the book, the appendix lists the basic steps needed to set up a lab environment with the databases needed to test the procedures given in the book.

Part I: Administering SQL Server Components

The administration of the different components of the SQL Server 2005 platform is covered in this part. The administration encompasses the configuration of the various components, including initial setup and adjustments during normal operations.

The chapters in this part cover the administration of the main components of SQL Server 2005.

Chapter 1: Administering SQL Server 2005 Database Engine

This chapter focuses on configuring the Database Services component, managing the server, and configuring the database properties of the SQL Server Database Engine after the product has been installed. Managing server and database configuration settings such as memory, processor performance, auditing, database files, and auto growth is covered in depth.

Chapter 2: Administering SQL Server 2005 Analysis Services

This chapter focuses on configuring the Analysis Services component for OLAP and business intelligence. Administration topics on how to manage OLAP cubes, partitions, database processing, and storage models are covered.

Chapter 3: Administering SQL Server 2005 Reporting Services

Reporting Services is a set of technologies utilized to deliver enterprise web-enabled reporting functionality. This chapter focuses on configuring the Reporting Services component, including Internet Information Services (IIS), and managing the Reporting Services settings.

Chapter 4: Administering SQL Server 2005 Notification Services

This chapter focuses on configuring the Notification Services component and managing the notification engine for generating and sending notifications.

Chapter 5: Administering SQL Server 2005 Integration Services

Integration Services is Microsoft's extract, transform, and load (ETL) tool for data warehousing and is a platform for building high-performance data integration and workflow solutions. This chapter focuses on installing the Integration Services component, saving packages, and executing packages.

Chapter 6: Administering SQL Server Replication

SQL Server Replication is another way of distributing data from a source SQL Server to either one or more target SQL Servers. The chapter focuses on replication components and provides a prelude to the different types of replication scenarios a database administrator can manage, such as Snapshot, Merge, and Transactional Replication.

Step-by-step replication configurations including the new peer-to-peer replication scenario, a new form of high availability, are discussed.

Part II: Managing SQL Server 2005

This part of the book covers the management of the SQL Server 2005 platform. This discussion encompasses the routine tasks needed to ensure that the platform is operating properly and at optimal levels.

This part includes topics such as conducting health checks, performing maintenance tasks, and generating indexes to keep SQL Server 2005 operating efficiently.

Chapter 7: Conducting a SQL Server 2005 Health Check

On many occasions IT professionals inherit a SQL Server implementation when they join an organization or through consultants who design and implement the SQL solution at their organization. It is imperative these IT professionals manage the new SQL installation; however, they are often unaware of what to review.

This chapter focuses on how to conduct a SQL Server health check so the organization's implementation is fully optimized and adheres to industry best practices.

Chapter 8: SQL Server 2005 Maintenance Practices

This chapter focuses on managing and maintaining a SQL Server environment. This discussion includes creating maintenance plans to check database integrity, shrink databases, reorganize indexes, and update statistics. Additionally, this chapter provides recommendations on daily, weekly, monthly, and quarterly maintenance practices that should be conducted on SQL Servers. This also includes managing replication.

Chapter 9: Managing and Optimizing SQL Server 2005 Indexes

Similar to an index found in a book, an index in SQL Server is utilized for fast retrieval of data from tables. This chapter focuses on index concepts, ways to design the appropriate index strategy to maximize performance, and data retrieval. In addition, the chapter shares best practices on implementing, managing, and optimizing indexes.

Chapter 10: Managing Full-Text Catalogs

More and more of today's applications leverage full text-search capabilities of the back-end database. This chapter covers administration concepts associated with full-text search and step-by-step instructions for performing tasks such as enabling full-text indexing, removing full-text indexing, and best practices for managing full-text indexing.

Chapter 11: Creating Packages and Transferring Data

A common database administrator task is to transfer data or databases between source and target environments. This chapter focuses on importing, exporting, and transforming data and databases via SQL Server Management Studio and the newly created ETL tool, Integration Services. The chapter covers using packages to transfer data and to automate maintenance tasks.

Part III: Securing the SQL Server Implementation

In this part of the book, the important topic of security is addressed.

Chapter 12: Hardening a SQL Server 2005 Environment

It is imperative that database administrators secure both the SQL Server installation and the data residing in it. This chapter provides an overview on how to manage a secure SQL Server implementation based on industry best practices so that vulnerabilities and security breaches are minimized.

The following security topics are covered: reducing the attack surface, applying security to dimensions, and securing reports. This chapter goes above and beyond the database engine and also focuses on the other SQL components such as Analysis Services, Reporting Services, and Internet Information Services.

Chapter 13: Administering SQL Server Security

This chapter focuses on how to administer SQL Server 2005 for role-based access and SQL authorization. This includes leveraging Active Directory to integrate the SQL Server 2005 security into the enterprise directory for single sign-on capabilities.

Chapter 14: Encrypting SQL Server Data and Communications

Securing SQL Server 2005 data while it is in databases and while it is being transmitted over the network is of paramount importance. In today's highly security conscious environment, it is critical that the database platform provide mechanisms to safeguard the integrity and confidentiality of the data no matter where it is.

This chapter covers the various options and methods of ensuring the confidentiality and integrity of the data both on the server and while on the network. The chapter also covers how to integrate with Public Key Infrastructure (PKI) to effectively use certificates in securing the data.

> **Note**
>
> The following sections can be found online. Go to www.informit.com/title/9780672329562 to register your book and download these chapters.

Part IV: SQL Server 2005 Overview

Chapter 15: SQL Server 2005 Technology Primer

This introductory chapter to SQL Server 2005 provides an overview of features, editions, and components. The Enterprise Edition is covered, as are the Database Services, Analysis Services, Reporting Services, Notification Services, and Integration Services.

Chapter 16: Tools of the Trade

This chapter covers the tools used to administer and manage SQL Server 2005. The platform encompasses a multitude of tools, so sometimes even finding the right tool is hard, even if you know the name of the tool.

This chapter gives you a complete overview of all the tools used to administer and manage SQL. This allows you to quickly access all the tools referred to in the book and provides a detailed understanding of the arsenal of SQL tools at your disposal.

Part V: Disaster Recovery and High Availability

Accidents happen, even in a perfect world. It is critical that the appropriate mechanism be put in place to ensure that SQL Server 2005 service can stay operational and recover from potential mishaps in the environment.

The chapters in this part address backup, recovery, and the various methods by which SQL Server 2005 can provide high availability.

Chapter 17: Backing Up and Restoring the SQL Server 2005 Environment

This chapter focuses on backing up and restoring the SQL Server 2005 environment, which includes the database engine, Analysis Services, Integration Services, and Reporting Services.

In addition, this chapter also focuses on recovery models, backup and restore best practices, and ways to correctly leverage technologies such as restoring a database to the point of failure, conducting online restores, and creating database snapshots.

Chapter 18: Administering and Managing Failover Clustering

How to configure and manage a single-instance and multiple-instance high-availability failover cluster is the main focus of this chapter. The chapter includes detailed step-by-step configurations on both single-instance and multiple-instance clusters, including building a Windows Server 2003 cluster. It also includes best practices from the field.

Chapter 19: Administering and Managing Database Mirroring

Most database administrators believe database mirroring is the top new feature of SQL Server 2005. This chapter focuses on configuring and managing database mirroring so that organizations can enhance the availability of their SQL Server systems, increase business continuity, and maintain a HOT standby of their database in another geographic location. The chapter includes detailed step-by-step configurations on all three database mirroring modes: high availability, high protection, and high performance.

This chapter also includes best practices from the field, case studies, and discussions of how to integrate database mirroring with other high-availability alternatives such as failover clustering and how to recover from a failed server.

Chapter 20: Administering and Managing Log Shipping

The focus of this chapter is on configuring and managing log shipping. The chapter includes step-by-step instructions on how to configure and maintain one or more "warm" standby databases typically referred to as *secondary databases*. Similar to the other chapters in this part, this chapter includes real-world examples and industry best practices.

Part VI: Monitoring and Troubleshooting SQL Server

When SQL Server 2005 is in operation, it is critical to monitor, tune, and troubleshoot the platform. Understanding what the platform is doing and resolving issues as they arise are key for the long-term health of the database environment.

Chapter 21: Monitoring SQL Server 2005

This chapter covers the native tools included with SQL Server for monitoring the SQL environment, including databases, performance, and auditing. Detailed explanations on how to utilize performance and optimization tools such as the Performance Monitor and SQL Server Profiler are included in this chapter. The chapter also covers using Operations Manager 2007 to monitor SQL Server 2005. This is Microsoft's premier tool for monitoring the Windows operating system and applications such as SQL Server 2005.

Chapter 22: Performance Tuning and Troubleshooting SQL Server 2005

After the SQL Server 2005 platform is placed in operation and is being monitored, it is important to take action on the findings that are uncovered. It is often difficult to anticipate real-world loads during the development phase of application deployment; thus, it is critical to adjust the parameters of the SQL Server 2005 platform to optimize the performance after it is deployed. And frequently you need to troubleshoot the performance of SQL Server 2005 to address problems that are uncovered by the monitoring.

This chapter focuses on how to tune and troubleshoot the performance of the SQL Server 2005 platform and the specific components, including the use of the Database Engine Tuning Advisor. The chapter also covers industry best practices in tuning the SQL platform.

Appendix

The appendix, "SQL Server 2005 Management and Administration," covers additional material that was not directly in line with the content of the book but that is potentially important to readers when using the examples given in the book.

The topics include the following:

- Basic installation of SQL Server 2005 including all components
- Installation of SQL Server 2005 Service Pack
- Configuration of the AdventureWorks OLTP sample database
- Configuration of the AdventureWorks OLAP sample database
- Basic installation of Certificate Service
- Basic installation of Operations Manger 2007

The appendix provides you with step-by-step instructions on how to conduct a basic installation of all the components that make up SQL Server 2005 and the supporting services such as certificate service. The installation is a prerequisite for following the examples in this book.

PART I

Administering SQL Server Components

IN THIS PART

CHAPTER 1

Administering SQL Server 2005 Database Engine

Although SQL Server 2005 is composed of numerous components, one component is often considered the foundation of the product. The Database Engine is the core service for storing, processing, and securing data for the most challenging data systems. Likewise, it provides the foundation and fundamentals for the majority of the core database administration tasks. As a result of its important role in SQL Server 2005, it is no wonder that the Database Engine is designed to provide a scalable, fast, and highly available platform for data access and other components.

This chapter focuses on administering the Database Engine component and managing the SQL server properties and database properties based on SQL Server 2005 Service Pack 2. Database Engine management tasks are also covered.

Even though the chapter introduces and explains all the management areas within the Database Engine, you are directed to other chapters for additional information. This is a result of the Database Engine component being so large and intricately connected to other features.

What's New for the Database Engine with Service Pack 2

- Upon the launch of SQL Server 2005, the installation of SQL Server 2005 Integration Services (SSIS) was warranted if organizations wanted to run maintenance plans. This has since changed. Integration Services is no longer required because maintenance plans are now a fully supported feature within the Database Engine.

■ Many enhancements have been made to maintenance plans in SQL Server 2005 with SP2 including support for environments with multiple servers, logging on to remote servers, and providing users with multiple schedules. Previously, maintenance plans could be run only on a server-only installation after SSIS was installed.

■ A new storage format is introduced with the release of SP2 to increase functionality and minimize disk space. The new format, known as vardecimal, stores decimal and numeric data as variable-length columns.

■ Logon triggers are included with SP2. In addition, SQL Server 2005 Enterprise Edition now has a Common Criteria Compliance Enabled option that follows common criteria for evaluating SP_CONFIGURE. See Common Criteria Certification in Books Online for more information.

■ Supported with SQL Server 2005 SP2 for the first time is the sqllogship application, which is responsible for operations involving backup, copy, and restore procedures. In addition, the application performs cleanup jobs for a log shipping configuration.

■ Plan cache improvements are part of the Database Engine enhancements with SP2, improving system performance and improving the use of the physical memory readily available to database pages. Plan cache improvements also can return XML query plans with an XML nesting level greater than or equal to 128 by using the new sys.dm_exec_ text_query_plan table-valued function. This feature is supported in SQL Server 2005 Express Edition SP2.

■ SQL Server Management Studio (SSMS) for Relational Engine features the following:

   ■ The Table.CheckIdentityValue() is supported only with the Express Edition of SQL Server 2005 and is involved in generating a schema name for an object name that meets the criteria.

   ■ The Column.AddDefaultConstraint() feature is also supported only with the Express Edition of SQL Server 2005. This feature is responsible for working against table columns for SQL Server 2000 database instances.

Administering SQL Server 2005 Server Properties

The SQL Server Properties dialog box is the main place you, as database administrator, configure server settings specifically tailored toward a SQL Server Database Engine installation.

You can invoke the Server Properties for the Database Engine by following these steps:

1. Choose Start, All Programs, Microsoft SQL Server 2005, SQL Server Management Studio.

2. Connect to the Database Engine in Object Explorer.

3. Right-click SQL Server and then select Properties.

The Server Properties dialog box includes eight pages of Database Engine settings that can be viewed, managed, and configured. The eight Server Properties pages include

- General
- Memory
- Processors
- Security
- Connections
- Database Settings
- Advanced
- Permissions

> **Note**
>
> Each SQL Server Properties setting can be easily scripted by clicking the Script button. The Script button is available on each Server Properties page. The Script options available include Script Action to New Query Window, Script Action to a File, Script Action to Clipboard, and Script Action to a Job.

The following sections provide examples and explanations for each page within the SQL Server Properties dialog box.

Administering the General Page

The first Server Properties page, General, includes mostly informational facts pertaining to the SQL Server 2005 installation, as illustrated in Figure 1.1. Here, you can view the following items: SQL Server Name; Product Version such as Standard, Enterprise, or 64 Bit; Windows Platform such as Windows 2000 or Windows 2003; SQL Server Version Number; Language Settings; Total Memory in the Server; Number of Processors; Root Directory; Server Collation; and whether the installation is clustered.

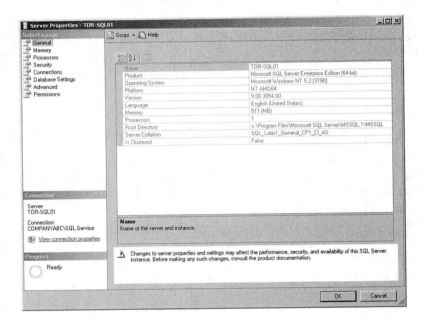

FIGURE 1.1
Administering the Server Properties General page.

Administering the Memory Page

Memory is the second page within the Server Properties dialog box. As shown in Figure 1.2, this page is broken into two sections: Server Memory Options and Other Memory Options. Each section has additional items to configure to manage memory; they are described in the following sections.

Administering the Server Memory Options

The Server Memory options are

- **Use AWE to Allocate Memory**—If this setting is selected, the SQL Server installation leverages Address Windowing Extensions (AWE) memory.

■ **Minimum and Maximum Memory**—The next items within Memory Options are for inputting the minimum and maximum amount of memory allocated to a SQL Server instance. The memory settings inputted are calculated in megabytes.

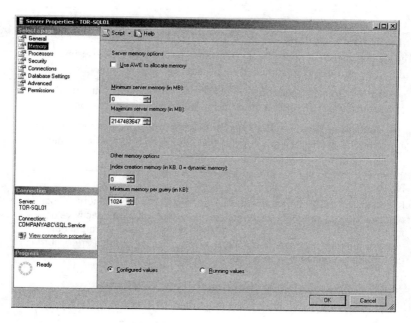

FIGURE 1.2
Administering the Server Properties Memory page.

The following Transact-SQL (TSQL) code can be used to configure Server Memory Options:

```
sp_configure 'awe enabled', 1
RECONFIGURE
GO
sp_configure 'min server memory', "MIN AMOUNT IN MB"
RECONFIGURE
GO
sp_configure 'max server memory', "MAX AMOUNT IN MB"
RECONFIGURE
GO
```

> **Note**
>
> The information in double quotes needs to be replaced with a value specific to this example. This applies to this Transact-SQL example and subsequent ones to follow in this chapter.

Other Memory Options

The second section, Other Memory Options, has two memory settings tailored toward index creation and minimum memory per query:

- **Index Creation Memory**—This setting allocates the amount of memory that should be used during index creation operations.

- **Minimum Memory Per Query**—This setting specifies the minimum amount of memory in kilobytes that should be allocated to a query.

> **Note**
>
> It is best to let SQL Server dynamically manage both the memory associated with index creation and for queries. However, you can specify values for index creation if you're creating many indexes in parallel. You should tweak the minimum memory setting per query if many queries are occurring over multiple connections in a busy environment.

Use the following TSQL statements to configure Other Memory Options:

```
sp_configure 'index create memory, "NUMBER IN KB"
RECONFIGURE
GO
sp_configure 'min memory per query, "NUMBER IN KB"
RECONFIGURE
GO
```

Administering the Processors Page

The Processor page, shown in Figure 1.3, should be used to administer or manage any processor-related options for the SQL Server 2005 Database Engine. Options include threads, processor performance, affinity, and parallel or symmetric processing.

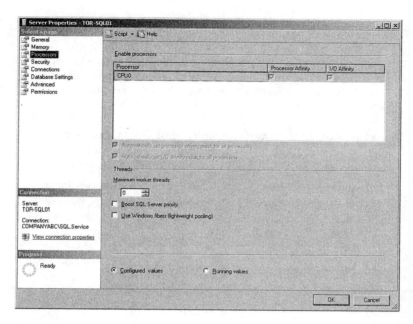

FIGURE 1.3
Administering the Server Properties Processor page.

Enabling Processors

Similar to a database administrator, the operating system is constantly multi-tasking. Therefore, the operating system moves threads between different processors to maximize processing efficiency. You should use the Processor page to administer or manage any processor-related options such as parallel or symmetric processing. The processor options include

- **Enable Processors**—The two processor options within this section include Processor Affinity and I/O Affinity. Processor Affinity allows SQL Server to manage the processors; therefore, processors are assigned to specific threads during execution. Similar to Processor Affinity, the I/O Affinity setting informs SQL Server on which processors can manage I/O disk operations.

> **Tip**
>
> SQL Server 2005 does a great job of dynamically managing and optimizing processor and I/O affinity settings. If you need to manage these settings manually, you should reserve some processors for threading and others for I/O operations. A processor should not be configured to do both.

- **Automatically Set Processor Affinity Mask for All Processors**—If this option is enabled, SQL Server dynamically manages the Processor Affinity Mask and overwrites the existing Affinity Mask settings.

- **Automatically Set I/O Affinity Mask for All Processors**—Same thing as the preceding option: If this option is enabled, SQL Server dynamically manages the I/O Affinity Mask and overwrites the existing Affinity Mask settings.

Threads

The following Threads items can be individually managed to assist processor performance:

- **Maximum Worker Threads**—The Maximum Worker Threads setting governs the optimization of SQL Server performance by controlling thread pooling. Typically, this setting is adjusted for a server hosting many client connections. By default, this value is set to 0. The 0 value represents dynamic configuration because SQL server determines the number of worker threads to utilize. If this setting will be statically managed, a higher value is recommended for a busy server with a high number of connections. Subsequently, a lower number is recommended for a server that is not being heavily utilized and has a small number of user connections. The values to be entered range from 10 to 32,767.

- **Boost SQL Server Priority**—Preferably, SQL Server should be the only application running on the server; thus, it is recommended to enable this check box. This setting tags the SQL Server threads with a higher priority value of 13 instead of the default 7 for better performance. If other applications are running on the server, performance of those applications could degrade if this option is enabled because those threads have a lower priority.

- **Use Windows Fibers (Lightweight Pooling)**—This setting offers a means of decreasing the system overhead associated with extreme context switching seen in symmetric multiprocessing environments. Enabling this option provides better throughput by executing the context switching inline.

Note

Enabling fibers is tricky because it has its advantages and disadvantages on performance. This is derived from how many processors are running on the server. Typically, performance gains occur if the system is running a lot of CPUs, such as more than 16; whereas performance may decrease if there are only 1 or 2 processors. To ensure the new settings are optimized, it is a best practice to monitor performance counters, after changes are made.

These TSQL statements should be used to set processor settings:

```
sp_configure 'affinity mask', "VALUE";
RECONFIGURE;
GO

sp_configure 'affinity 1/0 mask', :"VALUE";
RECONFIGURE;
GO
sp_configure 'lightweight pooling', "0 or 1";
RECONFIGURE;
GO

sp_configure 'max worker threads', :"INTEGER VALUE";
RECONFIGURE;
GO

sp_configure 'priority boost', "0 or 1";
RECONFIGURE;
GO
```

Administering the Security Page

The Security page, shown in Figure 1.4, maintains server-wide security configuration settings. These SQL Server settings include Server Authentication, Login Auditing, Server Proxy Account, and Options.

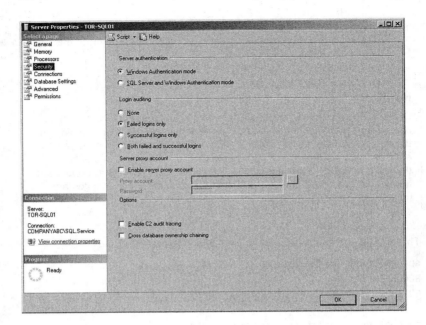

FIGURE 1.4
Administering the Server Properties Security page.

Server Authentication

The first section in the Security page focuses on server authentication. At present, SQL Server 2005 continues to support two modes for validating connections and authenticating access to database resources: Windows Authentication Mode and SQL Server and Windows Authentication Mode. Both of these authentication methods provide access to SQL Server and its resources.

> **Note**
>
> During installation, the default authentication mode is Windows. The authentication mode can be changed after the installation.

The **Windows Authentication Mode** setting is the default Authentication setting and is the recommended authentication mode. It tactfully leverages Active Directory user accounts or groups when granting access to SQL Server. In this mode, you are given the opportunity to grant domain or local server users access to the database server without creating and managing a separate SQL Server account. Also worth mentioning, when Windows Authentication mode is active, user accounts are subject to enterprise-wide policies enforced by the Active Directory domain, such as complex passwords, password history, account lockouts, minimum password length, maximum password length, and the Kerberos protocol. These enhanced and well-defined policies are always a plus to have in place.

The second Authentication Option is **SQL Server and Windows Authentication (Mixed) Mode.** This setting, which is regularly referred to as *mixed mode authentication*, uses either Active Directory user accounts or SQL Server accounts when validating access to SQL Server. SQL Server 2005 has introduced a means to enforce password and lockout policies for SQL Server login accounts when using SQL Server Authentication. The new SQL Server polices that can be enforced include password complexity, password expiration, and account lockouts. This functionality was not available in SQL Server 2000 and was a major security concern for most organizations and database administrators. Essentially, this security concern played a role in helping define Windows authentication as the recommended practice for managing authentication in the past. Today, SQL Server and Windows Authentication mode may be able to successfully compete with Windows Authentication mode.

Note

Review the authentication sections in Chapter 12, "Hardening a SQL Server 2005 Environment," for more information on authentication modes and which mode should be used as a best practice.

Login Auditing

Login Auditing is the focal point on the second section on the Security page. You can choose from one of the four Login Auditing options available: None, Failed Logins Only, Successful Logins Only, and Both Failed and Successful Logins.

Tip

When you're configuring auditing, it is a best practice to configure auditing to capture both failed and successful logins. Therefore, in the case of a system breach or an audit, you have all the logins captured in an audit file. The drawback to this option is that the log file will grow quickly and will require adequate disk space. If this is not possible, only failed logins should be captured as the bare minimum.

Server Proxy Account

You can enable a server proxy account in the Server Proxy section of the Security page. The proxy account permits the security context to execute operating system commands by the impersonation of logins, server roles, and database roles. If you're using a proxy account, you should configure the account with the least number of privileges to perform the task. This bolsters security and reduces the amount of damage if the account is compromised.

Additional Security Options

Additional security options available in the Options section of the Security page are

- **Enable Common Criteria Compliance**—When this setting is enabled, it manages database security. Specifically, it manages features such as Residual Information Protection (RIP), controls access to login statistics, and enforces restrictions where, for example, the column titled GRANT cannot override the table titled DENY.

> ### Note
> Enable Common Criteria Compliance is a new feature associated with SQL Server 2005 Service Pack 2 Enterprise Edition.

- **Enable C2 Audit Tracing**—When this setting is enabled, SQL Server allows the largest number of the success and failure objects to be audited. The drawback to capturing for audit data is that it can degrade performance and take up disk space.

- **Cross Database Ownership Chaining**—Enabling this setting allows cross database ownership chaining at a global level for all databases. Cross database ownership chaining governs whether the database can be accessed by external resources. As a result, this setting should be enabled only when the situation is closely managed because several serious security holes would be opened.

Administering the Connections Page

The Connections page, as shown in Figure 1.5, is the place where you examine and configure any SQL Server settings relevant to connections. The Connections page is broken up into two sections: Connections and Remote Server Connections.

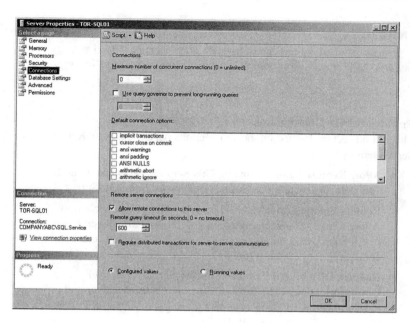

FIGURE 1.5
Administering the Server Properties Connections page.

Connections

The Connections section includes the following settings:

- **Maximum Number of Concurrent Connections**—The first setting determines the maximum number of concurrent connections allowed to the SQL Server Database Engine. The default value is 0, which represents an unlimited number of connections. The value used when configuring this setting is really dictated by the SQL Server hardware such as the processor, RAM, and disk speed.

- **Use Query Governor to Prevent Long-Running Queries**—This setting creates a stipulation based on an upper limit criteria specified on the time period in which a query can run.

- **Default Connection Options**—For the final setting, you can choose from approximately 16 advanced connection options that can be either enabled or disabled, as shown in Figure 1.5.

> **Note**
>
> For more information on each of the default Connection Option settings, refer to SQL Server 2005 Books Online. Search for the topic "Server Properties Connections Page."

Remote Server Connections

The second section located on the Connections page focuses on Remote Server settings:

- **Allow Remote Connections to This Server**— If enabled, the first option allows remote connections to the specified SQL Server.

- **Remote Query Timeout**—The second setting is available only if Allow Remote Connections is enabled. This setting governs how long it will take for a remote query to terminate. The values that can be configured range from 0 to 2,147,483,647. Zero represents infinite.

- **Require Distributed Transactions for Server-to-Server Communication**—The final setting controls the behavior and protects the transactions between systems by using the Microsoft Distributed Transaction Coordinate (MS DTC).

Administering the Database Settings Page

The Database Settings page, shown in Figure 1.6, contains configuration settings that each database within the SQL Server instance will inherit. The choices available on this page are broken out by Fill Factor, Backup and Restore, Recovery, and Database Default Locations.

Default Index Fill Factor

The Default Index Fill Factor specifies how full SQL Server should configure each page when a new index is created. The default setting is 0, and the ranges are between 0 and 100. The 0 value represents a table with room for growth, whereas a value of 100 represents no space for subsequent insertions without requiring page splits. A table with all reads typically has a higher fill factor, and a table that is meant for heavy inserts typically has a low fill factor. The value 50 is ideal when a table has plenty of reads and writes. This setting is global to all tables within the Database Engine.

For more information on fill factors, refer to Chapter 8, "SQL Server 2005 Maintenance Practices" and Chapter 9, "Managing and Optimizing SQL Server 2005 Indexes."

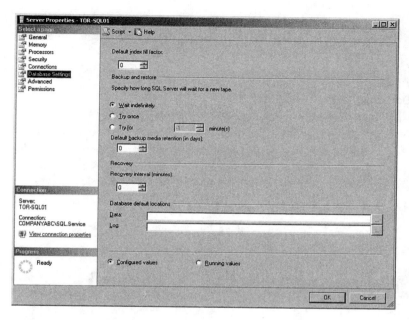

FIGURE 1.6
Administering the Server Properties Database Settings page.

Backup and Restore

The Backup and Restore section of the Database Settings page includes

- **Specify How Long SQL Server Will Wait for a New Tape**—The first setting governs the time interval SQL Server will wait for a new tape during a database backup process. The options available are Wait Indefinitely, Try Once, or Try for a specific number of minutes.

- **Default Backup Media Retention**—This setting is a system-wide configuration that affects all database backups, including the translation logs. You enter values for this setting in days, and it dictates the time to maintain and/or retain each backup medium.

Recovery

The Recovery section of the Database Settings page consists of

- **Recovery Interval (Minutes)**—Only one Recovery setting is available. This setting influences the amount of time, in minutes, SQL

Server will take to recover a database. Recovering a database takes place every time SQL Server is started. Uncommitted transactions are either committed or rolled back.

Database Default Locations

Options available in the Database Default Locations section are

- **Data and Logs**—The two folder paths for Data and Log placement specify the default location for all database data and log files. Click the ellipses on the right side to change the default folder location.

Administering the Advanced Page

The Advanced Page, shown in Figure 1.7, contains the SQL Server general settings that can be configured.

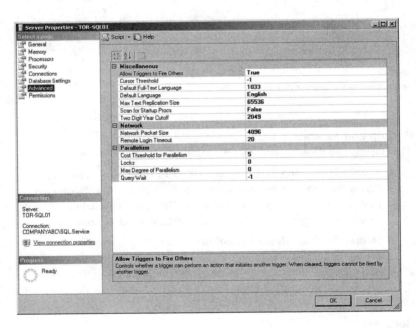

FIGURE 1.7
Administering the Server Properties Advanced Settings page.

Miscellaneous Settings

Options available on the Miscellaneous section of the Advanced page are

- **Allow Triggers to Fire Others**—If this setting is configured to True, triggers can execute other triggers. In addition, the nesting level can be up to 32 levels. The values are either True or False.

- **Cursor Threshold**—This setting dictates the number of rows in the cursor that will be returned for a result set. A value of 0 represents that cursor keysets are generated asynchronously.

- **Default Full-Text Language**—This setting specifies the language to be used for full-text columns. The default language is based on the language specified during the SQL Server instance installation.

- **Default Language**—This setting is also inherited based on the language used during the installation of SQL. The setting controls the default language behavior for new logins.

- **Max Text Replication Size**—This global setting dictates the maximum size of text and image data that can be inserted into columns. The measurement is in bytes.

- **Scan for Startup Procs**—The configuration values are either True or False. If the setting is configured to True, SQL Server allows stored procedures that are configured to run at startup to fire.

- **Two Digit Year Cutoff**—This setting indicates the uppermost year that can be specified as a two-digit year. Additional years must be entered as a four digits.

Network Settings

Options available on the Network section of the Advanced page are

- **Network Packet Size**—This setting dictates the size of packets being transmitted over the network. The default size is 4096 bytes and is sufficient for most SQL Server network operations.

- **Remote Login Timeout**—This setting determines the amount of time SQL Server will wait before timing out a remote login. The default time is 30 seconds, and a value of 0 represents an infinite wait before timing out.

Parallelism Settings

Options available on the Parallelism section of the Advanced page are

- **Cost Threshold for Parallelism**—This setting specifies the threshold above which SQL Server creates and runs parallel plans for queries. The cost refers to an estimated elapsed time in seconds required to run the serial plan on a specific hardware configuration. Set this option only on symmetric multiprocessors. For more information, search for "cost threshold for parallelism option" in SQL Server Books Online.

- **Locks**—The default for this setting is 0, which indicates that SQL Server is dynamically managing locking. Otherwise, you can enter a numeric value that sets the utmost number of locks to occur.

- **Max Degree of Parallelism**—This setting limits the number of processors (up to a maximum of 64) that can be used in a parallel plan execution. The default value of 0 uses all available processors, whereas a value of 1 suppresses parallel plan generation altogether. A number greater than 1 prevents the maximum number of processors from being used by a single query execution. If a value greater than the number of available processors is specified, however, the actual number of available processors is used. For more information, search for "max degree of parallelism option" in SQL Server Books Online.

- **Query Wait**—This setting indicates the time in seconds a query will wait for resources before timing out.

Administering the Permissions Page

The Permissions Page, as shown in Figure 1.8, includes all the authorization logins and permissions for the SQL Server instance. You can create and manage logins and/or roles within the first section. The second portion of this page displays the Explicit permission based on the login or role.

For more information on permissions and authorization to the SQL Server 2005 Database Engine, refer to Chapter 13, "Administering SQL Server Security."

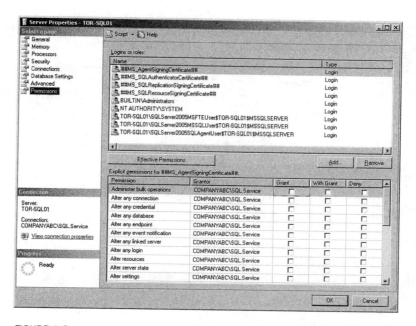

FIGURE 1.8
Administering the Server Properties Permissions page.

Administering the SQL Server Database Engine Folders

After you configure the SQL Server properties, you must manage the SQL Server Database Engine folders and understand what and how the settings should be configured. The SQL Server folders contain an abundant number of configuration settings that need to be managed on an ongoing basis. The main SQL Server Database Engine top-level folders, as shown in Figure 1.9, consist of

- Databases
- Security
- Server Objects
- Replication
- Management
- Notification Services

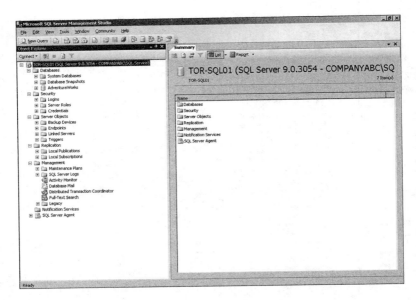

FIGURE 1.9
Viewing the Database Engine folders.

Each folder can be expanded upon, which leads to more subfolders and thus more management of settings. The following sections discuss the folders within the SQL Server tree, starting with the Databases folder.

Administering the Databases Folder

The Databases folder is the main location for administering system and user databases. Management tasks that can be conducted by right-clicking the Database folder consist of creating new databases, attaching databases, restoring databases, and creating custom reports.

The Databases folder contains subfolders as a repository for items such as system databases, database snapshots, and user databases. When a Database folder is expanded, each database has a predefined subfolder structure that includes configuration settings for that specific database. The database structure is as follows: Tables, Views, Synonyms, Programmability, Service Broker, Storage, and Security.

Let's start by examining the top-level folders and then the subfolders in subsequent sections.

Administering the System Databases Subfolder

The System Databases subfolder is the first folder within the Database tree. It consists of all the system databases that make up SQL Server 2005. The system databases consist of

- **Master Database**—The master database is an important system database in SQL Server 2005. It houses all system-level data, including system configuration settings, login information, disk space, stored procedures, linked servers, the existence of other databases, along with other crucial information.

- **Model Database**—The model database serves as a template for creating new databases in SQL Server 2005. The data residing in the model database is commonly applied to a new database with the Create Database command. In addition, the tempdb database is re-created with the help of the model database every time SQL Server 2005 is started.

- **Msdb Database**—Used mostly by the SQL Server Agent, the msdb database stores alerts, scheduled jobs, and operators. In addition, it stores historical information on backups and restores, SQL Mail, and Service Broker.

- **Tempdb**—The tempdb database holds temporary information, including tables, stored procedures, objects, and intermediate result sets. Each time SQL Server is started, the tempdb database starts with a clean copy.

Tip

It is a best practice to conduct regular backups on the system databases. In addition, if you want to increase performance and response times, it is recommended to place the tempdb data and transaction log files on different volumes from the operating system drive. Finally, if you don't need to restore the system databases to a point in failure, you can set all recovery models for the system databases to Simple.

Administering the Database Snapshots Subfolder

The second top-level folder under Databases is Database Snapshots. Database snapshots are a new technology introduced in SQL Server 2005. A *snapshot* allows you to create a point-in-time read-only static view of a database. Typical scenarios for which organizations use snapshots consist of running reporting queries, reverting databases to state when the snapshot was created in the event of an error, and safeguarding data by creating a snapshot before large bulk inserts occur. All database snapshots are created via TSQL syntax and not the Management Studio.

For more information on creating and restoring a database snapshot, view the database snapshot sections in Chapter 17, "Backing Up and Restoring the SQL Server 2005 Environment" (online).

Administering a User Databases Subfolder

The rest of the subfolders under the top-level Database folder are all the user databases. The user database is a repository for all aspects of an online transaction processing (OLTP) database, including administration, management, and programming. Each user database running within the Database Engine shows up as a separate subfolder. From within the User Database folder, you can conduct the following tasks: backup, restore, take offline, manage database storage, manage properties, manage database authorization, shrink, and configure log shipping or database mirroring. In addition, from within this folder, programmers can create the OLTP database schema, including tables, views, constraints, and stored procedures.

> **Note**
>
> Database development tasks such as creating a new database, views, or stored procedures are beyond the scope of this book, as this book focuses only on administration and management.

Administering the Security Folder

The second top-level folder in the SQL Server instance tree, Security, is a repository for all the Database Engine securable items meant for managing authorization. The sublevel Security Folders consist of

- **Logins**—This subfolder is used for creating and managing access to the SQL Server Database Engine. A login can be created based on a Windows or SQL Server account. In addition, it is possible to configure password policies, server role and user mapping access, and permission settings.

- **Server Roles**—SQL Server 2005 leverages the role-based model for granting authorization to the SQL Server 2005 Database Engine. Predefined SQL Server Roles already exist when SQL Server is deployed. These predefined roles should be leveraged when granting access to SQL Server and databases.

- **Credentials**—Credentials are used when there is a need to provide SQL Server authentication users an identity outside SQL Server. The principal rationale is for creating credentials to execute code in assemblies and for providing SQL Server access to a domain resource.

For more information on the Security folder, authorization, permission management, and step-by-step instructions on how to create logins, server roles, and credentials, refer to Chapter 13.

Administering the Server Objects Folder

The third top-level folder located in Object Explorer is called Server Objects. Here, you create backup devices, endpoints, linked servers, and triggers.

Backup Devices

Backup devices are a component of the backup and restore process when working with OLTP databases. Unlike the earlier versions of SQL Server, backup devices are not needed; however, they provide a great way for managing all the backup data and transaction log files for a database under one file and location.

To create a backup device, follow these steps:

1. Choose Start, All Programs, Microsoft SQL Server 2005, SQL Server Management Studio.

2. In Object Explorer, first connect to the Database Engine, expand the desired server, and then expand the Server Objects folder.

3. Right-click the Backup Devices folder and select New Backup Device.

4. In the Backup Device dialog box, specify a Device Name and enter the destination file path, as shown in Figure 1.10. Click OK to complete this task.

This TSQL syntax can be used to create the backup device:

```
USE [master]
GO
EXEC master.dbo.sp_addumpdevice  @devtype = N'disk',
@logicalname = N'Rustom''s Backup Device',
@physicalname = N'C:\Rustom''s Backup Device.bak'
GO
```

For more information on using backup devices and step-by-step instructions on backing up and restoring a SQL Server environment, refer to Chapter 17.

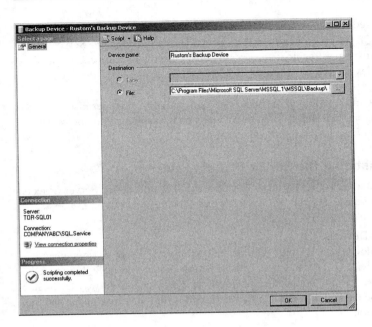

FIGURE 1.10
Creating a backup device with SQL Server Management Studio.

Endpoints

Applications must use a specific port that SQL Server has been configured to listen on to connect to a SQL Server instance. In the past, the authentication process and handshake agreement were challenged by the security industry as not being robust or secure. Therefore, SQL Server 2005 introduces a new concept called *endpoints* to strengthen the communication security process.

The Endpoint folder residing under the Server Objects folder is a repository for all the endpoints created within a SQL Server instance. The endpoints are broken out by system endpoints, database mirroring, service broker, Simple Object Access Protocol (SOAP), and TSQL.

The endpoint creation and specified security options are covered in Chapter 13.

Linked Servers

As the enterprise scales, more and more SQL Server 2005 servers are introduced into an organization's infrastructure. As this occurs, you are challenged by providing a means to allow distributed transactions and queries between different SQL Server instances. Linked servers provide a way for organizations to overcome these hurdles by providing the means of distributed transactions, remote queries, and remote stored procedure calls between separate SQL Server instances or non–SQL Server sources such as Microsoft Access.

Follow these steps to create a linked server with SQL Server Management Studio (SSMS):

1. Choose Start, All Programs, Microsoft SQL Server 2005, SQL Server Management Studio.

2. In Object Explorer, first connect to the Database Engine, expand the desired server, and then expand the Server Objects Folder.

3. Right-click the Linked Servers folder and select New Linked Server.

4. The New Linked Server dialog box contains three pages of configuration settings: General, Security, and Server Options. On the General Page, specify a linked server name, and select the type of server to connect to. For example, the remote server could be a SQL Server or another data source. For this example, select SQL Server.

5. The next page focuses on security and includes configuration settings for the security context mapping between the local and remote SQL Server instances. On the Security page, first click Add and enter the local login user account to be used. Second, either impersonate the local account, which will pass the username and password to the remote server, or enter a remote user and password.

6. Still within the Security page, enter an option for a security context pertaining to the external login that is not defined in the previous list. The following options are available:

   - **Not Be Made**—Indicates that a login will not be created for user accounts that are not already listed.

   - **Be Made Without a User's Security Context**—Indicates that a connection will be made without using a user's security context for connections.

   - **Be Made Using the Login's Current Security Context**— Indicates that a connection will be made by using the current security context of the user which is logged on.

   - **Be Made Using This Security Context**—Indicates that a connection will be made by providing the login and password security context.

7. On the Server Options page, you can configure additional connection settings. Make any desired server option changes and click OK.

> **Note**
>
> Impersonating the Windows local credentials is the most secure authentication mechanism, provided that the remote server supports Windows authentication.

Triggers

The final folder in the Server Objects tree is Triggers. It is a repository for all the triggers configured within the SQL Server instance. Again, creating triggers is a development task and, therefore, is not covered in this book.

Administering the Replication Folder

Replication is a means of distributing data among SQL Server instances. In addition, replication can also be used as a form of high availability and for offloading reporting queries from a production server to a second instance of SQL Server. When administering and managing replication, you conduct all the replication tasks from within this Replication folder. Tasks include configuring the distributor, creating publications, creating local subscriptions, and launching the Replication Monitor for troubleshooting and monitoring.

Administering, managing, and monitoring replication can be reviewed in Chapter 6, "Administering SQL Server Replication."

Administering the Notification Services Folder

Notification Services is used for developing applications that create and send notifications to subscribers. Because Notification Services is a SQL Server component, Chapter 4, "Administering SQL Server 2005 Notification Services," is dedicated to administering Notification Services.

Administering Database Properties

The Database Properties dialog box is the place where you manage the configuration options and values of a user or system database. You can execute additional tasks from within these pages, such as database mirroring and transaction log shipping. The configuration pages in the Database Properties dialog box include

- General
- Files
- Filegroups
- Options

- Permissions
- Extended Properties
- Mirroring
- Transaction Log Shipping

The upcoming sections describe each page and setting in its entirety. To invoke the Database Properties dialog box, perform the following steps:

1. Choose Start, All Programs, Microsoft SQL Server 2005, SQL Server Management Studio.

2. In Object Explorer, first connect to the Database Engine, expand the desired server, and then expand the Databases folder.

3. Select a desired database such as AdventureWorks, right-click, and select Properties. The Database Properties dialog box, including all the pages, is displayed in the left pane.

Administering the Database Properties General Page

General, the first page in the Database Properties dialog box, displays information exclusive to backups, database settings, and collation settings. Specific information displayed includes

- Last Database Backup
- Last Database Log Backup
- Database Name
- State of the Database Status
- Database Owner
- Date Database Was Created
- Size of the Database
- Space Available
- Number of Users Currently Connected to the Database
- Collation Settings

You should use this page for obtaining factual information about a database, as displayed in Figure 1.11.

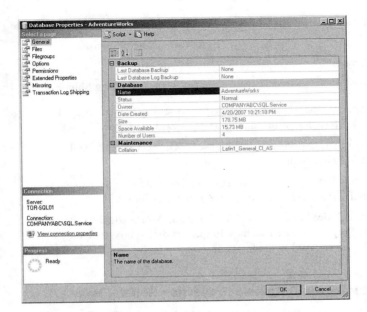

FIGURE 1.11
Viewing the General page in the Database Properties dialog box.

Administering the Database Properties Files Page

The second Database Properties page is called Files. Here, you can change the owner of the database, enable full-text indexing, and manage the database files, as shown in Figure 1.12.

Managing Database Files

The Files page is used to configure settings pertaining to database files and transaction logs. You will spend time working in the Files page when initially rolling out a database and conducting capacity planning. Following are the settings you'll see:

■ **Data and Log File Types**—A SQL Server 2005 OLTP database is composed of two types of files: data and log. Each database has at least one data file and one log file. When you're scaling a database, it is possible to create more than one data and one log file. If multiple data files exist, the first data file in the database has the extension *.mdf and subsequent data files maintain the extension *.ndf. In addition, all log files use the extension *.ldf.

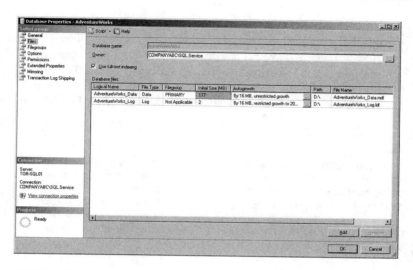

FIGURE 1.12
Configuring the database files settings from within the Files page.

> **Tip**
>
> To reduce disk contention, many database enthusiasts recommend creating multiple data files. The database catalog and system tables should be stored in the primary data file, and all other data, objects, and indexes should be stored in secondary files. In addition, the data files should be spread across multiple disk systems or Logical Unit Number (LUN) to increase I/O performance.

- **Filegroups**—When you're working with multiple data files, it is possible to create filegroups. A filegroup allows you to logically and physically group database objects and files together. The default filegroup, known as the Primary Filegroup, maintains all the system tables and data files not assigned to other filegroups. Subsequent filegroups need to be created and named explicitly.

- **Initial Size in MB**—This setting indicates the preliminary size of a database or transaction log file. You can increase the size of a file by modifying this value to a higher number in megabytes.

- **Autogrowth Feature**—This feature enables you to manage the file growth of both the data and transaction log files. When you click the ellipses button, a Change Autogrowth dialog box appears. The configurable settings include whether to enable autogrowth, and if autogrowth is selected, whether autogrowth should occur based on a percentage or in a specified number of megabytes. The final setting is whether to choose a maximum file size for each file. The two options available are Restricted File Growth (MB) or Unrestricted File Growth.

Tip

When you're allocating space for the first time to both data files and transaction log files, it is a best practice to conduct capacity planning, estimate the amount of space required for the operation, and allocate a specific amount of disk space from the beginning. It is not a recommended practice to rely on the autogrowth feature because constantly growing and shrinking the files typically leads to excessive fragmentation, including performance degradation.

- **Database Files and RAID Sets**—Database files should reside only on RAID sets to provide fault tolerance and availability, while at the same time increasing performance. If cost is not an issue, data files and transaction logs should be placed on RAID 1+0 volumes. RAID 1+0 provides the best availability and performance because it combines mirroring with stripping. However, if this is not a possibility due to budget, data files should be placed on RAID 5 and transaction logs on RAID 1.

Increasing Initial Size of a Database File

Perform the following steps to increase the data file for the AdventureWorks database using SSMS:

1. In Object Explorer, right-click the AdventureWorks database and select Properties.

2. Select the File Page in the Database Properties dialog box.

3. Enter the new numerical value for the desired file size in the Initial Size (MB) column for a data or log file and click OK.

Creating Additional Filegroups for a Database

Perform the following steps to create a new filegroup and files using the AdventureWorks database with both SSMS and TSQL:

1. In Object Explorer, right-click the AdventureWorks database and select Properties.

2. Select the Filegroups page in the Database Properties dialog box.

3. Click the Add button to create a new filegroup.

4. When a new row appears, enter the name of new the filegroup and enable the option Default.

Alternatively, you can use the following TSQL script to create the new filegroup for the AdventureWorks database:

```
USE [master]
GO
ALTER DATABASE [AdventureWorks] ADD FILEGROUP [SecondFileGroup]
GO
```

Creating New Data Files for a Database and Placing Them in Different Filegroups

Now that you've created a new filegroup, you can create two additional data files for the AdventureWorks database and place them on the newly created filegroup:

1. In Object Explorer, right-click the AdventureWorks database and select Properties.

2. Select the Files page in the Database Properties dialog box.

3. Click the Add button to create new data files.

4. In the Database Files section, enter the following information in the appropriate columns:

Columns	Value
Logical Name	AdventureWorks_Data2
File Type	Data
FileGroup	SecondFileGroup
Size	10 MB
Path	C:\
File Name	AdventureWorks_Data2.ndf

5. Click OK.

Note

For simplicity, the file page for the new database file is located in the root of the C: drive for this example. In production environments, however, you should place additional database files on separate volumes to maximize performance.

You can now conduct the same steps by executing the following TSQL syntax to create a new data file:

```
USE [master]
GO
ALTER DATABASE [AdventureWorks]
➥ADD FILE (NAME = N'AdventureWorks_Data2',
➥FILENAME = N'C:\AdventureWorks_Data2.ndf',
➥SIZE = 10240KB , FILEGROWTH = 1024KB )
➥TO FILEGROUP [SecondFileGroup]
GO
```

Configuring Autogrowth on a Database File

Next, to configure autogrowth on the database file, follow these steps:

1. From within the File page on the Database Properties dialog box, click the ellipses button located in the Autogrowth column on a desired database file to configure it.

2. On the Change Autogrowth dialog box, configure the File Growth and Maximum File Size settings and click OK.

3. Click OK on the Database Properties dialog box to complete the task.

You can use the following TSQL syntax to modify the Autogrowth settings for a database file based on a growth rate at 50% and a maximum file size of 1000MB:

```
USE [master]
GO
ALTER DATABASE [AdventureWorks]
MODIFY FILE ( NAME = N'AdventureWorks_Data',
MAXSIZE = 1024000KB , FILEGROWTH = 50%)
GO
```

Administering the Database Properties Filegroups Page

As stated previously, filegroups are a great way to organize data objects, address performance issues, and minimize backup times. The Filegroup page is best used for viewing existing filegroups, creating new ones, marking filegroups as read-only, and configuring which filegroup will be the default.

To improve performance, you can create subsequent filegroups and place data and indexes onto them. In addition, if there isn't enough physical storage available on a volume, you can create a new filegroup and physically place all files on a different volume or LUN if Storage Area Network (SAN) is being used.

Finally, if a database has static data, it is possible to move this data to a specified filegroup and mark this filegroup as read-only. This minimizes backup times; because the data does not change, SQL Server marks this file group and skips it.

Note

Alternatively, you can create a new filegroup directly in the Files page by adding a new data file and selecting New Filegroup from the Filegroup drop-down list.

Administering the Database Properties Options Page

The Options page, shown in Figure 1.13, includes configuration settings on Collation, Recovery Model, and other options such as Automatic, Cursor, and Miscellaneous. The following sections explain these settings.

Collation

The Collation setting located on the Database Properties Options page specifies the policies for how strings of character data are sorted and compared, for a specific database, based on the industry standards of particular languages and locales. Unlike SQL Server collation, the database collation setting can be changed by selecting the appropriate setting from the Collation drop-down box.

Recovery Model

The second setting within the Options page is Recovery Model. This is an important setting because it dictates how much data can be retained, which ultimately affects the outcome of a restore.

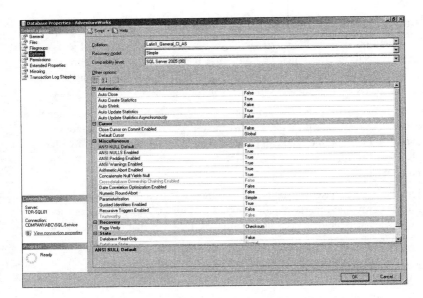

FIGURE 1.13
Viewing and configuring the Database Properties Options page settings.

Understanding and Effectively Using Recovery Models

Each recovery model handles recovery differently. Specifically, each model differs in how it manages logging, which results in whether an organization's database can be recovered to the point of failure. The three recovery models associated with a database in the Database Engine are

- **Full**—This recovery model captures and logs all transactions, making it possible to restore a database to a determined point-in-time or up-to-the-minute. Based on this model, you must conduct maintenance on the transaction log to prevent logs from growing too large and disks becoming full. When you perform backups, space is made available once again and can be used until the next planned backup. Organizations may notice that maintaining a transaction log slightly degrades SQL Server performance because all transactions to the database are logged. Organizations that insist on preserving critical data often overlook this issue because they realize that this model offers them the highest level of recovery capabilities.

- **Simple**—This model provides organizations with the least number of options for recovering data. The Simple recovery model truncates the transaction log after each backup. This means a database can be recovered only up until the last successful full or differential database backup. This recovery model also provides the least amount of administration because transaction log backups are not permitted. In addition, data entered into the database after a successful full or differential database backup is unrecoverable. Organizations that store data they do not deem as mission critical may choose to use this model.

- **Bulk-Logged**—This recovery model maintains a transaction log and is similar to the Full recovery model. The main difference is that transaction logging is minimal during bulk operations to maximize database performance and reduce the log size when large amounts of data are inserted into the database. Bulk import operations such as BCP, BULK INSERT, SELECT INTO, CREATE INDEX, ALTER INDEX REBUILD, and DROP INDEX are minimally logged.

  Since the Bulk-Logged recovery model provides only minimal logging of bulk operations, you cannot restore the database to the point of failure if a disaster occurs during a bulk-logged operation. In most situations, an organization will have to restore the database, including the latest transaction log, and rerun the Bulk-Logged operation.

  This model is typically used if organizations need to run large bulk operations that degrade system performance and do not require point-in-time recovery.

> **Note**
>
> When a new database is created, it inherits the recovery settings based on the Model database. The default recovery model is set to Full.

Next, you need to determine which model best suits your organization's needs. The following section is designed to help you choose the appropriate model.

Selecting the Appropriate Recovery Model

It is important to select the appropriate recovery model because doing so affects an organization's ability to recover, manage, and maintain data.

For enterprise production systems, the Full recovery model is the best model for preventing critical data loss and restoring data to a specific point in time. As long as the transaction log is available, it is possible to even get up-to-the-minute recovery and point-in-time restore if the end of the transaction log is backed up and restored. The trade-off for the Full recovery model is its impact on other operations.

Organizations leverage the Simple recovery model if the data backed up is not critical, data is static or does not change often, or if loss is not a concern for the organization. In this situation, the organization loses all transactions since the last full or last differential backup. This model is typical for test environments or production databases that are not mission critical.

Finally, organizations that typically select the Bulk-Logged recovery model have critical data, but logging large amounts of data degrades system performance, or these bulk operations are conducted after hours and do not interfere with normal transaction processing. In addition, there isn't a need for point-in-time or up-to-the-minute restores.

> **Note**
>
> It is possible to switch the recovery model of a production database and switch it back. This would not break the continuity of the log; however, there could be negative ramifications to the restore process. For example, a production database can use the Full recovery model and, immediately before a large data load, the recovery model can be changed to Bulk-Logged to minimize logging and increase performance. The only caveat is that the organization must understand it lost the potential for point-in-time and up-to-the-minute restores during the switch.

Switching the Database Recovery Model with SQL Server Management Studio

To set the recovery model on a SQL Server 2005 database using SSMS, perform the following steps:

1. Choose Start, All Programs, Microsoft SQL Server 2005, SQL Server Management Studio.

2. In Object Explorer, first connect to the Database Engine, expand the desired server, and then expand the database folder.

3. Select the desired SQL Server database, right-click on the database, and select Properties.

4. In the Database Properties dialog box, select the Options page.

5. In Recovery Model, select either Full, Bulk-Logged, or Simple from the drop-down list and click OK.

Switching the Database Recovery Model with Transact-SQL

It is possible not only to change the recovery model of a database with SQL Server Management Studio, but also to make changes to the database recovery model using Transact-SQL commands such as ALTER DATABASE. You can use the following TSQL syntax to change the recovery model for the AdventureWorks Database from Simple to Full:

```
--Switching the Database Recovery model
Use Master
ALTER DATABASE AdventureWorks SET RECOVERY FULL
GO
```

Compatibility Level

The Compatibility Level setting located on the Database Properties Options page is meant for interoperability and backward compatibility of previous versions of SQL Server. The options available are SQL Server 2005 (90), SQL Server 2000 (80), and SQL Server 7.0 (70).

Other Options (Automatic)

Also available on the Database Properties Options page are these options:

- **Auto Close**—When the last user exits the database, the database is shut down cleanly and resources are freed. The values to be entered are either True or False.

- **Auto Create Statistics**—This setting specifies whether the database will automatically update statistics to optimize a database. The default setting is True, and this value is recommended.

- **Auto Shrink**—Similar to the shrink task, if this setting is set to True, SQL Server removes unused space from the database on a periodic basis. For production databases, this setting is not recommended.

- **Auto Update Statistics**—Similar to the Auto Create Statistics settings, this setting automatically updates any out-of-date statistics for the database. The default setting is True, and this value is recommended.

- **Auto Update Statistics Asynchronously**—If the statistics are out of date, this setting dictates whether a query should be updated first before being fired.

Other Options (Cursor)

The following options are also available on the Database Properties Options page:

- **Close Cursor on Commit Enabled**—This setting dictates whether cursors should be closed after a transaction is committed. If the value is True, cursors are closed when the transaction is committed, and if the value is False, cursors remain open. The default value is False.

- **Default Cursor**—The values available include Global and Local. The Global setting indicates that the cursor name is global to the connection based on the Declare statement. During the Declare Cursor statement, the Local setting specifies that the cursor name is Local to the stored procedure, trigger, or batch.

Other Options (Miscellaneous)

The following options are also available on the Database Properties Options page:

- **ANSI Null Default**—The value to be entered is either True or False. When set to False, the setting controls the behavior to supersede the default nullability of new columns.

- **ANSI Null Enabled**—This setting controls the behavior of the comparison operators when used with null values. The comparison operators consist of Equals (=) and Not Equal To (<>).

- **ANSI Padding Enabled**—This setting controls whether padding should be enabled or disabled. Padding dictates how the column stores values shorter than the defined size of the column.

- **ANSI Warnings Enabled**—If this option is set to True, a warning message is displayed if null values appear in aggregate functions.

- **Arithmetic Abort Enabled**—If this option is set to True, an error is returned, and the transaction is rolled back if an overflow or divide-by-zero error occurs. If the value False is used, an error is displayed; however, the transaction is not rolled back.

- **Concatenate Null Yields Null**—This setting specifies how null values are concatenated. True indicates that string + NULL returns NULL. When False, the result is string.

- **Cross-Database Ownership Chaining**—Settings include either True or False. True represents that the database allows cross-database ownership chaining, whereas False indicates that this option is disabled.

■ **Date Correlation Optimization Enabled**—If this option is set to True, SQL Server maintains correlation optimization statistics on the date columns of tables that are joined by a foreign key.

■ **Numeric Round-Abort**—This setting indicates how the database will handle rounding errors.

■ **Parameterization**—This setting controls whether queries are parameterized. The two options available are Simple and Forced. When you use Simple, queries are parameterized based on the default behavior of the database, whereas when you use Forced, all queries are parameterized.

■ **Quoted Identifiers Enabled**—This setting determines whether SQL Server keywords can be used as identifiers when enclosed in quotation marks.

■ **Recursive Triggers Enabled**—When this setting is enabled by setting the value to True, SQL Server allows recursive triggers to be fired.

■ **Trustworthy**—This setting allows SQL Server to grant access to the database by the impersonation context. A value of True enables this setting.

■ **VarDecimal Storage Format Enabled**—When this option is set to True, the database is enabled for the VarDecimal storage format, which is a feature available only with Service Pack 2.

Other Options (Recovery)

Also available on the Database Properties Options page is

■ **Page Verify**—This option controls how SQL Server will handle incomplete transactions based on disk I/O errors. The available options include Checksum, Torn Page Detection, and None.

Other Options (State)

The following options are available on the Database Properties Options page:

■ **Read Only**—Setting the database value to True makes the database read-only.

The default syntax for managing the read-only state of a database is

```
ALTER DATABASE database_name
<db_update_option> ::=
    { READ_ONLY | READ_WRITE }
```

■ **State**—This field cannot be edited; it informs you of the state of the database. Possible states include Online, Offline, Restoring, Recovering, Recovery Pending, Suspect, and Emergency.

To change the state of a database with TSQL, use the default syntax:

```
ALTER DATABASE database_name
<db_state_option> ::=
    { ONLINE | OFFLINE | EMERGENCY }
```

■ **Restrict Access**—This setting manages which users can connect to the database. Possible values include Multiple, Single, and Restricted. The Multiple setting is the default state, which allows all users and applications to connect to the database. Single user mode is meant for only one user to access the database. This is typically used for emergency administration. The final setting, Restricted, allows only members of the db_owner, dbcreator, or sysadmin accounts to access the database.

The TSQL code for setting the Restrict Access value is as follows:

```
ALTER DATABASE database_name
<db_user_access_option> ::=
        { SINGLE_USER | RESTRICTED_USER | MULTI_USER }
```

Administering the Database Properties Mirroring Page

Most database administrators believe database mirroring is the paramount new feature included with the release of SQL Server 2005. Database mirroring is also a SQL Server high-availability alternative for increasing availability of a desired database. Database mirroring transmits transaction log records directly from one SQL Server instance to another SQL Server instance. In addition, if the primary SQL Server instance becomes unavailable, the services and clients automatically fail over to the mirrored server. Automatic failover is contingent on the settings and versions used.

The Database Properties Mirroring page is the primary tool for configuring, managing, and monitoring database mirroring for a database. The Mirroring page includes configuration settings for security; mirroring operating mode;

and the principal, mirror, and witness server network addresses. For more information on configuring database mirroring, review Chapter 19, "Administering and Managing Database Mirroring" (online).

Administering the Database Properties Permissions Page

The Database Properties Permissions page is used to administer database authorization and role-based access and to control permissions on the database. Chapter 13 covers these topics in their entirety.

Administering the Database Properties Extended Permissions Page

The Database Properties Extended Permissions page is used for managing extended properties on database objects, such as descriptive text, input masks, and formatting rules. The extended properties can be applied to schema, schema view, or column view.

Administering the Database Properties Transaction Log Shipping Page

The final Database Properties page is Transaction Log Shipping. Transaction log shipping is one of four SQL Server 2005 high-availability alternatives similar to database mirroring. In log shipping, transactions are sent from a primary server to the standby secondary server on an incremental basis. However, unlike with database mirroring, automatic failover is not a supported feature.

The configuration settings located on the Transaction Log Shipping page in the Database Properties dialog box are the primary place for you to configure, manage, and monitor transaction log shipping.

For more information on administering transaction log shipping, including step-by-step installation instructions, review Chapter 20, "Administering and Managing Log Shipping" (online).

SQL Server Database Engine Management Tasks

The following sections cover additional tasks associated with managing the SQL Server Database Engine.

Changing SQL Server Configuration Settings

Presently, most of the configuration settings can be changed from within SQL Server Management Studio. These settings can also be changed using the SP_CONFIGURE TSQL command. The syntax to change configuration settings is

```
SP_CONFIGURE ['configuration name'], [configuration setting
➥value]
GO
RECONFIGURE WITH OVERRIDE
GO
```

The *configuration name* represents the name of the setting to be changed, and the *configuration setting value* is the new value to be changed. Before you can change settings, however, you must use the SP_CONFIGURE command. You must enable advanced settings by first executing the following script:

```
SP_CONFIGURE 'show advanced options', 1
GO
RECONFIGURE
GO
```

For a full list of configuration options, see SQL Server 2005 Books Online.

Managing Database Engine Informational Reports

To succeed in today's competitive IT industry, you must be armed with information pertaining to SQL Server 2005. SQL Server 2005 introduces a tremendous number of canned reports that can be opened directly from within SQL Server Management Studio. These reports provide information that allows you to maximize efficiency when conducting administration and management duties.

You can open these canned reports by right-clicking a SQL Server instance in Management Studio and selecting Reports and then Standard Reports. The standard reports include

- Server Dashboard
- Configuration Changes History
- Schema Changes History
- Scheduler Health

- Memory Consumption
- Activity - All Blocking Transactions
- Activity - All Cursors
- Activity - Tip Sessions
- Activity - Dormant Sessions
- Activity - Top Connections
- Top Transactions by Age
- Top Transactions by Blocked Transactions Count
- Top Transactions by Locks Count
- Performance - Batch Execution Statistics
- Performance - Object Execution Statistics
- Performance - Top Queries by Average CPU Time
- Performance - Top Queries by Average IP
- Performance - Top Queries by Total CPU Time
- Performance - Top Queries by Total IP
- Server Broker Statistics
- Transaction Log Shipping Status

The standard report titled Server Dashboard, displayed in Figure 1.14, is a great overall report that provides an overview of a SQL Server instance, including activity and configuration settings.

Detaching and Attaching Databases

Another common task you must conduct is attaching and detaching databases.

Detaching a Database

When a database is detached, it is completely removed from a SQL Server instance; however, the files are still left intact and reside on the file system for later use. Before a database can be detached, all user connections must be terminated; otherwise, this process fails. The detach tool includes the options to automatically drop connections, update statistics, and keep full text catalogs.

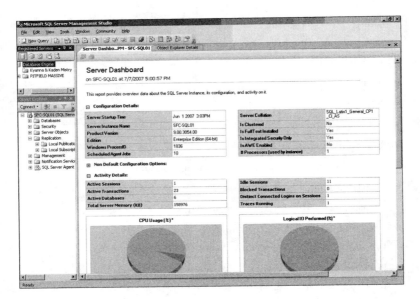

FIGURE 1.14
Viewing the standard Server Dashboard SQL Server canned report.

To drop the sample AdventureWorks database, follow these steps:

1. In Object Explorer, first connect to the Database Engine, expand the desired server, and then expand the Database folder.

2. Select the AdventureWorks database, right-click on the database, select Tasks, and then select Detach.

3. In the Detach Database dialog box, enable the following options, as displayed in Figure 1.15: Drop Connections, Update Statistics, and Keep Full Text Catalogs. Click OK.

Attaching a Database

Here's a common usage scenario for attaching databases: Say you need to move the database from a source to a target SQL Server. When a database is attached, the state of the database is exactly the same as when it was detached.

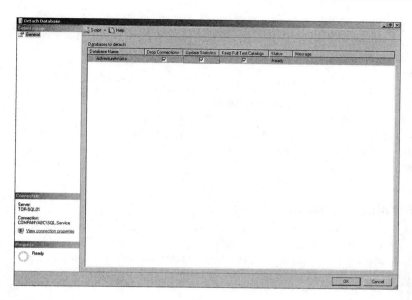

FIGURE 1.15
Specifying detach settings on the Detach Database dialog box.

The following steps illustrate how to attach a database with SQL Server Management Studio:

1. In Object Explorer, first connect to the Database Engine, expand the desired server, and then select the Database folder.

2. Right-click the Database folder and select Attach.

3. In the Attach Databases dialog box, click the Add button to add the database to be attached.

4. In the Locate the Database Files dialog box, specify the path to the *.mdf file and click OK.

5. Optionally, change the name or owner of the database.

6. Click OK to attach the database.

Alternatively, you can use the following TSQL syntax to attach the AdventureWorks database:

```
USE [master]
GO
CREATE DATABASE [AdventureWorks] ON
```

```
( FILENAME = N'D:\AdventureWorks_Data.mdf' ),
( FILENAME = N'D:\AdventureWorks_Log.ldf' )
 FOR ATTACH
GO
if exists (select name from master.sys.databases
➥sd where name = N'AdventureWorks' and
➥SUSER_SNAME(sd.owner_sid) = SUSER_SNAME() )
➥EXEC [AdventureWorks].dbo.sp_changedbowner @loginame=
➥N'COMPANYABC\SQL.Service', @map=false
GO
```

Scripting Database Objects

SQL Server 2005 has two levels of scripting functionality that assist you in automatically transforming a SQL Server task or action to a TSQL script. The scripting functionality is a great way to automate redundant administration responsibilities or settings. Moreover, you don't have to be a TSQL scripting expert to create solid scripts.

You can generate a script from within a majority of the SQL Server dialog boxes or pages. For example, if you make changes to the SQL Server Processor Properties page, such as enabling the options Boost SQL Server Priority or User Windows Fibers, you can click the Script button at the top of the screen to convert these changes to a script. In addition, this script can be fired on other SQL Servers to make the configuration automatically consistent across similar SQL Servers.

When you click the Script button, the options available are Script Action to New Query Window, Script Action to File, Script Action to Clipboard, and Script Action to Job.

Another alternative to creating scripts is right-clicking a specific folder within Object Explorer and selecting Script As or right-clicking a database, selecting Tasks, and then selecting Generate Script to invoke the Script Wizard. Some of these tasks include scripting database schemas, jobs, tables, stored procedures, and just about any object within SQL Server Management Studio. Additional scripting statements include Create, Alter, Drop, Select, Insert, and Delete.

Backing Up and Restoring the Database

Creating a backup and recovery strategy is probably the most important task you have on your plate. When you're creating backups, it is imperative that you understand the recovery models associated with each database such as

Full, Simple, and Bulk-Logged and understand the impact of each model on the transaction log and the recovery process. In addition, it is a best practice to back up the user databases, but to restore a full SQL Server environment, the system database should be included the backup strategy.

For more information on recovery models and backing up and restoring a SQL Server environment, see Chapter 17. That chapter focuses on backing up all components of SQL Server, such as the Database Engine, Analysis Services, Reporting Services, and Information Services.

Transferring SQL Server Data

There are many different ways to transfer data or databases from within SQL Server Management Studio. There are tasks associated with importing and exporting data and copying and/or moving a full database with the Copy Database Wizard. To use the transferring tasks, right-click a database, select Tasks, and then select Import Data, Export Data, or Copy Database.

Each of these ways to move data is discussed in its entirety in Chapter 11, "Creating Packages and Transferring Data."

Taking a SQL Server Database Offline

As a database administrator, you may sometimes need to take a database offline. When the database is offline, users, applications, and administrators do not have access to the database until it has been brought back online.

Perform the following steps to take a database offline and then bring it back online:

1. Right-click on a desired database such as AdventureWorks, select Tasks, and then select Take Offline.

2. In the Task Database Offline screen, verify that the status represents that the database has been successfully taken offline and then select Close.

Within Object Explorer, a red arrow pointing downward is displayed on the Database folder, indicating that the database is offline. To bring the database back online, repeat the preceding steps but select Online instead.

In addition, you can use the following TSQL syntax to change the state of a database from Online, Offline, or Emergency:

```
ALTER DATABASE database_name
<db_state_option> ::=
    { ONLINE | OFFLINE | EMERGENCY }
```

> **Note**
>
> When the database option is configured to an Emergency state, the database is considered to be in single-user mode; the database is marked as read-only. This mode is meant for addressing crisis situations.

Shrinking a Database

The Shrink Database task reduces the physical database and log files to a specific size. This operation removes excess space in the database based on a percentage value being entered. In addition, you can enter thresholds in megabytes, indicating the amount of shrinkage that needs to take place when the database reaches a certain size and the amount of free space that must remain after the excess space is removed. Free space can be retained in the database or released back to the operating system.

The following TSQL syntax shrinks the AdventureWorks database, returns freed space to the operating system, and allows for 15% of free space to remain after the shrink:

```
USE [AdventureWorks]
GO
DBCC SHRINKDATABASE(N'AdventureWorks', 15, TRUNCATEONLY)
GO
```

> **Tip**
>
> It is best practice not to select the option to shrink the database. First, when shrinking the database, SQL Server moves pages toward the beginning of the file, allowing the end of the files to be shrunk. This process can increase the transaction log size because all moves are logged. Second, if the database is heavily used and there are many inserts, the database files will have to grow again. SQL 2005 addresses slow autogrowth with instant file initialization; therefore, the growth process is not as slow as it was in the past. However, sometimes autogrow does not catch up with the space requirements, causing performance degradation. Finally, constant shrinking and growing of the database lead to excessive fragmentation. If you need to shrink the database size, you should do it manually when the server is not being heavily utilized.

Alternatively, you can shrink a database by right-clicking a database and selecting Tasks, Shrink, and Database or File.

Renaming a Database

The following steps illustrate how to change the name of a database by using SQL Server Management Studio:

1. In Object Explorer, right-click the name of the database and select Rename.

2. Type in the new name for the database and press Enter.

Administering the SQL Server Agent

The SQL Server Agent is a Microsoft Windows Service that executes scheduled tasks configured as SQL Server jobs. Ultimately, in SQL Server 2005, any task can be transformed into a job; therefore, the task can be scheduled to reduce the amount of time wasted on manual database administration. The SQL Server Agent can be managed from within SQL Server Management Studio.

Note

The SQL Server Agent service must be running to execute jobs and tasks. This is the first level of defense when you're troubleshooting why agent jobs are not firing.

Administering the SQL Server Agent Properties

Before utilizing the SQL Server Agent, you should first verify and configure the Agent properties to ensure that everything is copacetic.

The SQL Server Agent Properties dialog box has six pages of configuration settings, described in the following sections.

The General Page

The SQL Server Agent page maintains configurable settings such as Auto Restart SQL Server if It Stops Unexpectedly and Auto Restart SQL Server Agent if It Stops Unexpectedly.

From a best practice perspective, both the restart settings should be enabled on mission-critical databases. This prevents downtime in the event of a server outage because the service will restart if failure is inevitable.

You can change the error log path if preferred and configure a send receipt via the Net send command. In addition, you can include execution trace messages to provide meticulous information on SQL Server Agent operations.

The Advanced Page

The Advanced page controls the behavior of SQL Server Event Forwarding and Idle CPU conditions. It is possible to forward unhandled events, all events, or events based on predefined severity levels selected in the drop-down list to a different server. The target server must be specified in the server drop-down list. The differences between unhandled and handled events are that unhandled events forward only events that no alert responds to, whereas handled events forward both the event and the alert. The final section is tailored toward SQL Server Agent and CPU settings. These settings define the conditions when jobs will run based on values such as Average CPU Usage Falls Below in Percentage and And Remains Below This Level for In Seconds.

> **Note**
>
> In enterprise production environments, a SQL Server instance should have enough processing power that these CPU conditions settings are not required.

The Alert System Page

The Alert System page includes all the SQL Server settings for sending messages from agent alerts. The mail session settings are based on the prerequisite task of configuring SQL Server Database Mail. These topics are discussed in Chapter 21, "Monitoring SQL Server 2005" (online).

The Job System Page

The Job System page controls the SQL Server Agent shutdown settings. You can enter a numeric value based on a time increment that governs how long a job can run before automatically being shut down. It is also possible to specify a nonadministrator Job Step Proxy Account to control the security context of the agent; however, this option is available only when you're managing earlier SQL Server Agent versions.

The Connections Page

The Connections Page should be used to configure a SQL Server alias for the SQL Server Agent. An alias is required only if a connection to the Database

Engine will be made without using the default network transport or an alternate named pipe.

The History Page

You should use the final page, History, for configuring the limit size of a job history log setting. The options include setting maximum job history log size in rows and maximum job history rows per job.

Administering SQL Server Agent Jobs

The first subfolder located under the SQL Server Agent is the Job folder. Here, you create new jobs, manage schedules, manage job categories, and view the history of a job.

Follow these steps to create a new job:

1. In Object Explorer, first connect to the Database Engine, expand the desired server, and then expand the SQL Server Agent folder.

2. Right-click the Jobs folder and select New Job.

3. On the General page in the New Job dialog box, enter a name, owner, category, and description for the new job.

4. Ensure that the Enabled check box is set to True, as illustrated in Figure 1.16.

5. Click New on the Steps page. When the New Job Steps page is invoked, type a name for the step and enter the type of job this will be. The options range from Transact-SQL, which is the most common, to other items such as stored procedures, Integrations Services packages, and replication. For this example, select TSQL Type and enter the following TSQL syntax in the command window:

```
BACKUP DATABASE [AdventureWorks] TO  DISK =
➥N'C:\Program Files\Microsoft SQL Server
➥\MSSQL.1\MSSQL\Backup\AdventureWorks.bak'
➥WITH NOFORMAT, NOINIT,
➥NAME = N'AdventureWorks-Full Database Backup',
➥SKIP, NOREWIND, NOUNLOAD,  STATS = 10
GO
```

6. From within the General page, parse the command to verify that the syntax is operational and click the Advanced page.

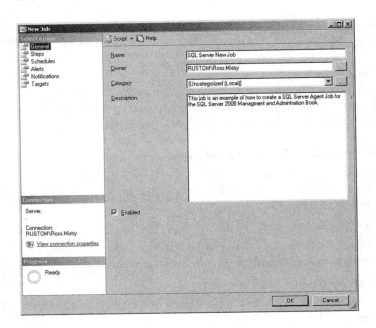

FIGURE 1.16
Specifying the Create New Job Details on the New Job dialog box.

7. The Advanced page includes a set of superior configuration settings. For example, you can specify actions on successful completion of this job, retry attempts including intervals, and what to do if the job fails. This page also includes Output File, Log to Table, History, and the potential to run the job under a different security context. Click OK to continue.

8. Within the New Job dialog box, you can use the Schedules page to view and organize schedules for the job. Here, you can create a new schedule or select one from an existing schedule.

9. Click OK to finalize the creation of the job.

Enabling or Disabling a SQL Server Agent Job

Each SQL Server Agent job can be either enabled or disabled by right-clicking the job and selecting either Enable or Disable.

Viewing SQL Server Agent Job History

From a management perspective, you need to understand whether a SQL Server Agent job was fired properly, completed successfully, or just outright failed. The Job History tool, which is a subcomponent of the Log File Viewer, provides thorough diagnostics and status of job history. Perform the following steps to review job history for a SQL Server Agent job from within SQL Server Management Studio:

1. In Object Explorer, first expand the SQL Server Agent and then the Jobs folder.

2. Right-click a desired job and select View Job History.

3. In the Log File Viewer, review the log file summary for any job from within the center pane.

4. Choose from additional options such as loading saved logs, exporting logs, creating a filter, parsing through logs with the search feature, and deleting logs.

Administering SQL Server Alerts and Operators

The SQL Server Alerts and Operators folders are used for monitoring the SQL Server infrastructure by creating alerts and then sending out notifications to operators. For more information on creating alerts and operators, review Chapter 21.

Administering SQL Server Proxies

The Proxies Folder found within the SQL Server Agent enables you to view or modify the properties of the SQL Server Agent Proxy account. You enter a proxy name and credentials and select the subsystem the proxy account has access to.

Administering SQL Server Error Logs

The final folder in the SQL Server is Error Logs. You can configure the Error Logs folder by right-clicking the folder and selecting Configure. The configuration options include modifying the error log file location, reducing the amount of disk space utilized by enabling the option Write OEM Error Log, and changing the Agent Log Level settings. These settings include enabling Error, Warnings, and/or Information.

Perform the following steps to view SQL Server Agent Error Logs:

1. In Object Explorer, first expand the SQL Server Agent and then the Error Logs folder.

2. When all the error logs are listed under the Error Logs folder, double-click any of the error logs to view them.

Summary

The Database Engine is the core component within SQL Server; it provides a key service for storing, processing, and securing data. SQL Server 2005 Service Pack 2 introduces many new features that improve your success at administering and managing this core component. In addition, reading this chapter will help you to fully understand how to manage and administer the SQL Server instance server properties, Database Engine folders, database properties, and SQL Server Agent.

Best Practices

Following is a summary of some of the best practices from the chapter:

- Leverage the scripting utility within SQL Server Management Studio to transform administration tasks into TSQL code.

- Unless there is a specific need to do otherwise, it is a best practice to allow SQL Server to dynamically manage the minimum and maximum amount of memory allocated to SQL Server. However, if multiple applications are running on SQL Server, it is recommended to specify minimum and maximum values for SQL Server memory. Therefore, the application cannot starve SQL Server by depriving it of memory.

- The preferred authentication mode is Windows Authentication over SQL Server Authentication because it provides a more robust authorization mechanism.

- Configuring SQL auditing is recommended to capture both failed and successful logins.

- Do not set the database to automatically shrink on a regular basis because this leads to performance degradation and excessive fragmentation over time.

- The first Database Engine administration task after a successful SQL installation should involve tuning and configuring the server properties.

- Configure the recovery model for each database accordingly and implement a backup and restore strategy. This should also include the system databases.

- Database files, transaction log files, and operating system files should be located on separate volumes for performance and availability.

- When multiple database files and transaction log files exist, organize them through the use of filegroups.

- Create basic reports in Management Studio to better understand the SQL Server environment.

- Automate administration tasks by using SQL Server 2005 Agent jobs.

CHAPTER 2

Administering SQL Server 2005 Analysis Services

Analysis Services is a SQL Server 2005 component that provides a foundation for business intelligence (BI) applications through online analytical processing (OLAP) and data mining functionality.

This chapter outlines the tasks associated with administering and managing an Analysis Services implementation. It starts with an overview of Analysis Services, which includes terminology, architecture, and a review of the different versions. In addition, this chapter highlights what is new with Service Pack 2. The chapter also includes step-by-step tasks for Analysis Services administration and management, such as processing cubes, using storage modes, monitoring performance, and creating backups and restores. The final sections focus on Analysis Services security and monitoring.

Because this book is an administration and management guide to SQL Server 2005, this chapter does not include programming or architecture of Analysis Services items such as modeling OLAP databases, designing OLAP cubes, or creating dimensions and measure groups.

Finally, all the examples in this chapter are based on the AdventureWorks data warehouse sample multidimensional database and Visual Studio AdventureWorks DW Analysis Services project included with SQL Server 2005 or available for download from the Microsoft site.

An Overview of Analysis Services

These days, business intelligence is almost a requirement because it allows organizations to make more informed business decisions by analyzing company data. Analysis Services is a component of SQL Server 2005 that provides business intelligence capabilities that help keep companies abreast of their current trends, provide the capacity for forecasting, and ultimately result in a competitive advantage.

Analysis Services Terminology

There are many new terms that you, as a database administrator, must become familiar with to manage Analysis Services. This section covers the key terms associated with Analysis Services and business intelligence.

- **Relational Database**—This database is a set of entities related to one another. Entities are tables that store data. This type of database adheres to the rules of normalization and is typically modeled based on the third normalized form. These databases are also referred to as online transaction processing (OLTP) databases and are used for managing transactions. The logical model and data are stored in the SQL Server Database Engine.

- **Multidimensional Database**—This database integrates data from different sources. An organization with a multidimensional database can conduct analysis, reporting, and decision making based on current and historical data. Unlike a relational database, a multidimensional database is not designed using the relational model. Data is stored in a multidimensional model. As a result, end users can achieve stronger analytical information by interactively exploring and navigating through the aggregated data by drilling down, slicing, dicing, and pivoting. Multidimensional databases are optimized to support decision making, whereas relational databases are meant for transactional inline business applications.

  The multidimensional database is also referred to as an online analytical processing (OLAP) database, an Analysis Services database, or a data warehouse. The actual data is stored in the Analysis Services component, not in the Database Engine like a traditional OLTP database. The process for moving data from the OLTP database to the OLAP database is known as extract, transform, and load (ETL).

> **Note**
>
> For the purpose of this chapter, the terms *OLAP database, multidimensional database, Analysis Services database,* and *data warehouse database* are all synonymous.

- **Extract, Transform, and Load (ETL)**—This triumvirate of data services from an OLTP database to a data warehouse is frequently referred to as *ETL*. The process encapsulates the extraction of data from a source, the transformation of the data to suit the requirements of the application, and finally the load of the data into a destination. The transformations can include normalizing, sanitizing, merging, aggregating, and copying the data. The sources and destinations for the data can be SQL databases, third-party ODBC data, flat files, or any number of other data locations.

- **Unified Dimensional Model (UDM)**—The UDM is the bridge between heterogeneous data sources and the user. When the UDM is contracted, end users issue queries directly to the UDM. As a result, they can obtain data from many disparate physical data sources.

- **Proactive Caching**—In today's business intelligence environments, the demand for real-time analytics is increasing. Proactive caching is a new technology introduced with SQL Server 2005 Analysis Services. It listens for changes in objects residing in the relational source and processes just those changes. This option provides an alternative for scheduled processing, while increasing performance.

- **Business Intelligence Development Studio**—The Business Intelligence Development Studio is essentially Microsoft Visual Studio 2005 with some additional SQL Server 2005 business intelligence project types. It is an applications development environment that allows developers to build Analysis Services multidimensional databases and measure groups, cubes, and all the other development components with BI.

Analysis Services Architecture

When you understand the terminology associated with Analysis Services, the next step is to understand the architecture.

The SQL Server technologies that make up business intelligence are as follows:

- **Analysis Services**—The component used for storing OLAP data, cubes, and solutions

- **Database Engine**—The component used for storing the relational database model and data associated with a multidimensional database

- **Reporting Services**—The component used for creating business intelligence reports

- **Integration Services**—The enterprise class data integration program for managing the ETL process from OLTP to OLAP

- **Business Intelligence Development Studio**—The development environment included with Visual Studio for creating, testing, and deploying BI projects

Analysis Services is the key component providing the backbone for business intelligence.

The Different Versions of Analysis Services

Analysis Services is supported only in the Standard and Enterprise Editions of SQL Server 2005. These editions are similar, but the Enterprise Edition of Analysis Services includes the following additional or enhanced features and functionality:

- **Advanced Business Analytics**—Includes metadata translation, account intelligence, perspective, and semi-additive measures.

- **Proactive Caching**—Provides automated caching based on an incremental time interval. Caching is dictated based on one of the three storage modes specified.

- **Advanced Data Management**—Provides flexibility for parallel processing, partitioned cubes, and server synchronization.

- **Full Writeback Support**—Provides dimension and cell writeback during processing.

- **Advanced Performance Tuning**—Increases accuracy, performance, and scalability. Options are included with this enterprise feature for tuning data mining models.

- **Integration Services Data Flow Integration**—Offers additional performance and scalability options within Integration Services for tuning data mining models. This feature is not available in other editions of SQL Server 2005.

- **Text Mining**—Includes additional options that pertain to text mining.

What's New with Service Pack 2 for Analysis Services

Compared to other SQL Server components, SQL Server 2005 Service Pack 2 fixes many known Analysis Services bugs and introduces an abundance of new features and functionality. The new items include

- Support of the new business intelligence features and functionality included with Microsoft Office 2007 and SQL Server 2005. (If Service Pack 2 is not installed, the new Office 2007 BI features are disabled.)

- Dramatically improved functionality of local and session cubes.

- Increased performance and scalability with improvements to unary operators, running sum calculations, partition query scalability, ragged hierarchies, cell writeback, visual totals, nonuniform memory access (NUMA) optimizations for partition-processing relational OLAP (ROLAP) dimensions, subselects, many-to-many dimensions, drillthrough, semi-additive measures, and stored procedures.

- Warning messages displayed if a user-defined hierarchy is not defined as a natural hierarchy.

- The introduction of a new argument for the MDX drilldown function. The argument allows you to specify drilldown on particular tuples.

- The addition of the SCOPE_ISOLATION property to the MDX CREATE method. This property enables session-scoped and query-defined calculations to be resolved before calculations in the cube rather than after.

- Improved functionality and performance through enhancements to incremental processing, cell writeback, usage-based aggregation, parent-child security, design algorithms, backward and forward compatibility, partition query scalability, and the Time Intelligence Wizard.

- Caching of commonly used attributes such as naïve bayes predictions to enhance performance.

- Improved neural network training as a result of better utilization of memory, with sparse training data sets and utilization of multiple threads during error computation (a SQL Server 2005 Enterprise Edition feature).

- The addition of limited support for data mining viewers with local mining models.

- The redistribution of data mining viewer controls that are now dependent on ADOMD.NET. (The new redistribution file will be available in a feature pack that will ship soon after Service Pack 2.)

Administering Analysis Services

SQL Server 2005 Analysis Services is composed of two distinct toolsets: SQL Server Management Studio (SSMS) and Business Intelligence Development Studio (BIDS). The toolsets are modeled after the responsibilities performed by both database administrators and database developers. The majority of the management and administration tasks are conducted by database administrators from within SQL Server Management Studio, whereas the greater part of the database developer duties are accomplished in Business Intelligence Developer Studio. Because the following sections focus on administration and management, the majority of the tasks illustrated here are conducted through SQL Server Management Studio.

Obtaining and Installing the Sample AdventureWorks DW Analysis Services Database

The AdventureWorks DW data warehouse sample database can be installed through the SQL Server 2005 installation process or by downloading the sample database directly from Microsoft Download Center.

To install the sample database from the Microsoft SQL Server 2005 installation DVD, you must select the sample database during the setup of SQL Server 2005. To locate the sample databases, follow these steps:

1. Select Workstation Components, Books Online, and Development tools on the Components to Install page.

2. Click Advanced and then expand Documentation, Samples, and Sample Databases.

3. Select Sample Code and Applications, expand Sample Databases, and choose the sample databases to install.

4. When the SQL Server 2005 installation is complete, choose Start, All Programs, Microsoft SQL Server 2005, Documentation and Tutorials, Samples and click Microsoft SQL Server 2005 samples to finalize the installation.

Alternatively, you can obtain the latest version of the sample database directly from the Microsoft Download Center. Using the latest version of the sample database is recommended because Microsoft updates the sample on a periodic basis.

Downloading the Latest AdventureWorks DW Sample Database

To obtain the latest AdventureWorks DW database from the Microsoft Download Center, perform the following steps. The latest version, as of this writing, is February 2007.

1. Download the latest AdventureWorks Business Intelligence Sample database from the Microsoft Download Center. The database choices are based on the processor version—x86, x64, or Itanium (IA64)—and whether the collation setting will be case-sensitive or not case-sensitive. For this example, the x64 file `AdventureWorksBICI_x64.msi` was used because it is not case-sensitive.

2. Double-click the appropriate MSI file to start the installation process.

3. On the Welcome to the Install Shield Wizard screen, click Next.

4. On the License Agreement screen, review the license, accept the terms, and click Next.

5. On the Destination Folder screen, install the sample database in the default location or click the Change command button and enter a folder of choice for the installation. Click Next to continue.

6. On the Ready to Install Program screen, click Install.

7. Click Finish.

Attaching the Latest AdventureWorks DW Sample Database

After you've downloaded and installed the latest database, the next step is to attach the database and transaction log files. To attach the sample AdventureWorks Business Intelligence database to a SQL Server instance using SSMS, perform the following steps:

1. Select Start, All Programs, Microsoft SQL Server 2005, SQL Server Management Studio.

2. In Object Explorer, connect to the Database Engine, expand the desired server, and expand the Database folder.

3. Right-click the Database folder and select Attach.

4. In the Attach Database dialog box, click the Add button in the Databases to Attach section.

5. Locate AdventureWorks database files, as shown in Figure 2.1, and click OK and then OK again in the Attach Databases screen to finalize.

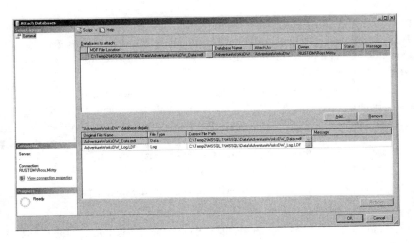

FIGURE 2.1
Attaching a database.

Note

The AdventureWorks sample database and transaction log files can be found in the destination folder that was used when installing the sample databases in the preceding steps. It is a best practice, for performance and availability, to isolate the database and transaction log files on separate hard drives.

Deploying Analysis Services Databases

After designing and creating the Analysis Services database with BIDS, you need to deploy the database to Analysis Services. The deployment process consists of wrapping the source definition files from BIDS with a Create command, which then sends them over to the server.

There are several options for deploying an Analysis Services database:

- Using the Analysis Services Deployment Wizard
- Using Business Intelligence Developer Studio
- Creating a SQL Server Integration Service Package
- Using the Synchronize Database Wizard

Deploying the initial database and then maintaining the ongoing changes are primary Analysis Services administration tasks you must conduct.

Using the Analysis Services Deployment Wizard

The Analysis Services Deployment Wizard is a tool used to deploy Analysis Services projects created in Business Intelligence Management Studio. The tool leverages the XML output files of a specified project and then deploys the project to a target SQL server of choice that is running an Analysis Services instance by using input scripts. You can invoke the tool by selecting Start, All Programs, Microsoft SQL Server 2005, Analysis Services, Deployment Wizard.

Using the Analysis Services Deployment Wizard is usually the preferred method for deploying an Analysis Services database. The reason is that the Deployment Wizard allows you to process the database into a production environment without overriding any existing Analysis Services server settings such as security and configuration. In addition, often if you're managing the Analysis Services instance, you do not have access to the Visual Studio Development environment; therefore, you may not have access to deploy directly from within the Business Intelligence project.

To deploy the AdventureWorks DW database with the Analysis Services Deployment Wizard, follow these steps:

1. Select Start, All Programs, Microsoft SQL Server 2005, Analysis Services, Deployment Wizard.

2. On the Analysis Services Welcome screen, click Next.

3. On the Specify Source Analysis Services Database screen, shown in Figure 2.2, click the ellipses button and specify the location of an Analysis Services database file. Click OK and then click Next to continue.

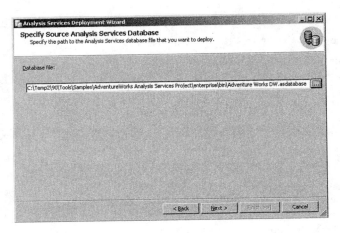

FIGURE 2.2
The Specify Source Analysis Services Database screen.

4. On the Installation Target screen, specify the target server and database name; then click Next.

5. The Specify Options for Partitions and Roles screen determines how existing partitions, roles, and members will be handled during deployment. Select the desired settings for the Partitions section and then Roles and Members section based on the explanations, as displayed in Figure 2.3. Click Next.

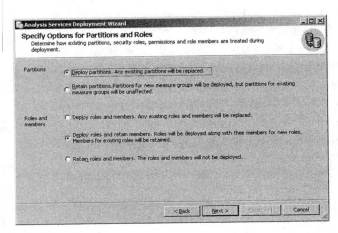

FIGURE 2.3
The Specify Options for Partitions and Roles screen.

6. The Specify Configuration Properties screen, shown in Figure 2.4, includes the configuration settings for each object being deployed. In addition, two Retain check boxes allow you to retain configuration and optimization settings for existing objects based on previous deployments. Select the appropriate Retain settings and change the properties as needed. Then click Next.

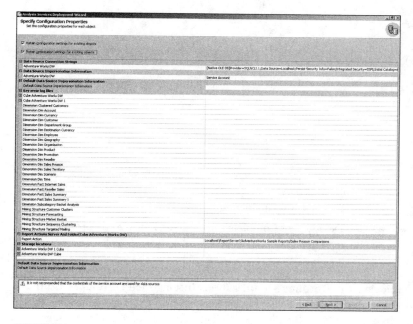

FIGURE 2.4
The Specify Configuration Properties screen.

7. On the Select Processing Options screen, shown in Figure 2.5, select the desired settings for the Processing Method and Writeback Table Options sections and whether to include all processing in a single transaction. Click Next to continue.

8. The final configuration screen, Confirm Deployment, allows you to create a deployment script by selecting the Create Deployment Script check box. Select the option to create a deployment script, enter a script location, and click Next to proceed.

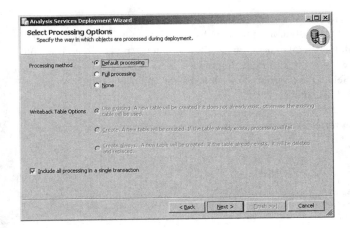

FIGURE 2.5
The Select Processing Options screen.

9. The Deploying Database screen provides configuration and status based on the deployment. Review the status for success or failure errors and click Next to continue.

10. On the Deployment Complete screen, click Finish to finalize the deployment process.

Deploying the Database via Business Intelligence Developer Studio

Another alternative for deploying an Analysis Services database is directly through the Business Intelligence Management Studio. A common usage scenario for this methodology includes deploying project design changes directly from the development environment to the production Analysis Services database.

Note

Unfortunately, if the database is deployed directly from within Business Intelligence Developer Studio and if the database already exists on Analysis Services, the existing configuration settings will be overwritten if you use this approach.

To deploy an Analysis Services Database via Business Intelligence Developer Studio, follow these steps:

1. Select Start, All Programs, Microsoft SQL Server 2005, SQL Server Business Intelligence Development Studio.

2. From within BIDS, select File, Open and click Project/Solution.

3. In the Open Project screen, select the Adventure Works.sln file and click Open.

Note

The Adventure Works.sln file is located in the \Microsoft SQL Server\90\Samples\AdventureWorks Analysis Services Project folder. The location of this folder is based on the installation method used for deploying the sample database. If the sample was installed with the default installation of SQL Server 2005, the folder is located in the installation path of SQL Server. If the sample was downloaded from the Microsoft website, the path is based on the location where the file was deployed.

---

4. From Solution Explorer, right-click the AdventureWorks DW project and select Deploy, as shown in Figure 2.6.

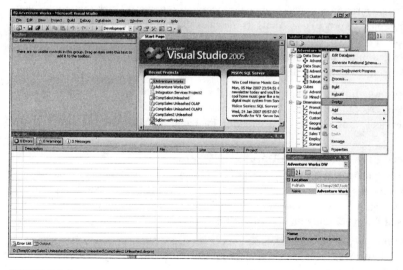

FIGURE 2.6
Deploying the database with Business Intelligence Developer Studio.

Note

When you deploy the sample database, the default server is set to localhost. If the target server name needs to be changed, right-click the server name and change it. This task should be conducted before the project is deployed.

Caution

If the AdventureWorks DW database already exists on the local host, a caution message box is displayed stating that the database will be overwritten if you continue this process.

Creating a SQL Server Integration Service Package

The SQL Server 2005 Integration Services (SSIS) component integrates data from different sources. This integration includes importing, exporting, and transforming data from disparate sources. The data can be copied, merged, restructured, and cleaned as part of the integration processing, which makes Integration Services a powerful tool in the development of data warehouses.

The Integration Services component includes a powerful task that allows you to deploy or process an Analysis Services database on a schedule. In addition, it is also possible to create a task that will schedule a deployment script, created in the previous steps by the Deployment Wizard or the Visual Studio Project, to occur at a desired time interval.

For more information on creating and scheduling Integration Services packages, refer to Chapter 5, "Administering SQL Server 2005 Integration Services," and Chapter 11, "Creating Packages and Transferring Data."

Using the Synchronize Database Wizard

The Synchronize Database Wizard is another technology within SQL Server that allows you to synchronize Analysis Services databases between Analysis Services instances. In addition to database synchronization, this tool is also used for synchronizing security settings.

To run the Synchronize Database tool, you right-click an Analysis Services Databases folder and select Synchronize from within Analysis Services on the Target server. You must specify the source and target server, security settings, whether to use compression, and finally either run the synchronization after the wizard is complete or generate a script that can be used later.

Processing Analysis Services Objects

Processing objects in Analysis Services means adding and updating data from a relational database to an Analysis Services database. This process is typically performed after the Analysis Services database has been deployed or when the Analysis Services database needs to be updated because changes have occurred on the relational side. The process loads the actual dimension and partitions with data.

The easiest approach to ensuring that the relational and multidimensional databases are consistent with one another is to process the entire database. When the entire database is processed, all the dimensions and cubes within the database are dropped and new ones are created, but end users still have access to the data during processing.

In many situations, it is not possible to process the full database at once due to the size constraints on a server and the shear amount of time to complete this task. Therefore, to address these challenges, you can process individual components, such as cubes or dimensions, separately to reduce the amount of processing time and space required. Users can still access the database during processing.

Analysis Services objects such as databases, cubes, partitions, measure groups, dimensions, mining models, and mining structures can be processed individually.

Processing the Full OLAP Database

To process a full Analysis Services multidimensional database from within SQL Server Management Studio, follow these steps:

1. Select Start, All Programs, Microsoft SQL Server 2005, SQL Server Management Studio.

2. In Object Explorer, connect to Analysis Services, expand the desired server, and then expand the desired database.

3. Right-click the database and select Process.

Note

Before processing the database, if desired, you can conduct a preliminary analysis of the processing job by clicking on the Impact Analysis button on the Process Database dialog box. The Impact Analysis dialog box is then invoked.

---

4. On the General page of the Process Database dialog box, the following process options are available for an object: Process Default, Process Full, and Unprocessed. Analysis Services automatically determines which processing option is the best fit for the scenario. You can over-write this automatic decision by selecting one of the processing options if desired. For this example, the Process Full option was selected to reprocess all the AdventureWorks DW objects, as shown in Figure 2.7.

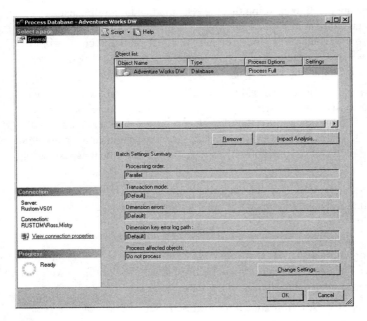

FIGURE 2.7
Specifying the process options for the AdventureWorks DW objects.

5. From within the same General page, you can specify customized settings for processing the cube by selecting the Change Settings button. The Change Settings dialog box contains two tabs for applying customized settings:

- **Processing Options Tab**—This tab, shown in Figure 2.8, contains Processing Order, Writeback Table Option, and Affected Objects settings.

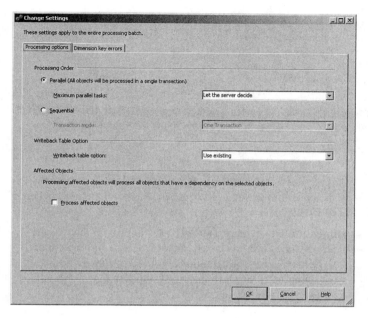

FIGURE 2.8
The Processing Options tab in the Change Settings dialog box.

The Processing Order section has two options: Parallel and Sequential. Parallel, just as it sounds, processes the objects in parallel. An additional drop-down setting, Maximum Parallel Tasks, can be configured when processing objects in parallel. This setting governs the number of tasks to execute in parallel when the operation is started. The default setting is Let the Server Decide, which allows Analysis Services to select an optional number of parallel tasks. You can also use the drop-down list and select a desired amount.

If you select Sequential, the objects are processed sequentially. The Transaction Mode drop-down list allows all objects to be processed in one selection or in multiple transitions. This option is available only if the Sequential option is selected.

Three Writeback Table settings are available from the drop-down menu: Create, Create Always, and Use Existing. The default, Use Existing, uses an existing writeback table. The Create option creates a writeback table if it does not exist, and the final setting, Create Always, creates a writeback table if it does not exist or overwrites the existing table if it does exist.

Note

Errors occur if the Create option is selected and a writeback table already exists and if the Use Existing option is selected and the table does not exist.

If the Process Affected Objects option is selected, processing occurs on all objects that have dependencies on the objects being processed.

■ **Dimension Key Errors Tab**—The second tab on the Change Settings dialog box, shown in Figure 2.9, contains two options: Use Default Error Configuration and Use Custom Error Configuration. If the Custom Error Configuration is selected, additional custom errors can be tuned.

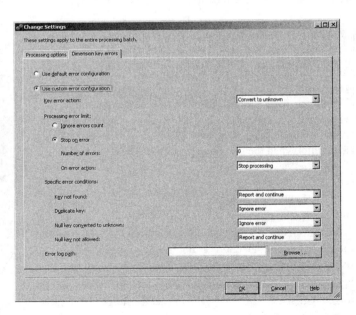

FIGURE 2.9
The Dimension Key Errors tab in the Change Settings dialog box.

6. From the Process Database dialog box, make the desired Batch Summary setting changes and click OK on the General page to commence processing.

7. Processing starts, and the Process Progress window displays status, start times, and the number of rows affected, as shown in Figure 2.10. For additional information, click the View Details or Copy button to paste the information into a document for later viewing; otherwise, click Close on the Process Progress window to continue.

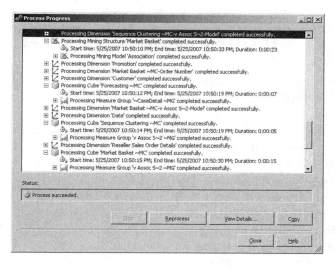

FIGURE 2.10
Reviewing the Process Progress window.

8. Click OK on the Process Database dialog box to complete the processing task.

Tip

To streamline the processing time of a multidimensional database, you may choose to process only subsets of the database such as a dimension and/or cube. These processing tasks can be accomplished by right-clicking on either a dimension and/or cube and selecting Process.

Analysis Services Management Tasks

When the Analysis Services administration tasks finish configuring server settings, deploying databases, and processing the data, ongoing management of Analysis Services is necessary. The following sections include some of the Analysis Services management tasks.

Analysis Services Properties Configuration

The Analysis Server Property dialog box is the place where you manage the behavior of an Analysis Services instance. This dialog box is invoked by launching SQL Server Management Studio, choosing Analysis Services in the Server Type drop-down list, and then right-clicking the Server name and selecting Properties.

When you're configuring Analysis Services properties, the dialog box is separated into three pages:

- **General Page**—This page allows you to set and modify basic and advanced general settings for an Analysis Server instance, as shown in Figure 2.11. General and advanced properties configuration is based on the following columns: Name, Value, Current Value, Default Value, Restart, Type, Units, and Category. In addition, from within this General page, you can reset defaults and display all advanced properties and modified properties.

- **Language/Collation Page**—This page allows you to set the server-wide collation and language settings for Analysis Services. The Collation setting manages the server behavior of both sorting and equivalence of strings, whereas the Language setting maintains the default language to be used.

- **Security Page**—This page allows you to grant a user or Windows group server-wide security privileges (server administrator role) for Analysis Services. When granting Analysis Services privileges from within this page, click the Add button to enter a name of a user or group.

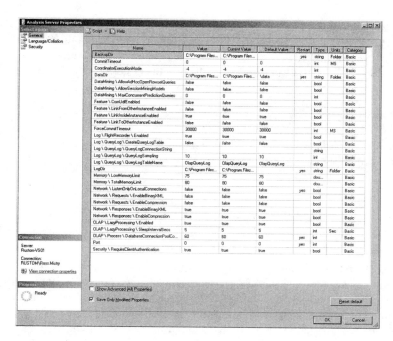

FIGURE 2.11
Reviewing the General page in the Analysis Server Properties dialog box.

Managing OLAP Storage Models

As a database administrator, you must first be aware of the storage models available in SQL Server 2005 Analysis Services to manage how each partition's data will be stored physically. The three OLAP storage models available for storing data are

- **Multidimensional OLAP (MOLAP)**—This storage model provides the best query performance, as detailed data and aggregations are kept in a multidimensional compressed proprietary format. The relational source is accessed only during initial processing, and queries are resolved exclusively from the multidimensional store.

- **Relational OLAP (ROLAP)**—This storage model is considered to be real-time, as detailed data and aggregations are stored in the relational source. This model supports real-time query processing. Data is fetched directly from the relational database, but performance degrades because queries tend to run slower as more aggregations are involved.

- **Hybrid OLAP (HOLAP)**—This storage model combines both MOLAP and ROLAP ideologies. Aggregations are stored in the multidimensional stores, whereas detailed data is found in the relational store. This storage model provides the benefits of both MOLAP and ROLAP.

Tip

It is a best practice to standardize and always use MOLAP unless there is a significant reason to leverage the other storage modes. MOLAP is optimized to provide the best query performance while providing efficient storage.

It is possible to configure the storage options for an OLAP cube or an individual partition with either Business Intelligence Developer Studio or, after initial deployment, with SQL Server Management Studio.

It is usually the responsibility of database architects or programmers to create the multidimensional environment. Database administrators typically administer the physical storage layout of a SQL Server environment. Therefore, it is common for these teams to work together on selecting the storage mode for a cube or partition; however, database administrators typically manage the storage model of an OLAP cube via SQL Server Management Studio.

Note

If SQL Server Management Studio is used to configure the storage mode of a cube or partition, after the initial deployment, the storage mode defined in the Visual Studio project via Business Intelligence Developer Studio will not be updated.

Managing Proactive Caching and the Storage Mode Settings

The storage options of an OLAP cube are configured with SQL Server Management Studio. The following example uses the AdventureWorks cube, which is located in the AdventureWorks DW multidimensional database.

1. Select Start, All Programs, Microsoft SQL Server 2005, SQL Server Management Studio.

2. In Object Explorer, connect to Analysis Services and expand the desired server.

3. Expand the Databases folder, the AdventureWorks DW folder, and the Cubes folder.

4. Right-click the AdventureWorks Cubes folder and select Properties.
5. In the Cube properties dialog box, select the Proactive Caching page.
6. On the Proactive Caching page, shown in Figure 2.12, select the Standard Setting option and choose the appropriate ROLAP, HOLAP, or MOLAP setting on the slider bar. Then click OK.

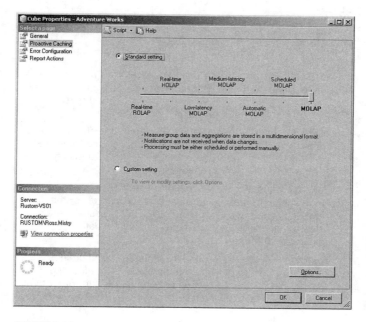

FIGURE 2.12
Managing the storage mode settings via the Proactive Caching page.

Table 2.1 summarizes the differences between the standard storage settings available on the Proactive Caching page.

Table 2.1   **Proactive Storage Settings Summary**

Storage Setting	Measure Group Data and Aggregations	Notifications	Processing
MOLAP	Stored in multi-dimensional format.	Not received when data changes.	Scheduled or performed manually.

Table 2.1   **continued**

Storage Setting	Measure Group Data and Aggregations	Notifications	Processing
Scheduled MOLAP	Stored in multi-dimensional format	Not received when data changes.	Performed automatically every 24 hours.
Automatic MOLAP	Stored in multi-dimensional format.	Server will listen for notifications when data changes.	Automatically with no restriction on latency.
Medium-latency MOLAP	Stored in multi-dimensional format.	Server will listen for notifications when data changes.	Performed automatically every 4 hours.
Low-latency MOLAP	Stored in multi-dimensional format.	Server will listen for notifications when data changes.	Performed automatically every 30 minutes.
Real-time HOLAP	Group data is stored in relational format and aggregates are stored in multi-dimensional format.	Server will listen for notifications when data changes.	All queries reflect the current state of data.
Real-time ROLAP	Stored in relational format.	Server will listen for notifications when data changes.	All queries reflect the current state of data.

> **Tip**
>
> For more customized and granular storage settings, use the Custom Setting option located on the Proactive Caching page.

Backing Up and Restoring Analysis Services

When you're managing Analysis Services, one of your most important tasks is creating an Analysis Services backup strategy. It is imperative that all the OLAP databases be backed up. In addition, based on the Analysis Services storage model being used on the OLAP database, you must not overlook backing up the OLTP databases associated with the data warehouse. After the backup is created, both the data and metadata are stored in a single file with the extension *.abf.

To initiate the backup and restore process, right-click the OLAP database and select either Backup or Restore. For more information and step-by-step instructions to back up and restore Analysis Services databases, review Chapter 17, "Backing Up and Restoring the SQL Server 2005 Environment" (online).

> **Tip**
>
> The Analysis Services database backup process can be automated by scripting the backup and creating a scheduled SQL Server Agent job.

Viewing and Managing Analysis Services Database Properties

You are able to manage and review the properties of each database by right-clicking the desired Analysis Services database and selecting Properties. The Properties page of a database includes general, security, and status settings.

Creating Standard Informational Database Reports

As a database administrator, you often are required to keep current on specific information and metrics on an Analysis Services database. Specific metrics include the estimated size of the database in bytes, date created, date last updated, date last processed, language settings, and collation settings. A standard report can be generated from within Analysis Services. To generate a report, right-click the Analysis Services database, select Standard Reports, and then select General. The results are displayed in the right pane.

Scripting Analysis Services Objects

Analysis Services includes a scripting wizard that automatically generates an XML script for almost any Analysis Services management task.

The wizard can automatically generate Create, Alter, and Delete scripts for Analysis Services objects such as data sources, cubes, measure groups, dimensions, mining structures, and roles. Basically, you choose the desired object to be scripted, right-click, and select Script.

The scripting wizard provides a solution for automating Analysis Services management tasks.

Securing Analysis Services

Similar to the Database Engine component, Analysis Services security management is tightly integrated with Windows authentication. Therefore, users or groups can be granted authorization at a macro or micro level.

From a security perspective, it is a best practice to first harden an Analysis Services installation and then grant access to the server and database objects based on a role-based strategy.

Hardening concepts for Analysis Services, such as using the Configuration tools, are covered in Chapter 12, "Hardening a SQL Server 2005 Environment." The following sections discuss granting administrative or database authorization based on a role model.

Granting Administrative Access to Analysis Services

The Server role, within Analysis Services, is the highest level of administrator access and control. If a user or group is added to this role, that user or group inherits full server-wide permissions and can fully manage all Analysis Services components, including objects and security.

To grant a user or group administrator privileges to Analysis Services, follow these steps:

1. Select Start, All Programs, Microsoft SQL Server 2005, SQL Server Management Studio.

2. In Object Explorer, connect to Analysis Services and expand the desired server.

3. Right-click the server name and select Properties.

4. Select the Security page in the Analysis Server Properties dialog box.

5. On the Security page, click Add To, select either the user or a Windows group, and click OK.

6. Click OK to finalize the settings.

> **Note**
>
> By default, members of the server's local Windows Administrators group are automatically enrolled for the Analysis Server role. Therefore, these members have full administrative control over any task within Analysis Server.

Creating Roles for Analysis Services Database Authorization

The high-level predefined database permissions for creating a new role on a selected Analysis Services database are

■ **Full Control**—This permission is equivalent to Administrator privileges on a specific database.

■ **Process Database**—This permission allows members of this newly created role to process the specified Analysis Services database. Members cannot view any data associated with this multidimensional database.

■ **Read Definition**—This permission grants authorization to members of this role for read permissions on all metadata associated with this database.

These three permissions should satisfy a majority of the database administration access requirement scenarios for Analysis Services databases. However, if more restriction and granularity are required, you can choose from additional security access items. The additional granular access rights include

■ Access

■ Administrator

■ AllowBrowsing

■ AllowDrillThrough

■ AllowedSet

■ AllowPredict

■ ApplyDenied

■ DefaultMember

■ DeniedSet

■ IsAllowed

■ Process

■ ReadDefinition

■ VisualTotals

These granular permissions can then be set on the database, data source, cube, cell, dimension, attribute, mining structure, and mining model levels.

Note

For a full description of each access right and permission available, refer to the topic "Permissions and Access Rights (SSAS)" in SQL Server 2005 Books Online.

To create a new role with Administrator privileges for the AdventureWorks multidimensional database, follow these steps.

1. Select Start, All Programs, Microsoft SQL Server 2005, SQL Server Management Studio.

2. In Object Explorer, connect to Analysis Services and expand the desired server.

3. Expand the Databases folder and the AdventureWorks DW multidimensional database.

4. Right-click the Roles folder and select New Role.

5. On the General page of the Create Role dialog box, enter a role name such as **Administrator Role** and enter a role description. Select the Full Control option to set the permissions for this role.

Note

The Process Database and Roll Definition permissions are automatically enabled when Full Control (Administrator) is selected.

---

6. On the Membership page, click Add To and specify the users and/or groups to be members of this newly created role. Click OK.

7. Click OK on the Create Role dialog box to complete the task.

Note

As stated earlier, it is possible to set granular permissions on a multidimensional database at the micro level. If this is warranted, you should leverage the additional pages from within the Edit Role dialog box such as Data Sources, Cubes, Cell Data, Dimensions, Dimension Data, and Mining Structures.

Tip

It is possible to duplicate an existing role to streamline the creation process of multiple roles with similar permissions. You can achieve this by right-clicking on the existing role and selecting Duplicate.

Administering and Monitoring Analysis Services Performance

Another common database administration task is administering and monitoring Analysis Services performance. The primary tools that should be leveraged to monitor performance include

- Performance Tuning Analysis Services with Profiler
- Flight Recorder

- Operations Manager
- Performance Monitor
- Analysis Services Log Files

Performance Tuning Analysis Services with Profiler

The SQL Server Profiler is a tool for capturing SQL Server 2005 events into a trace file. The trace file can be used to analyze a series of events, replay a series of events, or act as an auditing mechanism for security purposes.

This tool is also a great avenue, when used in conjunction with SQL Server 2005 Analysis Services, to view Analysis Services activity, monitor Analysis Services, or troubleshoot Analysis Services performance.

You can invoke SQL Server Profiler by choosing SQL Server Profiler under SQL Server 2005 Performance Tools.

Unfortunately, there isn't a specific profiler template tailored for Analysis Services. Therefore, the following events categories should be used when creating the Analysis Services trace: Command Events, Discovery Events, Discover Server State Events, Errors and Warning Events, Notification Events, Profess Reports Events, Queries Events, Security Audit Events, and Session Events.

Flight Recorder

SQL Server 2005 Analysis Services introduces a new logging technology that is similar to the black box found in commercial airplanes. The Analysis Services flight recorder constantly records Analysis Services activity to a trace file. The Flight Recorder trace options are specified in the Analysis Services server property settings. The settings include enabling flight recorder, size of the logs, and the location of the log file trace. The events can then be replayed for analysis by opening the trace file with SQL Server 2005 Profiler.

Monitoring Analysis Services with Operations Manager

Another great tool to proactively monitor Analysis Services is Microsoft Operations Manager (MOM). MOM includes a dedicated Microsoft Management Pack tailored for SQL Server. There is a subcomponent that focuses on SQL Server 2005 Analysis Services.

> **Note**
>
> For more information on proactively monitoring a database mirroring session with Microsoft Operations Manager, refer to Chapter 21, "Monitoring SQL Server 2005" (online).

Performance Tuning Analysis Services with Performance Monitor

Performance Monitor, included with Windows Server 2003, provides a plethora of newly created performance objects for monitoring and troubleshooting SQL Server 2005 Analysis Services. You can launch this tool by selecting Start, All Programs, Administrative Tools, Performance to discover the performance objects, counters, and explanations.

Summary

Analysis Services is a key Microsoft SQL Server 2005 component and is the foundation for providing business intelligence. You do not have to understand how to design multidimensional databases or be fluent with Business Intelligence Development Studio; however, you should understand how to conduct the following Analysis Services administration and management tasks: configuring Analysis Services server properties, deploying multidimensional databases, selecting the appropriate storage mode, and securing and monitoring Analysis Services.

Best Practices

- When deploying Analysis Services databases, use either the Analysis Services Deployment Wizard or Synchronize Database Wizard.

- Automate Analysis Services database backups by first scripting the backup task and then creating a scheduled job with the SQL Server Agent.

- Process individual Analysis Services components to reduce the processing time of a multidimensional database.

- Use Microsoft Operations Manager to proactively monitor an Analysis Services installation or infrastructure.

- Use 64-bit processors if there are more than 10 million members within a dimension.

- To minimize performance issues, tweak the following settings to avoid placing dimensions in ROLAP mode: Disable the Bring Online Immediately check box in the Storage Options dialog box and set the `OnlineMode` property to `OnCacheComplete`.

- Use a role-based security model that leverages Active Directory groups to maximize efficiency when granting authorization for BI data and for Analysis Services administration.

- When processing very large multidimensional databases, take advantage of processing individual components to reduce processing times and address lack of disk space issues.

- Standardize and always use MOLAP unless there is a significant reason to leverage the other storage modes. MOLAP is optimized to provide the best query performance while providing efficient storage.

CHAPTER 3

Administering SQL Server 2005 Reporting Services

SQL Server 2005 Reporting Services (SSRS) provides an enterprise-class reporting infrastructure by exposing multiple extensible components through numerous user and programmatic interfaces. SSRS uses these components to retrieve data from various sources, turn the data into a readable report, and deliver the data to specified targets. Targets can include a web browser for interactive reporting or an email account when report subscriptions are configured.

With the implementation of SSRS, an organization can centrally manage and secure reports through customizable roles. Analysts and developers can access data from numerous data sources through a standardized interface and development API, and data managers and report users are provided various viewing and report subscription functionality.

This chapter focuses on the day-to-day tasks and procedures needed to administer and troubleshoot SSRS. By exploring many of the typical administrative tasks, such as configuring report server components and defining site roles, you can achieve an in-depth understanding of the implementation. This knowledge will ultimately ensure the long-term health of the environment in which you work.

What's New for Reporting Services in Service Pack 2

Many new features and substantial improvements have been introduced with SQL Server 2005 Reporting Services, and with each new service pack, Microsoft continues to extend the functionality of the product.

In addition to improving performance and reliability, the following SSRS enhancements have been included with the SQL Server 2005 Service Pack 2 upgrade:

- **Usability**—When you're viewing reports, the Select All check box has been re-implemented for multiselect report parameters. This feature was originally removed during the SQL Server 2005 Service Pack 1 upgrade.

- **Development**—Numerous enhancements have been made for developers, such as the ability to access Hyperion System 9.3 BI+ Enterprise Analytics data sources and the ability to perform Report Model generation from Oracle data sources that run on version 9.2.0.3 or later.

- **Integration**—SharePoint Service 3.0 and Office 2007 SharePoint Server integration has been introduced in this service pack, allowing access to Reporting Services functionality from within the latest Microsoft SharePoint technologies.

Identifying Reporting Services Components

SQL Server 2005 Reporting Services is composed of several unique components, and all the components work together to provide a full-featured reporting solution. To help you administer and maintain SSRS, this chapter reviews the interaction between the different components.

Figure 3.1 illustrates the interaction the report server has with external elements such as remote databases and internal objects such as the processing and delivery component.

It is important to understand each of the SSRS components from an administrative perspective. Subsequent sections within this chapter identify and demonstrate common administrative processes and provide best practices to help ensure the environment operates as expected. This understanding will help you perform configuration changes as necessary to accommodate the dynamic needs of your organization and to troubleshoot the implementation if a problem should arise.

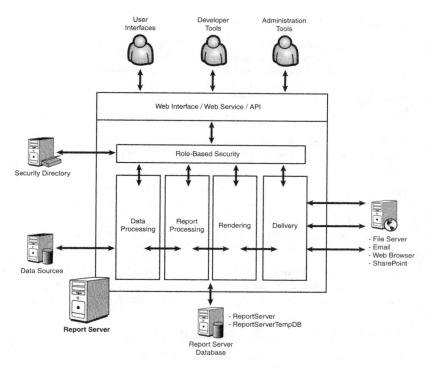

FIGURE 3.1
Report server components.

Understanding the Report Server

The report server resides on an Internet Information Server (IIS) and provides the core Reporting Services functionality through ASP.NET 2.0 web services. Each report server instance has two databases, and they are required for the implementation to operate successfully.

In a typical scenario, an Active Directory User, shown near the top of Figure 3.1, would access SSRS through the Report Manager web interface. The Report Manager is a component of the report server that provides browser-based access to Reporting Services.

Warning

When the Reporting Services web server is configured for Windows Integrated Authentication, the user account credentials are automatically passed through to Reporting Services if the address of the server is in the correct Internet Explorer security zone. By default, only the Intranet Zone allows passthrough authentication.

Before the user can access SSRS, an SSRS administrator must define a role allowing the user to perform specific tasks, such as viewing folders and running reports.

When the user executes a report by clicking on the report listed in the web browser, the data processing component retrieves the data from the data source, the data is then processed based on the business logic contained within the report, and the final report is rendered and displayed in the user's browser.

The user can then print or export the report using one of the predefined or custom-built extensions. Predefined extensions include the ability to export the report in HTML, MHTML, PDF, XML, CSV, TIFF, and Excel formats.

Understanding the Report Server Databases

SSRS uses two databases, and depending on how the system was designed, these databases can either be local on the same system as the report server or on a remote system SQL Server 2000 or 2005 Database Engine.

The web server gains access to these databases through the ASP.NET identity configured on the IIS 6.0 application pool assigned to the SSRS virtual directories. The Network Services account is the default identity for the SSRS application pool. Users browsing and running reports through SSRS do not require direct access to either of the SSRS databases.

Note

The local ASP.NET worker process identity is used to run the SSRS web services when installed on IIS 5.x. This account is subsequently used to access the report server database.

These two databases can be configured automatically during the installation of Reporting Services, if the automatic configuration option was selected during setup. When SSRS is configured automatically, the default names for the databases depend on the SQL instance SSRS was installed as. If SSRS was installed as the default instance, the database names are ReportServer and ReportServerTempDB. However, if SSRS was installed as a named instance, the instance name is appended to the database name. For example, if SSRS was installed as INSTANCE01, the default database names would be configured as ReportServer$INSTANCE01 and ReportServerTempDB$INSTANCE01.

If SSRS was not automatically configured during setup, the databases must be defined and the correct permission configured before the server can be used.

The ReportServer database is used to store metadata and object definitions. The following objects are kept in this database:

- Reports, report models, and report definitions
- Subscription and schedule definitions
- Report snapshots and report history
- System properties
- System-level security settings
- Report execution log data
- Symmetric keys
- Encrypted connection and credentials

The ReportServerTempDB database stores temporary information such as user session, execution data, and cached reports.

Understanding the Data Sources

The "data source" can refer to two different items. During day-to-day administration, you work with the data source object, which can be embedded within a report or shared among many reports in SSRS. The second type of data source is the external system or repository the data source object establishes a connection with. SSRS can establish a connection with the following:

- SQL Server 7.0/2000/2005
- SQL Server 2000/2005 Analysis Services
- Reporting Services Report Models
- Oracle
- SAP
- SAP NetWeaver Business Intelligence

- ODBC
- OLE DB
- XML
- Hyperion Essbase

New in SP2

The Hyperion System 9.3 BI+ Enterprise Analytics data source is new in SSRS Service Pack 2.

Identifying Reporting Service Administrative Tools

The report server is administered through the various tools included with SQL Server 2005, the IIS Manager, and various configuration files used by the SSRS web services.

To administer and effectively maintain the environment, you need an understanding of the SQL administration tools. SQL Server 2005 includes the following administrative tools:

- **SQL Server Configuration Manager**—This tool is used to administer different options associated with the service used to run each Reporting Services instance.

- **Report Server Configuration Manager**—This is the primary tool used to configure the report server, the key component of the Reporting Services implementation.

- **SQL Server Management Studio**—This new tool introduced with SQL Server 2005 provides administrative access to the SSRS site settings and objects such as data sources and reports.

- **Report Manager**—This web-based tool provides both administrative and user access to the SSRS instance.

- **SQL Server Surface Area Configuration**—This new tool introduced with SQL Server 2005 can be used to allow or prevent access to SSRS features and functionality to reduce the potential attack surface.

- **IIS Manager**—This console can be used to modify the Reporting Services website properties, security, and associated application pools.

You can find additional information on each of these tools in Chapter 16, "Tools of the Trade" (online). Also, this chapter does not discuss the SQL Server Surface Area Configuration tool, which is discussed in depth in Chapter 12, "Hardening a SQL Server 2005 Environment."

Using the SQL Server Configuration Manager

The SQL Server Configuration Manager, shown in Figure 3.2, is located in the Configuration Tools folder within the Microsoft SQL Server 2005 Start Menu program group. You can use this tool to administer the service used to run each SSRS instance.

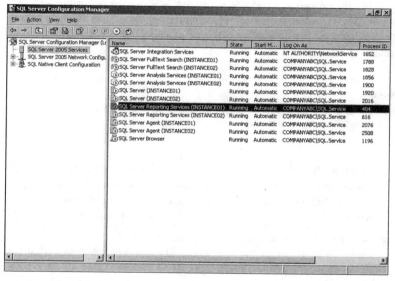

FIGURE 3.2
SQL Server Configuration Manager.

To configure SSRS, launch the SQL Server Configuration Manager tool and select the SQL Server 2005 Services node from the menu pane located on the left-side of the console. The SQL Server 2005 Service node displays the following information about SQL-related services and enables you to set service-related properties:

- **Name**—This column shows the service name and instance name of each SQL-related service.

- **Service State**—This column shows if the service is currently running, stopped, or suspended.

- **Service Start Mode**—This column shows if the service is configured to start automatically, manually, or if the service has been disabled.

- **Service Account**—This column shows the account configured to run the service.

- **Process ID**—This column shows the current process ID of the service.

- **Service Type**—This column shows the service association. Services associated with SSRS have been tagged with the ReportServer type.

To modify the properties of SSRS, right-click SQL Server Reporting Services from the list and select Properties. From within the Properties dialog box, the following tabs are listed, each providing basic service-related configuration options:

Note

Be sure to select the correct instance. The name of each instance is displayed in the Name column.

- **Log On**—This tab enables you to control the state of the service and is comparable to the Services console used to administer the operating system. This tab includes the ability to the launch the Reporting Services Configuration Manager by clicking the Configure button.

- **Service**—This tab displays general information about the service and enables you to change the start mode. The start mode controls what SSRS does when the underlying operating system is started. The SSRS start mode should be set to Automatic for normal operation, allowing the service to start without external interaction. Setting the service to Disabled prevents the service from starting or from being started manually, and setting the service to Manual allows the service to be started but doesn't allow the service to start automatically when the operating system starts.

- **Advanced**—This tab allows you to enable or disable Customer Feedback Reporting and Error Reporting. Customer Feedback Reporting provides Microsoft with basic information on how the product is being used. The Error Reporting feature sends Microsoft information when a problem with SSRS occurs. Both of these options are disabled by default. This tab also allows you to configure the path where the collected information is stored. If any settings are changed, the service must be restarted for changes to take effect.

Using the Reporting Services Configuration Manager

Configuration of the report server is primarily done through the Reporting Services Configuration Manager. This tool, shown in Figure 3.3, is located in the Configuration Tools folder within the Microsoft SQL Server 2005 Start Menu program group.

This tool is based on the Reporting Services WMI provider and provides a graphical interface into the configuration of SSRS.

Connecting to Reporting Services

When the Reporting Services Configuration Manager tool is launched, a dialog box is displayed requesting the report server and instance name. To connect to SSRS, type the name of the report server in the Machine Name field and then click the Find button. The Find button refreshes the Instance Name drop-down menu with each SSRS instance located on the specified server. After entering the correct machine and instance name, click the Connect button.

Note

If Reporting Services has been installed as the default instance, select MSSQLSERVER from the drop-down menu.

After the connection to the Report Server is established, the administration page opens. The administration page provides a navigation menu on the left side of the window and a details area for which the status of each item is displayed, along with component specific configuration options.

Each item in the navigation window can be selected and configured through this tool. To establish a new connection to a different server, click the Connect button located above the navigation menu.

The Reporting Services Configuration Manager tool, shown in Figure 3.3, shows the default configuration state if the SQL Server 2005 setup program

is allowed to configure the SSRS instance during installation. Each successfully configured item is identified with a green icon. If the setup program is
not allowed to configure SSRS during installation, the settings for each of the
components must be defined before SSRS can be used.

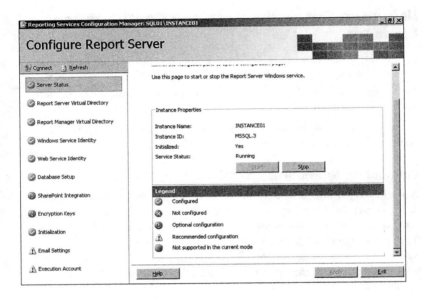

FIGURE 3.3
Reporting Services Configuration Manager.

Selecting an item from the navigation menu shows the current status of the
component and enables you to change the component's configuration. The
subsequent sections on this topic discuss configuration options for each item
listed in the navigation pane and demonstrate how to change each setting.

Identifying Server Status

The Server Status item shows the status of SSRS and provides a legend to
help identify the status of the other components. This item also allows starting and stopping the service responsible for running the selected SSRS
instance. To start or stop SSRS for the connected instance, click the Start or
Stop button on this page.

Configuring Report Server Virtual Directory

The Report Server virtual directory is used to access the SSRS web services. For example, the Rs utility can run configuration scripts written in VB .NET against the report server. When this utility is used, a connection is established with the SSRS web service endpoints available through the Report Server virtual directory. These endpoints expose the functionality used by the script to perform the desired action.

Use the following procedure to change the configuration from the current setting or to establish a new configuration on a system that has not been set up. This example creates a Report Server virtual directory called ReportServer on the Default Web Site. To create the report, do the following:

1. Select the Report Server Virtual Directory item from the navigation menu. If the default configuration was not selected during setup, the value in each field is empty.

2. Click the New button. A dialog box is displayed. This dialog box allows the selection of the website and enables you to change the name of the Report Server virtual directory. Select Default Web Site from the Website drop-down menu. Enter **ReportServer** in the Virtual Directory field and then click OK.

3. Several status messages are displayed describing each action executed to configure the Report Server virtual directory. The new Report Server virtual directory is ready after each task is successfully executed.

Warning

If the server will host more than one instance of SSRS, the Report Server virtual directory name should reflect the instance name to allow easy identification of the virtual directory associated with each instance.

If the virtual directory has been modified, the default setting can be easily reconfigured. To apply the default IIS settings, check the Apply Default Settings option and then click the Apply button located near the bottom of the page. This option resets the virtual directory with the default settings.

It is highly recommended to use an SSL certificate to secure the SSRS instance. If the SSRS web server has an SSL certificate installed, the option to enable SSL is available.

Use the following procedure to enable SSL on the Report Server virtual directory:

1. Enable the Require Secure Socket Layer (SSL) Connections option.

2. Select 3—All SOAP APIs from the Required For drop-down menu. This is the most secure connection option and ensures all communication is encrypted. Other options secure specific web service calls and data streams depending on the level.

3. Type the fully qualified computer name for the certificate in the Certificate Name field.

If you generate your own certificate, be sure to add the trusted root certificate to the machine certificate store. Simply double-clicking on the root certificate file only imports the root certificate to the users' personal certificate store. If the certificate is not trusted, SSRS does not use the certificate correctly. The following link provides additional information on Windows certificate management: http://www.microsoft.com/windowsserver2003/technologies/pki/default.mspx.

Configuring Report Manager Virtual Directory

The Report Manager virtual directory is used to access the Report Manager for administration of the site and by report users to run reports through the web browser.

Use the following procedure to change the configuration from the current setting or to establish a new configuration on a system that has not been set up. This example creates a Report Manager virtual directory called Reports on the Default Web Site. To create the virtual directory, do the following:

1. Select the Report Manager Virtual Directory item from the navigation menu. If the default configuration was not selected during setup, the value in each field is empty.

2. Click the New button. A dialog box is displayed. This dialog box allows the selection of the website and enables you to change the name of the Report Manager virtual directory. Enter **Reports** in the Virtual Directory field and then click OK.

3. Several messages are displayed describing each action executed to configure the virtual directory. The new Report Manager virtual directory is ready after each task is successfully executed.

Configuring the Windows Service Identity

The Windows Service Identity item allows you to configure or change the account used to run SSRS. This account can either be a Windows account or a built-in account.

For simplicity and security, the Network Service account can be used. This account has limited access to the operating system and is suitable for most installations. The Local System account is not recommended because this account has a very high level of access to the underlying operating system. If the SSRS instance running as Local System is compromised, the underlying operating system would also be compromised.

If the environment calls for low-level control over the service account, a Windows account can be specified. Time should be taken to configure this account with the least number of privileges necessary to run the service. It is not recommended to use an administrator account because this configuration could present a security risk if the server is compromised.

Use the following procedure to change the configuration from the current setting or to establish a new configuration on a system that has not been set up. This example configures SSRS to run under an account called SQL.Service located in the Companyabc domain. To configure SSRS, do the following:

1. Select the Windows Service Identity item from the navigation menu.

2. Select Windows Account and then enter the name of the service account in the account field. For example, to configure the SQL.Service account in the Companyabc domain, enter `Companyabc\SQL.Service` in the Account field.

3. Click the Apply button and wait for the configuration tool to reset the service account.

> **Warning**
>
> Previously used service accounts are not removed from the SSRS databases. These accounts should be manually removed if the account is no longer needed.

If the SSRS instance has already been initialized, several additional steps are necessary to reconfigure the Windows Service identity. The steps to reconfigure the Windows Service identity are as follows:

1. After you click the Apply button, a dialog box is displayed allowing the existing encryption keys to be saved to a password protected file.

2. Enter the password used to secure this file and the path to save the file; then click OK.

3. After you save the encryption keys, another dialog box is displayed. This dialog box requests an administrative account that can be used to grant the new service account the appropriate rights to the SSRS databases. Select Current User – Integrated Security from the Credentials Type drop-down list and then click OK. Wait for the configuration tool to complete the changes.

If Windows Authentication mode is not used, select SQL Server and enter the SQL logon credentials.

Configuring the Web Service Identity

The Web Service Identity item allows the configuration of the application pool account when SSRS is running on Internet Information Services 6.0. When SSRS is running under IIS 5.x, this item always uses the ASP.NET machine account.

Use the following procedure to change the configuration from the current setting or to establish a new configuration on a system that has not been set up. This example configures an application pool called ReportServer and assigns it to the Report Server and Report Manager virtual directories. To configure the Web Services identity, do the following:

1. Select the Web Service Identity item from the navigation menu. You can select an existing application pool from the list or create a new application pool for the SSRS virtual directories. It is recommended to use a different application pool for each SSRS instance.

2. Click the New button located next to the Report Server field. In the New Application Pool Properties dialog box, enter the name **ReportServer** in the Application Pool Name field. Select Built-in Account and then select Network Service from the drop-down menu. Click OK to start the creation of the application pool.

3. Select the ReportServer application pool from the Report Manager drop-down menu. The Report Server and Report Manager are now configured to use the same application pool.

4. After the application pool is created and assigned to each virtual directory, click the Apply button located near the bottom of the page to complete the change.

If Windows Authentication mode is not used, select SQL Server and enter the SQL logon credentials.

Configuring the Report Server Databases

The SSRS databases store information and objects as described in the previous section titled "Understanding the Report Server Databases."

Use the following procedure to change the configuration from the current setting or to establish a new configuration on a system that has not been set up. This example configures a database for the SSRS instance called ReportServer on INSTANCE01 of the local server. To configure the database for SSRS, do the following:

1. Select the Database Setup item from the navigation menu. If the default configuration was not selected during setup, the value in each field is empty.

2. In the Server Name field, select (LOCAL)\INSTANCE01 to create the database in INSTANCE01 on the local server. Click the New button and accept the default settings to establish a database called ReportServer. If this instance will be integrated with SharePoint, enable the Create the Report Server Database in SharePoint Integrated Mode option. Click OK to begin the creation of the database.

3. When the database has been successfully created, select Service Credentials from the Credentials Type drop-down menu. Click the Apply button to complete the changes and grant the IIS and SQL service accounts access to the SSRS database.

When prompted for the credentials to perform the operation, select Current User – Integrated Security from the Credentials Type drop-down list and then click OK. These credentials are used to grant the correct database permissions to the accounts specified on the Web Service Identity and Windows Service Identity configuration pages.

Configuring SharePoint Integration

SharePoint Integration is a new feature found in SQL Server 2005 Service Pack 2. It allows SSRS to integrate seamlessly into Windows SharePoint Services 3.0 and Microsoft Office SharePoint Services 2007, allowing you to publish and run reports though SharePoint.

The SharePoint Integration section is only available when the SSRS database is configured for SharePoint Integrated mode. By default SSRS configures the database for Native mode, but this can be changed in the Database Setup section. Once the database is configured for SharePoint integration mode, the SharePoint add-in component must be installed on the SharePoint server and permissions must be granted allowing both the SSRS web and windows service accounts access to the SharePoint database. For additional information on SharePoint integration, see the SQL Server 2005 Books Online.

Working with Report Server Encryption Keys

The Encryption Keys item allows management of the report server encryption keys. The report server uses encryption to store data such as usernames and passwords found in data sources. The encryption keys should be backed up to allow recovery of this information.

Use the following options when working with encryption keys:

- **Backup**—This button saves the current encryption keys to a password-protected file.

- **Restore**—This button restores the encryption keys from a password-protected file.

- **Change**—This button regenerates the encryption key and re-encrypts all data.

- **Delete**—This button deletes all encrypted content from the SSRS database.

Initializing the Report Server Instance

The Initialization item allows the SSRS instance to be activated when it's part of a scaled-out deployment. After the installation is activated, the implementation can be accessed by report users and report developers. A single server installation is automatically initialized.

Configuring Email Settings

The Email Settings item can be used to configure the server used to relay mail when a user subscribes to a report and specifies email delivery. This setting is optional; however, not configuring this item prevents users from creating email subscriptions.

Use the following procedure to change the configuration from the current setting or to establish a new configuration on a system that has not been set up. To configure the sender address as Ssrs@Companyabc.com and the SMTP Server address as mail.companyabc.com, do the following:

1. Select the Email Settings item from the navigation menu. If the default configuration was not selected during setup, the value in each field is empty.

2. Type `Ssrs@Companyabc.com` in the Sender Address field and `mail.companyabc.com` in the SMTP Server field. Click the Apply button to complete the changes.

This configuration option sets basic email settings for the SSRS sites. Additional options are available in the `RSreportserver.config` file and can be used for advanced email configuration. This file is located in the \Program Files\Microsoft SQL Server\<*Instance Name*>\Reporting Services\ ReportServer directory by default. The following parameters are available when configuring the file directly:

- `SMTPServer`—This parameter specifies the SMTP server used to deliver reports.

- `SMTPServerPort`—This parameter specifies the port used to access the SMTP server.

- `SMTPAccountName`—This parameter specifies the Microsoft Outlook Express account name.

- `SMTPConnectionTimeout`—This parameter specifies the number of seconds to wait for the SMTP server to respond. If the `SendUsing` parameter has a value of 2, this setting is ignored.

- `SMTPServerPickupDirectory`—This parameter specifies the local pickup directory if a local SMTP server is used.

- `SMTPUseSSL`—This parameter accepts 1 to enable SSL or 2 to disable SSL. The `SendUsing` parameter must have a value of 2 for this setting to work.

- `SendUsing`—A value of 1 specifies a local SMTP server, and a value of 2 specifies a remote SMTP server.

- `SMTPAuthenticate`—A value of 0 specifies no authentication, and a value of 2 specifies NTLM authentication.

- `From`—This parameter appears on the From line on the email message.

- `EmbeddedRenderFormats`—This parameter specifies the format of the email. Values can be MHTML or HTML4.0.

- `PrivilegedUserRenderFormats`—This parameter specifies the render formats available to the user creating the subscription.

■ ExcludedRenderFormats—This parameter specifies formats excluded from mail delivery.

■ SendEmailToUserAlias—This parameter accepts True when email subscriptions are sent to the person subscribing and False to allow the person subscribing to specify the To address.

■ DefaultHostName—This parameter specifies the default host name when the SendEmailToUserAlias parameter is set to True.

■ PermittedHosts—This parameter limits the hosts that can receive emails.

The following example is an excerpt of the RSreportserver.config file showing the different email options available:

```
<Extension Name="Report Server Email"
➥Type="Microsoft.ReportingServices.EmailDeliveryProvider.
➥EmailProvider,ReportingServicesEmailDeliveryProvider">
  <MaxRetries>3</MaxRetries>
  <SecondsBeforeRetry>900</SecondsBeforeRetry>
  <Configuration>
    <RSEmailDPConfiguration>
      <SMTPServer>mail.companyabc.com</SMTPServer>
      <SMTPServerPort></SMTPServerPort>
      <SMTPAccountName></SMTPAccountName>
      <SMTPConnectionTimeout></SMTPConnectionTimeout>
      <SMTPServerPickupDirectory>
          </SMTPServerPickupDirectory>
      <SMTPUseSSL></SMTPUseSSL>
      <SendUsing>2</SendUsing>
      <SMTPAuthenticate></SMTPAuthenticate>
      <From>Ssrs@companyabc.com</From>
      <EmbeddedRenderFormats>
        <RenderingExtension>MHTML</RenderingExtension>
      </EmbeddedRenderFormats>
      <PrivilegedUserRenderFormats>
        </PrivilegedUserRenderFormats>
      <ExcludedRenderFormats>
        <RenderingExtension>HTMLOWC
        </RenderingExtension>
        <RenderingExtension>NULL</RenderingExtension>
        <RenderingExtension>RGDI</RenderingExtension>
```

```
    </ExcludedRenderFormats>
    <SendEmailToUserAlias>True</SendEmailToUserAlias>
    <DefaultHostName></DefaultHostName>
    <PermittedHosts></PermittedHosts>
  </RSEmailDPConfiguration>
 </Configuration>
</Extension>
```

Configuring the Execution Account

The Execution Account item allows the report server to run jobs automatically.

Use the following procedure to change the configuration from the current setting or to establish a new configuration on a system that has not been set up. To configure the SQL.Service account found in the Companyabc domain as the SSRS execution account, do the following:

1. Select the Execution Account item from the navigation menu. If the default configuration was not selected during setup, the value in each field is empty.

2. Enable the Specify an Execution Account option, enter **Companyabc\SQL.Service** in the Account field, and then type the password in the Password and Verify Password fields.

3. Click the Apply button to save the changes.

Using the Reporting Services Administration Tools

Administration of SSRS sites is done through several tools: a graphical tool called the *SQL Server Management Studio*, a web-based tool called *Report Manager*, and several different command-line tools. The basic functionality of each tool is reviewed in the following sections. This basic tool operation allows a connection to be made to the different SSRS components. You need to be able to establish a connection to SSRS with the different components in demonstrations throughout the remainder of this chapter.

Administration with SQL Server Management Studio

The SQL Server Management Studio, shown in Figure 3.4, is a new and useful component included with SQL Server 2005. This tool allows the administration of almost every aspect of SSRS along with most other SQL 2005 components, all within a unified easy-to-use interface. This tool is normally located in the Microsoft SQL Server 2005 program group on a system with the client components installed.

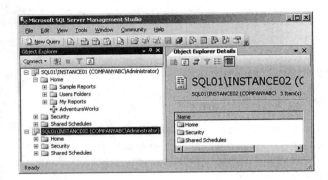

FIGURE 3.4
SQL Server Management Studio.

To open the SQL Server Management Studio, select Start, All Programs, Microsoft SQL Server 2005 and then click the SQL Server Management Studio shortcut. When the SQL Server Management Studio opens, the Connect to Server dialog box is displayed. This dialog box enables you to connect to a local or remote SSRS instance.

The following procedure demonstrates how to establish a connection to the report server as configured with the SQL Server 2005 sample installation found in the appendix, "Basic Installation of SQL Server Components." The sample installation configures the SQL Server for Windows Authentication mode. The name of the SQL server used in the example is SQL01 and the Reporting Services named instance is INSTANCE01. Do the following to configure the SQL Server for Windows Authentication mode:

1. Select Start, All Programs, Microsoft SQL Server 2005 and then click the SQL Server Management Studio shortcut to launch SQL Server Management Studio.

2. When the Connect to Server dialog box opens, select Reporting Services from the Server Type drop-down menu. Enter **SQL01\INSTANCE01** in the Server Name field.

3. Select Windows Authentication from the Authentication drop-down menu and then click the Connect button.

After the initial connection to the server has been established, additional connections can be made to other SQL components such as the Database Engine. To establish additional connections, select File, Connect Object Explorer from the menu. This reopens the Connect to Server dialog box. Additional connections are added to the Object Explorer pane located on the left side of the console window. The ability to open multiple connections to different components provides an efficient management environment for multiple components. Figure 3.4 shows the SQL Server Management Studio connected to multiple instances of SSRS; SQL01\INSTANCE02 has been highlighted in the Object Explorer navigation pane.

The SQL Server Management Studio shows each connected instance of Reporting Services in the Object Explorer pane. If the Object Explorer pane is not visible, select View, Object Explorer from the menu. Each SSRS instance can be expanded to reveal the Reporting Services folder hierarchy, along with site settings, reports, data sources, subscriptions, snapshots, schedules, and security information. The SQL01\INSTANCE01 instance shown in Figure 3.4 has been expanded to show the home folder, a data source called AdventureWorks, and some additional folders in the hierarchy.

Various configuration tasks are discussed throughout this chapter; however, generally, you can access configuration settings through each object simply by right-clicking the object and selecting Properties.

Administration with Report Manager

The Report Manager is a web-based administration tool for Reporting Services, shown in Figure 3.5. To access the Report Manager, type the URL of the Report Manager virtual directory in your browser's address bar. The virtual directory of the Report Manager can be identified and administered through the Reporting Services Configuration Manager tool; this tool is discussed in the section "Using the Reporting Services Configuration Manager" earlier in this chapter.

If the Reporting Services component was installed with the default settings, the URL includes the name of the SQL server followed by Reports. For example, to connect to Reporting Services installed as the default instance on the server SQL01, type **http://SQL01/Reports** in the address bar of the browser. To connect to Reporting Services installed as the named instance INSTANCE01, type **http://SQL01/Reports$INSTANCE01** in the address bar of the browser.

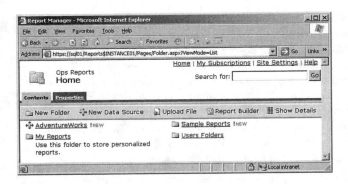

FIGURE 3.5
Report Manager.

After a connection has been established, the Reporting Services folder hierarchy is shown. By default, objects are shown in list view, and additional
details and options are hidden. While in list view, the button bar provides
buttons to facilitate creation of new folders and data sources. This view also
allows the uploading of files and launching the Report Builder tool. Figure
3.5 shows the Report Manager as seen browsing the Home folder in list view.
This is the same information available with the SQL Server Management
Studio shown in Figure 3.4.

The Show Details button located on the far right of the button bar changes
the list view to details view. While in details view, additional buttons are
displayed to allow moving or deleting objects found within the web page;
this includes folders, reports, data sources, and other objects such as shared
graphics. Also, while in the details view, additional information is shown for
each object, such as the object's description, creation date, person who last
modified the object, and time the object was last executed.

The site menu items located across the top right of the page are static. This
menu allows quick access to the Home folder, My Subscriptions area, and
Site Settings. You can use the Search field located under the site menu to find
reports based on the name of the report or description.

Various configuration tasks are discussed throughout this chapter. Most site
configuration options can be found within the Site Settings link located near
the top of the page. Figure 3.6 shows the site settings from within the Report
Manager.

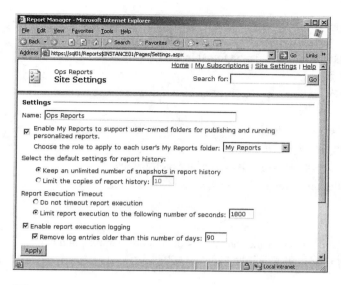

FIGURE 3.6
Site settings from within Report Manager.

Administration with the Command Line

The following three command-line utilities can be used to administer the Reporting Services implementation. Using these command-line utilities allows you to manage both report server components and objects found within Reporting Services. The three commands are

- RsConfig
- Rskeymgmt
- Rs

Each command-line utility has a -t option that enables writing data to the SSRS trace files. The default trace location is in the \Microsoft SQL Server\ <*SQL Server Instance*>\Reporting Services\LogFiles directory. For example, trace logs for SSRS installed as INSTANCE01 on the server SQL01 are in the D:\Program Files\Microsoft SQL Server\MSSQL.3\Reporting Services\LogFiles directory.

Each of the following trace files includes a time stamp appended to the name. For example, a Report Server Web service trace log file created on January

18, 2007, at 12:09:41AM would look like `ReportServer__01_18_2007_00_09_41.log`.

The following trace log files can be found in the log files directory on the SSRS server:

- **ReportServerService**—Report Server Windows service worker threads trace log
- **ReportServerService_main**—Report Server Windows service management threads trace log
- **ReportServerWebApp**—Report Manager trace log
- **ReportServer**—Report Server Web service trace log

Tip

To obtain a list of all command-line options along with examples and help, type `rsconfig -?` from within the command prompt.

Using the RSConfig Utility

The RSConfig command-line utility can be used to configure report server components. Table 3.1 shows the options available for this command.

Table 3.1 RSConfig **Utility Options**

Option	Description
-c *connection*	Sets the connection information to the report server database.
-e *executionaccount*	Sets the Unattended Execution Account used by the report server when executing reports.
-m *machinename*	(Optional) Sets the Universal Naming Convention (UNC) to *machinename* to configure; the default is localhost.
-i *instance name*	Sets the name of the Reporting Services instance; the default is MSSQLSERVER, which corresponds to the default instance.
-s *servername*	Sets the name of the SQL Server (including instance, if applicable) that hosts the report server catalog.
-d *databasename*	Sets the name of SQL Server catalog database.
-a *authmethod*	Sets the authentication type used to connect to the Report Server catalog. Can be SQL or Windows.

Option	Description
-u *username*	Sets the username used to connect to the server. Can be a SQL user or Windows user as DOMAIN\UserName. Optional for Windows authentication.
-p *password*	Sets the password used to connect to the server. Maybe a SQL or Windows password. Optional for Windows authentication.
-t *trace*	Includes trace information in error messages.

To open a command prompt, log on to the report server, select Start, Run, type **CMD**, and press Enter. You can use the following command to configure INSTANCE01 on the server SQL01 with the execution account SSRS.Exe located in the domain Companyabc:

```
RSConfig -e -m SQL01 -i INSTANCE01 -s SQL01\INSTANCE01
➥ -u Companyabc\SSRS.Exe -p Password1!! -t
```

Using the Rskeymgmt Utility

This Rskeymgmt command-line utility can be used to manage the SSRS encryption keys. Table 3.2 shows the options available for this command.

Table 3.2 Rskeymgmt **Utility Options**

Option	Description
-e *extract*	Extracts a key from a report server instance.
-a *apply*	Applies a key to a report server instance.
-s *reencrypt*	Generates a new key and re-encrypts all encrypted content.
-d *delete content*	Deletes all encrypted content from a report server database.
-l *list*	Lists the report servers announced in the report server database.
-r *installation ID*	Removes the key for the specified installation ID.
-j *join*	Joins a remote instance of report server to the scale-out deployment of the local instance.
-i *instance*	Sets the server instance to which operation is applied; the default is MSSQLSERVER.
-f *file*	Sets the full path and filename to read/write the key.
-p *password*	Sets the password used to encrypt or decrypt the key.

Table 3.2 **continued**

Option	Description
-m *machine name*	Sets the name of the remote machine to join to the scale-out deployment.
-n *instance name*	Sets the name of the remote machine instance to join to the scale-out deployment.
-u *user name*	Sets the username of an administrator on the machine to join to the scale-out deployment. If not supplied, the current user is used.
-v *password*	Sets the password of an administrator on the machine to join to the scale-out deployment.
-t *trace*	Includes trace information in error messages.

To open a command prompt, log on to the report server, select Start, Run, type **CMD**, and press Enter. You can use the following command to back up the encryption key used by INSTANCE01 on the local server:

```
skeymgmt -e -i INSTANCE01
➥-f c:\support\backupkey.snk -p Password1!! -t
```

Using the Rs Utility

The rs utility can execute code written in VB .NET against the SSRS web service endpoints. Table 3.3 shows the options available for this command.

Table 3.3 Rs **Utility Options**

Option	Description
-i *inputfile*	Sets the script file to execute.
-s *serverURL*	Sets the URL (including server and vroot) to execute the script against.
-u *username*	Sets the username used to log in to the server.
-p *password*	Sets the password used to log in to the server.
-e *endpoint*	Sets the Web service endpoint to use with the script. Options are Exec2005 - The ReportExecution2005 endpoint Mgmt2005 - The ReportService2005 endpoint Mgmt2000 - (Deprecated) The ReportService endpoint
-l *timeout*	Sets the number of seconds before the connection to the server times out. The default is 60 seconds, and 0 is infinite timeout.
-b	Runs as a batch and rolls back if commands fail.
-v *var=value*	Sets the variables and values to pass to the script.
-t *trace*	Includes trace information in error messages.

This utility is extremely powerful when used in conjunction with SQL Server Management Studio. From within SQL Server Management Studio, each action performed against the SSRS instance can be saved as a script. You can use this script and modify it to run against other servers. The following example demonstrates how to create a script that changes the SSRS site name:

1. Establish a connection to the Reporting Services instance with the SQL Server Management Studio.

2. Right-click the server name listed in the Object Explorer and select Properties.

3. When the Site Properties configuration window opens, select the General page from the menu on the left side of the window.

4. Type the new Reporting Services name in the field provided; for example, type **Administrative Reports** in the field.

5. Click the Script button at the top of the page to generate a script. The code for the script appears in a new window within SQL Server Management Studio, as shown in Figure 3.7. Close the Site Properties dialog box to view the code.

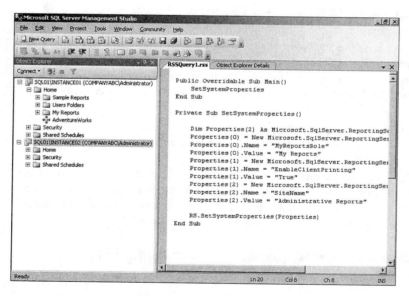

FIGURE 3.7
Code used to change the site name.

Often the code generated needs a bit of cleanup. As shown in Figure 3.7, the code not only changes the site name, but also references the My Reports and Client Printing parameters. The following code shows what the code looks like after some cleaning:

```
Public Overridable Sub Main()
    SetSystemProperties
End Sub


Private Sub SetSystemProperties()

    Dim Properties(0) As Microsoft.SqlServer
      ➡.ReportingServices2005.[Property]
    Properties(0) = New Microsoft.SqlServer
      ➡.ReportingServices2005.[Property]
    Properties(0).Name = "SiteName"
    Properties(0).Value = "Ops Reports"

    RS.SetSystemProperties(Properties)

End Sub
```

To execute the Site Name change code, copy the code into a text editor and save the file as **ChangeSiteName.rss**. From the command prompt, use the following command to connect to the Reporting Services instance and execute the code. This example changes the Reporting Services instance called INSTANCE01 on the server SQL02:

```
rs -i ChangeSiteName.rss
   ➡-s http://SQL02/ReportServer$INSTANCE01 -t
```

This command assumes the account used to execute the command has access to the Reporting Services instance on SQL02. If the account used to execute the command does not have access, additional options are needed to provide the username and password from the command line.

Administering Reporting Services Site Settings

Reporting Services site settings are global configuration options that control different aspects of the site. The following sections demonstrate configuration of the following site options:

- Site Name
- My Reports
- Report History

- Report Execution
- Report Execution Logging

Note

System-level role administration is discussed in the following section titled "Administering Reporting Services Security."

Each site setting can be changed through several different administration tools. For each site setting, the process necessary to make the change is demonstrated through the SQL Server Management Studio.

The SQL Server Management Studio can also be used to generate code that you can use to configure the site settings through the Rs command-line utility. Sample code is provided with each configuration as an example of the properties and values needed to make the change.

Alternatively, to access the site setting through the Report Manager, establish a connection to the SSRS instance. The site settings can be accessed through the Site Settings link located near the top of the page.

Configuring the Reporting Services Site Name

The name of the SSRS site is shown to users when they browse or run reports through the Report Manager. The name of the site appears at the top of the page and can help users identify the Reporting Service instance.

After a connection has been made to the report server with the SQL Server Management Studio, the site name can be changed by editing the site server properties. To locate the site server name, use the following procedure:

1. Establish a connection to the Reporting Services instance with the SQL Server Management Studio.

2. Right-click the server name listed in the Object Explorer and select Properties.

3. When the Site Properties configuration window opens, select the General page from the menu on the left side of the window.

4. Type the new Reporting Services name in the field provided; for example, type **Administrative Reports** in the field. Click OK to complete the change.

Configuring the My Reports Feature

Reporting Services can be configured to allow a feature called My Reports; this feature provides users with a personal "folder" within Reporting Services. The user can customize the My Reports folder by creating a folder hierarchy and can publish reports.

This feature is disabled by default on new installations of Reporting Services and can be enabled through each of the SSRS administration tools.

After making a connection to the report server with the SQL Server Management Studio, you can configure the My Reports feature through the site server properties. Use the following procedure to locate and enable the My Reports feature:

1. Establish a connection to the Reporting Services instance with the SQL Server Management Studio.

2. Right-click the server name listed in the Object Explorer and select Properties.

3. When the Site Properties configuration window opens, select the General page from the menu on the left side of the window.

4. Select the Enable a My Reports Folder for Each User option.

5. Select My Reports from the Select the Role to Apply to Each My Reports Folder drop-down menu and then click OK.

The preceding steps give the My Reports role access to the My Reports folder. If a user is not a member of the My Reports role, the link to the My Reports folder is not shown. Figure 3.8 shows the My Reports configuration page.

The following code provides an example of the properties and values needed to enable the My Reports feature with the Rs utility:

```
Public Overridable Sub Main()
    SetSystemProperties
End Sub


Private Sub SetSystemProperties()

    Dim Properties(1) As Microsoft.SqlServer
        ➥.ReportingServices2005.[Property]
    Properties(0) = New Microsoft.SqlServer
        ➥.ReportingServices2005.[Property]
```

```
Properties(0).Name = "EnableMyReports"
Properties(0).Value = "True"
Properties(1) = New Microsoft.SqlServer
   ➥.ReportingServices2005.[Property]
Properties(1).Name = "MyReportsRole"
Properties(1).Value = "My Reports"

RS.SetSystemProperties(Properties)

End Sub
```

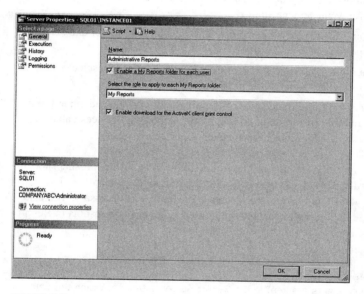

FIGURE 3.8
My Reports configuration page.

Configuring Report History

The Report History site setting configures the global default for report snap-shot retention. You can set this feature to keep a specific number of report snapshots or to keep all snapshots indefinitely.

> **Warning**
>
> When the retention period is set, existing report snapshots that exceed the new value are deleted from the database.

After making a connection to the report server with the SQL Server Management Studio, you can configure the Report History global settings through the site server properties. Use the following procedure to change the Report History setting for the site:

1. Establish a connection to the Reporting Services instance with the SQL Server Management Studio.

2. Right-click the server name listed in the Object Explorer and select Properties.

3. When the Site Properties configuration window opens, select the History page from the menu on the left side of the window.

4. Select the Limit the Copies of Report History option and enter **110** as the number of snapshots to keep in the Reporting Services database. Click OK to complete the change.

The preceding steps configured the site to allow only 110 report snapshots in the Reporting Services database. If a different number of snapshots is required, you should increase or decrease this option as necessary. You also can change the setting to Keep an Unlimited Number of Snapshots in Report History to keep all report snapshots indefinitely.

> **Warning**
>
> Report snapshots are kept in the Report Server database. Watch the database size on the busy system to ensure the database does not exhaust available space.

The following code provides an example of the properties and values needed to change the site to allow only 110 snapshots per report:

```
Public Overridable Sub Main()
    SetSystemProperties
End Sub

Private Sub SetSystemProperties()
```

```
Dim Properties(0) As Microsoft.SqlServer
    ➥.ReportingServices2005.[Property]
Properties(0) = New Microsoft.SqlServer
    ➥.ReportingServices2005.[Property]
Properties(0).Name = "SystemSnapshotLimit"
Properties(0).Value = "110"

RS.SetSystemProperties(Properties)

End Sub
```

Configuring Report Execution Timeout

The Report Execution site setting controls the global default for how long reports are allowed to run before the report processing engine stops them. The default configuration allows reports to run for 30 minutes (1800 seconds) before stopping the report and generating a timeout error. This feature can be set with the number of seconds to wait for a report or configured to allow reports to run indefinitely.

Warning

The execution timeout setting can be disabled completely, allowing reports to run indefinitely. This is not recommended for a production environment because an extremely large or poorly designed report can consume a large amount of system resources and negatively affect other users attempting to run reports.

After making a connection to the report server with the SQL Server Management Studio, you can configure the Report Execution Timeout global settings through the site server properties. Use the following procedure to change the Report Execution Timeout setting for the site:

1. Establish a connection to the Reporting Services instance with the SQL Server Management Studio.

2. Right-click the server name listed in the Object Explorer and select Properties.

3. When the Site Properties configuration window opens, select the Execution page from the menu on the left side of the window.

4. Select the Limit Report Execution to the Following Number of Seconds option and enter **3600** as the timeout value. Click OK to complete the change.

The preceding steps configure the site to allow reports to run for 3600 seconds (1 hour) before the processing engine stops the execution and returns a timeout error.

The following code provides an example of the properties and values needed to set the report execution timeout to 1 hour:

```
Public Overridable Sub Main()
    SetSystemProperties
End Sub

Private Sub SetSystemProperties()

    Dim Properties(0) As Microsoft.SqlServer
    ➥.ReportingServices2005.[Property]
    Properties(0) = New Microsoft.SqlServer
    ➥.ReportingServices2005.[Property]
    Properties(0).Name = "SystemReportTimeout"
    Properties(0).Value = "3600"

    RS.SetSystemProperties(Properties)

End Sub
```

Configuring Report Execution Logging

The Report Execution Logging setting allows the report server to record runtime information about report execution, such as who ran the report and whether any errors were generated. The Report Execution Logging setting found within the site settings allows the logging feature to be enabled or disabled. The feature also has a setting to groom old logs after a specific number of days.

After making a connection to the report server with the SQL Server Management Studio, you can configure the Report Execution Logging global settings through the site server properties. Use the following procedure to change the Report Execution Logging setting for the site:

1. Establish a connection to the Reporting Services instance with the SQL Server Management Studio.

2. Right-click the server name listed in the Object Explorer and select Properties.

3. When the Site Properties configuration window opens, select the Logging page from the menu on the left side of the window.

4. Select the Enable Report Execution Logging and Remove Log Entries Older Than This Number of Days options. Enter **90** for the number of days and then click OK.

The preceding steps configure the site to keep only 90 days' worth of report logs.

The following code provides an example of the properties and values needed to enable and set a 90-day limit on report execution logging:

```
Public Overridable Sub Main()
    SetSystemProperties
End Sub


Private Sub SetSystemProperties()

    Dim Properties(1) As Microsoft.SqlServer
    ➥.ReportingServices2005.[Property]
    Properties(0) = New Microsoft.SqlServer
    ➥.ReportingServices2005.[Property]
    Properties(0).Name = "ExecutionLogDaysKept"
    Properties(0).Value = "90"
    Properties(1) = New Microsoft.SqlServer
    ➥.ReportingServices2005.[Property]
    Properties(1).Name = "EnableExecutionLogging"
    Properties(1).Value = "True"

    RS.SetSystemProperties(Properties)

End Sub
```

Administering Reporting Services Security

SSRS provides access to the site through predefined noncustomizable tasks; each task is assigned to a customizable role. For example, a role called Browser is available by default. This role can view reports, view resources, view folders, manage personal subscriptions, and view models. A user or group assigned to this role subsequently can perform each of these tasks. Although the tasks cannot be modified, the roles and the application of roles on SSRS objects can be adjusted to secure the environment.

Warning

When you add a user to a group that is already part of a role assignment, you must reset Internet Information Services for the new role assignment to take effect for that user. You can accomplish this by using the IISRESET command.

The local administrators group on the report server can access Reporting Services and modify security settings. This configuration is provided to ensure the site doesn't become locked out if the permissions are inadvertently changed.

The difference between item and system roles is the tasks available for the role. System roles can be assigned only tasks that relate to system-wide function, whereas item roles can be assigned only tasks that can be performed on items, such as reports and data sources.

Administering Item Roles

The following tasks are available when configuring item roles:

- **Consume Reports**—Read report definitions.
- **Create Linked Reports**—Create linked reports and publish them to a report server folder.
- **Manage All Subscriptions**—View, modify, and delete any subscription regardless of who owns the subscription.
- **Manage Data Sources**—Create and delete shared data source items and modify data source properties.
- **Manage Folders**—Create, view, and delete folders and view and modify folder properties.
- **Manage Individual Subscriptions**—Each user can create, view, modify, and delete subscriptions that he or she owns.
- **Manage Models**—Create, view, and delete models and view and modify model properties.
- **Manage Report History**—Create, view, and delete report history snapshots and modify report history properties.

- **Manage Reports**—Create, view, and delete reports and modify report properties.

- **Manage Resources**—Create, modify, and delete resources and view and modify resource properties.

- **Set Security for Individual Items**—View and modify security settings for reports, folders, resources, and shared data sources.

- **View Data Sources**—View shared data source items in the folder hierarchy and view data source properties.

- **View Folders**—View folder items in the folder hierarchy and view folder properties.

- **View Models**—View models in the folder hierarchy, use models as data sources for a report, and run queries against the model to retrieve data.

- **View Reports**—View reports and linked reports in the folder hierarchy and view report history snapshots and report properties.

- **View Resources**—View resources in the folder hierarchy and view resource properties.

After making a connection to the report server with the SQL Server Management Studio, you can find the Item Roles by navigating to the Security/Roles folder. By default, five roles exist as part of the Reporting Services installation.

The following example demonstrates how to give a user access to the SSRS installation by assigning the user to the Browser role. This predefined role provides the user with limited access. The user account is called Test05 located in the domain Companyabc. Do the following to give a user access to the SSRS installation:

1. Establish a connection to the Reporting Services instance with the SQL Server Management Studio.

2. Expand the Security folder and then expand the Roles folder. The five default roles are listed.

3. Right-click the Home folder and select Properties. When the Folder Properties dialog box opens, click the Add Group or User button. In the field provided, type **Companyabc\Test05** and then click OK.

4. Enable the check box in the Browser column for user Test05. The properties dialog box should look similar to Figure 3.9.

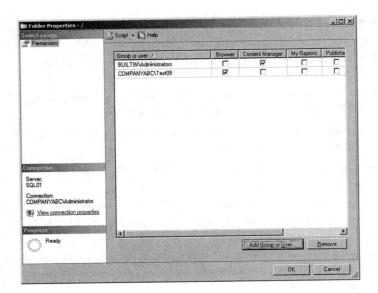

FIGURE 3.9
Home folder security.

Open the Report Manager with the account Test05 to verify that the user has access to each item in the console. To prevent a user from accessing a specific folder, do the following:

1. Establish a connection to the Reporting Services instance with the SQL Server Management Studio.

2. Right-click the Home folder and select New Folder to open the New Folder Properties dialog box. Enter **Secret Folder** in the Name field and then click OK. At this point, the test user can see the folder because it inherits permission from the parent object, the Home folder, and the test user has access to the Home folder.

3. Right-click the Secret Folder and select Properties. When the Folder Properties dialog box opens, select the Permissions page and then select Use These Roles for Each Group or User Account.

4. Highlight the Companyabc\Test05 account; then click the Remove button. Click OK to apply the changes.

The user Test05 no longer has access to the folder named Secret Folder. To restore access, go into the properties of the folder and add the user account or select the option Inherit Roles from the Parent Folder.

Administering System Roles

System roles can be assigned the following SSRS tasks:

- **Execute Report Definitions**—Start execution from report definition without publishing it to the report server.

- **Generate Events**—Allow an application to generate events within the report server namespace.

- **Manage Jobs**—View and cancel running jobs.

- **Manage Report Server Properties**—View and modify properties that apply to the report server and to items managed by the report server.

- **Manage Report Server Security**—View and modify system-wide role assignments.

- **Manage Roles**—Create, view, modify, and delete role definitions.

- **Manage Shared Schedules**—Create, view, modify, and delete shared schedules used to run reports or refresh a report.

- **View Report Server Properties**—View properties that apply to the report server.

- **View Shared Schedules**—View a predefined schedule that has been made available for general use.

After making a connection to the report server with the SQL Server Management Studio, you can find the Systems Roles by navigating to the Security/System Roles folder. By default, two roles exist on the Reporting Services.

The following example demonstrates how to add a system role called Job and Schedule Manager to the site. This role is given the ability to manage shared schedules and manage jobs for the site. To add a system role, do the following:

1. Establish a connection to the Reporting Services instance with the SQL Server Management Studio.

2. Expand the Security folder and then expand the System Roles folder. The two default roles, System Administrator and System User, are listed.

3. Right-click the System Roles folder and select New System Role. The New System Role window opens.

4. Enter the name `Job and Schedule Manager` in the Name field. Enter a description in the Description field. Enable the Manage Shared Schedules and Manage Jobs check boxes. Then click OK.

After the new role has been created, users or groups can be assigned to the role. When the role is assigned to a user or group, the tasks the role has been granted can be performed.

Use the following procedure to assign the account Test05 to the Job and Schedule Manager. This user has been created in the Companyabc domain. To assign the account, do the following:

1. Establish a connection to the Reporting Services instance with the SQL Server Management Studio.

2. Right-click the server name listed in the Object Explorer and select Properties.

3. When the Site Properties configuration window opens, select the Permissions page from the menu on the left side of the window.

4. Click the Add Group or User button and then type `Companyabc\Test05` in the field provided. Click OK to close the window.

5. When the Companyabc\Test05 account is listed, place a check in the Job and Schedule Managers column. Click OK to complete the change.

The user account Test05 is given the ability to manage shared schedules and jobs within reporting services. The user Test05 now has access to the Site Setting link when browsing the SSRS site. When the user clicks the link, only the options to manage shared schedules and jobs are listed.

Administering Shared Data Sources

A report uses a data source to establish a connection to a data warehouse, and after the connection is established, the report executes a query through the data source to get specific data needed for the report.

A shared data source can be implemented anywhere in the SSRS folder hierarchy. The connection properties within the shared data source can then be used by one or more reports found in the SSRS instance. A report-specific data source provides almost identical functionality to the shared data source, with one exception: The report-specific data source information is embedded in the report definition and cannot be shared with other reports.

If several reports require access to the same data, it is normally recommended to use a shared data source over a report-specific data source. This reduces the overhead of administering reports because the data source needs to be defined only once. For example, if the settings used to establish a connection to the data warehouse need to be changed, the shared data source can be easily modified. All reports using the shared data source then begin using the new settings without any additional modification.

Creating a Shared Data Source

This example assumes you installed the AdventureWorks database during the installation of SQL Server 2005. Additional information on the installation can be found in the appendix

The following procedure can be used to create a new data source. This data source is used to establish a connection to the AdventureWorks database and is used in the section "Administering Reports" later in this chapter.

1. Establish a connection to the Reporting Services instance with the SQL Server Management Studio and expand the Home folder.

2. To define a new data source in the root of the folder hierarchy, right-click on Home folder and select New Data Source. The New Data Source window opens.

3. On the General page, enter the name **AdventureWorks**. The name is important because the datasets defined in the report look for this name when executing the query.

4. Select the Connection page and then select Microsoft SQL Server from the Data Source Type drop-down menu.

5. Type the following connection string

    ```
    Data Source=SQL01\INSTANCE01;Initial Catalog=AdventureWorks
    ```

    This allows a connection to the AdventureWorks database on INSTANCE01 on the server SQL01.

To administer data source objects from within the Report Manager, establish a connection to the server with the browsers. The New Data Source button located on the button bar allows the creation of new data sources. To edit existing data sources, click the data source object in the web page to open the properties. The navigation menu on the left side and across the top of the properties page provides access to each configurable item.

Configuring Shared Data Source Credentials

The next step is to determine the credentials needed to attach to the data source. The following options are available on the Connection configuration page:

- **The Credentials Supplied by the User Running the Report**—When this option is selected, the user is asked to enter credentials when the report is executed. This option is generally inconvenient for the user running the report, especially if he or she will frequently access the report.

- **Credentials Stored Securely on the Report Server**—This option encrypts the credentials and stores them in the SSRS database. This is one of the best options because the person creating the data source can guarantee the account used to access the data has the least number of permissions necessary to run the report. The option Use as Windows Credentials When Connecting to the Data Source must be enabled when connecting to a SQL server using Windows Authentication mode. An option is available to impersonate authenticated users after a connection has been made. If the remote server allows impersonation, this can be used to filter data per user.

- **Windows Integrated Security**—This option passes the account credentials from the user running the report to the data source. This option is often not desirable because it is difficult to guarantee the data is accessed with the least number of permissions necessary to run the report.

- **Credentials Are Not Required**—This option should be used only when access to the data is controlled externally or in a nonproduction environment.

For demonstration purposes, this data source is configured to accept Windows integrated security. From within the New Data Source Properties dialog box, select Windows Integrated Security, then click OK to complete the changes.

Securing the Shared Data Source

The new data source object is now listed in the root of the SSRS site. It is viewable both in the SQL Server Management Studio and Report Manager. Additional settings can be found when administering existing data sources.

Right-click the newly created AdventureWorks data source and select Properties. Several new configuration pages are available in the Properties dialog box. The following configuration pages are available after the data source has been created:

- **Permissions**—This page allows the configuration of access to the data source. By default, the object inherits permissions from the parent object. If the data source is used to access sensitive data, select the Use These Roles for Each Group or User Account option and then add the users or groups allowed to use or manage this data source.

- **Dependent Items**—This option shows all the reports currently using this data source. If the data source is changed, the changes affect all dependent items.

Administering Reports

The term *report* can refer to both the final report that contains data or simply the object stored on the SSRS site.

For administration purposes, the term *report* is used to describe the report definition located on the SSRS server. The report definition contains the query used to retrieve data from the data source along with the layout of how the report should display data.

Reports can be administered through the SQL Server Management Studio, Report Manager, and command line. The following sections demonstrate how to manage reports through the SQL Server Management Studio.

Publishing and Viewing Reports

Before you can view a report, it must be published to the SSRS site. This example demonstrates how to upload and view reports found in the SQLServerSamples.msi file available with SQL Server 2005. Use the following procedure to extract the sample files on the server:

1. Browse to the location of the SQLServerSamples.msi file. By default, it is located in the D:\Program Files\Microsoft SQL Server\90\Tools\ Samples folder, if you chose to install the samples during the SQL Server 2005 installation. The latest samples can be downloaded from Microsoft at the following link: http://www.microsoft.com/downloads/ details.aspx?familyid=e719ecf7-9f46-4312-af89-6ad8702e4e6e& displaylang=en.

2. Double-click the MSI file to start the installation. The MSI file extracts the reports along with other samples to the C:\Program Files\Microsoft SQL Server\90\Samples\Reporting Services\Report Samples\ AdventureWorks Sample Reports folder.

Use the following procedure to upload the Employee Sales Summary.rdl sample reports to the Reporting Services site:

1. Establish a connection to the Reporting Services instance with the SQL Server Management Studio.

2. Expand the Home folder. Right-click Home and select New Folder. When the New Folder Properties dialog box opens, enter **Sample Report** in the Name field and then click OK.

3. Right-click the Sample Reports folder and select Import File. When the Import File window opens, browse to the C:\Program Files\Microsoft SQL Server\90\Samples\Reporting Services\Report Samples\AdventureWorks Sample Reports folder and select the `Employee Sales Summary.rdl` file.

4. When you select the RDL file, the name of the report is automatically filled in. Click OK to begin the upload process.

Viewing and Changing the Report Data Source

The properties of the report can be changed through the SQL Server Management Studio and Report Manager. Before viewing the report, you must specify the correct data source as follows:

1. Establish a connection to the Reporting Services instance with the SQL Server Management Studio.

2. Expand the Sample Reports folder and expand the Employee Sales Summary report. Notice the report has several folders that are used to store the data source, history, and subscription information.

3. Right-click the AdventureWorks data source listed beneath the Employee Sales Summary report and select Properties.

4. Ensure that A Shared Data Source is selected and click the Browse button. Choose the AdventureWorks data source created in the previous section "Administering Shared Data Sources" and click OK.

The report now uses the shared data source that was created earlier. To view the report, browse to the location of the report from within Report Manager, or right-click the report from within SQL Server Management Studio and select View Report from the menu.

When the report runs, choose the employee name from the Employee parameter list; then click the View Report button. A sales report for the employee is generated.

Viewing and Changing Report Properties

The following properties are available for the report:

- **Name & Description**—The name and description of the report are located on the General page of the report properties. These values can be changed to customize the name and description of the report.

- **Parameters**—Report parameters can be accessed on the Parameters page. Each parameter can be modified, the default value of the parameter can be set, the parameter can be hidden, and the parameter can be adjusted to prevent prompting the user for input.

- **Execution**—Execution settings can be accessed on the Execution properties page. The settings within this page provide customization for the way the report is executed. The SSRS site can be configured to cache the report after it's executed the first time or on a predefined schedule. Report snapshots can be configured and scheduled on this page, and the report can be configured to render from a snapshot instead of performing a query each time. The default report execution timeout settings can also be overridden from the site default.

- **History**—History settings can be accessed on the History properties page. The settings within this page allow history to be created manually, the report can be configured to keep a snapshot of every execution, and the number of snapshots for the report can also be overridden from the default site setting.

- **Permissions**—The report can be configured to inherit roles from the parent folder, or specific roles can be defined.

Administering a Report-Specific Data Source

A report-specific data source can be embedded directly within a report definition. Use the following procedure to configure a report-specific data source from within SQL Server Management Studio:

1. Establish a connection to the Reporting Services instance with the SQL Server Management Studio. Expand the Home folder and then expand the folder containing the report you want to modify.

2. Expand the report definition and then expand the Data Source folder beneath the report. Right-click the data source listed for the report and select Properties.

The properties page of the report lists the same options available when configuring the shared data source and one additional option at the top of the page. The following options allow the specification of a shared data source or a report-specific data source:

- **A Shared Data Source**—This option allows the person configuring the report to browse and select a predefined data source. This is the most common option because a single data source can be used for multiple reports with little configuration.

- **A Custom Data Source**—This option allows the configuration of data source parameters directly in the report definition. The same options are presented as with the shared data sources; however, this information is kept in the report and is not available for other reports.

Creating Linked Reports

A linked report provides a way to make a copy of an existing report. When the code within the original report is updated, the linked copy is also updated.

The benefit of having a linked report is that you can change the parameters of the linked copy. For example, if a default report is available but has numerous parameters allowing report users to select many different options, the report might be difficult to use. Creating a linked copy of a report allows you to change or hard-code the parameters. Users can then have a "custom" version of the original report with all the parameters they need preselected. To create a linked copy of a report, do the following:

1. Establish a connection to the Reporting Services instance with the SQL Server Management Studio.

2. Expand the Home folder and then expand the Sample Reports folder. Right-click the Employee Sales Summary report and select New Linked Report.

3. In the new Linked Report Properties dialog box, enter a name for the linked report; for example, enter **Sales for 2004**. Then click OK.

4. Locate the Sales for 2004 linked report, right-click the report, and select Properties. Then select the Parameters page to display the parameter options for the report.

5. In the ReportYear column, select 2004 as the default value and uncheck the Prompt User option. Click OK to apply the changes. Figure 3.10 shows the Parameters page of the Report Properties dialog box for the report.

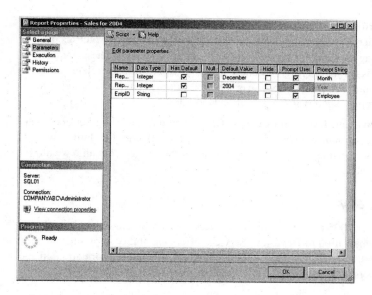

FIGURE 3.10
Report Parameters.

The linked report uses the same underlying report as Employee Sales Data. This report is configured not to prompt the user but to use predefined values instead. When the report titled Sales for 2004 is executed, the year prompt is missing because it's been hard-coded.

Troubleshooting Reporting Services

Troubleshooting problems in Reporting Services can be complex because many different components are working together to securely expose a reporting infrastructure. The log files available to troubleshoot problems are

- **Event Logs**—Reporting Services writes error information to the Windows event log. Be sure to monitor the event log on the report server and the SQL database servers because problems will likely be trends long before they turn into serious errors. Reporting Services also writes events to the event log when communication and configuration problems are encountered. Event numbers and descriptions greatly assist in the troubleshooting process. Because of the potential administrative overhead in monitoring event logs, an automated solution that can catch problem and filter noise is recommended.

- **Performance Logs**—SQL Server, Reporting Services, IIS, and the underlying operating system are collecting performance metrics on many aspects of the Reporting Services environment. These are good tools for identifying bottlenecks and other performance-related issues. Monitoring performance over a period of time provides a baseline to compare against if things start slowing down.

- **Trace and Execution Logs**—SQL Server and Reporting Services keep an enormous amount of data inside log files. Becoming familiar with these log files is highly recommended because they contain a wealth of data.

Summary

SQL Server 2005 Reporting Services offers a wealth of configurable options. An implementation of Reporting Services offers the ability to provide centralized, standardized, and scalable access to important information otherwise dispersed throughout the environment.

The key to administering the environment is to understand how each component interacts and how the feature set can be used to accommodate the objectives of the solution.

Best Practices

Following are best practices for administering SQL Server 2005 Reporting Services:

- Change the SSRS site name to allow easy identification of the report server.

- Keep a watchful eye on the event logs to catch trends before they become serious problems.

- Monitor performance counters to create a baseline detailing how the environment is performing.

- Configure the maximum number of report snapshots to avoid filling the Reporting Services database.

- Use SQL Server Management Studio to generate configuration scripts automatically.

- Allow only least-privileged access to a report database by configuring a shared data source with encrypted credentials stored in the report server.

- When you add a user to a group that is already part of a role assignment, reset Internet Information Services for the new role assignment to take effect for that user.

- Use SSL to secure the environment.

CHAPTER 4

Administering SQL Server 2005 Notification Services

SQL Server 2005 Notification Services provides a framework for creating notification applications. A notification application can generate and send immediate or scheduled messages to intended targets based on customizable subscription criteria.

This chapter helps identify the different Notification Services components and demonstrates the administrative processes necessary to keep a Notification Services implementation healthy and secure.

Identifying Notification Services Components

An understanding of the Notification Services components and terminology is important when administering a Notification Services implementation. Figure 4.1 shows how the different Notification Services components and external elements interact.

When a notification application is developed using the Notification Services framework, the features and functionality provided by SQL Server 2005 can be leveraged, including granular role-based security, high availability, and scalability.

Notification Services Instance

Each instance of SQL Server 2005 can host one or more Notification Services instances. Likewise, each Notification Services instance can host one or more notification applications.

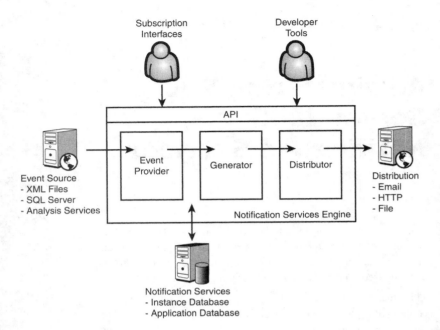

FIGURE 4.1
SQL Server 2005 Notification Services.

The Notification Services instance along with the notification applications can be configured programmatically through the Notification Services API, or the entire configuration can be defined through XML-based configuration files.

The configuration of the Notification Services instance and application defines how the Notification Services engine components, shown in Figure 4.1, are used to create the notification solution. This configuration essentially defines the business logic use to connect to the data source, analyze events, and deliver notifications.

The developer of the notification application is normally responsible for creating and providing the XML configuration files used to configure the instance and the notification applications. The configuration file used to configure the Notification Services instance is commonly referred to as the *instance configuration file* or the *ICF*.

Following are some of the configurable items associated with the Notification Services instance:

■ Notification Services instance name

■ Database Engine instance name

■ Deliver protocols

■ Delivery channels

■ Encryption

■ Instance version

■ Instance history

■ Configuration parameters

■ Associated notification applications

The XML file used to configure the application is commonly referred to as the *application definition file* or the *ADF*. The ICF references one or more ADFs, essentially allowing each instance to host multiple applications.

Following are the different Notification Services application-configurable items:

■ Notification application database name

■ Event information

■ Event Providers

■ Subscription information

■ Notification information

■ Generator settings

■ Distributor settings

■ Application execution settings

■ Application version

■ Configuration parameters

If the notification application and Notification Services instance are configured programmatically, you, as the administrator, are still responsible for granting the necessary rights and ensuring the environment is secure.

Notification Services Engine

As shown in Figure 4.1, the Notification Services engine runs the Event Provider, Generator, and Distributor components. These components provide the foundation on which the notification application is built.

The engine for each Notification Services instance can be configured to run as a Windows service or as part of an external application. When the Notification Services instance is configured to run as a Windows service, the process of registering the instance also creates the service. The service name is NS$ with the Notification Services instance name as a suffix. For example, if the Notification Services instance name is Accounting, the service name is NS$Accounting.

A Windows service is not created when the engine is hosted by an external application, although the process of registering the instance is still performed. When the engine is hosted by an external application, the Windows service is not necessary because an instance of each component is defined within the external application. When the component is defined within an external application, the functionality of those components is exposed to the developer through the Notification Services API.

The components of the Notification Services engine are

- **Event Provider**—This component is used to collect events from event sources for the Notification Services application.

- **Generator**—This component is used to analyze collected events and generate notifications if the event data matches criteria defined within the subscription.

- **Distributor**—This component is used to deliver the notification to the subscriber through one or more of the predefined channels.

- **Application Programming Interface (API)**—The Notification Services Managed Objects expose the functionality of Notification Services to external applications. This functionality is then used to integrate the Notification Services engine into external applications, build a user interface to manage subscriptions, and otherwise programmatically configure and control the Notification Services framework.

The Notification Services engine components can be placed on a single server or distributed across multiple servers to effectively distribute load and potentially handle a much higher volume of data. When distributed across multiple servers in a scaled-out scenario, the application configuration defines what engine components to run on each server. The server names of each server are either hard-coded in the configuration or configured through parameters when the Notification Services instance and notification application are created.

The Event Provider component can also work outside the Notification Services engine. This configuration is applicable when the Notification Services instance is run by a Windows service or as part of an external application. When the Event Provider runs outside the Notification Services engine, it is commonly referred to as a nonhosted Event Provider.

Examples of nonhosted Event Providers include applications that use the Notification Services SQL views to insert events directly into the notification applications' event tables. The Generator component still analyzes the events and matches subscriptions, and the Distributor component is still responsible for delivery of notifications to subscribers.

Notification Services Databases

The configuration settings for the Notification Services instance and notification applications can be stored in different places depending on the characteristics of the notification solution. The developer of the notification application may allow the storage of instance and application data within custom tables created directly in the source database. Alternatively, the Notification Services instance and application data can be stored in separate databases created specifically for the notification solution.

Subscriber data and subscription data are kept separately. This design characteristic allows subscriber data to be reused much more effectively by other notification applications hosted by the Notification Services instance, while each application stores unique subscriptions for each subscriber. When the instance and application data are stored in separate databases, subscriber data is kept in the instance database, whereas the actual subscription data is then kept in the application database.

The database names for the instance and application databases can be customized. However, both databases have default values if the names are not explicitly defined in the configuration. The instance database is called NSMain with the name of the Notification Services instance as a prefix. Each application database is named after the notification application with the Notification Services instance name as a prefix.

For example, if the Notification Services instance is called Accounting and the instance hosts the EmployeeAlerts and EmployeeNewsletter notification applications, three databases are created. The instance database is called AccountingNSMain; this database will store subscriber details, such as the names of the subscribers and the devices the subscribers would like notifications sent to. The application databases are called AccountingEmployeeAlerts and AccountingEmployeeNewsletter; these databases will store different subscriptions each employee creates.

Notification Services Security

Understanding the different rights and permissions needed for each Notification Services component is important. Each component is responsible for a different aspect of the solution and must be configured accordingly.

Notification Services enables developers to configure components to run on different servers or to host components within other applications. It is important to communicate with the developers to determine what service accounts are being used for each component and to ensure the correct permissions are assigned.

> **Note**
>
> As a best practice, accounts should always be implemented with the least number of rights necessary to accomplish the defined task.

Notification Services uses a role-based security model to help ensure only the required amount of access is granted to each component used in the Notification Services solution.

Identifying Accounts Used by Notification Services

It is recommended to run the Notification Services engine as a restricted Windows domain user account. A domain account can be easily granted access to other servers and services in the environment while maintaining centralized administration of the account. Using the built-in service accounts to access the database is not recommended because the service is then granted explicit access to the different databases used by the notification application. If the service account is also running other programs, the other programs also have access to the different databases.

When the Notification Services engine is configured to run as a Windows service, a service account must be provided. The Windows account provided to run the service can be used to access the Notification Services databases directly, or the service can be configured to provide the credentials of a SQL account to access the Notification Services databases. The account used to access the Notification Services database must be placed in the appropriate database role.

Figure 4.2 shows an example of running the Notification Services engine under a Windows service account while providing access to the database with a different SQL account. This configuration is done during the registration of the Notification Services instance and is described in the "Registering a Notification Services Instance" section later in this chapter.

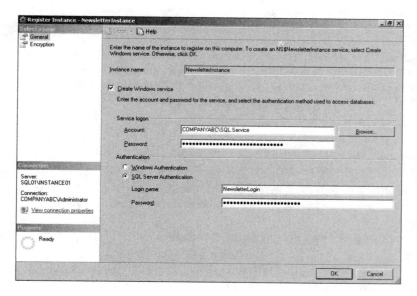

FIGURE 4.2
Instance service and access accounts.

When the Notification Services engine is hosted by an external application, the account used by the external application to access the Notification Services databases is controlled by the developer. This account must be placed in the appropriate database role to allow the appropriate access to the Notification Services instance.

Providing Access to the Notification Services Instance

The Notification Services engine runs the hosted Event Provider, Generator, and Distributor. Each component requires access to the Notification Services instance and application databases.

If each component is installed on the same computer, one account is responsible for running all components. In this scenario, the Windows or SQL account used by the service must be added to the NSRunService database role on the instance and application database.

In a scaled-out deployment, the Event Provider, Generator, and Distributor can each run on a different system, and each system can be configured with unique credentials used to access the Notification Services databases. In this scenario, the Windows or SQL account used to access the database for each component is placed in the role specific to that component. For example, the account running the Event Provider component must be added to the NSEventProvider role, the account running the Generator component must be added to the NSGenerator role, and the account running the Distributor component must be added to the NSDistributor role. These roles must be configured on both the instance and application databases.

A nonhosted Event Provider runs outside the Notification Services engine as an external application. When a nonhosted Event Provider is used, the account used to run this component must be added to the NSEventProvider role for both the instance and application database.

The account used by the Subscription Management interfaces must be added to the NSSubscriberAdmin role for both the instance and application database.

Providing Access to External Components

The service account used to run the Notification Services engine must be a member of the SQLServer2005NotificationServicesUser$ group. This is a local group on the server where Notification Services has been installed. This group provides access to the binaries used to run the Windows service. When the Notification Services instance is registered, the corresponding Windows service account is automatically added to this group. External applications hosting the Notification Services engine must be manually added to this group if they required access to the Notification Services binaries. The service account used by the Notification Services engine must also be able to write to the Windows event log.

When the Event Provider component hosts a Windows service, the service account must have access to the event source to retrieve event-related data. For example, if the Event Provider needs to query a remote database, the service account used by the Event Provider must be granted the appropriate rights to query the data in the remote database. Likewise, if the Event Provider reads events from a folder on a server, the service account used by the Event Provider must be granted the appropriate rights to read and write to the folder. Nonhosted Event Providers must also have access to the event source.

Just as the Event Provider component requires access to read event-related data from the event source, the Distributor component requires access to external components to deliver the notifications. This can include writing notifications to a file server, sending a notification email, or delivering notifications to a web server. The Distributor component also requires access to any supporting files such as XSL Transform (XSLT) content formatter used to format email before delivery to the intended recipient. When the Distributor sends email messages through a local SMTP server, the service account must be in the local administrators group.

Administering Notification Services Components

Administration of Notification Services can be performed through the SQL Server Management Studio and with the nscontrol.exe and NsService.exe command-line utilities. Although the SQL Server Management Studio is the primary administration tool, the different command-line utilities provide an effective way to script or automate administrative tasks. The command-line utilities are also necessary in a scaled-out deployment because the SQL Server Management Studio is unavailable. In a scaled-out deployment, the Notification Services engine components are implemented across multiple servers to improve both the performance and scalability of the Notification Services application.

To demonstrate the various administrative processes, you need a working Notification Services application. Demonstrations throughout subsequent sections in this chapter use the Inventory Tracker Notification Services example provided with SQL Server 2005. This example allows subscriptions to be made based on the inventory of items found within the AdventureWorks database. When the inventory count of an item changes, an event is sent by a nonhosted Event Provider to the notification application, the event is evaluated, and if a subscription for the item has been created and the criterion of the subscription matches the event, a notification is sent to the subscriber.

If you want to successfully run this sample, several prerequisites must be met. Following are the Inventory Tracker Notification Services prerequisites:

- **Database Engine**—The Database Engine component can be installed by selecting the SQL Server Database Services component during the SQL Server 2005 installation. This component hosts the AdventureWorks database along with the Notification Services instance and application data.

- **Notification Services Engine**—The Notification Services engine can be installed by selecting the Notification Services component during the SQL Server 2005 setup. This component hosts the Notification Services instance and notification application.

- **Workstation Components**—The workstation components, including the SQL Server Management Studio, can be installed by selecting the Client Components during the SQL Server 2005 setup. The SQL Server Management Studio is used to configure and administer Notification Services.

- **AdventureWorks Database**—The AdventureWorks database can be installed by selecting Sample Databases during the SQL Server 2005 setup. This database is used as the event source for the notification application.

- **SMTP Service**—The Simple Mail Transfer Protocol service can be installed by enabling the SMTP Service component of Internet Information Services (IIS). The SMTP service is used to deliver notifications to the intended subscribers.

- **.NET Framework 2.0**—The .NET Framework 2.0 can be downloaded from Microsoft (http://www.microsoft.com/downloads/details.aspx?familyid=0856eacb-4362-4b0d-8edd-aab15c5e04f5&displaylang=en). The .NET Framework is used to build part of the notification application used to demonstrate administrative processes.

The installation of the Database Engine, Notification Services engine, Workstation Components, and AdventureWorks sample database is performed through the SQL Server 2005 setup. The appendix, "SQL Server 2005 Management and Administration" (online), provides additional information on how to install the required SQL Server 2005 components. The Database Engine instance, SQL01\INSTANCE01, is used to host the Notification Services instance.

You can install the SMTP Service through the following procedure:

1. Click Start, Control Panel, Add or Remove Programs. The Add or Remove programs window opens.

2. Click the Add/Remove Windows Components button.

3. Select Application Server and click Details; then select Internet Information Services (IIS) and click Details.

4. Enable the SMTP Service component. Click OK and complete the Windows Components Wizard.

Note

Stop and disable the Simple Mail Transfer Protocol (SMTP) service to prevent notifications from being delivered during the demonstration.

You can install the Notification Services examples by running the Microsoft SQL Server 2005 Samples installer. To locate the installer, click Start, All Programs, Microsoft SQL Server 2005, Documentation and Tutorials, Samples and then click the Microsoft SQL Server 2005 Samples shortcut. When the installation wizard opens, click the Next button on each page to extract the samples to the default directory.

The Notification Services examples are located in the C:\Program Files\ Microsoft SQL Server\90\Samples\Notification Services directory after the Microsoft SQL Server 2005 Samples have been installed. The Inventory Tracker example used in this demonstration is located in the InventoryTracker folder.

Defining Notification Services Accounts

The Inventory Tracker example uses several different accounts to access the Notification Services instance and application data.

The NSRulesEvaluator account is hard-coded in the application definition file and is used by the Generator component to communicate with the application database when evaluating subscription rules.

Follow these steps to create the NSRulesEvaluator SQL account:

1. Establish a connection the Database Engine instance SQL01\INSTANCE01 with the SQL Server Management Studio. Expand the Security/Logins node from within the Object Explorer pane.

2. Right-click Logins and select New Login to open the login creation window. Type **NSRulesEvaluator** in the Login Name field and then select SQL Server authentication.

3. Enter and confirm the password. Uncheck the User Must Change Password at Next Login option and then click OK.

You can use the following SQL code to add the NSRulesEvaluator login to the Database instance. Remember to change the password in the command by changing the password to the actual password you want to assign to the account:

```
USE [master]
GO
CREATE LOGIN [NSRulesEvaluator ]
  WITH PASSWORD=N'password',
  DEFAULT_DATABASE=[master],
  CHECK_EXPIRATION=ON,
  CHECK_POLICY=ON
GO
```

The Inventory Tracker instance uses a Windows Service to run the Notification Services engine. The Inventory Tracker engine hosts the Generator and Distributor components; the Event Provider component is nonhosted because it is external to the engine. The Windows domain account, SQL.NSInventory, is used to run the Inventory Tracker service.

In this demonstration, an Active Directory user account is created and this account will ultimately run the Notification Services engine, which is described later in the chapter. If the Notification Services computer is not a member of an Active Directory domain, a local account can be used. To add a local account to the computer, right-click My Computer and select Manage; accounts are located under the Local Users and Groups node.

Use the following process to create the SQL.NSInventory Windows domain user account:

1. On the Notification Services server, select Start, Run; type **dsa.msc** in the Open field; and then click OK. The Active Directory Users and Computer console opens.

2. Right-click the Users container; then select New, User to open the New User Object window.

3. Type **SQL.NSInventory** in the First Name and User Logon Name fields. Click Next.

4. Type and confirm the password for the account. Uncheck the User Must Change Password at Next Logon option and then click Next. Click the Finish button to create the service account.

The account's NSRulesEvaluator login doesn't need to be assigned any rights; this is done automatically when the Notification Services instance is created. The SQL.NSInventory account must be added to the Local Administrators group on the Notification Services server. Local administrative rights are necessary when notifications are delivered through a local SMTP instance.

To add the SQL.NSInventory Windows domain user account to the Local Administrators group on the Notification Services server, follow these steps:

1. On the Notification Services server, select Start, Run; type **compmgmt.msc** in the Open field; and then click OK. The Computer Management console opens.

2. From within the navigation pane, expand Local Users and Group and then select the Group node.

3. Double-click the Administrators group to open the properties window. Click the Add button and add the SQL.NSInventory account to the group. Click OK to complete the change.

Creating a Notification Services Instance

The Database Engine instance, SQL01\INSTANCE01, is used to host the Notification Services instance. To create the Notification Services instance, you use the instance configuration file.

Follow these steps to create the Notification Services instance used to run the Inventory Tracker example:

1. Establish a connection to SQL01\INSTANCE01 with the SQL Server Management Studio. Expand the instance name and select the Notification Services node from within the Object Explorer pane. By default, the Notification Services node is empty because no instances have been established.

2. Right-click the Notification Services node and select New Notification Services Instance. The New Notification Services Instance window opens.

3. Click the Browse button and navigate to the location of the Inventory Tracker instance configuration file. The ICF is located in the C:\Program Files\Microsoft SQL Server\90\Samples\Notification Services\InventoryTracker folder. Select the instance configuration file InstanceConfig.xml and click Open.

4. The Notification Services Instance window now lists the required parameters. Enter the correct settings in the Value field for the instance to run as intended.

5. In the `SqlServer` parameter, type **SQL01\INSTANCE01**. This is the name of the SQL instance used to host the Inventory Tracker application databases.

6. In the `SampleDirectory` parameter, type **C:\Program Files\ Microsoft SQL Server\90\Samples\Notification Services\ InventoryTracker**. This is the default installation directory of the Inventory Tracker example.

7. In the `NotificationServicesHost` parameter, type **SQL01**. This is the server used to run the Inventory Tracker instance. After the parameters have been entered, click OK.

8. A series of actions run against the SQL server; these actions create the Notification Services instance for the Inventory Tracker application based on the settings in the configuration files and the parameters provided. Click the Close button to return to the SQL Studio Management Studio.

If any errors were reported, click the error message for additional information. The error messages are often useful when you're trying to resolve issues.

The following settings are contained within the Inventory Tracker ICF file. The ICF defines the instance database and references the InventoryTracker application along with the corresponding ADF. This ICF also defines the SMTP and File delivery channels used to get notification to the intended targets:

```
<?xml version="1.0" encoding="utf-8"?>
➡<NotificationServicesInstance
xmlns:xsd= xmlns:xsi="http://www.w3.org/2001/XMLSchema-instance"
xmlns="http://www.microsoft.com/
➡MicrosoftNotificationServices/ConfigurationFileSchema">
  <InstanceName>InventoryTrackerInstance</InstanceName>
  <SqlServerSystem>%SqlServer%</SqlServerSystem>

  <!-- Specify the Database and schema name
  the InventoryTracker instance data will be installed into.-->
  <Database>
    <DatabaseName>AdventureWorks</DatabaseName>
    <SchemaName>NS_InventoryTrackerInstance</SchemaName>
  </Database>
```

```xml
<Applications>
  <Application>
    <ApplicationName>InventoryTracker</ApplicationName>
    <BaseDirectoryPath>%SampleDirectory%\AppDefinition
➥</BaseDirectoryPath>
    <ApplicationDefinitionFilePath>appADF.xml
➥</ApplicationDefinitionFilePath>
      <Parameters>
        <!-- These parameters are defined as environment
             variables or as command line arguments.
             They are passed to the ADF file. -->
        <Parameter>
          <Name>_DBSystem_</Name>
          <Value>%SqlServer%</Value>
        </Parameter>
        <Parameter>
          <Name>_NSSystem_</Name>
          <Value>%NotificationServicesHost%</Value>
        </Parameter>
        <Parameter>
          <Name>_BaseDirectoryPath_</Name>
          <Value>%SampleDirectory%</Value>
        </Parameter>
        <Parameter>
          <Name>_EventsDir_</Name>
          <Value>%SampleDirectory%\Events</Value>
        </Parameter>
      </Parameters>
  </Application>
</Applications>
<DeliveryChannels>
    <DeliveryChannel>
    <DeliveryChannelName>FileChannel</DeliveryChannelName>
    <ProtocolName>File</ProtocolName>
    <Arguments>
      <Argument>
        <Name>FileName</Name>
        <Value>
        %SampleDirectory%\Notifications\
          ➥FileNotifications.txt
```

```
        </Value>
      </Argument>
    </Arguments>
  </DeliveryChannel>
  <DeliveryChannel>
    <DeliveryChannelName>EmailChannel</DeliveryChannelName>
    <ProtocolName>SMTP</ProtocolName>
  </DeliveryChannel>
 </DeliveryChannels>
</NotificationServicesInstance>
```

> **Note**
>
> Parameters are used in the Inventory Tracker application to allow easy modifications to the Notification Services applications during deployment.

The following settings are contained within the Inventory Tracker ADF file. The ADF for the Inventory Tracker application defines several key components, including the application database name, event classes, subscription classes, notification classes, Provider settings, Generator settings, Distributor settings, and the application execution settings.

```
<Database>
  <DatabaseName>AdventureWorks</DatabaseName>
  <SchemaName>NS_InventoryTrackerApplication</SchemaName>
</Database>

<EventClasses>
  <EventClass>
    <EventClassName>InventoryTrackerEvents</EventClassName>
    <Schema>
      <Field>
        <FieldName>ProductId</FieldName>
        <FieldType>int</FieldType>
      </Field>
      <Field>
        <FieldName>ProductName</FieldName>
        <FieldType>nvarchar(50)</FieldType>
      </Field>
      <Field>
```

```
          <FieldName>ProductNumber</FieldName>
          <FieldType>nvarchar(25)</FieldType>
        </Field>
        <Field>
          <FieldName>Quantity</FieldName>
          <FieldType>int</FieldType>
        </Field>
        <Field>
          <FieldName>LocationName</FieldName>
          <FieldType>nvarchar(50)</FieldType>
        </Field>
      </Schema>
    </EventClass>
  </EventClasses>

  <SubscriptionClasses>
    <SubscriptionClass>
      <SubscriptionClassName>
      InventoryTrackerSubscriptions
      </SubscriptionClassName>
      <Schema>
        <Field>
          <FieldName>DeviceName</FieldName>
          <FieldType>nvarchar(255)</FieldType>
        </Field>
        <Field>
          <FieldName>SubscriberLocale</FieldName>
          <FieldType>nvarchar(10)</FieldType>
        </Field>
      </Schema>
      <EventRules>
        <EventRule>
          <RuleName>InventoryTrackerRule</RuleName>
          <ConditionAction>
            <SqlLogin>NSRulesEvaluator</SqlLogin>
            <SqlUser>NSRulesEvaluator</SqlUser>
            <InputName>InventoryTrackerEvents</InputName>

<InputSchema>NS_InventoryTrackerApplication</InputSchema>
            <SqlExpression>
```

```
INSERT INTO
[NS_InventoryTrackerApplication]
  ➡.[InventoryTrackerNotifications]
(
[SubscriberId],
[DeviceName],
[SubscriberLocale],
[ProductId],
[ProductName],
[ProductNumber],
[Quantity],
[LocationName]
)

(
SELECT
r.[Subscription.SubscriberId],
r.[Subscription.DeviceName],
r.[Subscription.SubscriberLocale],
r.[Input.ProductId],
r.[Input.ProductName],
r.[Input.ProductNumber],
r.[Input.Quantity],
r.[Input.LocationName]

FROM [NS_InventoryTrackerApplication].
➡InventoryTrackerRule AS r
)
            </SqlExpression>
          </ConditionAction>
          <EventClassName>InventoryTrackerEvents</EventClassName>
        </EventRule>
      </EventRules>
    </SubscriptionClass>
  </SubscriptionClasses>

  <NotificationClasses>
    <NotificationClass>
      <NotificationClassName>InventoryTrackerNotifications
➡</NotificationClassName>
      <Schema>
```

```
<Fields>
  <Field>
    <FieldName>ProductId</FieldName>
    <FieldType>Int</FieldType>
  </Field>
  <Field>
    <FieldName>ProductName</FieldName>
    <FieldType>nvarchar(50)</FieldType>
  </Field>
  <Field>
    <FieldName>ProductNumber</FieldName>
    <FieldType>nvarchar(25)</FieldType>
  </Field>
  <Field>
    <FieldName>Quantity</FieldName>
    <FieldType>int</FieldType>
  </Field>
  <Field>
    <FieldName>LocationName</FieldName>
    <FieldType>nvarchar(50)</FieldType>
  </Field>
</Fields>
</Schema>
<ContentFormatter>
  <ClassName>XsltFormatter</ClassName>
  <Arguments>
    <Argument>
      <Name>XsltBaseDirectoryPath</Name>
      <Value>%_BaseDirectoryPath_%\AppDefinition</Value>
    </Argument>
    <Argument>
      <Name>XsltFileName</Name>
      <Value>Application.xslt</Value>
    </Argument>
  </Arguments>
</ContentFormatter>
<DigestDelivery>true</DigestDelivery>
<Protocols>
<Protocol>
<ProtocolName>File</ProtocolName>
    <Fields>
```

```xml
            <Field>
                <FieldName>ProductId</FieldName>
                <FieldReference>ProductId</FieldReference>
            </Field>
            <Field>
                <FieldName>ProductName</FieldName>
                <FieldReference>ProductName</FieldReference>
            </Field>
            <Field>
                <FieldName>ProductNumber</FieldName>
                <FieldReference>ProductNumber</FieldReference>
            </Field>
            <Field>
                <FieldName>Quantity</FieldName>
                <FieldReference>Quantity</FieldReference>
            </Field>
            <Field>
                <FieldName>LocationName</FieldName>
                <FieldReference>LocationName</FieldReference>
            </Field>
        </Fields>
    </Protocol>


    <Protocol>
        <ProtocolName>SMTP</ProtocolName>
        <Fields>
            <Field>
                <FieldName>Subject</FieldName>
                <SqlExpression>
                    'InventoryTracker notification:
                        ➥ '+CONVERT (NVARCHAR(30), GETDATE())
                </SqlExpression>
            </Field>
            <Field>
                <FieldName>BodyFormat</FieldName>
                <SqlExpression>'html'</SqlExpression>
            </Field>
            <Field>
                <FieldName>From</FieldName>
                <SqlExpression>'InventoryTracker@AdventureWorks'
                    ➥</SqlExpression>
```

```
          </Field>
          <Field>
            <FieldName>Priority</FieldName>
            <SqlExpression>'Normal'</SqlExpression>
          </Field>
          <Field>
            <FieldName>To</FieldName>
            <SqlExpression>DeviceAddress</SqlExpression>
          </Field>
        </Fields>
      </Protocol>
    </Protocols>
    <ExpirationAge>PT2H</ExpirationAge>
  </NotificationClass>
</NotificationClasses>

<Providers>
  <NonHostedProvider>
    <ProviderName>SQLTriggerEventProvider</ProviderName>
  </NonHostedProvider>
</Providers>

<Generator>
  <SystemName>%_NSSystem_%</SystemName>
</Generator>

<Distributors>
  <Distributor>
    <SystemName>%_NSSystem_%</SystemName>
    <QuantumDuration>PT15S</QuantumDuration>
  </Distributor>
</Distributors>

<ApplicationExecutionSettings>
  <QuantumDuration>PT15S</QuantumDuration>
  <PerformanceQueryInterval>PT5S</PerformanceQueryInterval>
  <SubscriptionQuantumLimit>1</SubscriptionQuantumLimit>
  <ChronicleQuantumLimit>1</ChronicleQuantumLimit>
  <Vacuum>
    <RetentionAge>P0DT00H00M01S</RetentionAge>
    <VacuumSchedule>
```

```
<Schedule>
  <StartTime>23:00:00</StartTime>
  <Duration>P0DT02H00M00S</Duration>
</Schedule>
</VacuumSchedule>
</Vacuum>
</ApplicationExecutionSettings>
```

The Inventory Tracker adds information directly to the AdventureWorks source database instead of creating a new database. From within the SQL Studio Management Studio, expand Databases, expand AdventureWorks, and then expand the Tables node. The tables with the NS prefix hold the Notification Services instance and application data.

Enabling a Notification Services Instance

Several additional steps are required before the Inventory Tracker is ready. From within the SQL Studio Management Studio, select the Notification Services node; the Notification Services instance InventoryTrackerInstance is now listed. The next step is to enable the instance.

To enable the Notification Services instance, right-click InventoryTrackerInstance and select Enable. A confirmation dialog box is displayed. Click Yes to enable the instance.

To view the current status of the Inventory Tracker application, right-click InventoryTrackerInstance and select Properties. Figure 4.3 shows each of the components of the InventoryTracker application.

The Application, Subscriptions, and Event Provider components have all been enabled. The Generator and Distributor components are listed as Enable Pending because the service used to run those components has not yet been created. The process of registering the instance creates the service.

Registering a Notification Services Instance

The Notification Services instance can be configured to run the engine components under a Windows service or integrated within an external application. When the instance is configured to host the engine components in an external application, the instance registration process simply allows the external application to communicate with the Notification Services instance and application. When the instance is configured to run the engine under a Windows service, the registration process creates the service used to run the engine. A different service is used for each Notification Services instance.

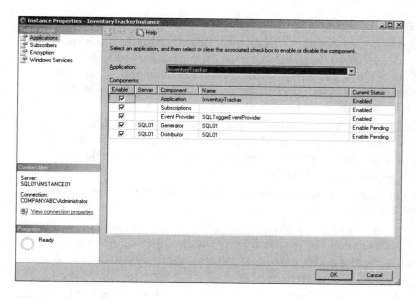

FIGURE 4.3
Inventory Tracker instance properties.

The Notification Tracker example is configured to run the components as a Windows service. Follow these steps to register the Notification Tracker instance:

1. From within SQL Server Management Studio, right-click the InventoryTrackerInstance and select Tasks, Register. The Register Instance window opens.

2. Enable the Create Windows Service option. Click the Browse button and locate the SQL.NSInventory account that was created in the section "Defining Notification Services Accounts" earlier in this chapter. Enter the password for this account and select Windows Authentication as the authentication type.

3. Click OK to begin the registration process. The registration creates the Windows service used to run the Notification Services engine. When the registration process is complete, click the Close button.

After the instance has been registered, the service account must be granted the appropriate permissions to be able to access the database and underlying operating system.

Granting Access to the Instance and Application Data

Before the service used to run the Notification Services engine is started, the service account must be allowed to access the instance and application data. If the Notification Services instance will read data from a file server or another database, the correct permissions must also be granted on those external objects.

The Inventory Tracker instance is configured to run each component with a Windows service. The service account must be added to the NSRunService role on the AdventureWorks database because this database holds the instance and application data.

Follow these steps to allow the SQL.NSInventory service account access to the databases:

1. From within SQL Server Management Studio, expand Security and then select Logins. The Security node lists each defined login account. Right-click the Logins node and select New Login to open the New Login configuration window.

2. Ensure that Windows authentication option has been selected; then click the Search button and find the SQL.NSInventory account in the directory.

3. Click the User Mapping page from the menu on the left. Enable the AdventureWorks database from the database list. In the lower pane, enable the NSRunService role.

4. Figure 4.4 shows how the Logon Permissions should be configured. Click OK to complete the Login configuration for the service account.

The service account also needs access to the pickup and drop locations in the operating system. However, because the account is a Local Administrator, it already has access to these areas. File notifications for the application are written to the C:\Program Files\Microsoft SQL Server\90\Samples\ Notification Services\InventoryTracker\Notifications folder by default.

Configuring a Nonhosted Event Provider

When the inventory count for an item in the AdventureWorks database changes, a trigger is executed, and the change is sent to the Notification Services application as an event. The Inventory Tracker application is an example of a nonhosted Event Provider because events are inserted directly into the application's event tables independently of the engine.

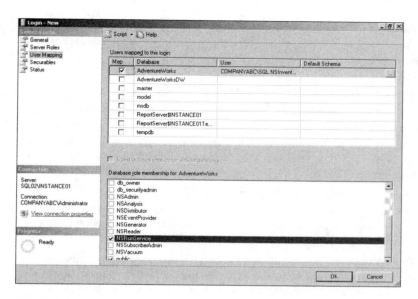

FIGURE 4.4
AdventureWorks database role membership.

The nonhosted Event Provider is external from the service running the engine. If the Inventory Tracker service is stopped, the nonhosted Event Provider is unaffected and continues to operate and insert events. However, notifications for these events are not delivered if the service is stopped because the Generator and Distributor components are essentially stopped.

Use the following process to configure the nonhosted Event Provider (SQL trigger) for the Inventory Tracker application:

1. Establish a connection to the SQL01\INSTANCE01 Database Engine component with the SQL Server Management Studio.

2. Select File, Open, File from the menu. Open the SetupInventoryTrackerSample.sql file. This file is located in the C:\Program Files\Microsoft SQL Server\90\Samples\Notification Services\InventoryTracker\SQLScripts directory.

3. Click the F5 button or select Query, Execute from the menu. The "Command(s) completed successfully" message should be displayed in the messages window.

The trigger is added to the Production.ProductInventory table in the AdventureWorks database. Any time the inventory for an item is changed, an event is inserted in the Inventory Tracker event tables.

Starting the Notification Services Instance

The instance is almost ready to be used. The configuration has been set, the correct permissions have been granted, and the nonhosted Event Provider has been configured. The next step is to start the Inventory Tracker instance. You can do this from the Windows service console or from within the SQL Server Management Studio.

From within SQL Server Management Studio, right-click InventoryTrackerInstance and select Start. A dialog box opens asking for confirmation. Click the Yes button. When the instance is started, the associated Windows service is started.

To view the current status of the Inventory Tracker application, right-click InventoryTrackerInstance and select Properties. Figure 4.5 shows each of the components of the InventoryTracker application. Each component is now enabled and ready.

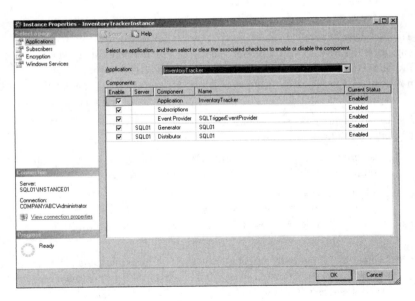

FIGURE 4.5
Inventory Tracker instance properties.

Adding Subscribers and Subscriptions

Adding subscribers and subscriptions is a bit more complicated because you need to manually develop a subscription interface. Luckily for us, the Inventory Tracker example can programmatically add subscribers and subscriptions, because developing an interface is beyond the responsibility of the administrator and the scope of this book.

The program used to add subscriptions must be compiled; this can be done from within Visual Studio .NET 2005 or from the MSBuild.exe command-line utility. The MSBuild.exe command-line utility is available after the .NET Framework 2.0 has been installed.

Before building the solution, you must use the Strong Name tool (Sn.exe) to generate the key pair used by the solution. Follow these steps to generate a key pair:

1. From the Notification Services Server, click Start, Run; type **CMD** in the Open field; and then click OK. The Windows command prompt opens.

2. Change to the C:\Program Files\Microsoft Visual Studio 8\SDK\v2.0\ Bin directory from within the command prompt.

3. Type **sn -k C:\samplekey.snk** to generate a new key pair that will be used to build the project. The key pair is written to the root of the C: drive.

4. Copy the samplekey.snk key from the root of the C: drive to the C:\Program Files\Microsoft SQL Server\90\Samples\Notification Services\InventoryTracker directory.

After copying the key pair to the Inventory Tracker sample directory, you can build the project. The MSBuild.exe tool can be used to build the solution; this tool is located in the C:\WINDOWS\Microsoft.NET\Framework\ v2.0.50727 directory after the .NET Framework 2.0 has been installed.

Follow these steps to build the Subscriber and Subscription programs for the Inventory Tracker:

1. From the Notification Services Server, click Start, Run; type **CMD** in the Open field; and then click OK. The Windows command prompt opens.

2. Change to the C:\WINDOWS\Microsoft.NET\Framework\v2.0.50727 directory from within the command prompt.

3. Type **msbuild "C:\Program Files\Microsoft SQL Server\ 90\Samples\Notification Services\InventoryTracker\ InventoryTracker.sln"**.

The command prompt shows several pages of output as each program within the Visual Studio project is built. When the build process is complete, the message "Build succeeded" is displayed in green text.

The build process essentially compiles all the different applications used by the Inventory Tracker sample; this includes an application to add subscribers and subscriptions. These two applications are responsible for interfacing with Notification Services and take the place of a proper interface, such as a web page, that would allow an operator to add this information. Although the development of this type of application is beyond the scope of this book, the code used to interface with Notification Services can be examined by loading the project into Visual Studio .NET 2005. To add subscribers, navigate to the C:\Program Files\Microsoft SQL Server\90\Samples\Notification Services\ InventoryTracker\AddSubscribers\cs\AddSubscribers\bin\Debug folder and double-click AddSubscribers.exe. A list of subscribers and subscriber devices is added to the application. Press Enter to exit the program.

The subscribers and devices that were added by this program can be viewed through the NSSubscriberView and NSSubscriberView views in the AdventureWorks database. The following query shows the subscribers along with the devices for each subscriber created by the AddSubscriptions.exe program.

```
USE AdventureWorks
SELECT *
FROM
NS_InventoryTrackerInstance.NSSubscriberView
 AS SV
   INNER JOIN
NS_InventoryTrackerInstance.NSSubscriberDeviceView
 AS SD
  ON SV.SubscriberID = SD.SubscriberID
```

To add subscriptions for the subscribers, navigate to the C:\Program Files\ Microsoft SQL Server\90\Samples\Notification Services\InventoryTracker\ AddSubscriptions\cs\AddSubscriptions\bin\Debug folder and double-click the AddSubscriptions.exe program. Two subscriptions are added. Press Enter to exit the program.

The subscriptions added by this program can be viewed through the NSInventoryTrackerSubscriptionsView in the AdventureWorks database. The following query shows the subscriptions for the different subscribers. When you run the query, notice only two subscriptions were created, although four subscribers were added:

```
USE AdventureWorks
SELECT *
FROM
NS_InventoryTrackerApplication.NSInventoryTrackerSubscriptionsView
```

Normally, the process used to add subscribers and subscription data involves a subscriber going to a web page and actually making a subscription to data of interest. The programs provided with the Inventory Tracking example have simplified the process by directly adding subscribers and subscription data for demonstration purposes.

Viewing Subscription Data and Notifications

Several views are added to the instance database. The following two views can be used to manage subscribers and subscriber devices:

- NSSubscriberView
- NSSubscriberDeviceView

To view the subscribers for the instance, establish a connection to the server with the SQL Server Management Studio. Expand Databases/AdventureWorks/Views. Right-click the NSSubscriberView and select Open. The details pane lists the subscribers added with the AddSubscriber.exe utility.

Many SQL views are added to the application database; these views are used for an assortment of functionality. The following two views are used to manage subscription and track notifications:

- NS<*SubscriptionClassName*>View
- NS<*NotificationClassName*>NotificationDistribution

Use the following process to change inventory in the AdventureWorks database and generate a notification:

1. Establish a connection to the SQL01\INSTANCE01 Database Engine component with the SQL Server Management Studio.

2. Select File, Open, File from the menu. Open the UpdateProductInventory.sql file. This file is located in the C:\Program Files\Microsoft SQL Server\90\Samples\Notification Services\InventoryTracker\SQLScripts directory.

3. Click the F5 button or select Query, Execute from the menu to run the code.

This code essentially changes the inventory count for specific items in the AdventureWorks database. Each item has corresponding subscriptions that were created with the AddSubscriptions.exe program. When the inventory count of these items is below a specific level, a notification is sent to the subscriber.

The primary method to validate notifications in a production environment is to query the NotificationDistribution view. This view has the Notification Class Name as a prefix. In the Inventory Tracking example, the full name of the view is NSInventoryTrackerNotificationsNotificationDistribution.

The Inventory Tracker application is configured to send email notifications. If the SMTP service is stopped, the email message resides in the Pickup directory. This directory is commonly located in the C:\Inetpub\mailroot folder. Navigate to the Pickup directory and verify the EML message is present. Then open the EML message with a program such as Outlook Express. Notice that the email has been formatted for the recipient.

The Inventory Tracker is also configured to deliver text file–based notifications. Look in the C:\Program Files\Microsoft SQL Server\90\Samples\ Notification Services\InventoryTracker\Notifications folder for a file called FileNotifications.txt. Open the text file to review the notifications.

Use the following process to reset the inventory count to the original values. After the values have been reset, you can run the UpdateProductInventory. sql file again to generate new notifications.

1. Establish a connection to the SQL01\INSTANCE01 Database Engine component with the SQL Server Management Studio.

2. Select File, Open, File from the menu. Open the ResetProductInventory.sql file. This file is located in the C:\Program Files\Microsoft SQL Server\90\Samples\Notification Services\InventoryTracker\SQLScripts directory.

3. Click the F5 button or select Query, Execute from the menu to run the code.

Updating a Notification Services Instance

The settings for the notification application can be updated with new settings in the Instance and Application configuration files.

Follow these steps to update an existing Notification Services instance along with any hosted applications:

1. Establish a connection to SQL01\INSTANCE01 with the SQL Server Management Studio. Expand the instance name and select the Notification Services node from within the Object Explorer pane.

2. Right-click the Notification Services instance node and select Tasks, Update. The Update Instance window opens.

3. Click the Browse button and navigate to the location of the new Inventory Tracker instance configuration file.

4. The Notification Services Instance window now lists the required parameters. You must enter the correct settings in the Value field for the instance to run as intended. Enter any new parameters required; then click OK.

5. A series of actions runs against the SQL Server; these actions update the Inventory Tracker instance and application with any new settings specified in the configuration files. If any errors are reported, click the error message for additional information. Click the Close button to return to the SQL Studio Management Studio.

Administration from the Command Line

Notification Services instances and applications can be administered from the command line with the `nscontrol.exe` command-line utility. The `NsService.exe` command-line utility is used by developers when debugging custom applications. This utility is used to run the Notification Services instance as a console application to facilitate debugging in Visual Studio .NET.

Table 4.1 lists `nscontrol.exe` commands in the Configuration category.

Table 4.1   Configuration Commands

Configuration	Description
Register	Establishes Registry entries and performance counters
Unregister	Clears Registry entries and performance counters
ListVersions	Displays the registered versions and instances
DisplayArgumentKey	Displays the argument encryption key for an instance

Table 4.2 lists `nscontrol.exe` commands found in the Creation/Deletion/ Maintenance category.

Table 4.2   **Creation/Deletion/Maintenance Commands**

Creation/ Deletion	Description
Create	Creates a Notification Services instance
Delete	Removes a Notification Services instance
Update	Updates a Notification Services instance
Upgrade	Upgrades an instance to a new version or edition
Enable	Enables instance or application components
Disable	Disables instance or application components
Status	Shows the status of an instance or application
Export	Serializes an instance and its applications to XML
Repair	Repairs metadata for a Notification Services instance

Developers use the NsService.exe command-line utility when debugging custom applications. This utility is used to run the Notification Services instance as a console application to facilitate debugging in Visual Studio .NET.

Troubleshooting Notification Services

Notification Services provides independent logging capabilities for each component to help troubleshoot potential problems.

The first source for troubleshooting information is the Windows event logs. Both Windows and Notification Services write information to these logs, so this should be the first place to look when you encounter a problem. By default, all Notification Services error and warning events are logged to the Windows application log. You can increase the level of logging by changing the settings within the NSservice.exe.config file. This file is located in the C:\Program Files\Microsoft SQL Server\90\NotificationServices\9.0.242\ bin folder by default.

To increase the logging level, change the default 2 to a 4. A value of 4 configures verbose logging. The following code demonstrates what the configuration file looks like with the logging level set to verbose:

```
<?xml version="1.0" encoding="UTF-8"?>
<!--
    The default logging levels for all components is Warning

    Off = 0 < Error = 1 < Warning = 2 < Info = 3 < Verbose = 4
```

```
Change the values of the value attribute to change the
➥logging level.

Setting the logging level enables all log events which are
➥less than or equal to the log level setting
-->
<configuration>
    <system.diagnostics>
        <switches>
            <add name="LogAdministrative" value="4"/>
            <add name="LogService" value="4"/>
            <add name="LogEventProvider" value="4"/>
            <add name="LogEventCollector" value="4"/>
            <add name="LogGenerator" value="4"/>
            <add name="LogDistributor" value="4"/>
            <add name="LogVacuumer" value="4"/>
            <add name="LogOther" value="4"/>
            <add name="LogPerformanceMonitor" value="4"/>
        </switches>
    </system.diagnostics>
</configuration>
```

The Notification Services instance must be restarted for the changes to take effect. Remember to change the logging level to level 2 after the problem is resolved to avoid additional overhead created with excessive logging.

The different logging levels are stated in the text file and can be read as "No logging = 0," "Error Messages = 1," "Error and Warning Messages = 2," "Error, Warning, and Info Messages = 3," and "Log Everything = 4."

It is highly recommended to monitor for errors in the application log programmatically, especially if the Notification Services application is scaled out across different servers. This can be accomplished with a product such as Microsoft Operations Manager.

Each Notification Services instance provides a set of performance counters. These performance counters can also be used to troubleshoot bottlenecks and other potential performance-related issues. It is recommended to monitor the performance counters on an ongoing basis to analyze environmental trends.

Summary

Any size organization can benefit by using the Notification Services framework to build notification applications and quickly and easily provide notification capabilities for existing applications. Allowing subscriptions to be made to data increases productivity by providing timely access to important information.

Notification Services provides developers with a standardized framework that leverages the many different features found within SQL Server 2005, such as high availability and scalability.

Best Practices

The following best practices can be taken from this chapter:

- Understand how the components interact. Notification Services has many different components and can use several different accounts to access different internal and external elements. Understanding how the components interact substantially reduces issues related to permissions and other configuration areas.

- It is important to communicate with the developers to determine what service accounts are being used for each component to ensure the correct permissions are assigned.

- Always implement accounts with the least number of rights necessary to accomplish the defined task.

- Programmatically monitor event logs. Errors and warnings are recorded in the Application event logs by default; it is important to respond to error conditions before they become serious problems.

- Monitor performance for each instance. Understanding the performance trends and scalability of the environment is important because the needs of the organization may change from time to time.

CHAPTER 5

Administering SQL Server 2005 Integration Services

SQL Server 2005 Integration Services (SSIS) replaces the SQL Server 2000 Data Transformation Services (DTS). SSIS provides for the following data services:

- Extraction
- Transformation
- Loading

This triumvirate of data services is frequently referred to as ETL. The process encapsulates the extraction of data from a source, the transformation of the data to suit the requirements of the application, and finally the load of the data into a destination. The transformations can include normalizing, sanitizing, merging, aggregating, and copying the data. The sources and destinations for the data can be SQL databases, third-party ODBC data, flat files, or any number of other data locations.

SSIS delivers high-performance ETL services with a rich set of tools for designing, testing, executing, and monitoring these integrations. The subject of SSIS is broken down into administration and development. This chapter addresses the topic of SSIS administration, and Chapter 11, "Creating Packages and Transferring Data," covers development.

What's New in Integration Services with Service Pack 2

There are a number of new features and enhancements to SSIS in SQL Server 2005 Service Pack 2. The principal changes are

- SQL Server Import and Export Wizard supports Office 12, providing connectivity to Access 2007 and Excel 2007.
- The package's interaction with external data sources is now logged for troubleshooting.
- Data flow components now support combo boxes for variables.
- The Execute SQL task now has a `ParameterSize` property for string values.
- The `IsNull` property of columns in the Script Component raises a warning when it is used incorrectly.
- The Lookup transformation reports the final count of cached rows.

In addition, the overall performance of SSIS has been improved in Service Pack 2. This allows faster package execution and higher data throughput.

Understanding Integration Services

SSIS is fundamentally a service for storing and executing packages. Administration and management are covered in this chapter; this principally is the administration and management of package storage and execution.

Much of the complexity in integrating disparate data stores is pushed down into the packages themselves. This level of detail is examined in Chapter 11.

Integration Services Object Model

The Integration Services Object Model is the collection of objects and the interactions between them. Objects within SSIS are

- Packages
- Control Flows
- Data Flows
- Connections

- Variables
- Event Handlers
- Log Providers

For the administration of SSIS, the main consideration is packages. The package object contains all the preceding objects and provides the most granular level of SSIS administration. The package is almost an atomic entity from the perspective of Integration Services.

Packages

Packages are the core structure for Integration Services. They contain the logic that defines how the data will be integrated. They contain control flows (that is, control tasks) and data flows (that is, data tasks). When packages are executed, the control and data flows are executed.

Packages can be stored in SQL Server 2005, to the Integration Services package store, or to a file system.

The internal objects within packages, ways to create packages in Business Intelligence Development Studio, and various options within packages are covered in Chapter 11.

Projects and Solutions

Packages are organized into *solutions* and *projects*, which are, respectively, containers used to facilitate the development of packages and groups of packages that accomplish a business purpose.

Projects are containers for the packages, and a single project can contain multiple packages. Solutions are containers for projects, and a single solution can contain multiple projects. The solutions, projects, and packages are created, tested, and deployed from SQL Server 2005 Business Intelligence Development Studio.

Although solutions and projects are used to organize the packages, ultimately, the packages are what SSIS uses to actually do work. These units are executed to actually manipulate data. Integration Services fundamentally does not interact with the overarching solution and project organizing containers.

This chapter does not address the creation of solutions and projects. This topic is covered in Chapter 11.

Integration Services Service

Integration Services is a Windows service that manages SSIS packages. The IS service handles the following:

- Starting and stopping packages
- Importing and exporting packages

- Managing the SSIS Package Storage

- Providing integration with SQL Server Management Studio

The service is not required for the design and running of packages, but it facilitates the monitoring of packages in the SSIS package store in the SQL Server Management Studio.

If the service is stopped, packages can still be executed using other tools such as the execute package utility, SSIS Designer, SQL Server Import and Export Wizard, or dtexec command-line utility.

64-Bit Limitations of Integration Services

Not all features of SSIS are available in 64-bit versions, so you need to take care with some issues. And there are further limitations when comparing AMD and Itanium 64-bit platforms.

> **Note**
>
> This problem is not unique to SSIS. Many other applications have limitations and provisos when you're installing on 64-bit platforms and Itanium 64-bit platforms.

SQL Server 2005 64-bit installs all the possible design and run components of SSIS, placing the 32-bit-only versions in "Program Files (x86)" and the 64-bit versions in "Program Files."

Some of the compatibility issues and limitations of the 64-bit version of SSIS include

- **Business Intelligence Development Studio is not supported on Itanium 64-bit.** This component is not supported on Itanium 64-bit computers and is not installed on this platform. It is installed and supported on AMD 64-bit computers.

- **A limited number of native 64-bit tools is supported.** The only native 64-bit SSIS tools are dtexec, dtutil, and the SQL Server Import and Export Wizard. All the other tools are 32-bit versions when SSIS is installed on 64-bit servers.

- **The execute package utility is 32-bit.** The UI version of the dtexec utility that runs packages from within SQL Server Management Studio, the dtexecui utility, is 32-bit and runs packages in 32-bit mode.

■ **The SQL Server message queue task is either 64-bit or 32-bit.** The Message Queue task only runs in packages that are running in the same mode as the SQL Server installation. If a 64-bit version of SQL is installed, then the Message Queue task only runs in packages that are running in 64-bit mode. The Message Queue task does not run using the execute package utility, which is only 32-bit.

■ **The SQL Server Agent is only 64-bit.** The SQL Server Agent runs in 64-bit mode on 64-bit platforms, so jobs with SSIS package-execution-type steps use the 64-bit dtexec utility and run in 64-bit mode. To run packages in 32-bit mode, you must use the operating-system-type step and use the 32-bit version of the dtexec in the command line.

■ **SSIS is not backward compatible with DTS jobs in 64-bit.** The 64-bit SQL Server 2005 does not support any backward compatibility with DTS packages created in earlier versions of SQL.

When using a mixed environment of 64-bit and 32-bit SQL Server 2005 Integration Services, you must take care to ensure that compatibility issues do not arise.

There are also some package development issues that need to be taken into account; they're covered in Chapter 11.

Managing Integration Services

Much of the management of Integration Services revolves around packages. The tasks that you need to perform as database administrator are essentially package tasks, including creating, storing, and running packages, and other package-specific tasks.

Creating an Integration Services Package

Using the SQL Server Import and Export Wizard is one of the easiest ways to create a basic package. Sophisticated package creation is done through the Business Intelligence Development Studio (BIDS).

This example creates a package that will import comma-delimited data from biometric monitors for patients in a vaccination study. The biometric data consists of a patient number and a series of measurements of the patient's temperature, pulse, respiration, and blood pressure.

The blank database named BioData already exists on the SQL Server 2005 server named SQL01. The biometric data will be refreshed periodically, so you need a package to import the data for ease of scheduling. To create it, follow these steps:

1. Open SQL Server Management Studio.

2. Connect to the Database Engine of the SQL01 SQL server.

3. Expand the Databases folder in Object Explorer.

4. Right-click on the BioData database.

5. Select Tasks, Import Data.

6. Click Next.

7. From the Data source drop-down, select Flat File Source.

8. Enter the filename of the source data, in this case **biodata.txt**.

9. A warning appears in the messages window, stating "Columns are not defined for this connection manager."

10. Check the box Column Names in the first data row.

11. Click Next.

12. Click Next to leave the destination defaults.

13. Click Edit Mappings.

14. Check the box Drop and Re-create Destination Table. This setting overwrites the table each time the package is run.

15. Click OK.

16. Click Next.

17. Check the box Save SSIS Package and click Next. This saves the package to the SQL Server.

18. Enter a name for the package, in this case **BioDataImport**.

19. Click Next and then Finish.

The package execution results are summarized in a window, as shown in Figure 5.1. Note that the package completed with one error, which was due to the BioData table not existing on the first run. As you can see from the figure, more than 7 million rows were imported into the table.

The package was installed to the SQL Server. To confirm this, you can connect the Integration Services instance using the following steps:

1. In SQL Server Management Studio Object Explorer, click on the Connect drop-down and select Integration Services.

2. Click Connect to connect with the current credentials.

3. Expand the Stored Packages folder in the Object Explorer window.

4. Expand the MSDB folder to see the BioDataImport package.

At this point, you should see the package in the folder.

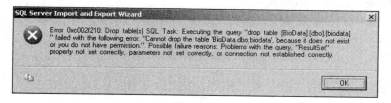

FIGURE 5.1
Using the SQL Server Import and Export Wizard.

Storing Packages

Packages can be stored in the SQL Server MSDB database, SSIS package storage, or file system. Only the SQL Server storage and SSIS file system storage are managed by SSIS.

Folders and subfolders can be created in either the MSDB storage or the SSIS file system storage to help organize the packages.

Packages stored in the MSDB database are stored in the sysdtspackages90 table. Folders within the MSDB are stored as rows within the database.

Packages stored in the SSIS file system storage are stored by default in the %Program Files%\Microsoft SQL Server\90\DTS\Packages\ directory. Packages can be viewed and managed in these folders from the Object Explorer within SSIS, as well as the file system. Folders created in the file system are actually file folders in the directory structure.

Note

Unfortunately, packages cannot be dragged and dropped within the folder structure of the SSIS storage. You must use the export and import feature to move the packages around.

However, you can drag and drop files within the native Windows file system. When you do, the changes are reflected in the SSIS file system folder.

Importing and Exporting Packages

Packages can be imported and exported from the SSIS storage. This can be done with the Object Explorer in SQL Server Management Studio or the file system in Windows.

Packages can be exported to

- Back up the packages
- Move the packages to a different SQL Server
- Include the packages in a project or solution using SQL Server Business Intelligence Development Studio

Packages can be exported to SQL Server (that is, the MSDB database), the SSIS package store, or the file system. The destination can be local or on another server, such as another SQL Server or even just a file share on another server. The saved file will have a .dtsx extension.

To export a package, such as the BioDataImport package, from SSIS to a backup file, follow these steps:

1. Open SQL Server Management Studio.
2. Select Integration Services from the Server Type drop-down.
3. Click Connect.
4. Expand the Stored Packages folder.
5. Expand the MSDB folder.
6. Right-click on a package to export, in this case the BioDataImport package.
7. Select Export Package.
8. Select the destination of the package, in this case File System.
9. Enter the path and filename for the package. The path must exist already for the package to be saved.
10. Alternatively, click on the button next to the Package path field to browse for a location.
11. Click OK to save the package.

These steps save the package in XML format, which you can then import into another server with SQL Server Management Studio or into a project in the Business Intelligence Development Studio.

To import a package in SQL Server Management Studio, follow these steps:

1. Open SQL Server Management Studio.
2. Select Integration Services from the Server Type drop-down.
3. Click Connect.
4. Expand the Stored Packages folder.
5. Right-click on the File System folder.
6. Select Import Package.
7. Select the source of the package, in this case File System.
8. Enter the path and filename for the package. Alternatively, click on the button next to the Package path field to browse for a package. In this case, the package named `PatientStatusImport.dtsx` is imported to load patient status. This package imports data from a file named `PatientStatus.txt`.
9. Click in the Package Name field. The package name is filled in automatically but can be changed if needed.
10. Click OK to save the package.

The package is then displayed in the File System folder. You can now run the package from there.

Running Packages

You can trigger the packages from within the SQL Server Management Studio and monitor their execution progress in detail. The contents of packages cannot be reviewed within the tool. To do that, you must export the package and then open it in the Business Intelligence Development Studio (see Chapter 11).

To run a package (using the newly imported PatientStatusImport package) within SSIS, do the following:

1. Open SQL Server Management Studio.
2. Select Integration Services from the Server Type drop-down.
3. Click Connect.
4. Expand the Stored Packages folder.
5. Expand the File System folder.
6. Right-click the PatientStatusImport package imported earlier and select Run Package.

7. The execute package utility runs.

8. In the General options page, there is the package source, the server, the authentication, and the package name.

9. Click the Reporting options page to see the reporting options available.

10. Click the Command Line options page to see the command-line version of the execution. This capability is useful to automate the package execution in the future.

> **Note**
>
> You can add parameters to the command line by selecting the Edit the Command Line Manually option.

11. Click Execute to run the package.

12. The Package Execution Progress window opens, displaying the package progress and information as shown in Figure 5.2. The message indicated shows that 10,000 rows were written to the table.

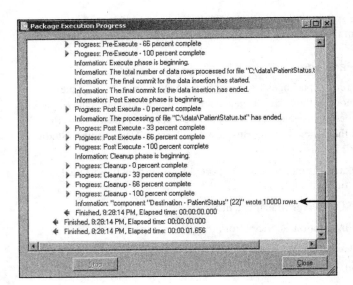

FIGURE 5.2
Package Execution Progress window.

13. Click Close to close the progress window.

14. Click Close to close the execute package utility.

The execution of the package logs a pair of events in the Windows NT Application event log. These events are from source SQLISPackage with event ID 12288 when the package starts and 12289 when the package finishes successfully. If the package fails, the event ID logged is 12291.

Scheduling Packages

Packages can be scheduled to run automatically using the SQL Server Agent. The packages need to be stored in the SSIS package store, either the MSDB or the file system, to be scheduled.

In the example, the Patient Status Data package needs to be run every day at 6 a.m. to update the patient status. To schedule a package for execution, follow these steps:

1. Open SQL Server Management Studio.

2. Connect to the Database Engine of the SQL Server.

3. Right-click on SQL Server Agent and select New, Job.

4. In the General options page, enter the name of the job, in this example **Daily Patient Status Update**.

5. Select the Steps option page.

6. Click New to create a new step.

7. Enter the Step name, in the example **Update Patient Status**.

8. In the Type pull-down, select SQL Server Integration Services Package.

9. In the Package Source pull-down, select the SSIS package store.

10. In the Server pull-down, select the server name.

11. Click on the Package selection button to the right of the Package field.

12. Browse the Select an SSIS Package window to find the package, in this example the PatientStatusImport package imported earlier.

13. Click OK.

14. Click OK to save the step.

15. Select the Schedules option page.

16. Click New to create a new job schedule.

17. In the Name field, enter **Daily at 6am**.

18. In the Occurs pull-down, select Daily.

19. Change the Daily Frequency to 6:00:00 AM.

20. Click OK to save the schedule.

21. Click OK to save the job.

The job will now run the SSIS package at 6 a.m. every day. The job is saved in the database and can be reviewed in the Jobs folder within the SQL Server Agent. You can test it by right-clicking on the job and selecting Start Job.

Jobs can run a series of packages in a sequence of steps and even with conditional branches that depend on the output of the preceding packages. This allows packages to be chained together to complete a larger task.

Managing the Running Packages

You can view the running packages in the SQL Server Management Studio connection to Integration Services. The list of running packages is located under the Running Packages folder.

To generate a report of the running package, right-click on the running package and select General. The report, shown in Figure 5.3, is not very detailed. The main information is in the Execution Started and Executed By fields.

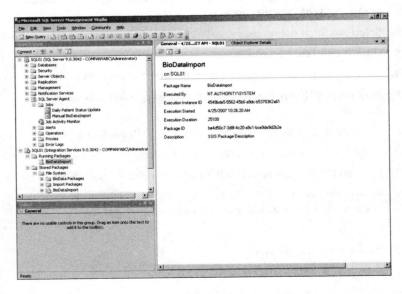

FIGURE 5.3
Running package.

You also can stop the package from the Integration Services Object Explorer Running Packages window. Simply right-click on the running package and select Stop.

Unfortunately, the management of running packages within the SQL Server Management Studio is limited and the information presented minimal. The tool gives only a general sense of what the packages are doing, rather than the details you might be looking for.

Removing Packages

To remove the packages from the Integration Services package store, follow these steps:

1. Open SQL Server Management Studio.
2. Select Integration Services from the Server Type drop-down.
3. Click Connect.
4. Expand the Stored Packages folder.
5. Expand the File System folder.
6. Right-click the PatientStatusImport package imported earlier and select Delete.
7. Click on Yes to confirm the deletion of the package.

When a package is deleted, it cannot be retrieved except by restoring from a backup. There is no "undo" function within the tool, so delete packages carefully and only after exporting the packages for safekeeping.

Administering Integration Services

Administering the SQL Server 2005 Integration Services consists of administering the Integration Services service and packages. There are relatively few administration activities directly related to SSIS itself because it is mainly a vehicle for running and storing packages.

Administering the Integration Services Service

The default behavior of the Integration Services service can be modified to suit the needs of the application. Three options can be configured for the Integration Services service:

- Stopping packages when the service stops
- Changing the File System folder default location
- Changing the default root folders to display

The configuration file, named MsDtsSrvr.ini,xml, is located in %Program Files%\Microsoft SQL Server\90\DTS\Binn\. The configuration file is loaded when the service starts.

The default configuration file for the Integration Services service is

```
<?xml version="1.0" encoding="utf-8"?>
<DtsServiceConfiguration xmlns:xsd=http://www.w3.org/2001/
➥XMLSchema
 xmlns:xsi="http://www.w3.org/2001/XMLSchema-instance">
  <StopExecutingPackagesOnShutdown>true
 ➥</StopExecutingPackagesOnShutdown>
  <TopLevelFolders>
    <Folder xsi:type="SqlServerFolder">
      <Name>MSDB</Name>
      <ServerName>.</ServerName>
    </Folder>
    <Folder xsi:type="FileSystemFolder">
      <Name>File System</Name>
      <StorePath>..\Packages</StorePath>
    </Folder>
  </TopLevelFolders>
</DtsServiceConfiguration>
```

You can change the service configuration simply by modifying the configuration file and then restarting the service.

For example, if you want to configure the service not to stop packages on shutdown and to add the SQL Server folder (MSDB database) to the Object Explorer view, your modified configuration file would look like this:

```
<?xml version="1.0" encoding="utf-8"?>
<DtsServiceConfiguration xmlns:xsd=http://www.w3.org/2001/
➥XMLSchema
  xmlns:xsi="http://www.w3.org/2001/XMLSchema-instance">
  <StopExecutingPackagesOnShutdown>false
 ➥</StopExecutingPackagesOnShutdown>
  <TopLevelFolders>
    <Folder xsi:type="SqlServerFolder">
      <Name>MSDB</Name>
      <ServerName>.</ServerName>
    </Folder>
    <Folder xsi:type="SqlServerFolder">
      <Name>SQL02MSDB</Name>
```

```
    <ServerName>SQL02</ServerName>
    </Folder>
    <Folder xsi:type="FileSystemFolder">
      <Name>File System</Name>
      <StorePath>..\Packages</StorePath>
    </Folder>
  </TopLevelFolders>
</DtsServiceConfiguration>
```

This example shows how the file would be modified for a SQL Server named SQL01 to be able to explore the packages in the MSDB on SQL02. After you modified the configuration file, there would be an additional root folder SQL02MSDB showing packages stored in the SQL Server Store of SQL02. And packages running on SQL01 would not stop when the service was stopped.

Monitoring Package Execution

Integration Services exposes a number of performance counters that allow the monitoring of package execution in real-time or the capture for historical reference. This shows the number of rows being processed, the memory being used in different capacities, and the impact of certain data types on the package performance. The counters can be used to tune the performance of the package and see the impact of the changes.

A couple of terms used in the counters bear explanation. *Flat buffers* are blocks of memory that a component uses to store data. A flat buffer is a large block of bytes that is accessed byte by byte. *Binary large objects (BLOBs)* are data types used in SQL to store large binary data such as images or unstructured text. They can be large objects and can affect the performance of a package, so understanding how much data is from this type is important.

The object is the SQLServer:SSIS Pipeline, and the various counters are listed in Table 5.1.

Table 5.1   **Integration Services Package Counters**

Performance Counter	Description
Rows read	The number of rows that a source produces. This counter is for the life of the SSIS instance and resets if the service is restarted.
Rows written	The number of rows offered to a destination. This counter is for the life of the SSIS instance and resets if the service is restarted.

Table 5.1   **continued**

Performance Counter	Description
Buffer memory	The amount of memory in use.
Buffers in use	The number of buffer objects that all data flow components and the data flow engine are currently using.
Buffers spooled	The number of buffers currently written to the disk.
Private buffer memory	The total amount of memory in use by all private buffers.
Private buffers in use	The number of buffers that transformations use.
BLOB bytes read	The number of bytes of BLOB data that the data flow engine has read from all sources.
BLOB bytes written	The number of bytes of BLOB data that the data flow engine has written to all destinations.
BLOB files in use	The number of BLOB files that the data flow engine currently is using for spooling.
Flat buffer memory	The total amount of memory, in bytes, that all flat buffers use.
Flat buffers in use	The number of flat buffers that the data flow engine uses. All flat buffers are private buffers.

The counters can be used directly from the Performance Microsoft Management Console (MMC) for a real-time view of the package performance or can be used with a monitoring tool such as Microsoft Operations Manager (MOM) 2007.

Logging Packages Execution

The two main types of logging possible with packages in SSIS are

- **Logging within the Package**—Logging within the package is logging tasks that are built into the package at design time using the SSIS Designer. This form of logging is covered in Chapter 11.

- **Console Logging**—This form of logging is independent of the package design and is handled by the tool executing the package. This is the type of logging covered in this section.

Console logging shows the progress and status of the package execution. The messages are informative and even give optimization tips to make the package more efficient in addition to just status and error messages.

When running from the execute package utility (the UI for the dtexec utility), the Reporting options specify the level of console logging to do. The default is Verbose, meaning that all events will be displayed.

To capture the console log, use the dtexec utility and pipe the input into a text file. An example is the following command:

```
dtexec /DTS "\File System\PatientStatusImport" /SERVER SQL01
       /MAXCONCURRENT " -1 " /CHECKPOINTING OFF  /REPORTING V >
➡c:\log.txt
```

This command executes the package PatientStatusImport from the SSIS file system package store with Verbose console logging and saves the output into the text file c:\log.txt.

More granular logging requires a bit more effort and forethought during the design of the package. This is covered in Chapter 11.

Backing Up and Restoring Packages

Backing up packages needs to include some additional steps because packages in the SSIS file system store are, in reality, stored in the file system. Even packages stored in the SQL Server, that is, the MSDB, might have some configuration or data files stored in the file system depending on the package.

In addition to the procedures outlined in the Chapter 17, "Backing Up and Restoring the SQL Server 2005 Environment" (online), it is critical to back up the file system as well. This includes the SSIS file system store directory, which by default is %Program Files%\Microsoft SQL Server\90\DTS\Packages\. Backing up this directory backs up all the packages stored in the SSIS file system package store.

Securing Integration Services

SQL Server Integration Services supports a number of security features. These security features protect the packages from unauthorized execution, modification, sensitive information, and even the entire contents of the packages. This section describes the database roles and the protection levels for packages.

In addition to the roles and protection levels, packages can also be signed with certificates to verify the authenticity of the packages. This security feature is examined in Chapter 11.

> **Note**
>
> In addition to the security that SSIS provides to packages, you must also be concerned with other areas of security with regards to packages. Packages frequently use data files, configuration files, and log files. These files are not protected by the security mechanisms within SSIS.
>
> To ensure that confidential information is not exposed, you must protect the locations of these files as well. Typically, you do this at the operating system level through ACL controls and the Encrypting File System (EFS).

SSIS has three database roles for controlling access to packages. They roughly fall into the categories of administrator, user, and operator. If more granularity is needed in the rights assignment, you can create user-defined roles.

The fixed database level roles and their rights are listed in Table 5.2.

Table 5.2   **Fixed Security Roles**

Role	Read Action	Write Action
db_dtsadmin or sysadmin	Enumerate own packages. Enumerate all packages. View own packages. View all packages. Execute own packages. Execute all packages. Export own packages. Export all packages. Execute all packages in SQL Server Agent.	Import packages. Delete own packages. Delete all packages. Change own package roles. Change all package roles.
db_dtsltduser	Enumerate own packages. Enumerate all packages. View own packages. Execute own packages. Export own packages.	Import packages. Delete own packages. Change own package roles.
db_dtsoperator	Enumerate all packages. View all packages. Execute all packages. Export all packages. Execute all packages in SQL Server Agent.	None
Windows administrators	View execution details of all running packages.	Stop all currently running packages.

Protection levels are set on packages when they are created in the Business Intelligence Development Studio or the wizards. These protection levels prevent the unauthorized execution or modification of packages. Protection levels can be updated on packages when they are imported into the SSIS package store.

The protection levels refer to sensitive information in what they protect or not, which is defined as

- The password part of a connection string is sensitive information.

- The task-generated XML nodes that are tagged as sensitive are considered sensitive information.

- Any variable marked as sensitive is considered sensitive information.

The options for protection levels are listed in the following sections.

Do Not Save Sensitive (DontSaveSensitive)

The DontSaveSensitive option suppresses sensitive information in the package when it is saved. This protection level does not encrypt; instead, it prevents properties that are marked sensitive from being saved with the package and therefore makes the sensitive data unavailable to other users. If a different user opens the package, the sensitive information is replaced with blanks and the user must provide the sensitive information.

Encrypt All with Password (EncryptAllWithPassword)

The SensitiveWithPassword option encrypts the whole package by using a password. The package is encrypted by using a password that the user supplies when the package is created or exported. To open the package in SSIS Designer or run the package by using the dtexec command prompt utility, the user must provide the package password. Without the password, the user cannot access or run the package.

Encrypt All with User Key (EncryptAllWithUserKey)

The EncryptAllWithUserKey option encrypts the whole package by using a key based on the user profile. Only the same user using the same profile can load the package. The package is encrypted by using a key that is based on the user who created or exported the package. Only the user who created or exported the package can open the package in SSIS Designer or run the package by using the dtexec command prompt utility.

Encrypt Sensitive with Password (EncryptSensitiveWithPassword)

The EncryptSensitiveWithPassword option encrypts only the sensitive information in the package by using a password. Data Protection Application Programming Interface (DPAPI), a standard Windows cryptography component, is used for this encryption. Sensitive data is saved as a part of the package, but that data is encrypted by using a password that the current user supplies when the package is created or exported. To open the package in SSIS Designer, the user must provide the package password. If the password is not provided, the package opens without the sensitive data and the current user must provide new values for sensitive data. If the user tries to execute the package without providing the password, package execution fails. For more information about passwords and command-line execution, see dtexec Utility in the SQL Server Books Online.

Encrypt Sensitive with User Key (EncryptSensitiveWithUserKey)

The EncryptSensitiveWithUserKey option is the default setting for packages. It encrypts only the sensitive information in the package by using keys based on the current user. Only the same user using the same profile can load the package. If a different user opens the package, the sensitive information is replaced with blanks and the current user must provide new values for the sensitive data. If the user attempts to execute the package, package execution fails. DPAPI is used for this encryption.

Rely on Server Storage for Encryption (ServerStorage)

The EncryptSensitiveWithUserKey option protects the whole package using SQL Server database roles. This option is supported only when a package is saved to the SQL Server MSDB database. It is not supported when a package is saved to the file system from Business Intelligence Development Studio.

Command Prompt Utilities

There are two Integration Services–specific command-line utilities. These two utilities allow you to manage, configure, and execute packages from a command line.

Executing Packages with dtexec

The dtexec utility configures and executes SSIS packages from a command line. These packages can be stored in the SSIS package store, a SQL Server, or on a file system. The dtexec utility replaces the dtsrun utility from SQL Server 2000.

The dtexec utility runs in four phases when executing a package:

- **Command Sourcing**—The command line is parsed.

- **Package Load**—The package is loaded from the source specified on the command-line arguments.

- **Configuration**—The command line and package options are processed.

- **Validation and Execution**—Finally, the package is run or validated.

At the end of the execution, the dtexec utility returns an exit code in the ERRORLEVEL variable for use in batch files or other execution agents. The various exit codes are given in Table 5.3.

Table 5.3   dtexec **Utility Exit Codes**

Exit Code	Description
0	The package executed successfully.
1	The package failed.
3	The package was canceled by the user.
4	The utility was unable to locate the requested package. The package could not be found.
5	The utility was unable to load the requested package. The package could not be loaded.
6	The utility encountered an internal error of syntactic or semantic errors in the command line.

These error codes can be used to determine the status of the execution or to branch within the batch file.

The dtexec command line options are

```
Usage: DTExec /option [value] [/option [value]] ...
Options are case-insensitive.
A hyphen (-) may be used in place of a forward slash (/).
/CheckF[ile]          [Filespec]
/Checkp[ointing]      [{On | Off}] (On is the default)
/Com[mandFile]        Filespec
/Conf[igFile]         Filespec
/Conn[ection]         IDOrName;ConnectionString
```

/Cons[oleLog]	[[DispOpts];[{E | I};List]] DispOpts = any one or more of ➡N, C, O, S, G, X, M, or T. List = {EventName | SrcName | SrcGuid}[;List]
/De[crypt]	Password
/DT[S]	PackagePath
/F[ile]	Filespec
/H[elp]	[Option]
/L[ogger]	ClassIDOrProgID;ConfigString
/M[axConcurrent]	ConcurrentExecutables
/P[assword]	Password
/Rem[ark]	[Text]
/Rep[orting]	Level[;EventGUIDOrName[;EventGUIDOrName[...]] Level = N or V or any one or more of ➡E, W, I, C, D, or P.
/Res[tart] ➡default)	[{Deny | Force | IfPossible}] (Force is the
/Set	PropertyPath;Value
/Ser[ver]	ServerInstance
/SQ[L]	PackagePath
/Su[m]	
/U[ser]	User name
/Va[lidate]	
/VerifyB[uild]	Major[;Minor[;Build]]
/VerifyP[ackageid]	PackageID
/VerifyS[igned]	
/VerifyV[ersionid]	VersionID
/W[arnAsError]	

Of particular note, the /set option allows you to change the value of any property in the package. This allows the configuration to be adjusted at runtime or variables to be populated. This makes the package execution eminently customizable.

For a detailed description of each option, see the SQL Server Books Online.

> **Note**
>
> The `dtexec` command-line options are processed in the order in which they appear on the command line. Unfortunately, the parser does not report an error if the same option appears twice in the command line.
>
> If the same option is configured on the command line, the last specified option is used.

Managing Packages with `dtutil`

The `dtutil` utility allows you to manage packages from the command line. It allows access to packages stored in the SSIS package store, SQL Server, and the file system.

With `dtutil`, you can perform all the tasks that can be performed through the SQL Server Management Server Studio when connected to an Integration Services instance. These tasks include

- Copying packages
- Deleting packages
- Moving packages
- Signing packages

At the end of the execution, the `dtutil` utility returns an exit code in the ERRORLEVEL variable for use in batch files or other execution agents. The various exit codes are given in Table 5.4.

Table 5.4 `dtutil` **Utility Exit Codes**

Exit Code	Description
0	The utility executed successfully.
1	The utility failed.
4	The utility cannot locate the requested package.
5	The utility cannot load the requested package.
6	The utility encountered an error in the command line.

These error codes can be used to determine the status of the execution or to branch within the batch file.

The dtutil command-line options are

```
Usage: DTUtil /option [value] [/option [value]] ...
Options are case-insensitive.
A hyphen (-) may be used in place of a forward slash (/).
The vertical bar (|) is the OR operator and is used
➥to list possible values.
For extended help use /help with an option.
For example: DTUtil /help Copy
```

```
/C[opy]                {SQL | FILE | DTS};Path
/Dec[rypt]             Password
/Del[ete]
/DestP[assword]        Password
/DestS[erver]          Server
/DestU[ser]            User name
/DT[S]                 PackagePath
/En[crypt]             {SQL | FILE | DTS};Path;ProtectionLevel
➥[;Password]
/Ex[ists]
/FC[reate]             {SQL | DTS};ParentFolderPath;NewFolderName
/FDe[lete]             {SQL | DTS};ParentFolderPath;FolderName
/FDi[rectory]          {SQL | DTS}[;FolderPath[;S]]
/FE[xists]             {SQL | DTS};FolderPath
/FR[ename]             {SQL | DTS};ParentFolderPath;OldFolderName;
➥NewFolderName
/Fi[le]                Filespec
/H[elp]                [Option]
/I[DRegenerate]
/M[ove]                {SQL | FILE | DTS};Path
/Q[uiet]
/R[emark]              [Text]
/Si[gn]                {SQL | FILE | DTS};Path;Hash
/SourceP[assword]      Password
/SourceS[erver]        Server
/SourceU[ser]          User name
/SQ[L]                 PackagePath
```

For a detailed description of each option, see the **SQL Server Books Online**.

Summary

SQL Server 2005 Integration Services provides a set of strong extraction, transformation, and loading (ETL) services that are fast and robust. These services include many features and options for ensuring that data integration is handled effectively. This feature was somewhat lacking in previous versions of SQL Server, but SQL Server 2005 improves on it immensely.

For more detailed information on the creation of packages and numerous options within them, see Chapter 11.

Best Practices

Some important best practices from the chapter include

- Export packages before deleting them.
- Take care when mixing 32-bit and 64-bit versions of SSIS to ensure full interoperability.
- Create user-defined security roles to ensure the least privilege security principle.

CHAPTER 6

Administering SQL Server Replication

Replication serves many purposes. Most people are aware of its use through organizations that copy databases from one server instance to another SQL Server instance. It can also be used for data distribution, synchronization, fault tolerance, disaster recovery, load balancing, reporting, and testing. When configuring replication, an organization can choose to replicate the full database or partial components of a database, such as tables, views, and stored procedures. SQL Server 2005 has added to this list a new replication topology called *peer-to-peer transactional replication*. Peer-to-peer replication is one of four SQL Server high-availability alternatives discussed in this chapter.

This chapter focuses on explaining the replication components and then providing an overview of replication, including prerequisites and a feature comparison. The chapter also includes step-by-step administration procedures such as configuring snapshot replication and peer-to-peer replication. The final sections of this chapter include replication management and monitoring tasks augmented with replication best practices.

What Is New for Replication with Service Pack 2?

SQL Server 2005 Service Pack 2 introduces the following changes and improvements for replication:

- You can use a database snapshot to initialize subscriptions to snapshot and transactional publications. You can do this only when using the Enterprise Edition of SQL Server, however. You must specify a database snapshot value in the sync_method publication property.

■ You can use a new stored procedure that re-creates triggers, stored procedures, and views. These objects are used to track and apply data changes for merge replication.

SQL Server 2005 Replication Essentials

Many pieces make up a replication topology. As a database administrator, you must fully comprehend these items to successfully administer, manage, and monitor replication. The following sections examine these topics in more detail.

SQL Server 2005 Replication Roles

Before installing SQL Server 2005 replication, you need to understand not only the underlying model, but also the replication roles available. This is necessary for you to successfully configure, administer, and manage replication. Take a look at the various replication roles:

■ **Publisher**—SQL Server publisher is a replication component responsible for producing the data that will be available in the replication topology for subscription. The publisher is configured on the instance of SQL Server where the database to be replicated resides. Although a replicated environment can consist of many subscribers, there can be only one publisher for each article published for replication.

■ **Distributor**—The distributor is responsible for circulating the published data for replication from the SQL Server publisher to the SQL Server subscribers. The replication metadata, history, and other pertinent replication information are stored in a replication database on the SQL Server hosting the distributor role. The distributor role can reside on the same SQL Server instance as the publisher, or it can be isolated where it resides on a different SQL Server for performance reasons.

■ **Subscriber**—The subscriber receives published data meant for replication from the distributor. When configuring a subscriber, you have the flexibility to choose if you want to subscribe to all publications, a specific publication, or a subset of specific publications available at the publisher/distributor.

Additional Replication Components

When you and your organization understand the replication roles, you must then turn your attention to understanding other replication components and terminology to successfully implement replication. The additional components are:

- **Articles**—Articles are database items that have been selected for publication. They include tables, stored procedures, views, indexed views, and user-defined functions. When creating articles for publication, you can create filters that exclude unwanted rows and columns from published tables.

- **Publications**—Publications consist of either a single article or group of articles available for replication. It is beneficial to group more than one article into a single publication instead of replicating each article separately.

- **Push Subscriptions**—A push subscription is used when distributing data; the distributor is responsible for providing data and subsequent updates to subscribers.

- **Pull Subscriptions**—Pull subscriptions are the opposite of push subscriptions. For this type of subscription, subscribers initiate replication based on a scheduled task, or they do so manually.

SQL Server 2005 Replication Agents

SQL Server 2005 replication uses a number of agents to effect replication. These agents, as described here, are programs run as SQL Server jobs by the SQL Server Agent:

- **Snapshot Agent**—This agent is used by all three types of replication. It sets up the initial data files and updates the synchronization information in the distribution database. It runs on the distributor role.

- **Log Reader Agent**—This agent is used by transactional replication. There is an instance of this agent on the distributor role for each database using transactional replication. The log reader agent moves the transactions from the publisher to the distributor database.

- **Distribution Agent**—This agent is used by both transactional and snapshot replication. It creates the initial snapshot on the subscriber and moves transactions to the subscriber from the distribution database. This agent runs on the distributor for push replication or on the subscriber for pull replication.

- **Merge Agent**—This agent works with merge replication to create the initial snapshot on the subscribers. It then transfers and reconciles data changes. Each merge subscription has its own instance of this agent. This agent runs on the distributor for push replication or on the subscriber for pull replication.

- **Queue Reader Agent**—This agent works with transactional replication and runs on the distributor. This agent is used only when the queued updating option is used, allowing changes made at the subscriber to be replicated back to the publisher.

Note that these agents handle the actual work of the replication process and run on a schedule.

The Types of Replication Alternatives Available

When configuring and administering replication, you need to consider three types of replication:

- **Snapshot**—Snapshot replication distributes data by copying the entire contents of a published article from the distributor to the subscriber data based on a specific point in time. Any modified changes to the source database are not reflected on the subscriber, which causes the subscriber to be out of date until the subsequent snapshot occurs. In addition, the data residing on the subscriber is read-only and cannot be updated.

- **Transactional Replication**—Transactional replication keeps the publisher and subscriber in sync with each other and up to date by first replicating the initial snapshot and then applying any incremental changes made to articles from the publisher to the distributor and finally to the subscriber.

- **Merge Replication**—Merge replication is similar to transactional replication; however, it is possible to independently update the database on both the publisher and subscriber using this replication. When configuring merge replication, the initial snapshot copies the published articles to the subscriber. Periodically, changes on the publisher and subscriber are then merged together.

Each replication type offers different setup features and functionality regarding distributing and replicating data between SQL Server instances.

SQL Server 2005 Replication Topologies

There are many ways to configure replication based on how data will be distributed throughout the organization. The flow of data and placement of the publisher, distributor, and subscriber dictate the topology that an organization uses. Beyond the basic server-to-server replication strategy, some of the intricate replication topologies include

- **Central Publisher/Single or Multiple Subscribers**—A central publisher replication topology, as shown in Figure 6.1, typically consists of a single server configured as a publisher and distributor. There can be either one or more servers within the topology configured as subscribers. In addition, a dedicated distributor may be used to relieve workload from the publisher. This model is commonly used by retail organizations. In this situation, retail organizations typically replicate product and pricing information from the central headquarters to all their stores.

CENTRAL PUBLISHER/MULTIPLE SUBSCRIBERS REPLICATION TOPOLOGY

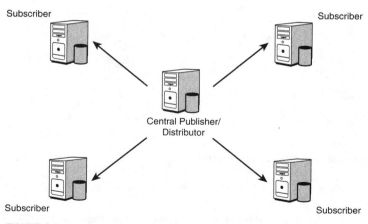

FIGURE 6.1
Central publisher/multiple subscribers model.

- **Central Subscriber/Multiple Publishers**—A central subscriber is a single server configured as a subscriber that accepts replication data from one or more publishers. This model is typically used when there is a need to centralize data from many sites or SQL Server instances. For example, this model may be used by an organization with manufacturing facilities all over the world and a business requirement to centralize manufacturing data from each site and store it in a central location such as the headquarters for reporting purposes. This type of organization would be an ideal candidate for the central subscriber/ multiple publisher model. The central subscriber/multiple publishers model is depicted in Figure 6.2.

CENTRAL SUBSCRIBER/MULTIPLE PUBLISHERS REPLICATION TOPOLOGY

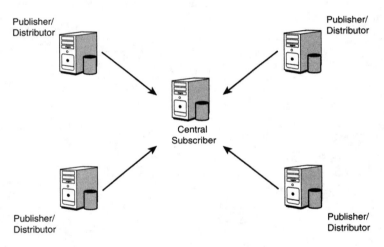

FIGURE 6.2
Central subscriber/multiple publishers model.

Note

When you use the central subscriber model, data is consolidated from many databases into a single database. Therefore, each article partaking in the replication topology must have a unique ID that is typically a site identifier as the primary key. Otherwise, replication will fail when data is consolidated due to duplicate primary key violations.

- **Peer-to-Peer**—Peer-to-peer replication is a new replication model introduced with SQL Server 2005, as illustrated in Figure 6.3. This model acts as a high-availability mechanism because all participants in the replication topology are peers. There isn't a hierarchy as with normal transactional replication models. In addition, data can be updated on all databases configured in the peer-to-peer replication topology. For instance, one of the advantages of peer-to-peer replication is witnessed when one of the peers is unavailable. In this situation, the traffic can be redirected to another peer as a form of high availability. In addition, because all peers are updatable and support bidirectional replication, this model can be used for load-balancing clients across multiple SQL Server instances.

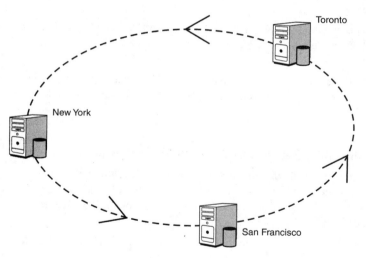

PEER-TO-PEER
REPLICATION TOPOLOGY

FIGURE 6.3
Peer-to-peer publishers model.

SQL Server 2005 Replication Prerequisites

Configuring replication is not as simple as clicking through a few screens of a SQL Server installation wizard. A number of prerequisite steps must be fulfilled before a replication can be configured and implemented.

Before you install SQL Server replication, ensure the following prerequisites are met or understood:

- The SQL Server hosting the Replication folder needs enough free space to support the replication scenario. Typically, the snapshot files are the same size as the database.

- You need to understand the locking ramifications of the snapshot agent on the published table. The agent locks the whole table when it copies data from the publisher to the distributor; therefore, you must carefully identify and choose the time and frequency of the snapshots to ensure end users and applications are not affected by these table locks.

- The distribution database needs to have ample hard disk space to support the distribution database transaction log. The size of the distribution database log grows based on the frequency of the transactional replication model. All transactions are logged to the distribution database between snapshots and cleared only after the new snapshot is created.

- When you use transactional replication, all tables included in the replication article must have a primary key associated with the published table.

- If you use peer-to-peer transactional replication, the distribution must be configured first on each peer node, and then the database and schema must be initialized.

Comparing SQL Server 2005 Replication Features

Replication is included with all editions of SQL Server. However, like any Microsoft product, the Enterprise Edition includes all replication features, and the other editions have limited features and functionality to lower the cost of the product.

SQL Server 2005 replication can interoperate with Oracle. The capability to use transactional replication with an Oracle database as a publisher is supported only on the Enterprise Edition of SQL Server 2005. The limitations with the Express Edition are evident when using merge or transactional replication because only subscribers are supported. It is not possible to set up a distribution or publication. The Workgroup Edition, on the other hand, allows both the publisher and subscriber roles. When you use merge replication with this edition, up to 25 subscribers can be published. However, when transactional replication is used, only 5 subscribers are supported.

Knowing When to Implement SQL Server 2005 Replication

There can be many reasons behind an organization's implementation of SQL Server replication. Following are some of the situations organizations try to address by using SQL Server 2005 replication:

- **Distributing Data**—This involves distributing data from one server to another server. For example, an organization must make data such as pricing or sales data residing at corporate headquarters readily available to all field offices.

- **Consolidating Data**—An organization may be interested in consolidating data from many servers to one server for centralized reporting, analysis, or business intelligence. Examples include consolidating data from field offices, manufacturing facilities, or data residing in PDAs or mobile devices to a centralized SQL Server.

- **Ensuring High Availability**—Replication is one of four SQL Server 2005 high-availability alternatives. It can be used to maintain redundant copies of a database on multiple servers residing in different locations. Peer-to-peer transaction replication is the latest alternative provided with SQL Server 2005 and is discussed later in this chapter. When replication is used for high availability, it does not provide automatic failover or automatic client redirect like failover clustering or database mirroring does.

- **Reporting**—If you want to minimize performance degradation on production databases/servers, it is advantageous to offload reporting from production database servers to dedicated reporting servers. Although there are a number of ways of achieving this goal, transactional replication provides a means of replicating data to one or more reporting servers with minimal overhead on the production database. Unlike with database mirroring, the reporting database can be accessed for reporting purposes in real-time without the need for creating database snapshots.

- **Distributing or Consolidating Database Subsets**—Unlike other high-availability alternatives or data distribution methods such as log shipping or database mirroring, replication offers a means to copy or replicate only a subset of the database if needed. For example, you can choose to replicate only a table, rows based on a filter, specific columns, or stored procedures.

- **Ensuring Scalability**—The goal is to scale the workload across multiple databases with replication. This provides increased performance and availability.

Combining Replication with Other SQL Server High-Availability Alternatives

Other SQL Server high-availability alternatives can be combined with replication to create maximum availability, business continuity, and disaster recovery. As such, replication can be configured in conjunction with failover clustering, database mirroring, and log shipping.

Combining Replication with Database Mirroring

When combining replication with database mirroring, you should take into account the following:

- To increase fault tolerance, you should use a remote distributor.

- Immediate updating subscribers, Oracle publishers, and peer-to-peer publishers are now supported.

- Mirroring copies only the publication database; therefore, login accounts, jobs, and objects outside the server must be copied to the mirror server manually.

- Mirroring should use the same distributor as the publisher.

- Replication agents should be configured for failover.

Combining Replication with Log Shipping

Replication and log shipping can coincide with one another; however, replication does not continue in the event that a log shipping failover occurs. Unfortunately, if the primary server is permanently down, replication needs to be reconfigured.

If log shipping and transactional replication are combined, it is recommended to configure the Sync with Backup Option on the publication and distribution databases. This option ensures that transactions on the publication database are not sent to the distribution database unless they have been backed up.

Although these technologies are supported, it is probably not a great idea to combine replication and log shipping in mission-critical environments and organizations trying to achieve high availability of five 9s (99.999%).

Combining Replication with Failover Clustering

If there is a need to combine replication with another SQL Server high-availability alternative, failover clustering is the most practical. Failover clustering offers high availability for publication and distribution databases with no impact to the subscribers in the event of a server failover. All in all, failover clustering is the best alternative because it requires the least amount of administrative effort and all failovers are seamless.

Administering SQL Server Replication

Now that you've had the opportunity to examine an overview of SQL Server replication and familiarize yourself with the replication terminology, components, models, and prerequisites when administering SQL Server replication, it's time to administer replication. The following sections include step–by–step procedures on how to configure snapshot and peer-to-peer replication.

Configuring Snapshot Replication

The following example illustrates the centralized publisher and multiple subscribers' replication model. Snapshot replication is used to distribute AdventureWorks data from a centralized publisher residing in CompanyABC's San Francisco headquarters to two sales offices residing in New York and Toronto.

As a prerequisite task, ensure that all three SQL servers reside in a domain such as the CompanyABC domain and each server is successfully registered in SQL Server Management Object (SSMO) on the SFC-SQL01 server. Table 6.1 summarizes CompanyABC's snapshot replication information based on items and descriptions for this example.

Table 6.1   **CompanyABC's Snapshot Replication Information**

Item	Description
SFC-SQL01	PUBLISHER/DISTRIBUTOR
NYC-SQL01	SUBSCRIBER
TOR-SQL01	SUBSCRIBER
Publication Name	AdventureWorks-Snapshot-Publication
Articles	AdventureWorks Tables : Customer(Sales) and CustomerAddress(Sales)
Replication Type	Snapshot Replication

Using the information in Table 6.1, you can now turn your attention to preparing the distributor for replication on SFC-SQL01.

Configuring the Distributor for Replication

The first step to configuring snapshot replication in a centralized publisher/multiple subscriber topology is to configure the distributor for replication. Follow these steps to configure SFC-SQL01 as a distributor:

1. From the San Francisco server (SFC-SQL01), choose Start, All Programs, Microsoft SQL Server 2005, SQL Server Management Studio.

2. In Object Explorer, first connect to the Database Engine, expand the desired server (SFC-SQL01), and then expand the Replication folder.

3. Right-click the Replication folder and select Configure Distribution.

4. On the Configure Distribution Welcome screen, select Next.

5. On the Distributor page, shown in Figure 6.4, you can configure the distributor on the local server or a remote server. For this example, select the first option, SFC-SQL01\Principal, which acts as its own distributor, and then click Next.

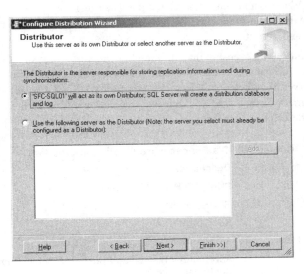

FIGURE 6.4
Selecting the SQL Server to host the distributor role.

6. On the Snapshot Folder page, specify the physical location of the Snapshot folder and then click Next. It is recommended to use a network path so that distribution and merge agents can access the path of the snapshots over the network if they are used.

7. On the Distribution Database page, shown in Figure 6.5, specify the location of the distribution database and log files and then click Next. The drive letters you use must exist on the server that hosts the role of the distributor.

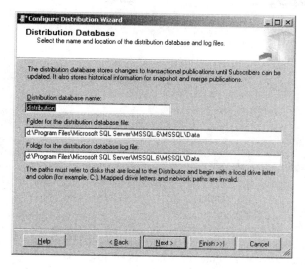

FIGURE 6.5
Specifying the distribution database options.

8. On the Publishers screen, shown in Figure 6.6, add additional publisher servers within the infrastructure that can use this server as a distributor. For this example, enter SFC-SQL01. Click Next to continue.

9. On the Wizard Actions page, select the options Configure Distribution and Generate a Script File with Steps to Configure Distribution and then click Next.

10. The Script File Properties page is displayed because the option to save the script was selected in the preceding step. Specify the location of the file, whether to append or overwrite the existing file, and the final format, either International Text (Unicode) or Windows Text (ANSI). Then click Next to continue.

11. The final configuration step involves verifying the choices made in the Complete the Wizard page. Click Finish to complete the distributor configuration.

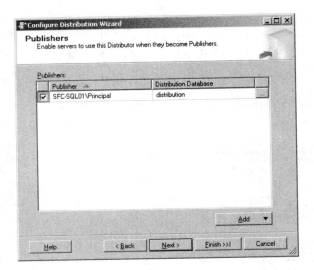

FIGURE 6.6
Enabling servers to use the distributor.

12. Verify the distributor is configured successfully and the publisher is enabled, as demonstrated in Figure 6.7. Then click Close.

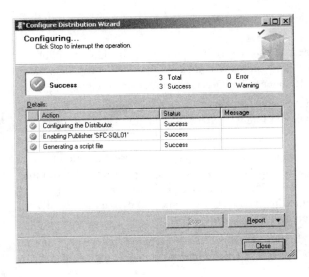

FIGURE 6.7
Configuring the distributor status.

Transact-SQL (TSQL) can also be used to configure the distributor. You can use the TSQL script, ConfigureDistribution.sql, in Listing 6.1 to create a distributor based on the preceding example.

Listing 6.1 ConfigureDistribution.sql—**Configuring the Distributor with Transact-SQL**

```
/****** Scripting replication configuration for server
➝SFC-SQL01. Script Date: 5/30/2007 4:8:49 PM ******/
/****** Please Note: For security reasons, all password
➝parameters were scripted with either NULL or
➝an empty string. ******/

/****** Installing the server SFC-SQL01 as a
➝Distributor. Script Date: 5/30/2007 4:8:49 PM ******/
use master
exec sp_adddistributor @distributor
➝= N'SFC-SQL01', @password = N''
GO
exec sp_adddistributiondb @database = N'distribution',
➝@data_folder = N'C:\Program Files\Microsoft
➝SQL Server\MSSQL.1\MSSQL\Data', @log_folder =
➝N'C:\Program Files\Microsoft SQL Server\
➝MSSQL.1\MSSQL\Data', @log_file_size = 2,
➝@min_distretention = 0, @max_distretention = 72,
➝@history_retention = 48, @security_mode = 1
GO
use [distribution]
if (not exists (select * from sysobjects where name =
➝ 'UIProperties' and type = 'U '))
    create table UIProperties(id int)
if (exists (select * from ::fn_listextendedproperty
➝ ('SnapshotFolder', 'user', 'dbo', 'table',
➝'UIProperties', null, null)))
    EXEC sp_updateextendedproperty N'SnapshotFolder',
➝ N'C:\Program Files\Microsoft SQL Server\MSSQL.1\
➝MSSQL\ReplData', 'user', dbo, 'table', 'UIProperties'
else
    EXEC sp_addextendedproperty N'SnapshotFolder',
➝ 'C:\Program Files\Microsoft SQL Server\
➝MSSQL.1\MSSQL\ReplData', 'user', dbo, 'table',
➝'UIProperties'
```

Listing 6.1   **continued**

```
GO

exec sp_adddistpublisher @publisher = N'SFC-SQL01',
➥ @distribution_db = N'distribution',
➥@security_mode = 1, @working_directory =
➥ N'C:\Program Files\Microsoft SQL Server\
➥MSSQL.1\MSSQL\ReplData', @trusted = N'false',
➥@thirdparty_flag = 0, @publisher_type = N'MSSQLSERVER'
GO
```

Configuring Publications for the AdventureWorks Database

The second step when configuring snapshot replication in a centralized publisher/multiple subscriber topology involves configuring the publisher and selecting the articles that will be replicated. Follow these steps to define the articles for publication on SFC-SQL01:

1. From the San Francisco server (SFC-SQL01), choose Start, All Programs, Microsoft SQL Server 2005, SQL Server Management Studio.

2. In Object Explorer, first connect to the Database Engine, expand the desired server (SFC-SQL01), expand Replication folder, and then expand Local Publications.

3. Right-click the Local Publication folder and select New Publication.

4. On the New Publication Wizard screen, select Next.

5. Choose the AdventureWorks database on the Publication Database screen because it contains the data that will be replicated. Then click Next.

6. On the Publication Type page, select the desired publication type that supports the replication model. For this example, choose Snapshot Publication and then click Next.

7. On the next page, Articles, you can choose the objects you want to publish, such as tables, stored procedures, views, indexed views, and user-defined functions. For this example, CompanyABC's business requirement is to publish all the AdventureWorks customer tables. In the Objects to Publish section, select the Customer(Sales) and CustomerAddress(Sales) tables, as shown in Figure 6.8, and then click Next.

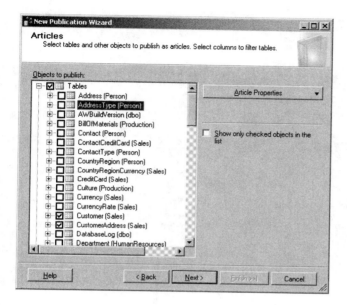

FIGURE 6.8
Choosing the articles for publication.

8. The Filter Table page allows you to create horizontal or vertical filters on the articles selected. For this example, do not leverage filters. Click Next to proceed.

9. On the Snapshot Agent screen, enable the two options Create a Snapshot Immediately and Keep the Snapshot Available to Initialize Subscriptions and Schedule the Snapshot Agent to Run at the Following Times, as shown in Figure 6.9. These options control the frequency with which snapshots will be created. In addition, click the Change button to schedule the Snapshot Agent to run once every hour or enter a specific time value. Then click Next.

10. On the next screen, Agent Security, you can specify accounts and security settings for all replication agents on this page. Click the Security Settings command button and enter a Windows account for the snapshot agent and publisher, as shown in Figure 6.10. Click OK to close the Snapshot Agent Security screen and then click Next.

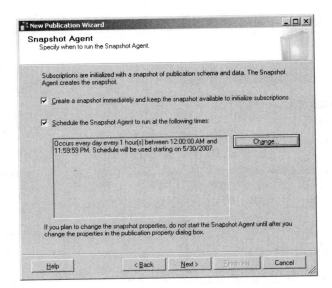

FIGURE 6.9
Specifying the snapshot initialization settings.

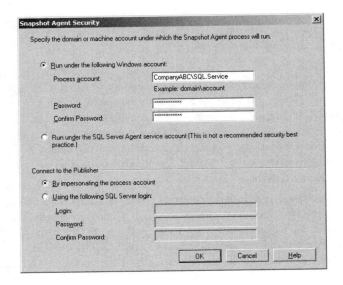

FIGURE 6.10
Entering the snapshot agent authentication credentials.

11. On the Wizard Actions page, select the options Create the Publication and Generate a Script File with Steps to Create the Publication and then click Next.

12. The Script File Properties page is displayed because the option to save the script was selected in the preceding step. Specify the location of the file, whether to append or overwrite the existing file, and the final format, either International Text (Unicode) or Windows Text (ANSI). Then click Next to continue.

13. On the Complete the Wizard screen, review the configuration settings and then enter a name for the publication, as shown in Figure 6.11. Click Finish to finalize the configuration.

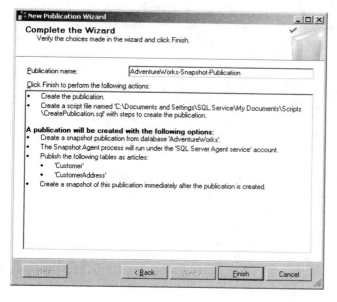

FIGURE 6.11
Finalizing the publication summary settings.

14. On the final screen titled Creating Publication, verify in detail the status of each action in the publication and then click Close to finalize.

15. In Object Explorer, expand the Local Publication folder to view the newly created publication for the AdventureWorks database.

> **Note**
>
> When creating the publication, specify a domain account to simplify the authentication process between the servers by the Snapshot Agent.

Alternatively, you can use the following TSQL syntax instead of SQL Server Management Studio to configure the publication. The TSQL script, CreatePublication.sql, in Listing 6.2, is based on the preceding example.

Listing 6.2   CreatePublication.sql—Creating a Publisher with Transact-SQL

```
/****** Scripting replication configuration for server
➥ SFC-SQL01. Script Date: 5/30/2007 4:8:49 PM ******/
/****** Please Note: For security reasons, all password
➥ parameters were scripted with either NULL or
➥ an empty string. ******/

/****** Installing the server SFC-SQL01 as a Distributor.
➥ Script Date: 5/30/2007 4:8:49 PM ******/
use master
exec sp_adddistributor @distributor = N'SFC-SQL01',
➥ @password = N''
GO
exec sp_adddistributiondb @database = N'distribution',
➥ @data_folder = N'C:\Program Files\Microsoft
➥ SQL Server\MSSQL.1\MSSQL\Data', @log_
➥ folder = N'C:\Program Files\Microsoft SQL
➥ Server\MSSQL.1\MSSQL\Data', @log_file_size = 2,
➥ @min_distretention = 0, @max_distretention = 72,
➥ @history_retention = 48, @security_mode = 1
GO

use [distribution]
if (not exists (select * from sysobjects
➥ where name = 'UIProperties' and type = 'U '))
➥create table UIProperties(id int)
if (exists (select * from ::fn_listextendedproperty
➥ ('SnapshotFolder', 'user', 'dbo', 'table',
➥ 'UIProperties', null, null)))
```

Listing 6.2 **continued**

```
    EXEC sp_updateextendedproperty N'SnapshotFolder',
➥  N'C:\Program Files\Microsoft SQL Server\
➥ MSSQL.1\MSSQL\ReplData', 'user', dbo, 'table',
➥'UIProperties'
else
    EXEC sp_addextendedproperty N'SnapshotFolder',
➥   'C:\Program Files\Microsoft SQL Server\
➥MSSQL.1\MSSQL\ReplData', 'user', dbo, 'table',
➥'UIProperties'
GO

exec sp_adddistpublisher @publisher = N'SFC-SQL01',
➥  @distribution_db = N'distribution',
➥ @security_mode = 1, @working_directory =
➥ N'C:\Program Files\Microsoft SQL Server\
➥ MSSQL.1\MSSQL\ReplData', @trusted = N'false',
➥ @thirdparty_flag = 0, @publisher_type = N'MSSQLSERVER'
GO
```

Configuring Subscriptions for the AdventureWorks Database

Now that both the distributor and publication roles have been initialized and configured, the final step is to subscribe to the publication created. You carry out this task by creating a subscription on all servers that will receive the published articles. To create the subscription, first conduct the following steps on NYC-SQL01 and then repeat them on TOR-SQL01:

1. From the New York server (NYC-SQL01), choose Start, All Programs, Microsoft SQL Server 2005, SQL Server Management Studio.

2. In Object Explorer, first connect to the Database Engine, expand the desired server (NYC-SQL01), expand Replication folder, and then expand Local Subscriptions.

3. Right-click the Local Subscriptions folder and select New Subscriptions.

4. On the New Subscription Wizard screen, select Next.

5. On the Publication page, select the desired publisher server, such as SFC-SQL01 for this example. Then from the Database and

Publications section, choose the publication based on the publication created in the previous example (AdventureWorks-Snapshot-Publication), as shown in Figure 6.12. Then click Next.

Note

If the desired SQL Server publisher is not available, select Find SQL Server Publisher from the Publisher drop-down list.

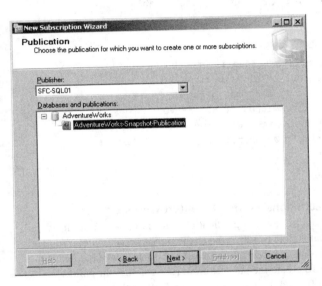

FIGURE 6.12
Subscribing to the publication already created.

6. The next screen provides two options where the distribution agents can run. The default option on the Distribution Agent Location screen is Pull Subscription. The alternative is Push Subscription. Select the option Run Each Agent at Its Subscriber (Pull Subscriptions) and then click Next.

7. On the Subscribers screen, ensure the appropriate SQL Server subscriber (NYC-SQL01) is selected and then select the Subscription database. Click Next to continue. For this example, the AdventureWorks database does not exist on NYC-SQL01; therefore, select New Database from the Subscription Database drop-down list and create a new AdventureWorks database.

8. On the New Database page, enter the database name (AdventureWorks), select the appropriate path for the database and log files, and then click OK. Click Next on the Subscribers page to continue.

9. Enter the appropriate user account and password for both the distributor and subscriber connections by clicking the ellipses on the Distribution Agent Security page, as shown in Figure 6.13.

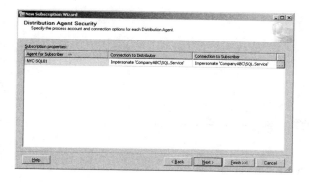

FIGURE 6.13
Specifying the process account and connection options for each distribution agent.

10. On this screen, specify the context for the distribution agent, distributor, and subscriber. Click OK to return to the Distribution Agent Security page and then click Next.

11. On the Synchronization Schedule page, set the agent schedule. The options available include Run Continuously, Run On Demand Only, and Define Schedule. For this example, select Run Continuously, as illustrated in Figure 6.14, and click Next.

12. On the Wizard Actions page, select the options Create the Subscription and Generate a Script File with Steps to Create the Subscriptions and then click Next.

13. On the Initialize Subscriptions page, ensure that the Initialize check box is enabled and that Immediately is selected in the Initialize drop-down box. Click Next to continue.

14. The Script File Properties page is displayed because the option to save the script was selected in the step 12. Specify the location of the file, whether to append or overwrite the existing file, and the final format, either International Text (Unicode) or Windows Text (ANSI).

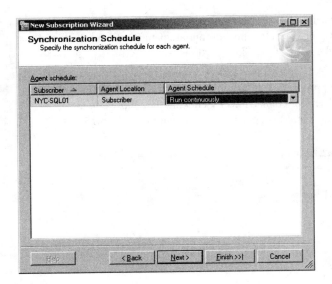

FIGURE 6.14
Specifying the agent synchronization schedule.

15. On the Complete the Wizard screen, review the configuration settings and click Finish.

16. On the final screen, Creating Subscription(s), verify the status details of each action in the subscription and click Close to finish.

17. To create an additional subscriber on the Toronto SQL Server, repeat steps 1–16 on the Toronto SQL Server instance.

Just as with some of the earlier sets of instructions, you can use TSQL syntax instead of SQL Server Management Studio to create the subscription. The TSQL syntax, NewSubscription.sql, shown in Listing 6.3 configures the Subscription based on the preceding example depicted for NYC-SQL01.

Listing 6.3   NewSubscription.sql—**Creating a Subscription with Transact-SQL**

```
----------------BEGIN: Script to be run
    at Publisher 'SFC-SQL01'----------------
use [AdventureWorks]
exec sp_addsubscription @publication = N
    'AdventureWorks-Snapshot-Publication',
    @subscriber = N'NYC-SQL01',
```

Listing 6.3 **continued**

```
➥    @destination_db = N'AdventureWorks',
➥    @sync_type = N'Automatic',
➥    @subscription_type = N'pull',
➥    @update_mode = N'read only'
GO
----------------END: Script to be run at
➥    Publisher 'SFC-SQL01'----------------

----------------BEGIN: Script to be run
➥    at Subscriber 'NYC-SQL01'----------------
use [AdventureWorks]
exec sp_addpullsubscription @publisher =
➥ N'SFC-SQL01', @publication = N
➥ 'AdventureWorks-Snapshot-Publication',
➥    @publisher_db = N'AdventureWorks',
➥    @independent_agent = N'True',
➥    @subscription_type = N'pull', @description = N'',
➥    @update_mode = N'read only', @immediate_sync = 1

exec sp_addpullsubscription_agent @publisher
➥ = N'SFC-SQL01', @publisher_db = N'AdventureWorks',
➥@publication = N'AdventureWorks-Snapshot-Publication',
➥@distributor = N'SFC-SQL01', @distributor_security_mode =
➥1, @distributor_login = N'', @distributor_password = null,
➥@enabled_for_syncmgr = N'False', @frequency_type = 64,
➥@frequency_interval = 0, @frequency_relative_
➥interval = 0,
➥@frequency_recurrence_factor = 0, @frequency_subday = 0,
➥@frequency_subday_interval = 0,
➥@active_start_time_of_day = 0, @active_end_time_of_day =
➥235959,
➥@active_start_date = 20070530,
➥@active_end_date = 99991231, @alt_snapshot_folder = N''
➥, @working_directory = N'', @use_ftp = N'False',
➥@job_login = N'CompanyABC\SQL.Service', @job_password =
➥null, @publication_type = 0
GO
----------------END: Script to be run at Subscriber
➥'NYC-SQL01'----------------
```

Testing Snapshot Replication

Any changes made to the data residing in the AdventureWorks database on the publisher are propagated through replication to the subscribers based on the snapshot interval. To test the replication topology, make changes on the Customer(Sales) and CustomerAddress(Sales) tables located on the publisher. The changes should be addressed on the subscriber AdventureWorks database.

Configuring Peer-to-Peer Transactional Replication

The following example illustrates the new peer-to-peer transactional replication topology among three SQL Server instances for CompanyABC. Each SQL Server instance is located in different geographical regions such as San Francisco, New York, and Toronto. This is summarized in Table 6.2.

As a prerequisite task, make sure that all three SQL Server nodes reside in a domain such as the CompanyABC and each server is successfully registered in SQL Server Management Studio on the SFC-SQL01 server to ensure proper connectivity.

Table 6.2   **CompanyABC's Peer-to-Peer Replication Summary**

Item	Description
SFC-SQL01	Peer-to-Peer Member
NYC-SQL01	Peer-to-Peer Member
TOR-SQL01	Peer-to-Peer Member
Publication Name	AdventureWorks-Publication
Articles	All AdventureWorks Tables
Replication Type	Transactional Replication

Configuring the Distributor for Replication

The first step in configuring peer-to-peer transactional replication topology is to configure all peer nodes as a distributor for replication. Conduct the following steps to configure SFC-SQL01, NYC-SQL01, and TOR-SQL01 as distributors:

1. From the San Francisco server (SFC-SQL01), choose Start, All Programs, Microsoft SQL Server 2005, SQL Server Management Studio.

2. Expand the desired server (SFC-SQL01); then expand the Replication folder.

3. Right-click the Replication folder and select Configure Distribution.

4. On the Configure Distribution Welcome screen, select Next.

5. On the Distributor page, select the option Act as Its Own Distributor and click Next.

Note

When configuring peer-to-peer replication, you can use a remote distributor. If a remote distributor is used, it is not a best practice to have all peers use the same remote distributor because it would be a single point of failure.

---

6. On the Snapshot Folder page, specify a network share location of the Snapshot folder, as shown in Figure 6.15, and then click Next. It is recommended to use a network path; therefore, the replication peers can access the snapshots over the network.

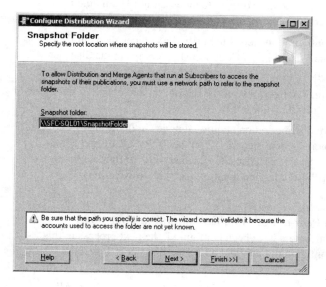

FIGURE 6.15
Specifying the root location for the Snapshot folder.

> **Note**
> The network share used for the Snapshot folder should be secured with NTFS permissions.

7. On the Distribution Database page, specify the location of the distribution database and log files and then click Next.

8. On the Publishers screen, add additional publisher servers within the infrastructure that can use this server as a distributor. For this example, enter only SFC-SQL01 and click Next.

9. On the Wizard Actions page, select the options Configure Distribution and Generate a Script File with Steps to Configure Distribution and click Next.

10. The Script File Properties page is displayed because the option to save the script was selected in the preceding step. Specify the location of the file, whether to append or overwrite the existing file, and the final format, either International Text (Unicode) or Windows Text (ANSI).

11. The final configuration step is to verify the choices made in the Complete the Wizard page. Click Finish to complete the distributor configuration.

12. Verify that the configuration of the distributor and enabling publisher was successful. Click Close.

13. To configure distribution on additional nodes in the peer-to-peer replication topology, repeat steps 1–12 on the TOR-SQL01 and NYC-SQL01 SQL Server instances. On each server, configure a secure shared Snapshot folder and configure a local distributor.

Configuring the Peer-to-Peer Publication on the First Node

After all three distributors have been configured, the next process in this procedure is to configure the publication on the first node. Just follow these steps:

1. From the San Francisco server (SFC-SQL01), choose Start, All Programs, Microsoft SQL Server 2005, SQL Server Management Studio.

2. In Object Explorer, first connect to the Database Engine, expand the desired server (SFC-SQL01), and expand Replication folder and then Local Publications.

3. Right-click the Local Publication Folder and select New Publication.

4. On the New Publication Wizard screen, select Next.

5. Choose the AdventureWorks database on the Publication Database screen because it contains the data that will be replicated and click Next.

6. On the Publication Type page, choose Transactional Publication and click Next.

7. On the next page, Articles, select the database objects to publish, such as the Customer(Sales) table, as shown in Figure 6.16. Then click Next to continue.

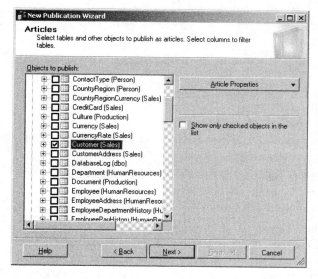

FIGURE 6.16
Selecting articles for peer-to-peer replication.

8. Click Next on the Filter Table Rows page because peer-to-peer replication does not support Filtering.

9. On the Snapshot Agent screen, clear the options Create a Snapshot Immediately and Keep the Snapshot Available to Initialize Subscriptions and Schedule the Snapshot Agent to Run at the Following Times, as shown in Figure 6.17. Then click Next.

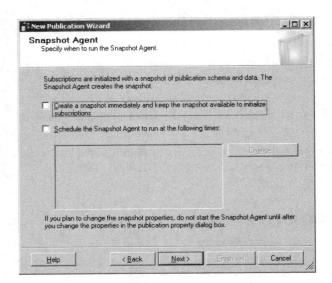

FIGURE 6.17
Clearing the snapshot initialization and schedule settings.

10. On the Agent Security page, enter credentials for the Snapshot Agent and Log Reader Agent and click Next.

11. On the Wizard Actions page, select the options Configure the Publication and Generate a Script File with Steps to Create the Publication and click Next.

12. The Script File Properties page is displayed because the option to save the script was selected in the preceding step. Specify the location of the file, whether to append or overwrite the existing file, and the final format, either International Text (Unicode) or Windows Text (ANSI).

13. On the Complete the Wizard screen, review the configuration settings, enter a peer-to-peer-publication as the publication name, and click Finish.

14. On the final screen, Creating Publication, verify the detail status of each action in the publication and click Close to finalize.

15. Expand the Local Publication folder to view the newly created publication for the AdventureWorks database.

Enabling the Publication for Peer-to-Peer Replication

The next step is to enable the publication for peer-to-peer replication via the publication properties as follows:

1. From the San Francisco server (SFC-SQL01), expand the Replication folder and then Local Publications.

2. Right-click on the publication you created in the previous steps and select Properties.

3. On the Subscriptions Options page of the Publication Properties dialog box, set the Allow Peer-to-Peer Subscriptions to True, as shown in Figure 6.18, and then click OK.

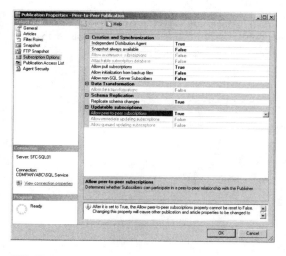

FIGURE 6.18
Enabling peer-to-peer replication settings.

> **Note**
>
> After the peer-to-peer subscription setting has been enabled, the property cannot be disabled; therefore, you are forced to remove replication.

Configuring the Peer-to-Peer Topology

Before configuring the subscriptions on the nodes that will act as subscribers in the peer-to-peer replication topology, you must first initialize the peers with the source database schema and data. You can initialize the schema and database on the peers by creating a database package using SQL Server 2005 Integration Services (SSIS) or by backing up and restoring the source database. For more information on how to copy a database from one SQL Server instance to another, see Chapter 11, "Creating Packages and Transferring Data."

Follow these steps to configure the peer-to-peer topology:

1. From the San Francisco server (SFC-SQL01), expand the Replication folder and then Local Publications.

2. Right-click on the publication you created in the previous steps and select Configure Peer-to-Peer Topology.

3. On the Configure Peer-to-Peer Topology Wizard screen, click Next.

4. On the Publication screen, expand the AdventureWorks database and select the peer-to-peer publication you created in the previous steps (Peer-to-Peer-Publication), as illustrated in Figure 6.19. Click Next to continue.

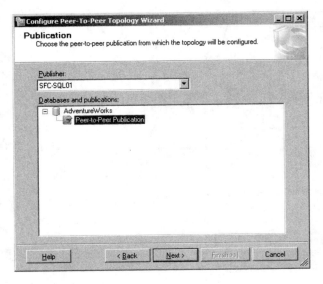

FIGURE 6.19
Configuring the peer-to-peer publication.

5. On the next screen displayed, you can select the server instances and database to be configured as peers. On the Peers screen, first click Add

SQL Server and then add the Peer Server Instances such as NYC-SQL01 and TOR-SQL01. Ensure that the peer database selected is AdventureWorks, as shown in Figure 6.20, and then click Next.

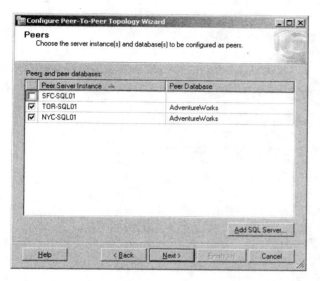

FIGURE 6.20
Adding SQL Server instances to be configured as peers.

Note

When choosing the server instances and database to be configured as peers, you cannot choose the original SQL Server instance hosting the peer database. In this example, the database would be SFC-SQL01.

---

6. On the Log Reader Agent Security screen, enter the appropriate Log Reader Agent user account and password for both the connections to the distributor and subscriber by clicking the ellipses on the Distribution Agent Security page. For this example, enable Use the First Peer's Security Settings for All Other Peers and click Next.

7. On the Distribution Agent Security screen, enter the appropriate Distribution Agent user account and password for both the connections to the distributor and subscriber by clicking the ellipses. For this example, enable Use the First Peer's Security Settings for All Other Peers option and then click Next.

8. On the next screen, New Peer Initialization, select the option I Created the Peer Database Manually, or I Restored a Backup of the Original Publication Database Which Has Not Been Changed Since the Backup Was Taken, as shown in Figure 6.21, and then click Next.

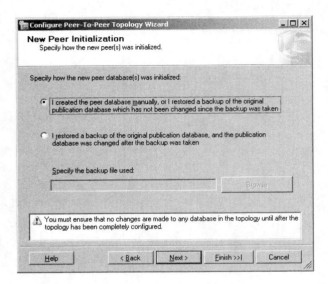

FIGURE 6.21
Specifying how peers will be initialized.

9. On the Complete the Wizard screen, review the configuration settings selected and then click Finish.

Note

An error may arise on the SFC-SQL01 server stating that the publication or its log reader agent already exists and will not be modified. This error is erroneous and should be disregarded.

---

10. Review the status of each action; then click Close to finalize the building of the peer-to-peer topology.

11. To validate that the peer-to-peer replication topology has been created, expand both the Local Publication and Local Subscription folders on each SQL Server peer node. The appropriate publication and subscriptions should be created as shown in Figure 6.22.

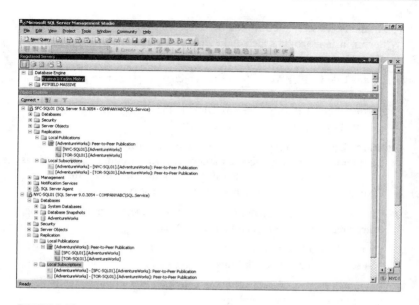

FIGURE 6.22
Viewing the peer-to-peer publications and subscriptions via SSMS.

Adding a Node to an Existing Peer-to-Peer Replication Topology

Sometimes you may need to add new peer nodes to the existing peer-to-peer
replication topology after it has been created and initialized. If necessary,
follow these high-level steps:

1. On the new server, first configure distribution based on the steps
   described previously.

2. Initialize the schema and data by either backing up and restoring the
   source database or by creating an SSIS package.

3. From a SQL Server instance, expand the Replication folder and then
   Local Publications.

4. Right-click on the publication you created in the previous steps and
   select Configure Peer-to-Peer Topology.

5. On the Configure Peer-to-Peer Topology Wizard screen, click Next.

6. On the Publication screen, expand the AdventureWorks database and
   select the peer-to-peer publication created in the previous steps.

7. On the Peers screen, click Add SQL Server. Connect to the new SQL Server instance to be added and then select the new server as a peer. Click Next to continue.

8. On the Log Reader Agent Security screen, enter the appropriate Log Reader Agent user account and password for both the connections to the distributor and subscriber by clicking the ellipses on the Distribution Agent Security page. Click Next to continue.

9. On the Distribution Agent Security screen, enter the appropriate Distribution Agent user account and password for both the connections to the distributor and subscriber by clicking the ellipses on the Distribution Agent Security page and then click Next.

10. On the New Peer Initialization screen, specify the option I Created the Peer Database Manually and then click Next.

11. On the Complete the Wizard screen, review the configuration settings you selected and then click Finish.

12. Review the status of each action and click Close to finalize the building of the peer-to-peer topology.

Managing SQL Server 2005 Replication

The following sections focus on management tasks after SQL Server 2005 replication has been implemented. These tasks are in no particular order and can be configured via SSMS or TSQL.

Managing the Distributors Properties

The Distributors Properties screen allows you to manage distributor configuration settings and tasks. The settings and tasks on the General and Publishers Pages on the Distributor Properties include

- Transaction Retention per Distribution Database in Hours

- History Retention per Distribution Database in Hours

- Setting the Queue Reader Agent

- Adding Additional Publishers

- Setting the Administrative Link password which the Publisher requires to connect to the Distributor

You can invoke the Distributors Properties screen by right-clicking the Replication folder and selecting the distributor's properties.

Disabling Publishing and Distribution

In some situations, either you or your organization may decide to remove replication from within the SQL Server infrastructure.

If this is necessary, follow these steps to disable publishing and distribution with SSMS:

1. From the San Francisco server (SFC-SQL01), choose Start, All Programs, Microsoft SQL Server 2005, SQL Server Management Studio.

2. In Object Explorer, first connect to the Database Engine, expand the desired server (SFC-SQL01), and then expand the Replication folder.

3. Right-click the Replication folder and select Disable Publishing and Distribution.

4. On the Disable Publishing and Distribution Wizard, select Next.

5. On the Disable Publishing screen, choose the option Yes; Disable Publishing on This Server, as shown in Figure 6.23. Click Next to continue.

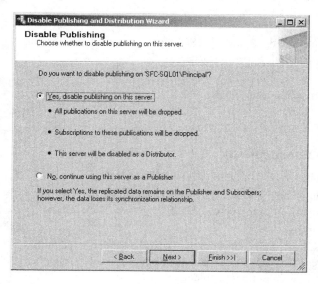

FIGURE 6.23
Disabling publications and distribution.

> **Note**
>
> Any publication or subscriptions are dropped if you decide to disable publishing and distribution.

6. If a publication exists, the Confirm Dropping of Publications screen is induced; click Next to continue.

7. On the Wizard Actions page, select the options Disable Publishing and Distribution and Generate a Script File with Steps to Create the Publishing and Distribution and then click Next.

8. The Script File Properties page is displayed because the option to save the script was selected in the preceding step. Specify the location of the file, whether to append or overwrite the existing file, and the final format, either International Text (Unicode) or Windows Text (ANSI).

9. On the Complete the Wizard screen, verify the disabling choices and click Finish to proceed.

10. On the Disabling Distribution screen, verify that each item successfully completed and click Close.

Alternatively, you can use the following TSQL syntax to remove publishing and distribution from a SQL Server instance:

```
use [master]
exec sp_dropdistributor @no_checks = 1
GO
```

Deleting Local Subscriptions

Follow these steps to delete local subscriptions with SSMS:

1. From the San Francisco server (SFC-SQL01), choose Start, All Programs, Microsoft SQL Server 2005, SQL Server Management Studio.

2. In Object Explorer, first connect to the Database Engine, expand the desired server (SFC-SQL01), expand the Replication folder, and then expand the Local Subscriptions folder.

3. Right-click the desired subscription to delete and select Delete.

4. Confirm the deletion warning message and click Yes.

Deleting Local Publications

Follow these steps to delete local subscriptions with SSMS:

1. From the San Francisco server (SFC-SQL01), choose Start, All Programs, Microsoft SQL Server 2005, SQL Server Management Studio.

2. In Object Explorer, first connect to the Database Engine, expand the desired server (SFC-SQL01), expand the Replication folder, and then expand the Local Publications folder.

3. Right-click the desired publication to delete and select Delete.

4. Confirm the deletion warning message and click Yes.

Deleting the Distribution Database

Before the distribution database can be deleted, all publications and subscriptions must be deleted. In addition, all publishers using the distributor must be disabled and/or deleted.

Follow these steps to delete the distribution database with SSMS:

1. From the San Francisco server (SFC-SQL01), choose Start, All Programs, Microsoft SQL Server 2005, SQL Server Management Studio.

2. In Object Explorer, first connect to the Database Engine, expand the desired server (SFC-SQL01), expand the Database folder, and then expand the System Databases folder.

3. Right-click the Distribution database and select Delete.

4. Confirm the deletion warning message and click Next.

Managing Replication Passwords

SQL Server 2005 comes with a utility for managing SQL Server passwords. To launch the utility, right-click the Replication folder from within SQL Server 2005 Management Studio and then select Update Replication Passwords. When the Update Replication Passwords utility is invoked, you can update a replication username and password. The password is updated throughout the replication topology.

Generating Replication Scripts

Automatically generating scripts for replication jobs is a new feature included with SQL Server 2005 replication and a recommended best practice. Replication scripts can be created during the configuration of a replication component such as a publisher, distributor, or subscription or after the replication topology has been implemented. The replication scripts can be used for disaster recovery or to reduce the amount of time associated by creating repetitive replication tasks.

Tip

All replication components should be scripted and used as a form of backup and disaster recovery. In addition, scripts should be updated when changes to the replication environment take place.

To generate replication scripts, follow these steps:

1. From the San Francisco server (SFC-SQL01), choose Start, All Programs, Microsoft SQL Server 2005, SQL Server Management Studio.

2. In Object Explorer, first connect to the Database Engine, expand the desired server (SFC-SQL01), and then expand the Replication folder.

3. Right-click the Replication folder and then select Generate Scripts.

4. In the Generate SQL Script screen, select the desired scripting functionality and then click Script to File.

Backing Up and Restoring Replication

Similar to any production database, the replicated databases residing on a publisher, distributor, or subscriber should be backed up on a regular basis. In addition, the associated replication system database called Distribution should also be included in the backup strategy; it is equally important to back up this system database because it holds the replication configuration information.

When you're using transactional replication, it is a best practice to leverage the Sync with Backup option on the distribution and publication databases. This setting ensures consistency and that the transaction logs on the publication database are not truncated until the distribution database has been successfully backed up. Therefore, transactions are not lost in the event of a database disaster because uncommitted transactions are replayed in the event of a database restore.

Configuring the Sync with Backup Option

The first step is to configure Sync with Backup option on the publisher by executing the following TSQL syntax. The default syntax to enable coordinated backups for transactional replication is

```
sp_replicationdboption [ @dbname= ] 'db_name'
        , [ @optname= ] 'optname'
        , [ @value= ] 'value'
    [ , [ @ignore_distributor= ] ignore_distributor ]
    [ , [ @from_scripting = ] from_scripting
```

This stored procedure should be executed on the publisher. The @optname value should be set to sync with backup and the @value should be set to true.

The next step is to execute the TSQL syntax on the distribution database. Similar to the publisher script, the @optname value for this stored procedure should be set to sync with backup and the @value should be set to true.

The default syntax to enable coordinated backups on the distribution database is

```
sp_replicationdboption [ @dbname= ] 'db_name'
        , [ @optname= ] 'optname'
        , [ @value= ] 'value'
    [ , [ @ignore_distributor= ] ignore_distributor ]
    [ , [ @from_scripting = ] from_scripting ]
```

Note

Latency between the publication and distribution databases occurs when using the Sync with Backup option for transitional consistency. The reason is that transactions will not be transferred to the distribution database until they have been successfully backed up on the publisher.

There are different strategies for recovering replication based on which topology and model are selected. For more information on the sequences of restoring replication based on a specific replication topology, see the topic "Strategies for Backing Up and Restoring Snapshot and Transactional Replication" in SQL Server 2005 Books Online.

> **Tip**
>
> When you're restoring the distribution database, it is a best practice to use the same server to preserve replication settings. If a new server is warranted, you must re-create all the publications and subscriptions.

Monitoring and Troubleshooting SQL Server Replication

After configuring replication, you should turn your attention to understanding the tools available for monitoring and managing the replication topology. The main goals for monitoring replication are to identify system performance, determine how long replication takes, and understand how to identify replication anomalies. The following tools for monitoring replication should be leveraged:

- Replication Monitor tool
- Systems Monitor
- Microsoft Operations Manager

Using the Replication Monitor Tool to Monitor Replication

The Replication Monitor tool is included with SSMS and should be used as a central monitoring tool for analyzing and tuning publications, subscriptions, and replication jobs. You can invoke the Replication Monitor tool by right-clicking the Replication folder and then selecting Launch Replication Monitor from within SSMS.

Follow these steps to launch the Replication Monitor tool and see how to register servers and monitor a replication topology:

1. Using the San Francisco server (SFC-SQL01), in Object Explorer, right-click the Replication folder and then select Launch Replication Monitor.

2. Add all publishers in the replication topology that will be monitored. To do this, in the left pane in the Replication Monitor screen, right-click Replication Monitor and select Add Publisher.

3. On the Add Publisher screen, click the Add button to register the publishers to be monitored. Register the server in the default My Publishers group or create a new publisher group by clicking New Group. For this example, add the SFC-SQL01 and NYC-SQL01 publishers and then click OK.

After the tool is launched and the publishers or distributors have been registered, you can carry out the following replication tasks from within the Replication Monitor console:

- Configure publisher settings
- Monitor publications
- Monitor subscriptions
- Reinitialize and validate subscriptions
- Generate snapshots
- Review agent properties
- Configure replication alerts

Monitoring and Managing Publishers

When a SQL Server instance is highlighted from within Replication Monitor, the right pane includes these three tabs for monitoring and managing publishers:

- **Publications Tab**—This tab provides status on each publication included within a registered publisher. The Status column indicates whether the publication is operational or experiencing issues. In addition, the Publications tab also includes columns that point out the number of subscriptions per publication, synchronization metrics per publication, and performance indicators based on Current Average Performance and Current Worst Performance.

- **Subscription Watch List Tab**—The goal of this tab is to display subscription status and information based on a registered publisher. Replication Monitor first illustrates the status of each subscription and then indicates the status of the subscription. The subscription status can be OK, Error, Performance Critical, Long-Running Merge, Expiring Soon/Expired, Uninitialized Subscription, Retrying Failed Command, Synchronizing, or Not Synchronized.

  The next few columns display the names of the subscription and publication. The final columns provide information on performance and latency. The Performance column indicates the performance of the subscription based on the values Excellent, Good, Fair, and Poor, and the Latency column specifies the latency based on a time value.

  You can also filter the information displayed in the Subscription Watch List tab by choosing to show information based on Transactional,

Merge, or Snapshots Subscriptions. An additional filter is included to show information based on All Subscriptions, 25 Worst Performing Subscriptions, 50 Worst Performing Subscriptions, Errors and Warnings Only, Errors Only, Warnings Only, Subscriptions Running, and Subscriptions Not Running. This is illustrated in Figure 6.24.

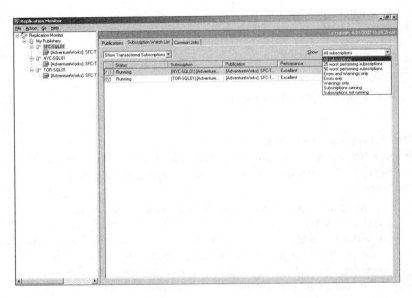

FIGURE 6.24
The Subscription Watch List tab located within Replication Monitor.

■ **Common Jobs Tab**—This tab provides job information and status on all publications on the publisher. For each common job, the following information is displayed: Status, Job Name, Last Start Time, and Duration.

Monitoring and Managing Subscriptions

By further expanding the publisher server name and then clicking on a publication, you have access to more tools to monitor subscriptions. The tabs include

■ **All Subscriptions**—This tab is similar to the Publications tab; however, this tab displays information on subscriptions, of course, and not publications. The information displayed based on the columns available includes the status of each subscription, the subscription name, performance, and latency, as shown in Figure 6.25. In addition, it is possible to filter subscriptions based on All Subscriptions, 25 Worst Performing Subscriptions, 50 Worst Performing Subscriptions, Errors and Warnings Only, Errors Only, Warnings Only, Subscriptions Running, and Subscriptions Not Running.

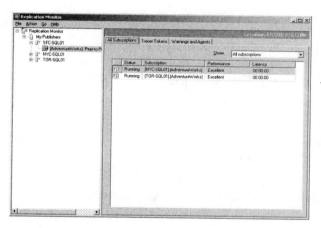

FIGURE 6.25
Displaying the All Subscriptions tab in Replication Monitor.

- **Tracer Tokens**—The second tab is a great utility to test the replication topology, including performance, by placing an artificial synthetic transaction into the replication stream. By clicking the Insert Tracer command button shown in Figure 6.26, you can review and calculate performance metrics between the publisher to distributor, distributor to subscriber, and finally the total latency for the artificial transaction.

- **Warnings and Agents**—When you're monitoring subscriptions, the final tab allows you to configure alerts and notifications on subscriptions. Each of these predefined replication alerts can be configured and customized based on a SQL Server event, SQL Server performance condition alert, WMI event alert, error numbers, and severity. In addition, a response can be created for each alert. These responses can execute a specific job or notify an operator on each replication alert that has been customized. The predefined alerts include

  - Replication Warning: Long merge over dialup connection (Threshold:Mergelowrunduration)

- Replication Warning: Long merge over LAN connection (Threshold: mergefastrunduration)
- Replication Warning: Slow merge over dialup connection (Threshold: mergeslowrunspeed)
- Replication Warning: Slow merge over LAN connection (Threshold: mergefastrunspeed)
- Replication Warning: Subscription expiration (Threshold: expiration)
- Replication Warning: Transactional replication latency (Threshold: latency)
- Replication: Agent custom shutdown
- Replication: Agent failure
- Replication: Agent retry
- Replication: Agent success
- Replication: Expired subscription dropped
- Replication: Subscriber has failed data validation
- Replication: Subscriber has passed data validation
- Replication: Subscription reinitialized after validation failure

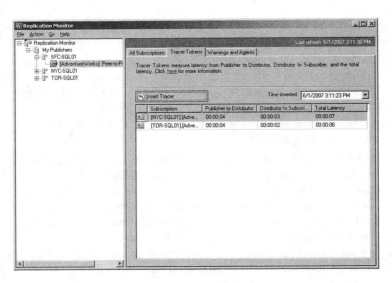

FIGURE 6.26
Inserting synthetic transactions into the replication topology.

Monitoring Replication with Systems Monitor

The Replication Monitor tool is a great starting point for monitoring and managing SQL Server 2005 replication. However, sometimes you may need to dive deeper and obtain additional metrics when monitoring replication. The System Monitor performance monitoring tool included with Windows Server 2003 can be used to obtain additional replication metrics. You can launch this tool by choosing Start, All Programs, Administrative Tools and Performance.

The specific performance object, counters, and descriptions that provide information on the SQL Server replication can be found in Performance Monitor under SQLServer: Replication.

Table 6.3 describes the performance objects and counters.

Table 6.3   Replication Objects and Counters in Performance Monitor

Agent	Performance Object	Counter	Description
All agents	Microsoft SQL Server: Replication Agents	Running	The number of replication agents currently running.
Snapshot Agent	SQL Server: Replication Snapshot	Snapshot: Delivered Cmds/sec	The number of commands per second delivered to the distributor.
Snapshot Agent	SQL Server: Replication Snapshot	Snapshot: Delivered Trans/sec	The number of transactions per second delivered to the distributor.
Log Reader Agent	SQL Server: Replication Logreader	Logreader: Delivered Cmds/sec	The number of commands per second delivered to the distributor.
Log Reader Agent	SQL Server: Replication Logreader	Logreader: Delivered Trans/sec	The number of transactions per second delivered to the Distributor.
Log Reader Agent	SQL Server: Replication Logreader	Logreader: Delivery Latency	The current amount of time, in milliseconds, elapsed from when transactions were applied at the publisher to when they are delivered to the distributor.
Distribution Agent	SQL Server: Replication Dist.	Dist: Delivered Cmds/sec	The number of commands per second delivered to the subscriber.

Table 6.3   **continued**

Agent	Performance Object	Counter	Description
Distribution Agent	SQL Server: Replication Dist.	Dist: Delivered Trans/sec	The number of transactions per second delivered to the subscriber.
Distribution Agent	SQL Server: Replication Dist.	Dist: Delivery Latency	The current amount of time, in milliseconds, elapsed from when transactions were delivered to the distributor to when they are applied at the subscriber.
Merge Agent	SQL Server: Replication Merge	Conflicts/sec	The number of conflicts per second occurring during the merge process.
Merge Agent	SQL Server: Replication Merge	Downloaded Changes/sec	The number of rows per second replicated from the publisher to the subscriber.
Merge Agent	SQL Server: Replication Merge	Uploaded Changes/sec	The number of rows per second replicated from the subscriber to the publisher.

Collecting and analyzing the metrics in Table 6.3 assists organizations when there is a need to monitor SQL Server replication, set up performance baselines, or address performance issues. In addition to the SQL Server counters listed here, it is also a best practice to analyze physical disk, processor, system, I/O, network and CPU time.

Monitoring Replication with Operations Manager

Another great tool to proactively monitor a replication topology—including the health of the distributor, publisher, subscriber, publications, subscriptions, and articles—is Operations Manager 2007. Operations Manager includes a dedicated Microsoft Management Pack tailored toward SQL Server and rules that center on replication.

Note

For more information on proactively monitoring a database mirroring session with Operations Manager 2007, refer to Chapter 21, "Monitoring SQL Server 2005" (online).

Summary

Replication in SQL Server 2005 is a mature technology and a great utility to copy data among SQL Server instances. For the most part, replication is predominantly used for distributing data between physical sites within an organization. However, it is also commonly used for creating redundant read-only copies of a database for reporting purposes and for consolidating data from many locations.

Although replication can be used as a form of high availability or for disaster recovery, failover clustering, log shipping, and database mirroring are preferred alternatives because they guarantee transaction safety in the event of a disaster.

Best Practices

Some of the best practices that apply to replication include

- Create a backup and restore strategy after the replication topology has been implemented. Don't forget to include the distribution, MSDB, and master databases on the publisher, distributor, and all subscribers.

- Script all replication components from a disaster recovery perspective. Scripts are also useful for conducting repetitive tasks. Finally, regenerate and/or update scripts whenever a replication component changes.

- Use Replication Monitor and Performance Monitor to create baseline metrics for tuning replication and validating that the hardware and network infrastructure live up to the replication requirements and expectations.

- When using replication topologies that allow updates to occur on both the publisher and subscriber, validate that the data is consistent on a periodic basis. For example, if transitional or merge replication is used, data should be checked on both the publisher and subscriber to guarantee that the data is consistent and no errors are occurring within the replication topology.

- Familiarize yourself on how to modify database schema and publications after replication has been configured. Some replication items can be changed on the fly, whereas others require you to create a new snapshot.

- Place the Distribution system database on either a RAID 1 or RAID 1+0 volume other than the operating system. Finally, set the recovery model to Full to safeguard against database failures and set the size of the database to accommodate the replication data.

- When configuring replication security, apply the principle of least privilege to ensure that replication is hardened and unwanted authorization is prevented.

- To address performance degradation on the publisher, configure a distributor on its own server.

PART II

Managing SQL Server 2005

IN THIS PART

CHAPTER 7

Conducting a SQL Server 2005 Health Check

If SQL Servers are left unkept or unmanaged, maintaining them can become overwhelming. Even then, some of the most maintained SQL Servers still have room for improvement. Health checks are meant to assist you, as database administrator (DBA), by providing more information on current issues or uncovering potential issues and then recommending best practice recommendations or resolutions based on experience.

Typically, organizations budget a health check annually as a part of their routine maintenance plan. However, health checks are not always planned events.

Consider this example: You just inherited the responsibility to manage a SQL Server 2005 environment. In this case, it would be a good idea to conduct a health check to uncover any potential issues so that you're not caught off-guard. By performing a health check at this point, you might find that database growth was originally set for autogrowth as opposed to being planned, causing the free space on the volume to drop to dangerous levels. If this situation is left uncorrected, the database would not be able to expand, causing unscheduled downtime for production. Although this is an extreme example, it illustrates why you need to conduct a health check.

During a SQL health check, numerous tasks need to be completed. This chapter focuses on the three key steps of conducting a SQL Server 2005 health check: data gathering, data analysis and reporting, followed by best practices.

The overall goal of a health check is to

- Ensure optimal efficiency of SQL Server 2005
- Provide more information on current issues or uncover potential issues
- Suggest and/or apply best practice recommendations and solutions

This sounds like a simple list from a high level. When SQL Server is broken down all the way to the components, meeting these three objectives of a health check can become a daunting task! We start by examining the first key step at a high level, the gathering of data.

In the data gathering stage (step 1), the following tasks are to be completed:

- Conducting initial meeting with the DBA
- Collecting performance information
- Collecting log information
- Collecting security information
- Collecting log shipping (if applicable)
- Collecting location and size of SQL databases
- Collecting transaction logs
- Collecting backup strategy
- Collecting business continuity strategy

As you guessed, this information takes a long time to gather. When the information is compiled, it needs to be analyzed. This leads to the second key step, data analysis and reporting.

During data analysis and reporting (step 2), the information compiled in the preceding step is to be analyzed. Depending on the complexity of the environment, this step can potentially take longer than gathering the data itself. In this stage, the following tasks are to be completed:

- Analyzing all collected information during the preceding stage
- Comparing findings to best practices
- Creating a report summarizing all the issues and suggested best practice resolutions

In the last major section of this chapter, "Health Areas to Look Out For," we review the most common best practices recommended during health checks (step 3). They include

- Checking the server configuration and disk placement
- Planning for database file capacity
- Reviewing backup strategy and business continuity
- Making post-installation updates and patches
- Documenting
- Monitoring
- Reviewing antivirus configuration
- Reviewing security

Data Gathering for the Health Check

The data gathering step can be the most challenging and time-consuming step during a health check. We can be thankful that Microsoft has developed a number of tools to help make this process a lot less painful. This following sections break down the entire process, from the initial meeting to kick off the health check, to which types of data to gather, then how to go about gathering the information. The corresponding tools are described; however, detailed information on the tools appears later in the chapter.

The initial meeting to begin the health check should involve the person facilitating the health check, the DBA, and any other interested parties.

The agenda for this meeting should include the following points:

- Review and discuss the tasks to be completed during the health check.
- Review and discuss which tasks require more attention.
- Review and discuss the key components of SQL Server 2005 (such as Analysis Services, Database Engine, Integration Services, and Replication).

  For example, when reviewing and discussing the Database Engine, review, discuss, and then rank each online SQL database. A one to five scale is recommended, five being mission critical.

- Review and discuss any and all issues the DBA is experiencing.

The goals of this meeting are to

- Understand the environment.
- Understand the issues at hand.
- Define the scope of work.
- Review and rank each database.
- Set expectations.

Collecting Information: The Tools

Before you learn how to go about collecting the information, pause for a moment to look at the tools in use during a health check to programmatically gather the information. Without these tools, manually collecting such information could take exponentially longer and may not be as accurate.

The following sections describe the tools in use in terms of brief history, the information the tool targets, and the way the tool functions. These sections do not cover how to install the tools, as well as how and when to use the tools. We cover the "how and when" when we review how to go about gathering the information.

SQLDIAG

In previous versions of SQL Server (SQL 7.0 and SQL 2000), DBAs could rely on the PSSDiag utility to assist in collecting the information. The PSSDiag utility's core collection engine ships with SQL Server 2005 under the name SQLDIAG.EXE, replacing the PSSDIAG.EXE found with earlier versions of SQL.

The SQLDIAG utility, by default, can gather information from the Event Viewer, Performance Monitor, Profiler Traces, and Sysmon logs as well as provide detailed blocking information. Using this tool, you can collect information from SQL Server 2005 programmatically instead of having to manually collect information. Following are a few examples:

- Contents of the servername.txt file
- Operating system version report
- System report
- Output from specific stored procedures
- Sysprocesses
- SPIDs and deadlock information

- Microsoft diagnostics report for server
- Processor list
- Video display report
- Hard drive report
- Memory report
- Services report
- Drivers report
- IRQ and port report
- DMA and memory report
- Network report
- SQL Database size
- The last 100 queries and exceptions

SQLDIAG is included with a default SQL Server 2005 installation and is located in C:\Program Files\Microsoft SQL\90\Tools\Binn.

If additional information outside the defaults is needed, you can modify the ##SQLDIAG.XML configuration file to include additional criteria. You can specify how to add criteria in the following form:

```
</PerfmonObject>
<PerfmonObject name="\MSFTESQL:FD(*)" enabled="true">
<PerfmonCounter name="\*" enabled="true" />
</PerfmonObject>
```

The configuration file is created on the first execution of the SQLDIAG tool and is stored in the C:\Program Files\Microsoft SQL\90\Tools\Binn\ SQLDIAG\ folder.

By default, SQLDIAG establishes communication with SQL Server 2005 using Windows Authentication, and it is assumed that the tool is launched with Administrative (Windows) and SysAdmin (SQL) rights.

If default settings do not match the configuration, SQLDIAG can be configured to use SQL authentication and can be launched by a user without Administrative (Windows) and SysAdmin (SQL) rights by specifying the /G switch.

The SQLH2 Tool

Microsoft's Health and History tool, SQLH2, was created to collect data from single or multiple instances of SQL Server to determine how it is being used. In a nutshell, SQLH2 targets WMI information on configurations and hardware, events and outages, and SQL Server (such as instances, profiler traces, partition schemes, endpoints, server broker settings). Using this tool, you can store the information and then report on it.

By default, the SQLH2 tool is configured to gather 27 performance counters from the local machine, including 15 system counters and 12 SQL Server counters. If additional counters are required, you can make changes to the H2PerfConfigFile.XML file by simply adding the following text to the document:

```
<PERFCOUNTER Object="REPLACEME" Counter="REPLACEME"/>
```

Here's an example:

```
<PERFCOUNTER Object="SQLServer:Locks" Counter="Page" />
```

Additional servers can be added with the following syntax:

```
<TARGET Name="Alameda-SP01">
      <PERFCOUNTER Object="PROCESSOR" Counter="% Processor time"
   </TARGET>
```

You can download SQLH2 from http://www.microsoft.com/downloads. SQLH2, by default, installs in the root of the primary volume under SQLH2, and the data files are stored two levels further under perfcollector\data.

SQLH2 installs as a system service. While the service is running, data is collected every 120 seconds. By default, the output is saved to C:\SQLH2\Data\; remember, this option is configurable during the install. It is important to understand where you're storing the collected data. If you use SQLH2's default collection option for a single server, the data file should grow at an estimated 1600 bytes per data capture (estimated 1.2MB per day). SQLH2 can collect data from more than one server, so take the necessary precautions when installing and using this tool.

SQL Best Practice Analyzer

Introduced for SQL Server 2000, SQL Best Practice Analyzer (BPA) makes its return for SQL Server 2005, reporting on SQL Server configurations and then comparing them against Microsoft recommendations and best practices.

The BPA functions by checking for specific configurations and settings within an instance of SQL Server 2005. The information gathered is compared against the BPA's updatable XML file; then specific recommendations are highlighted to help you quickly identify and report on issues. SQL Server 2005 BPA focuses on the following key areas of SQL Server 2005:

- **Analysis Services**—Focuses on user hierarchies, aggregatable attributes

- **Database Engine**—Focuses on various database objects and settings such as file placement, I/O, database functions (blocks, BULK INSERTS)

- **Integration Services**—Focuses on package usage, package content (ActiveX scripting)

- **Replication**—Focuses on replication publishing and subscribing, alerts, violations

The BPA provides solutions in the form of recommendations or best practices. The BPA also can report on recent changes to further assist you in troubleshooting.

You can find the SQL Server 2005 BPA tool by browsing to http://www. microsoft.com/downloads and searching for the keywords *SQL 2005 BPA*. The BPA installs by default to C:\Program Files\Microsoft SQL Server 2005 Best Practices Analyzer.

SQL BPA functions in Windows Authentication mode and assumes the user has the necessary credentials within SQL. When a user does not have the necessary credentials, an error occurs. If the proper authentication is not present, the tool reports that it is unable to connect to the specified server(s), with the error message "Please ensure that the target server is running and you have provided correct user credentials."

When the tool is first launched, it queries Microsoft for any updates for its configuration (XML) file. This is normal behavior and can be canceled at any time.

We reserve the steps of launching a scan for the section on gathering information and the same for viewing reports, which are covered during the data analysis and reporting step in this chapter.

Other Tools

The tools listed in this section are optional and can be called on during the information-gathering stage. A brief overview of the tools is provided in the event a health check could benefit from them.

- **Log File Viewer**—This reporting tool is integrated with SQL Server 2005, providing a one-stop shop for viewing log files from SQL Server and the Windows operating system.

- **Activity Monitor**—Another reporting tool integrated into SQL Server 2005, this tool allows you to identify every current process running on SQL Server 2005 and what those processes are doing.

- **SQL Server Profiler**—This tool can monitor and record virtually every facet of SQL Server 2005 activity, usually used when performance is in question.

- **SQL Server Trace**—Performing a trace can provide detailed information on why deadlocks are occurring. Data collected during the trace is analyzed using the profiler.

Collecting Core Performance Information

Now that the tools are identified, the next task is to actually collect the information needed for the health check using the three main tools.

SQLH2

The process starts with gathering information using SQLH2, which functions as a local service, gathering data locally for the network.

It is recommended that this tool be started first because it collects data over a period of time. While this tool is in operation, you can continue gathering additional information. You can find the output file in the installation directory under the data folder, by default, C:\SQLH2\PerfCollector\Data.

To initiate SQLH2's data capture, either open services.msc and start Microsoft SQLH2 Performance Collector, or open a command prompt and type **net start "microsoft sqlh2 performance collector"**. After the service starts, explore to C:\SQLH2\PerfCollector\Data to confirm file growth within the next 5–10 minutes.

SQLDIAG

Moving the focus to collecting data from the core of SQL server, you use the SQLDIAG tool to gather specific core information. A few sample targets are the operating system, hardware configuration, SQL installation and configuration, database status, size of the operating system, and online/offline SQL databases. To accomplish this task, you use SQLDIAG's default settings, which report on more than 60 stored procedures on all online databases.

To launch the tool, simply open a command prompt and type **SQLDIAG.EXE**. Figure 7.1 shows the typical result of this command.

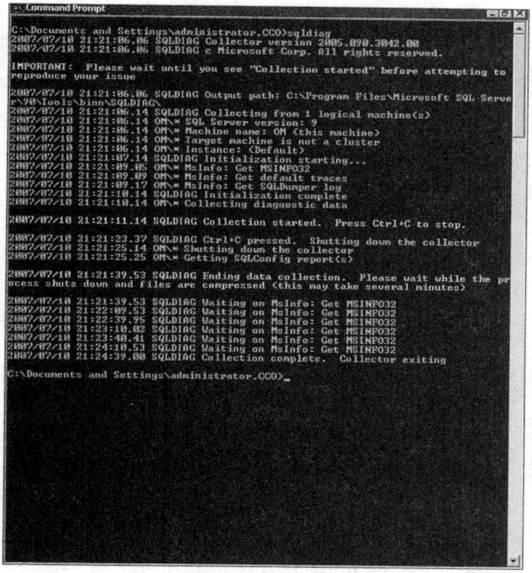

FIGURE 7.1
SQLDIAG output.

While the output lines are self-explanatory, notice the line that states SQLDIAG Collection Started. During this period, you may perform tasks that cause SQL to produce an error. SQLDIAG can capture detailed information and provide more direction on the root cause of the problem.

The output of this tool can be found, by default, in C:\Program Files\ Microsoft SQL\90\Tools\Binn\SQLDIAG. Out of the 12 files in the folder, the 2 files you need are

■ <HOSTNAME>_SP>SQLDIAG_SHUTDOWN.OUT—This file contains all SQL information that is required during a health check (for example, stored procedures, database location and size, blocks).

■ <HOSTNAME>_MSINFO32.TXT—This file contains all the information needed about the operating system, installed drivers, and hardware.

Both files are massive and are easiest to view using Excel. The next section covers what to look for in these two files.

Collecting SQL Core Services Information

To collect information from core services, you can use the SQL Server 2005 BPA. It targets the Analysis Services, Database Engine, Integration Services, and Replication components and then compares the findings against a predetermined list of best practices and recommendations from Microsoft. As mentioned earlier, this tool is regularly updated by Microsoft and provides the timeliest solutions to review these components of SQL Server 2005.

To use the BPA, follow these steps:

1. Open Microsoft SQL Server Best Practices Analyzer 2.0.

2. After allowing the updater to complete, follow the Go to the Welcome Screen link in the right pane.

3. Click Select Options for a New Scan. Take caution on which SQL Server component is selected; there isn't a Back button for this application. However, at the last screen to confirm your selections, you are able to change options.

4. To scan based on computer name for this example, select the computer name under Select SQL Server Components(s) By.

5. Type the server name hosting the database that you want to analyze and click List SQL Server Components.

6. When the server and component services are displayed, as shown in Figure 7.2, select what you want to review and click Configure/Add Selected Service(s).

7. When you are prompted to select the databases to be scanned, select the corresponding databases and click Next.

8. On the following screen to configure Analysis Services scan options, if the service instance is not running, your only option is to click Continue.

9. The following screen confirms the target database. If step 8 did not contain any options, this screen is grayed out and the only option is to click Next.

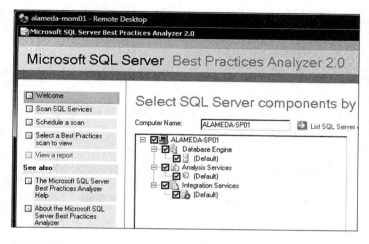

FIGURE 7.2
Selecting components using SQL Server BPA 2.0.

10. On the following screen, select which Integration Services packages to scan. Click Next.

11. The last screen confirms the selections before the scan.

12. Select Detailed Scan and enter a name to further describe this scan for documentation.

13. Click Scan Selected Components to launch the scan.

14. After the scan is complete, save the completed scan as an XML document and exit the application.

Collecting Log Shipping Information

Using SQL Server 2005's built-in reporting tool is the easiest way to gather information pertaining to log shipping. The report uses the SP_help_log_ shipping_monitor stored procedure to query related tables. There are some conditions to using this reporting feature.

If a monitoring server is in use, the name and status of every primary and secondary server are visible.

For primary servers running the report, the name, status, and primary database names are made visible, as well as backup job status reports and secondary server status.

For secondary servers, the name, status, secondary database name, and restore status appear.

To use this reporting tool, follow these steps:

1. Open Microsoft SQL Server Management Studio.

2. From the Object Explorer, select Server.

3. Right-click on the server and select Reports, Standard Reports to see all the available reports.

4. Select the Transaction Log Shipping Status report.

5. Allow the report to generate and then either export to Excel or print.

If this report does not provide enough information, refer to Table 7.1 for stored procedures that contain relevant data to be queried.

Table 7.1   **Stored Procedures for Tracking Log Shipping**

Stored Procedure	Description
`log_shipping_monitor_alert`	Stores alert job ID.
`log_shipping_monitor_error_detail`	Stores error details for log shipping jobs.
`log_shipping_monitor_history_detail`	Contains history details for log shipping agents.
`log_shipping_monitor_primary`	Contains a single monitor record for the primary database in each log shipping configuration. This includes information about the last backup file and last restored file.
`log_shipping_monitor_secondary`	Stores one monitor record for each secondary database, including information about the last backup file and last restored file.

Reviewing Transaction Logs

Transaction logs play an important role in SQL Server 2005, so it is important to understand how large logs are and how much actual space is being used. These next few steps run a query in SQL Server 2005 to return the desired information:

1. Open Microsoft SQL Server Management Studio.

2. Click on the New Query button.

3. Type in **DBCC SQLPERF(LOGSPACE)**" and execute the query.

The result should look similar to Figure 7.3.

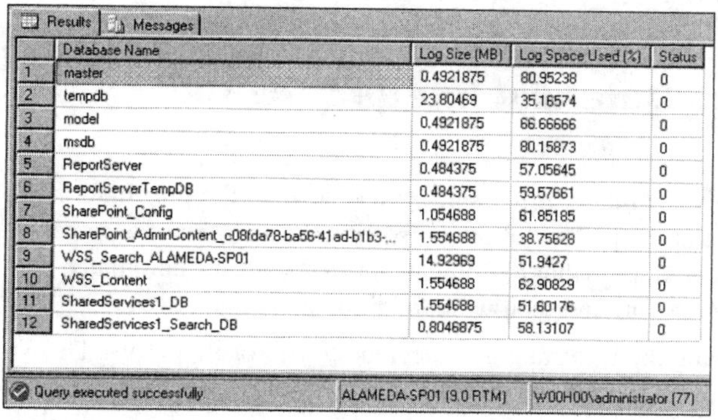

	Database Name	Log Size (MB)	Log Space Used (%)	Status
1	master	0.4921875	80.95238	0
2	tempdb	23.80469	35.16574	0
3	model	0.4921875	66.66666	0
4	msdb	0.4921875	80.15873	0
5	ReportServer	0.484375	57.05645	0
6	ReportServerTempDB	0.484375	59.57661	0
7	SharePoint_Config	1.054688	61.85185	0
8	SharePoint_AdminContent_c08fda78-ba56-41ad-b1b3-...	1.554688	38.75628	0
9	WSS_Search_ALAMEDA-SP01	14.92969	51.9427	0
10	WSS_Content	1.554688	62.90829	0
11	SharedServices1_DB	1.554688	51.60176	0
12	SharedServices1_Search_DB	0.8046875	58.13107	0

FIGURE 7.3
Reviewing transaction logs.

Reviewing the Backup Strategy and Business Continuity Plan

One of the most important tasks that you are charged with as a database administrator is ensuring the survival of the database and the information within. Reviewing the backup strategy requires gathering information pertaining to how you back up the SQL Server 2005 environment. It is also critical to understand how the backup strategy plays into the business continuity plan. Here are a few examples of what types of information to collect:

- Backup type (full, incremental, log files only)
- Backup frequency (hourly, daily)
- Backup storage policy (offsite, onsite, protected environment)
- Business continuity plan
- Business continuity drills (simulating a disaster and enacting the business continuity plan's instructions)

Reviewing Antivirus Configuration

Improperly configured antivirus software can affect performance of SQL Server 2005. Therefore, you need to gather the following information when reviewing antivirus configuration:

- Antivirus exclusions (rule sets, policies)
- Scan behavior

- Scheduled scans
- Antivirus software behaviors (updating, patching)

Analyzing the Data and Interpreting the Data Output

During the data analysis and reporting step, you review all the information gathered in the previous step. The following sections explain how to process the information gathered and what to do next, starting with the automated tools provided by Microsoft and then using additional best practices.

We begin by reviewing the information collected by Microsoft's tools. This is a necessary step because the information collected from the tools may be cryptic and nested in odd locations. The goal is to provide answers to eliminate wasted time.

Capturing data isn't always the same experience with each tool. Some outputs are easy to read, whereas others are not. You often understand what the tool is meant to do, such as capture data, but not always how to understand it. These sections focus on the three main tools in use during a health check: SQLDIAG, SQLH2, and SQL Server 2005 BPA.

SQLDIAG Results

Taking the file `<servername>_sp_sqldiag_shutdown.OUT` into focus, `SQLDIAG.EXE`, by default, captures data in more than 60 locations. The following information reflects where SQLDIAG is gathering the data for the `.OUT` file. The data within the `.OUT` file should be reviewed, and optimizations should be recommended as necessary.

It is recommended that you use Excel to open this file. By default, the file should be located in C:\Program Files\Microsoft SQL Server\90\Tools\Binn\SQLDIAG.

Following are a number of stored procedures from which SQLDIAG gathers data. To obtain a complete list of the store procedures targeted, reference the `.OUT` file. In addition, to understand additional information on the stored procedures, refer to SQL Server 2005 Books Online.

- `sp_configure`—Updates the currently configured value (the `config_value` column in the `sp_configure` result set) of a configuration option changed with the `sp_configure` system stored procedure.
- `sp_who`—Provides information about current users, sessions, and processes in an instance of the Microsoft SQL Server Database Engine.

The information can be filtered to return only those processes that are not idle, that belong to a specific user, or that belong to a specific session.

- **sp_helpd**—Reports information about a specified database or all databases.

- **sp_helpextendedproc**—Reports the currently defined extended stored procedures and the name of the dynamic link library (DLL) to which the procedure (function) belongs.

- **Sysprocesses**—Contains information about processes that are running on an instance of Microsoft SQL Server.

Following are a few sample tables where SQLDIAG gathers data. To obtain a complete list of the tables targeted, reference the .OUT file. In addition, to understand more information on the tables, refer to SQL Server 2005 Books Online.

- **sys.dm_exec_sessions**—Returns one row per authenticated session on Microsoft SQL Server.

- **fn_virtualservernodes**—Returns a list of failover clustered instance nodes on which an instance of SQL Server can run. This information is useful in failover clustering environments.

- **sysdevices**—Contains one row for each disk backup file, tape backup file, and database file.

- **sysdatabases**—Contains one row for each database in an instance of Microsoft SQL Server 2005. When SQL Server is first installed, sysdatabases contain entries for the master, model, msdb, and tempdb databases.

- **sys.dm_tran_database_transactions**—Contains information about transactions at the database level.

Using the table sys.dm_io_virtual_file_stats as an example, review the output from SQLDIAG on the sample server in Figure 7.4. Again, sys.dm_io_virtual_file_stats reports I/O statistics for data and log files.

Notice in Figure 7.4 that a number of databases are consuming more I/O bandwidth than the other databases. Users have also been complaining about wait times for process reports from this server. From this information, you can determine that you need to tune the performance to meet the bandwidth needs of the in-demand databases on this instance of SQL. Refer to Chapter 22, "Performance Tuning and Troubleshooting SQL Server 2005" (online), for steps on how to do this. After optimizations have occurred, to see the results of the performance tuning, you can execute SQLDIAG again or apply a direct query to the table (in this example, the table is sys.dm_io_virtual_file_stats).

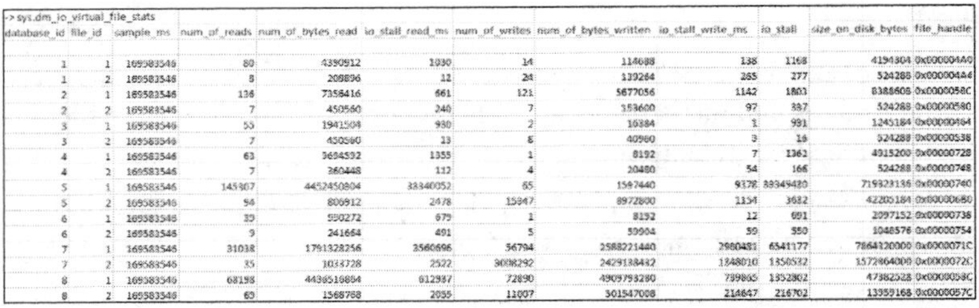

-> sys.dm_io_virtual_file_stats

database_id	file_id	sample_ms	num_of_reads	num_of_bytes_read	io_stall_read_ms	num_of_writes	num_of_bytes_written	io_stall_write_ms	io_stall	size_on_disk_bytes	file_handle
1	1	169583546	80	4390912	1030	14	114688	138	1168	4194304	0x000004A0
1	2	169583546	8	208896	12	24	139264	265	277	524288	0x000004A4
2	1	169583546	136	7356416	661	121	5677056	1142	1803	8388608	0x0000058C
2	2	169583546	7	450560	240	7	153600	97	337	524288	0x00000580
3	1	169583546	55	1941504	930	2	16384	1	931	1245184	0x00000464
3	2	169583546	7	450560	13	8	40960	3	16	524288	0x00000538
4	1	169583546	63	3694592	1355	1	8192	7	1362	4915200	0x00000728
4	2	169583546	7	360448	112	4	20480	54	166	524288	0x00000748
5	1	169583546	145807	4452450804	38340052	65	1597440	9378	38349430	719323136	0x00000740
5	2	169583546	94	806912	2478	15947	8972800	1154	3632	42205184	0x00000680
6	1	169583546	33	990272	679	1	8192	12	691	2097152	0x00000736
6	2	169583546	9	241664	491	5	59904	59	550	1048576	0x00000754
7	1	169583546	31038	1791328256	3560696	56794	2588221440	2980481	6541177	7864320000	0x0000071C
7	2	169583546	35	1033728	2522	3008292	2429138432	1348010	1350532	1572864000	0x0000072C
8	1	169583546	68198	4436516864	612937	72890	4909793280	739865	1352802	47382528	0x0000058C
8	2	169583546	63	1568768	2055	11007	301547008	214647	216702	13959168	0x0000057C

FIGURE 7.4
SQLDIAG output.

Here is a sample syntax for a query that can be used where the first `NULL` represents the `database_id`, and the second `NULL` represents the `file_id`. `NULL` specifies the query to return with all databases in the instance of SQL and all files on the database.

```
Select * from sys.dm_io_virtual_file_stats (NULL,NULL)
```

SQLH2 Results

Viewing the output for SQLH2 isn't as straightforward as it should be, as shown in the following results:

```
1,5,1.072439E+09,6310,4/17/2007 9:38:05 AM
1,6,1.972543E+09,6310,4/17/2007 9:38:05 AM
1,7,10,6310,4/17/2007 9:38:05 AM
1,8,497.4487,6310,4/17/2007 9:38:05 AM
1,9,0,6310,4/17/2007 9:38:05 AM
1,10,0,6310,4/17/2007 9:38:05 AM
1,11,0.0004512368,6310,4/17/2007 9:38:05 AM
```

As such, there is a supplemental download for SQLH2. A `.CAB` file is required to help interpret the data, and it can be found at www.microsoft.com/downloads under the name `ReportV2.cab`. This download contains 11 reports to help you process the information faster.

The files contained in SQLH2's `ReportV2.cab` file provide reports on the following topics:

- Changes made to the server in a specific time frame
- Changes made to SQL Server instances
- Number of features enabled in SQL Server 2005
- SQL database and instances
- Server information
- SQL Server availability
- SQL Server "space dynamics" details

Also included are two script files, `Dictionaries.sql` and `Procs.sql`; these scripts are meant to process against the repository database created by SQLH2. The `Dictionaries.sql` file stores descriptions for values throughout the database, and the `Procs.sql` creates a number of stored procedures used for a specific report (availability).

If you want to access the reports provided in the `.CAB` file, you must complete a series of steps to prep Web Report Services:

1. Process the two `.SQL` files in Microsoft SQL Server Management Studio against SQLH2's Repository Database.

2. Open a web browser to the desired SQL Server's Reporting Services web interface (for example, http://<*servername*>/reports or http://localhost/reports).

3. Create a data source. If you name the data source SQLH2Repository, any uploaded `.RDL` files will be automatically associated.

4. Upload the reports by selecting the Load link.

5. Access the newly uploaded reports by clicking on the Report link.

SQL 2005 BPA Results

The Best Practices Analyzer is the most efficient way of checking on the key components of SQL: Database Engine, Analysis Services, Integration Services, and Replication. As of April 2007, the BPA scans for

- 12 best practice scenarios in Security
- 44 best practice scenarios for the Database Engine
- 34 best practice scenarios for the Analysis Services
- 5 best practices for the Integration Services
- 5 best practices in Replication

When you're viewing BPA reports, you can choose from three main selections:

- **List Reports**—There are two subviews: a Critical Issues tab, which reports all critical issues; and an All Issues tab, which provides a tiered view, grouping the items by issue, severity, and class.

- **Tree Reports**—Information is grouped by focus; for example, the BPA might recommend that a service start under a Network Service account. However, this information is shown only when the parent is expanded upon. In this example, because the recommendation relates to the Analyzing Host portion of the report, the recommendation is shown only when the entire tree is expanded.

- **Other Reports**—The selection provides more verbose information. The Hidden Items tab details additional issues. The Run-Time Log details what actions transpired during the scan.

For this example, you can use the most effective view—the List Reports selection with the All Issues tab arranged by Issue configurations. This view is captured in Figure 7.5. Note that the report is sorted by issue.

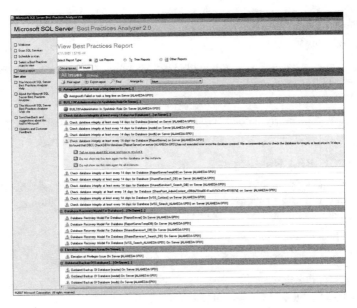

FIGURE 7.5
All Issues view of BPA results.

Notice that in Figure 7.6, if a recommendation is expanded upon, the following three options are prompted:

- **Tell Me More About This Issue and How to Resolve It**—This option opens a new window from the local Compiled HTML (CHM) help file to the specific recommendation, if a recommendation is applicable.

- **Do Not Show Me This Item Again for This Database on This Instance**—This option suppresses the recommendation for this database only, at which point you can reassociate the recommendation in the Other Reports selection.

- **Do Not Show This Item Again for All Instances**—This option suppress the recommendation for all instances. The recommendation maybe reassociated in the Other Reports selection.

FIGURE 7.6
BPA recommendations.

If Tell Me More About This Issue and How to Resolve It is selected (see Figure 7.7), the BPA displays a new window relating to the issue from its local CHM file, suggesting a best practices resolution. Notice that not just a recommendation is being suggested; supporting information is also provided—in this case, a table with detailed information and a hyperlink linking directly to Microsoft at the bottom of the page.

The BPA has a large emphasis on security; therefore, this next example focuses on a recommended security best practice. Notice that in Figure 7.8, if the warning is expanded, a message detailing the issue is displayed immediately.

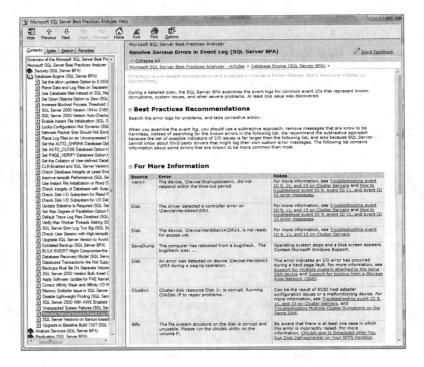

FIGURE 7.7
BPA recommendation details link.

Follow the issue deeper by selecting **Tell Me More About This Issue** and **How to Resolve It** to be linked again to the CHM (see Figure 7.9). Not only is a resolution displayed, but also a hyperlink to SQL 2005 Books Online for more information.

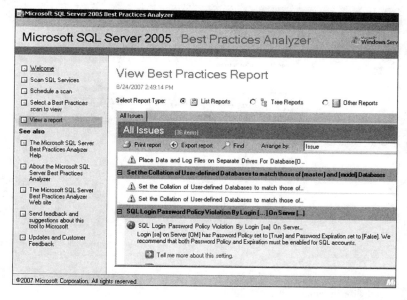

FIGURE 7.8
BPA security recommendation.

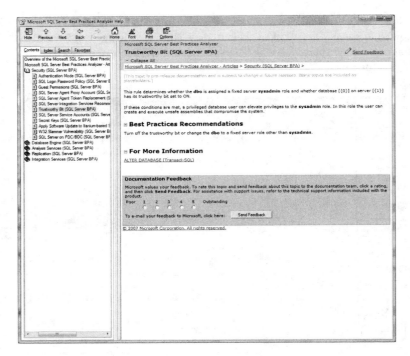

FIGURE 7.9
Security recommendation details.

Health Areas to Look Out For

Health checks consist not only of monitoring performance or looking for error events, but also looking at issues that might result in problems down the line. This includes proper backup methods, space allocations, and other areas. The goal of the following sections is to highlight recommended best practices that you can use in a health check to determine whether the SQL Server 2005 system is deployed and maintained in a healthy way. If a system is not following a best practice recommendation, it is not in a healthy state.

While a plethora of best practices exist, these sections describe the most common best practices reviewed and suggested during a health check.

Server Configuration and Disk Placement

During a health check, look at the server's configuration in terms of disk placement. Best practice recommends that when you're using locally attached storage, the operating system needs to be isolated from the database and transaction logs, preferably on separate RAID volumes. For the transaction log files, it is recommended that you use RAID 1 volumes. For the operating system and database, it is recommended that you use separate RAID 5 or RAID 1+0 volumes. The goal in using a configuration such as this would be to provide maximum throughput, fault tolerance, and recoverability.

A question could be which storage solution to implement—the preceding scenario or network-based storage (NAS/SAN). Without going into too much detail, NAS devices rely on Universal Naming Convention (UNC) shares. Aside from this type of file-based access degrading performance, situations requiring heavy I/O bandwidth suffer horrible performance hits.

SAN devices are more suited for SQL Server 2005 because the data is transported via Small Computer Systems Interface (SCSI). Using SAN software, unlike NAS, multiple volumes can be configured and published to servers.

The choice whether to go network or locally based depends on the demands of the environment. A one-to-one type scenario ensures that only one server has full exclusive access to the disk system, whereas a network-based storage system may not.

Database File Capacity Planning

For a health check, look for how the transaction logging is configured. It is recommended that mission-critical databases and transaction logs be allocated enough space to accommodate their growth.

While anticipating growth can become complicated, best practice suggests that to anticipate growth, the DBA or database owner can do two things: manually increase the database at a scheduled time or choose a defined amount for the logs to grow by. If you use the second option, it is important not to define a size that cannot be managed efficiently or a size so small that expansion will occur too frequently.

If database file capacity planning does not occur, performance will constantly degrade as the log files continue to grow unmanaged. It is important to remember that, once growth as been initiated, the transactions must wait until the database growth has stopped.

Reviewing Backup Strategy and Business Continuity

During a health check, you need to understand how the organization performs backups and how this plays into the organization's overall business continuity plan.

Many consider the backup and restore operations to be the most crucial tasks that DBAs are charged with. Some of these operations ensure that the database will survive a massive hardware failure. Fortunately, you can create a backup strategy on each database with knowledge of many different backup options. If a failure occurs, an organization must depend on its backup(s) to return the database to full service. Backup operations are typically consistent and should be set to Full. The Full recovery model uses database backups and transaction log backups to provide complete protection and the potential to recover the database to the point of failure. If this level of recovery is not required, the Simple Recovery model should be used because this model allows the database to be recovered to the point of the last successful backup.

Best practice recommends that all organizations design and implement a backup and restore strategy, in conjunction with a business continuity plan. This strategy should allow an organization to completely restore mission-critical databases in the event of a disaster. The business continuity plan should detail how to restore critical infrastructure, systems, and services in the event of a disaster. Disaster recovery drills must also be completed routinely. By performing this task, you ensure that the backups captured contain valid and good data and also validate the business continuity plan. By paying full attention to the backup activity and working in conjunction with the parties responsible for the business continuity plan, you can not only avoid mistakes, but also guarantee the safety of an organization's SQL Server environment.

Reviewing Post-Installation Updates and Patches

During a health check, look at how the organization is applying updates and/or patches. SQL Server 2005 is part of a constantly evolving set of technologies released by Microsoft. Whether to increase stability or address a threat or exploit, SQL Server occasionally requires patching and updating until its official support ends. As such, best practice recommends that SQL Server be updated with the latest service packs and/or patches on a regular basis. A maintenance plan should be in place to check for updates, test the updates, and deploy the updates to production systems.

Reviewing Documentation

During a health check, look to see if the organization is current with all its documentation. Best practice recommends that documentation be created and associated with production and test SQL Server(s) to supplement operations and routine maintenance. These documents should include

- **Server Build Documents**—How servers are configured and how SQL is installed
- **Backup and Restore Strategies**—How backup jobs are configured
- **Database Layouts Including Schemas**—How database structure and design are documented
- **SLA Agreement**—How to recover from disk failure
- **Maintenance Plans**—How to test a service pack before deployment to production systems
- **Monitoring Events**—How to automate log shipping reports

Reviewing Monitoring

During a health check, look to see whether the organization is actively monitoring the overall state of the SQL server.

Most organizations are not actively monitoring their SQL Server environment. Whether the environment is a single server or server farm, best practice recommends a third-party application to monitor SQL current status. With a monitoring application, it is possible to create alerts and monitoring within SQL Server. The ultimate monitoring strategy for SQL Server includes the use of Microsoft Operations Manager 2007. Operations Manager 2007 offers an unprecedented level of proactive management and monitoring capabilities that enable you to react to problems and recover from them more quickly.

Microsoft also has a specific management pack that focuses on SQL Server. The management pack delivers event log consolidation, advanced alerting capabilities, performance monitoring, and built-in reports. Operations Manager 2007 is recommended because it is the best-of-breed product for SQL Server 2005 monitoring. Organizations typically have it in place to monitor other infrastructure servers such as Exchange, SMS, and Active Directory.

Reviewing Antivirus Configuration

During a health check, look to see whether the organization is using antivirus protection and, if so, how it is configured. Best practice is to have some type of managed antivirus application installed on the SQL Server 2005 system.

For this, it is recommended that exclusions be configured for backup files, SQL transaction logs, and any other type of SQL data (see the Knowledgebase article KB309422 for an official word from Microsoft).

If exclusions are not configured, SQL performance could be negatively affected because most default antivirus applications are configured to scan files that are accessed. In the event that the servers are clustered, if the files are scanned during a failover, this could interrupt how soon the server can come online (unless the antivirus application is cluster-aware).

In relation to best practice antivirus application management, another best practice addresses how to schedule virus scans. A common oversight in the scheduling of antivirus protection scans is not having a scan scheduled. Every database is different, and as such, different scans may be required to address the different needs. If nonproduction hours do not allow for a full backup nightly, a schedule must be created to ensure antivirus protection is met. As an example, the schedule might include a full backup before the weekend and incremental backup throughout the week.

Reviewing Security

During a health check, security is a major concern. With all the different facets of security to review, this helps to start the process.

Best practice recommends that SQL Server 2005 be deployed in a data center, which should be reviewed as part of a health check. Typically, data centers are shielded with firewalls and other advanced filtering technologies. Based on this recommendation, the server is protected based on its environment.

The following would be looked at during a health check:

- **Service Account (SA)**—Rename the service account. No one should log on as SA, and should always use Windows Integrated Authentication.

- **Windows Authentication Is Strongly Recommended**—If SQL authentication is used, enforce the usage of strong passwords.

- **Securing SQL Server**—Audit principals regularly disable any unused network protocols, remove or disable any unnecessary applications, and remove or disable any unnecessary services.

- **Securing SQL Data**—Restrict privileges on accounts used for SQL services. When applicable, use on-the-wire encryption (such as IPSec) to protect your data in transit and store backups in a secured location at a minimum to protect backups.

- **Securing SQL Hardware**—When applicable, place the server(s) in a limited access data center and minimize the visibility of the server.

Summary

Conducting a SQL Server 2005 health check can be an overwhelming task for the uninitiated. It is important to remember the three main goals of conducting such a health check: Ensure optimal efficiency of SQL Server 2005, provide more information on current issues or uncovering potential issues, and suggest and/or apply best practice recommendations and solutions.

Nested within the two high-level steps are many substeps; what makes the entire process a bit easier are the tools released by Microsoft.

Built-in tools such as SQLDIAG allow you to dig deep into SQL Server to gather detailed information. Tools that are available for download allow you to target different sets of information. For example, SQL Server 2005 BPA focuses on the core components of SQL Server 2005, reporting dynamic suggestions based on Microsoft's best practice; whereas SQLH2 reports on topics relating to the overall health of SQL Server 2005.

Although the tools allow you to quickly gather the information systematically, you must analyze the data to determine the best course of action to be recommended. Included in the report to be created are a number of frequently recommended best practices.

Above all, while conducting a health check, you must refrain from trying to fix each issue as it appears. It's important to document all the issue(s) and then bring the information back to the core group with recommendations/ suggestions and to develop a game plan to address all the issues encountered.

Best Practices

Some important best practices from the chapter include

- Conduct general health checks every 6 to 12 months.

- Create documentation and associate it with production and test SQL Server(s) to supplement operations and routine maintenance.

- Identify all the health issues during the health check and then develop a remediation plan. Don't try to fix the issues during the health check because doing so muddles the results and slows down the health check process. And the fix for one issue might affect another.

- Retain all health check documentation and information for future use.

- In general, all organizations design and implement a backup and restore strategy in conjunction with a business continuity plan.

■ Using SQL Server 2005 BPA is the most efficient way to scan the core components of SQL Server 2005 (for example, Security, Database Engine, Analysis Services, Integration Services, and Replication).

■ The SQLDIAG utility, by default, can gather information from the Event Viewer, Performance Monitor, Profiler Traces, and Sysmon logs as well as provide detailed blocking information.

■ SQLH2 (Microsoft's Health and History tool, H2) was created to collect data from single or multiple instances of SQL Server to determine how it is being utilized.

■ When using a locally attached storage, isolate the operating system from the database and transaction logs, preferably on separate RAID volumes.

■ Place the hardware in a protected location, such as a data center.

■ Allocate enough space on mission-critical databases and transaction logs to accommodate their growth.

■ Update SQL Server with the latest service packs and/or patches. A maintenance plan should be in place to check for updates, test the updates, and deploy the updates to production systems.

■ Use Microsoft System Center Operations Manager 2007 or a third-party application to monitor SQL current status.

■ Manage antivirus scanning, excluding specific files within SQL Server.

■ Use Windows Authentication.

■ No one should log in as the Service Account to do administration.

CHAPTER 8

SQL Server 2005 Maintenance Practices

For SQL Server databases to perform at optimal levels, a database administrator (DBA) should conduct routine maintenance on each database. Some of these routine database tasks involve rebuilding indexes, checking database integrity, updating index statistics, and performing internal consistency checks and backups. These routine database maintenance tasks are often overlooked because they are redundant, tedious, and often time consuming. Moreover, today's DBAs are overwhelmed with many other tasks throughout the day. In recognition of these issues, SQL Server provides a way to automate or manually create these routine DBA chores with a maintenance plan. After the maintenance tasks are identified and created, routine maintenance should commence daily, weekly, monthly, or quarterly, depending on the task. Ultimately, these tasks will put organizations on the path to having healthier, consistent, and more trustworthy databases.

What's New for Maintenance with Service Pack 2

With SQL Server Service Pack 2, many new improved features and fixes have bolstered the maintenance plan creation experience. These changes include the following:

- The Maintenance Plan designer supports multiple subplans within a maintenance plan and the functionality to create independent schedules for each subplan. Multiple Schedules is a highly anticipated feature that can be leveraged to set separate schedules for items such as backups, updating statistics, and executing SQL Server jobs.

- Upon the launch of SQL Server 2005, the installation of SQL Server Integration Services (SSIS) was warranted if organizations wanted to run maintenance plans. This has since changed. Integration Services is no longer required because maintenance plans are now a fully supported feature within the Database Engine.

- For increased administration, maintenance plans now support multi-server environments and logging maintenance plan information to remote servers. You can now configure maintenance plans for all target servers from one central master server.

- The Maintenance Cleanup Task, which first appeared in SQL Server 2000, has reemerged in the maintenance plans to be enjoyed by every DBA. To review, this task removes any remaining files that were part of the maintenance plan execution.

Other improvements and enhancements are seen with the introduction of SQL Server 2005 Service Pack 2. The following reveals some of the fixes that more than a few people have anticipated to improve specific tasks.

- With the release of SQL Server 2005 Service Pack 2, new backup expiration options have been added to the Database Backup maintenance plan task. You can specify backup expiration options, such as having the backup set expire after a specific date or on a specific date. This feature existed in SQL Server 2000; however, it was not available when SQL Server 2005 was released.

- If you select a specific location to store the backup folder, the Database Backup maintenance plan task will not reset this option.

- In the past, when using the Backup Database maintenance plan task, it was possible to create differential and transaction log backup plans on system databases that were using the Simple Recovery model. This bug has been addressed.

- The History Cleanup maintenance plan task offers the option to delete files by selecting a unit of time in hours, ultimately reducing manual work.

- The Update Statistics task includes options for full scan or for sample size, as was available in SQL Server 2000 maintenance plans.

Establishing a SQL Server Maintenance Plan

A maintenance plan performs a comprehensive set of SQL Server jobs that run at scheduled intervals. The maintenance plan conducts scheduled SQL

Server maintenance tasks to ensure that relational databases within the database engine are performing optimally, conducting regular backups, and checking for anomalies. The Database Maintenance Plan, a feature included within the SQL Server Database Engine, can be used to automatically create and schedule these daily tasks. A comprehensive maintenance plan includes these primary administrative tasks:

- Running database integrity checks
- Updating database statistics
- Reorganizing database indexes
- Performing database backups
- Cleaning up database historical operational data
- Shrinking a database
- Cleaning up leftover files from the maintenance plan
- Executing SQL Server jobs
- Cleaning up maintenance tasks

Note

Unlike SQL Server 2000, Log Shipping is no longer a task included with the maintenance plan. Log Shipping can be configured at the database level in SQL Server Management Studio (SSMS) or via Transact-SQL (TSQL) scripts.

Check Database Integrity Task

The Check Database Integrity Task verifies the health and structural integrity of both user and system tables within relational databases selected in the SQL Server Database Engine. When running this task, you have the option to also check the integrity of all index pages. This specific task can be created in the Maintenance Plan Wizard, which will manually create a Maintenance Task. On the other hand, you can use TSQL to create this task. When you create the Database Integrity task, the database options available include all system databases, all user databases, or specific databases.

Although the following is a basic syntax, it supplies the information you need to assess the health and integrity of the database on the AdventureWorks database.

```
USE [AdventureWorks]
GO
DBCC CHECKDB WITH NO_INFOMSGS
GO
```

Shrink Database Task

The Shrink Database Task reduces the physical database and log files to a specific size, similar to the Automatic Shrink Task available in SSMS. When creating a maintenance task, you can shrink all databases, all system databases, all user databases, or specific databases within a single task. This operation removes excess space in the database based on a percentage value you enter. In addition, thresholds in MB can be entered, indicating the amount of shrinkage that needs to take place after the database reaches a certain size and the amount of free space that must remain after the excess space is removed. Finally, free space can be retained in the database or released back to the operating system.

This TSQL syntax shrinks the AdventureWorks database, returns freed space to the operating system, and allows for 15% of free space to remain after the shrink:

```
USE [AdventureWorks]
GO
DBCC SHRINKDATABASE(N'AdventureWorks', 15, TRUNCATEONLY)
GO
```

Tip

When you create maintenance plans, it is a best practice not to select the option to shrink the database. First, when shrinking the database, SQL Server moves pages toward the beginning of the file, allowing the tail end of the files to be shrunk. This process can increase the transaction log size because all moves are logged. Second, if the database is heavily used and there are many inserts, the database files will have to grow again. SQL Server 2005 addresses slow autogrowth with instant file initialization; therefore, the growth process is not as slow as it was in the past. However, at times autogrow does not catch up with the space requirements, causing performance degradation. Third, constant shrinking and growing of the database leads to excessive fragmentation. If you need to shrink the database size, it should be done manually when the server is not being heavily utilized.

Reorganize Index Task

When there is a need to improve index scanning performance, look toward the Reorganize Index Task. This task defragments and compacts clustered and nonclustered indexes on all tables or views, or a particular table or view. The Reorganize Index Task can also be applied to all databases, system databases, user databases, or individually targeted databases. By also selecting an additional option, large object (LOB) data types such as images or text will also be included in the compacting process.

To gain better insight into the operation of this task, use the TSQL syntax that follows to reorganize indexes for the AdventureWorks [Sales]. [SalesOrderDetail] table. This example also includes the option to compact large objects:

```
USE [AdventureWorks]
GO
ALTER INDEX [AK_SalesOrderDetail_rowguid]
ON [Sales].[SalesOrderDetail]
REORGANIZE WITH ( LOB_COMPACTION = ON )
GO
USE [AdventureWorks]
GO
ALTER INDEX [IX_SalesOrderDetail_ProductID]
ON [Sales].[SalesOrderDetail]
REORGANIZE WITH ( LOB_COMPACTION = ON )
GO
USE [AdventureWorks]
GO
ALTER INDEX [PK_SalesOrderDetail_SalesOrderID_SalesOrderDetailID]

ON [Sales].[SalesOrderDetail]

REORGANIZE WITH ( LOB_COMPACTION = ON )
```

Rebuild Index Task

The Rebuild Index Task aims at eliminating fragmentation by reorganizing all the table indexes in the database. This task is particularly good for ensuring that query performance and application response do not degrade. Therefore, when SQL is called on to conduct index scans and seeks, it operates at its full potential. In addition, this task optimizes the distribution of data and free space on the index pages, which allows for growth to take place faster.

The two rebuild index free space options consist of the following:

- **Reorganize Pages with the Default Amount of Free Space**—Drop the indexes on the tables in the database and re-create them with the fill factor that was specified when the indexes were created.

- **Change Free Space per Page Percentage To**—Drop the indexes on the tables in the database and re-create them with a new, automatically calculated fill factor, thereby reserving the specified amount of free space on the index pages. The higher the percentage, the more free space is reserved on the index pages, and the larger the index grows. Valid values are from 0 through 100.

The rebuild index task advanced options consist of the following:

- **Sort Results in tempdb**—The Sort Results in tempdb is the first Advanced option available in the Rebuild Index Task. This option is comparable to the SORT_IN_TEMPDB option for the index. When this option is enabled, the intermediate results are stored in tempdb during the rebuild of an index.

- **Keep Index Online While Reindexing**—The second advanced option allows users to access the underlying table, clustered index data, and the associated indexes during the index rebuild operation.

Armed with the knowledge of what the Rebuild Index Task can do, use the following information to gain some hands-on experience. Use the Rebuild Index syntax that follows to rebuild indexes for the AdventureWorks [Sales]. [SalesOrderDetail] table. The option to Reorganize Pages Using the Default Amount of Free Space has been selected. This example will also sort results in tempdb and keep the index online while reindexing.

```
USE [AdventureWorks]
GO
ALTER INDEX [AK_SalesOrderDetail_rowguid]
➥ ON [Sales].[SalesOrderDetail]
REBUILD WITH ( PAD_INDEX = OFF, STATISTICS_NORECOMPUTE =
➥ OFF, ALLOW_ROW_LOCKS = ON, ALLOW_PAGE_LOCKS = ON,
➥ SORT_IN_TEMPDB = ON, IGNORE_DUP_KEY = OFF, ONLINE = ON )
GO
```

```
USE [AdventureWorks]
GO
ALTER INDEX [IX_SalesOrderDetail_ProductID]
➥ ON [Sales].[SalesOrderDetail]
REBUILD WITH ( PAD_INDEX = OFF, STATISTICS_NORECOMPUTE = OFF,
➥ ALLOW_ROW_LOCKS = ON, ALLOW_PAGE_LOCKS = ON,
➥ SORT_IN_TEMPDB = ON, ONLINE = ON )
GO
USE [AdventureWorks]
GO
ALTER INDEX [PK_SalesOrderDetail_SalesOrderID_SalesOrderDetailID]
➥ ON [Sales].[SalesOrderDetail]
REBUILD WITH ( PAD_INDEX = OFF, STATISTICS_NORECOMPUTE = OFF,
➥ ALLOW_ROW_LOCKS = ON, ALLOW_PAGE_LOCKS = ON,
➥  SORT_IN_TEMPDB = ON, ONLINE = ON )
```

Update Statistics Task

The Update Statistics Task ensures the data in the tables and indexes on one or more SQL Server databases are up to date by resampling the distribution statistics of each index on user tables.

There are numerous choices available to customize this task. Each of the options is explained next:

- **Databases**—First select the databases that will be impacted by this task. The choices range from All Databases, System Databases, or User Databases and These Databases.

- **Object**—After the databases are selected, decide in the Objects box whether to display both tables and views or only one of these options.

- **Selection**—Choose the tables or indexes that will be impacted. If the Tables and Views option was selected in the Objects box, this box will be unavailable.

- **Update**—The Update box offers three choices. Select All existing statistics if you need to update both columns and indexes. Select Column statistics if you need to update only column statistics, and select Index Statistics if you need to update only index statistics.

- **Scan Type**—The Scan Type section allows you to update statistics based on a Full Scan or by entering a Sample By value. The Sample By values can be either a percentage or a specific number of rows.

The syntax to update statistics on the AdventureWorks [Sales].
[SalesOrderDetail] table with the advanced options to update all existing
statistics and conduct a full scan is as follows:

```
use [AdventureWorks]
GO
UPDATE STATISTICS [Sales].[SalesOrderDetail]
WITH FULLSCAN
```

History Cleanup Task

The History Cleanup Task offers organizations the perfect opportunity to
remove historical data in a few simple steps. You can delete several types
of data using this task. The following explains the options associated with
this task.

- **Historical Data to Be Deleted**—Use the Maintenance Plan Wizard to
  purge several types of data, including Backup and Restore history, SQL
  Server Agent Job history, and Maintenance Plan history.

- **Remove Historical Data Older Than**—Use the wizard also to select
  the age of the data you want to delete. For example, you can choose to
  periodically remove older data based on daily, weekly, monthly, and
  yearly increments.

When the History Cleanup Task is complete, you can save a report to a text
file or email the report to an operator by clicking Next. The Select Report
Options screen is invoked and you must enable the check box Write a Report
to a Text File, and then the storage location of the report by specifying the
file and folder location.

The following TSQL example removes historical data older than four weeks
for the following items: Backup and Restore history, SQL Server Agent Job
history, and Maintenance Plan history.

```
declare @dt datetime select @dt =
➥ cast(N'2006-12-28T09:26:24' as datetime)
➥ exec msdb.dbo.sp_delete_backuphistory @dt
GO
EXEC msdb.dbo.sp_purge_jobhistory
➥ @oldest_date='2006-12-28T09:26:24'
GO
EXECUTE msdb..sp_maintplan_delete_log null,
➥ null,'2006-12-28T09:26:24'
```

Execute SQL Server Agent Job

The Execute SQL Server Agent Job task allows you to run SQL Server Agent jobs that already exist as well as SSIS packages as part of the maintenance plan. This is done by selecting the job in the Available SQL Server Agent Jobs section in the Define Execute SQL Server Agent Job Task screen. Alternatively, TSQL syntax can be used to execute a job by entering the appropriate Job ID of a specific job that already exists.

The syntax to execute a SQL Server Agent Job is as follows:

```
EXEC msdb.dbo.sp_start_job @job_
➥id=N'35eca119-28a6-4a29-994b-0680ce73f1f3'
```

Back Up Database Task

The Back Up Database Task is an excellent way to automate and schedule full, differential, or transaction log backups.

You can choose from an expanded set of options when creating full, differential, or transaction log backups with maintenance plans. With these expanded options, you can choose to back up a database or an individual component, set expiration dates, verify integrity, and even determine whether to use disk or tape. Each of the backup options is described in more detail next:

- **Specify the Database**—A maintenance plan can be generated to perform a variety of backups, including backing up a single database, all databases, system databases, or all user databases.

- **Backup Component**—The Backup Component section offers the option of either backing up the entire database or individual files or filegroups.

- **Backup Set Will Expire**—To stipulate when a backup set will expire and can be overwritten by another backup, you need only to specify the number of days or enter a hard date such as September 5th, 1974, for the set to expire.

- **Backup Up To**—This option allows the backup to be written to a file or a tape. A tape drive must be present on the system to back up to tape. The other option is having a backup written to a file residing on a network share.

- **Back Up Databases Across One or More Files**—When selecting the backup destination, you can either add or remove one or more disk or tape locations. In addition, you can view the contents of a file and append to the backup file if it already exists.

- **Create a Backup File for Every Database**—Instead of selecting the preceding option, Back Up Databases Across One or More Files, you can let SQL Server automatically create a backup file for every database selected. In addition, you can automatically create a subdirectory for each database selected.

Note

If the Automatically Create a Subdirectory option is selected, the new subdirectory created will inherit permissions from the parent directory. NTFS permissions should be used to secure the root folder to restrict unauthorized access.

- **Verify Backup Integrity**—This option verifies the integrity of the backup when it is completed by firing a TSQL command that determines whether the backup was successful and is accessible.

Note

For a more thorough and detailed discussion of full, differential, and transaction log backups, see Chapter 17, "Backing up and Restoring the SQL Server 2005 Environment" (online).

You can choose to back up a database in one of three ways when you create a maintenance plan. Select the Define Back Up Database (Full) Task when it is necessary to capture the full database. Similarly, select Define Back Up Database (Differential) Task if it is important to record only data that has changed since the last full backup, or select the Define Back Up Database (Transaction Log) Task, which will back up only entries that are recorded to logs. The backup file extension for the Full and Differential Task is *.bak, whereas the Transaction Log Task is *.trn. Other than these noted differences, the options for each task are the same.

Caution

It is probably abundantly clear by now that maintenance plans are regularly used by DBAs to back up databases, including the transaction logs. A problem may occur during the restore process if you create a transaction log backup with the maintenance plan on a database that has already been configured for log shipping. Ultimately, two sets of transaction log backups are created, one from the maintenance task and the other from the log shipping task. Therefore, if a restore is needed, a combination of the transaction log backups is required to conduct the restore; otherwise, it is not possible to restore the database to the point of failure. If transaction log backups already exist based on log shipping, it is a best practice not to create additional transaction log backups with the maintenance plan. This will eliminate confusion and the potential of a botched restore resulting in lost data.

Maintenance Cleanup Task

The Maintenance Cleanup Task is used to delete files such as backups and reports that reside on the database after the maintenance plan is completed. There are many options for deleting data using this task:

- **Delete Files of the Following Type**—You can choose to delete database backup files or maintenance plan text reports.

- **File Location**—You can also choose to delete a specific file using the File Name box.

- **Search Folder and Delete Files Based on an Extension**—You can delete numerous files with the same extension within a specified folder using this option; for example, all files with the extension *.txt. You can also select to delete all first-level subfolders within the folder identified with this option.

- **File Age**—Files can be deleted by age. You will need to indicate the age of the files to be deleted. For example, you may choose to delete files older than two years. The unit of time also includes hours, days, weeks, and months.

Creating a Maintenance Plan

You can use several methods for creating a maintenance plan. You can use the Database Maintenance Plan Wizard from SQL Server Management Studio (SSMS), or you can manually create a maintenance plan using the tasks associated with the Maintenance Plan Tasks Toolbox. Review the next sections to appreciate how easy and straightforward it is to create a maintenance plan manually and with the wizard.

Creating a Maintenance Plan with the Wizard

Maintaining SQL Server databases is a vital activity for DBAs everywhere. A well-maintained system requires the use of a maintenance plan that automates administrative tasks according to each organization's needs. In this section the Maintenance Plan Wizard is used to create a customized maintenance plan of all system and user databases.

For this example, the steps include the following maintenance tasks: Check Database Integrity, Reorganize Index, Rebuild Index, Update Statistics, and Clean Up History. In a production environment, you should not include both the Reorganize Index and Rebuild Index task in the same plan. These tasks would be considered redundant because one task rebuilds the indexes from scratch and the other reorganizes the indexes. They have only been included for explanation purposes.

Note

A discussion of how to create databases and transaction log backups with the Maintenance Plan Wizard is discussed in Chapter 17 in the section titled "Automating Backups with a Maintenance Plan" (online).

---

1. Choose Start, All Programs, Microsoft SQL Server 2005, SQL Server Management Studio.

2. In Object Explorer, first connect to the Database Engine, expand the desired server, expand the Management folder, and then the Maintenance Plans folder.

3. Right-click Maintenance Plans and choose Maintenance Plan Wizard.

4. In the Welcome to the Database Maintenance Plan Wizard screen, read the message and then click Next.

5. In the Select Plan Properties screen, enter a name and description for the maintenance plan.

6. Choose either the first option (Separate Schedules for Each Task) or the second option (Single Schedule for the Entire Plan or No Schedule). For this example, a separate schedule will be created for the backup plan. Click Next as shown in Figure 8.1.

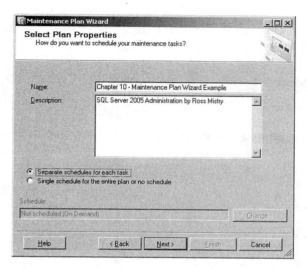

FIGURE 8.1
Scheduling and selecting the Maintenance Plan properties.

New Feature with Service Pack 2

The capability to create separate independent schedules for each subtask within a single maintenance plan is a new feature supported only with Service Pack 2.

7. On the Select Maintenance Tasks screen, as shown in Figure 8.2, place a check on the following maintenance tasks: Check Database Integrity, Reorganize Index, Rebuild Index, Update Statistics, and Clean Up History, and then click Next.

8. On the Select Maintenance Task Order page, select the order that the tasks should be executed and then click Next.

Tip

Many maintenance tasks, including reindexing or updating statistics, alter the database when they run. In recognition of this situation, it is a best practice to make the full database backup maintenance task the first order of operation when prioritizing maintenance tasks. This ensures that the database can be rolled back if the maintenance plan tasks that change the database fail.

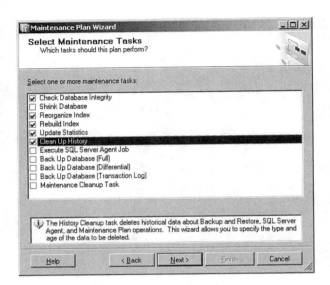

FIGURE 8.2
Selecting database maintenance tasks.

9. The first option in the maintenance plan is checking the database integrity. In the Define Database Check Integrity Task page, select All Databases from the drop-down list. The next item is to accept the defaults. Do this by validating that the Include Indexes Check is enabled, which will ensure all index pages and table databases have an integrity check run against them. Proceed to change the schedule by clicking Change and then set this task so it reoccurs every week starting during nonpeak times, such as Sunday at midnight. Click Next to proceed as in Figure 8.3.

10. The second option selected is to Reorganize Index. From the drop-down on the Define Reorganize Index Task page, select All Databases. Ensure the option for Compact Large Objects is enabled. Set this task to occur once a week. Click Next to proceed as in Figure 8.4

11. The Rebuild Index is the third task selected in the maintenance plan. On the Define Rebuild Index Task page, first select All Databases and then proceed to schedule this task to occur once a week. Select the Free Space Options to Reorganize Pages with the Default Amount of Free Space. In the Advanced Options section, enable Sort Results in tempdb and Keep Index Online While Reindexing, as shown in Figure 8.5. Click Next to proceed.

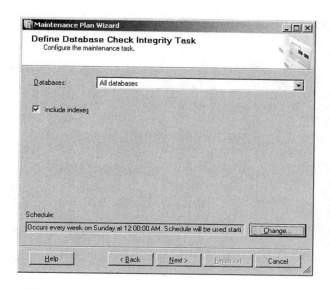

FIGURE 8.3
The Define Database Check Integrity Task screen.

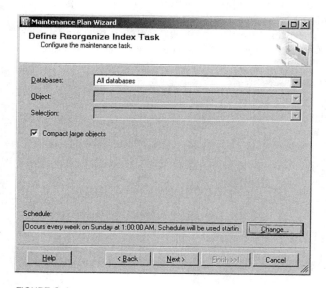

FIGURE 8.4
The Define Reorganize Index Task screen.

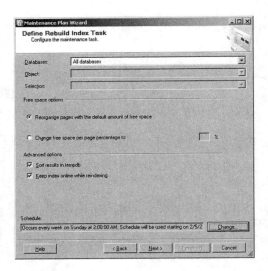

FIGURE 8.5
The Define Rebuild Index Task screen.

12. For the fourth task, select All Databases from the database drop-down
    list in the Define Update Statistics Task page. Ensure that the default
    settings for All Existing Statistics update and Full Scan type are selected.
    Set this task to reoccur weekly. Click Next to proceed as in Figure 8.6.

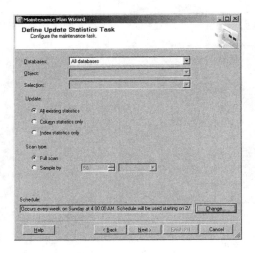

FIGURE 8.6
Specifying options on the Define Update Statistics Task screen.

13. In the Define History Cleanup Task page, select the historical data to delete options, such as Backup and Restore History, SQL Server Agent Job History, and Maintenance Plan History. Select a value that will communicate when historical data will be deleted. This value should be based on the organization's retention requirements, as shown in Figure 8.7. Schedule the task to reoccur on a weekly basis and then click Next.

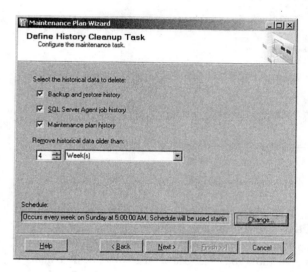

FIGURE 8.7
Specifying options on the Define History Cleanup Task screen.

14. In the Select Report Options page, set the option to either write a report to a text file and enter a folder location or email the report. To email the report, Database Mail must be enabled, configured, and an Agent Operation with a valid email address must already exist. Click Next to continue.

15. The Complete the Wizard page summarizes the options selected in the Maintenance Plan Wizard. It is possible to drill down on a task to view advanced settings. Review the options selected, and click Finish to close the summary page.

16. In the Maintenance Plan Wizard Progress screen, review the creation status as shown in Figure 8.8, and click Close to end the Maintenance Plan Wizard.

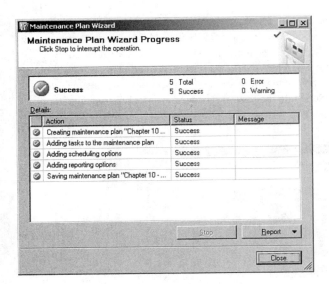

FIGURE 8.8
Viewing the Maintenance Plan Wizard Progress screen.

Manually Creating a Maintenance Plan

Maintenance plans can also be created manually with the aid of the Maintenance Plan (Design Tab). You can create a much more flexible maintenance plan with an enhanced workflow using the Maintenance Plan Design Tab compared to the Maintenance Plan Wizard, because it is equipped with better tools and superior functionality.

The experience of creating a maintenance plan manually has been further enhanced with the introduction of Service Pack 2. Maintenance plan history can now be logged to a remote server when you're creating a manual plan. This is a great new feature when managing many SQL Servers within an infrastructure because all data that is logged can be rolled up to a single server for centralized management.

Note

Creating manual maintenance plans with the Maintenance Plan (Design Tab) is very similar to the design surface available when creating packages with SSIS. For more information on creating Integration Service projects, see Chapter 5, "Administering SQL Server 2005 Integration Services."

The Maintenance Plan design surface, as shown in Figure 8.9, can be launched by right-clicking the Maintenance Plans folder and selecting New Maintenance Plan.

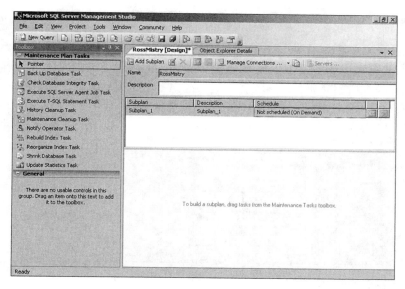

FIGURE 8.9
Viewing the Maintenance Plan design surface and toolbar screen.

You will find the Maintenance Tasks toolbox in the left pane of the Maintenance Plan (Design Page). You can drag maintenance tasks from this toolbox to the design surface in the center pane. If more than one task is dragged to the designer, it is possible to create a workflow process between the two objects by establishing relationships between the tasks. The workflow process can consist of precedence links. As such, the second task will only execute based on a constraint, which is defined in the first task such as "on success, failure or completion." For example, you can choose to create a workflow that will first back up the AdventureWorks database and then, on completion, rebuild all the AdventureWorks indexes, as illustrated in Figure 8.10.

The precedence constraint link between two objects can control the workflow if there is a statement to execute the second rebuild index task when the first backup task is successful. In this situation, when a backup task fails, the second task will not fire. As for creating a precedence constraint, you should first highlight both of the maintenance tasks in the designer, right-click, and then choose Add Precedence Constraint. Once the Precedence Constraint is created, either double click the connector arrow or right-click it and select Edit. This will bring up the Precedence Constraint Editor where you can define the constraint options, as shown in Figure 8.11.

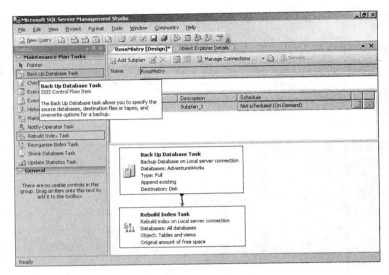

FIGURE 8.10
Implementing a Precedence Constraint between two maintenance plan tasks.

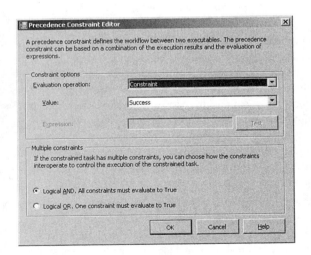

FIGURE 8.11
Setting the Precedence Constraints on the Maintenance Plan Tasks screen.

In addition to creating precedence links, you also can execute tasks simultaneously. This is known as task parallelism and is commonly used when executing the same type of maintenance tasks on different SQL Servers. For example, you can execute a full backup of the master database on all the SQL servers from a central master SQL Server starting on Sunday at 9:00 p.m.

The final item worth mentioning is the reporting capabilities. After the maintenance plan is completed, you can create a report. To do this, locate the Reporting and Logging icon in the Maintenance Plan designer. The Reporting and Logging dialog box as shown in Figure 8.12 displays options such as Generate a Text File Report and Send Reports to an Email Recipient. Additional logging functionality exists, such as log extended information and log maintenance plan history to a remote server. The latter is a new Service Pack 2 feature.

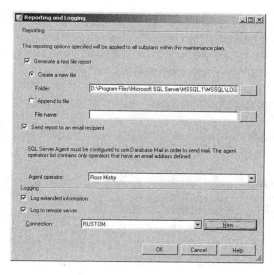

FIGURE 8.12
Configuring Maintenance Plan Reporting and Logging options.

Tip

When working with maintenance plan tasks, you can use a View TSQL command button to convert the options selected for the task into TSQL syntax. This is a great feature for many DBAs who do not have an extensive background in programming.

Viewing Maintenance Plans

All maintenance plans can be viewed under the Maintenance Plan folder in SSMS and stored in SQL Server as jobs. They require the SQL Server Agent to be running to launch the job at the scheduled interval. If the SQL Server Agent is stopped, the jobs will not commence. In addition, all jobs can be edited or changed for ongoing support or maintenance.

Follow these steps to view the maintenance plan jobs in SQL Server Management Studio:

1. Choose Start, All Programs, Microsoft SQL Server 2005, SQL Server Management Studio.

2. In Object Explorer, first connect to the Database Engine, expand the desired server, expand SQL Server Agent, and then expand the jobs folder.

3. Click Jobs to see a list of jobs created by the Maintenance Plan Wizard. The jobs are displayed in the Object Explorer Details tab located in the right pane; otherwise, the jobs are displayed under the Jobs folder in Object Explorer. This is shown in Figure 8.13.

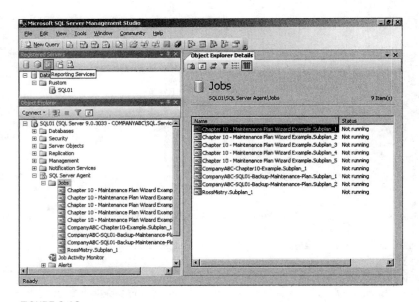

FIGURE 8.13
Viewing Maintenance Plan scheduled jobs.

> **Note**
>
> One major difference with the scheduled job for the maintenance plan in SQL Server 2005 is that the scheduled job executes an SSIS package. The scheduled job in SQL Server 2000 used the SQLMAINT utility instead.

If the SQL Server Agent is not running, a dialog box appears, stating that the SQL Server Agent on the target server is not running. The SQL Server Agent must be started for SQL Server jobs to commence. Follow these steps to start the SQL Server Agent:

1. Choose Start, All Programs, Microsoft SQL Server 2005, SQL Server Management Studio.

2. In Object Explorer, first connect to the Database Engine, and then expand the desired server.

3. Right-click SQL Server Agent and then click Start.

Creating Multiserver Maintenance Plans

In the past, DBAs encountered numerous challenges when managing more than one maintenance plan within their SQL infrastructure. The task of creating maintenance plans in a multiserver environment was exceedingly tedious because a maintenance plan had to be created on each and every server. Moreover, the task of verifying success, failure, and job history was equally difficult and time consuming; it had to be conducted on each server because a method to centrally manage these plans did not exist. To clearly illustrate just how difficult life could get for DBAs, it is worth mentioning that a typical global organization may have well over 100 SQL servers within its infrastructure; therefore, imagine the heartache and lack of operational efficiency that came along with managing maintenance plans.

Today, these nuisances have been alleviated. SQL Server 2005 Service Pack 2 offers support for multiserver maintenance plans. Specifically, you can now create maintenance plans for each of your SQL servers from a single central master server. This provides a significant difference in operational efficiency and administration.

To take full advantage of this new feature in Service Pack 2, a multiserver environment containing one master server and one or more target servers must be constructed before a multiserver maintenance plan can be created. It should be mentioned that target servers can be used only to view the maintenance plans. As a result, multiserver maintenance plans must be created and maintained on the master server so that you can provide regular maintenance of them.

> **Note**
>
> To create or manage multiserver maintenance plans, you must be a member of the sysadmin fixed server role on each of the SQL Servers.

Multiserver maintenance plans can be created with either the Maintenance Plan Wizard or by manually using the Maintenance Plan (Design Tab).

Establishing Maintenance Schedules for SQL Server

With each new release, SQL Server has become more self-maintaining. However, even with self-maintenance and automated maintenance plans, DBAs must conduct additional maintenance. Some maintenance procedures require daily attention, whereas others may require only yearly checkups. The maintenance processes and procedures that an organization follows depend strictly on the organization's individual environment.

The categories described in the following sections and their corresponding procedures are best practices for organizations of all sizes and with varying IT infrastructures. The following sections will help organizations establish sound maintenance practices to help them ensure the health of their SQL Server Database Engine. The suggested maintenance tasks that follow are based on daily, weekly, monthly, and quarterly schedules.

Daily Routine Maintenance Tasks

Maintenance tasks requiring close and regular attention are commonly checked each day. DBAs who take on these tasks daily ensure system reliability, availability, performance, and security. Some of the daily routine maintenance tasks include the following:

- Check that all required SQL Server services are running.
- Check Daily Backup logs for success, warnings, or failures.
- Check the Windows Event logs for errors.
- Check the SQL Server logs for security concerns such as invalid logins.

- Conduct full or differential backups.

- Conduct Transaction Log backups on databases configured with the Full or Bulk-Logged recovery model.

- Verify that SQL Server jobs did not fail.

- Check that adequate disk space exists for all database files and transaction logs.

- At least monitor processor, memory, or disk counters for bottlenecks.

Weekly Routine Maintenance Tasks

Maintenance procedures that require slightly less attention than daily checking are categorized in a weekly routine and are examined in the following list:

- Conduct full or differential backups.

- Review Maintenance Plan reports.

- Check database integrity.

- Shrink the database if needed.

- Compact clustered and nonclustered tables and views by reorganizing indexes.

- Reorganize data on the data and index pages by rebuilding indexes.

- Update statistics on all user and system tables.

- Delete historical data created by backups, restores, SQL Server agent, and maintenance plan operations.

- Manually grow database or transaction log files if needed.

- Remove files left over from executing maintenance plans.

Monthly or Quarterly Maintenance Tasks

Some maintenance task are managed more infrequently, such as on a monthly or quarterly basis. Do not interpret these tasks as unimportant because they don't require daily maintenance. These tasks also require maintenance to ensure the health of their environment, but on a less regular basis because they are more self-sufficient and self-sustaining. Although the following tasks may appear mundane or simple, they should not be overlooked during maintenance.

- Conduct a restore of the backups in a test environment.

- Archive historical data if needed.

- Analyze collected performance statistics and compare them to baselines.

- Review and update maintenance documentation.

- Review and install SQL Server patches and service packs (if available).

- Test failover if running a cluster, database mirroring, or log shipping.

- Validate that the backup and restore process adheres to the Service Level Agreement defined.

- Update SQL Server build guides.

- Update SQL Server disaster recovery documentation.

- Update maintenance plan checklists.

- Change Administrator passwords.

- Change SQL Server service account passwords.

Summary

The maintenance plan feature alone should be one of the key selling points for SQL Server 2005. The capability to use a wizard that is uncomplicated to automate administrative tasks that SQL Server will perform against a single database or multiple databases has decreased the amount of manual work DBAs must do and ensures that tasks do not get overlooked. You can also create plans manually. This is a good option for those looking for a lot of flexibility on advanced workflow.

SQL Server 2005 Service Pack 2 has also allowed organizations to extend their use of maintenance plans. The following are just some of the features Service Pack 2 has brought to the table. SQL Server 2005 Service Pack 2 offers support for multiserver maintenance plans, SQL Server 2005 no longer requires SSIS to be installed, and Service Pack 2 offers the potential for remote logging.

In the end, the most important thing to take away from this chapter is the importance of having a maintenance plan in place early and ensuring that maintenance is scheduled accordingly to preserve the health of each database.

Best Practices

Some important best practices from the chapter include the following:

- DBAs should fully understand all maintenance activities required and implemented within the SQL Server environment.

- Use the Maintenance Plan Wizard to automate and schedule routine maintenance operations.

- When creating maintenance plans with the wizard, leverage the new features included in SQL Server Service Pack 2 and create independent schedules for subtasks.

- Maintenance tasks should be scripted, automated, and fully documented.

- Maintenance tasks should be conducted during nonpeak times or after hours, such as on weekends and after midnight.

- When you configure the order of the maintenance tasks, backups should be executed first, and then other tasks that change the database.

- Do not include the Shrink Task when creating Maintenance Plans. Manually shrink the database if needed during nonpeak hours.

- Maintenance tasks should be grouped into daily, weekly, and monthly schedules.

- Schedule and conduct routine maintenance tasks on a daily, weekly, and monthly basis.

- For a large enterprise environment running many SQL Servers, take advantage of subplans and the multiserver maintenance plan.

CHAPTER 9

Managing and Optimizing SQL Server 2005 Indexes

SQL Server 2005 uses indexes to structure and optimize access to data found within the tables of a database. Index design, maintenance, and optimization are key factors that contribute to how well a database performs. Although the lack of indexes or the use of poorly designed indexes, along with inadequate maintenance, can lead to performance degradation, well-designed and maintained indexes can significantly improve the overall performance of a database by reducing the cost associated with locating data.

When you are performing management and administrative tasks on indexes, it is important to understand the different options and powerful tools that help make indexing management and optimization decisions.

The Importance of Indexes

A well-planned indexing strategy allows fast and efficient access to the underlying data. Indexes can be created on tables or views and ideally allow SQL Server to locate and manage data more efficiently. When efficiency is improved, the amount of time each operation takes is reduced, along with the cost associated with performing the operation.

Index design is typically performed during development of the database application. The reason is that the ability to create effective indexes is based on understanding how application queries are coded and how the data is stored in the database. However, indexes also require management after the database application is deployed and as usage patterns emerge or change.

Managing and optimizing indexes as an ongoing process allow potential performance improvements without requiring changes to the underlying code. As data is queried, the SQL Server query optimizer automatically determines the best method to access the data based on the type of operation and the available indexes.

How Indexes Work

The data within a SQL Server 2005 database is stored within tables. The data within a table is grouped together into allocation units based on the column data type. The data within each allocation unit is physically stored in 8KB pages.

> **Note**
>
> For efficiency, groups of eight pages are physically managed together. This 64KB group of pages is referred to as an *extent*.

Pages within a table store the actual data rows along with the different structures to facilitate locating the data. When the data associated with a table is not logically sorted, the table is referred to as a *heap* structure.

When an index is created, the data in the heap can be rearranged and becomes part of the index, as in the case of a clustered index. An index can also be created as a separate structure that simply points to the location of the data in the heap or clustered index, as in the case of a nonclustered index. A new type of index is also available in SQL Server 2005; this new index can be created on XML columns in the table to improve the efficiency of XML queries.

The different types of indexes have advantages and disadvantages along with different characteristics that need to be considered as part of the ongoing indexing maintenance strategy.

Heap Structures

A heap structure is often the least efficient method of querying data rows in a table because all rows in the table are scanned each time the data is queried. For example, when a specific row of data is needed or when a range of data is needed, all pages in the table are scanned to ensure the correct result is returned.

The heap structure can be the most efficient structure when dealing with small tables, infrequently accessed tables, or when large amounts of data are frequently written to or deleted from the table. The index maintenance cost can often outweigh any potential performance improvement on these types of tables. It is often recommended to avoid creating indexes on tables that fall into these categories.

Clustered Indexes

Clustered indexes are tables that have been sorted based on one or more table columns, commonly referred to as *key* columns. When a clustered index is created, the table is sorted into a *b-tree* structure allowing SQL Server to quickly locate the correct data. Figure 9.1 shows an example of a clustered index b-tree.

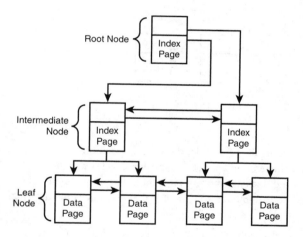

FIGURE 9.1
Clustered index b-tree structure.

The top of the index contains the root node, the starting position for the index. The intermediate level contains the index key data; the index data can point to other intermediate pages or the data in the leaf level. The leaf level nodes located at the bottom of the b-tree contain the actual table data. When the data in the table is queried, the Database Engine can quickly navigate the b-tree structure and locate specific data without having to scan each page.

Nonclustered Indexes

Nonclustered indexes are implemented as a separate b-tree structure that does not affect the pages in the underlying table. Figure 9.2 shows an example of a nonclustered index b-tree.

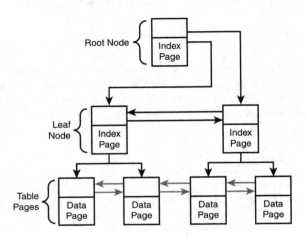

FIGURE 9.2
Nonclustered index b-tree structure.

The top of the index contains the root node, the starting position for the index. However, unlike clustered indexes, a nonclustered index does not contain any data pages and does not modify the data in the source table. The index pages on the leaf node contain a *row locator* that references the data in the associated table.

If the underlying table is also clustered, as in a clustered index, leaf node pages in the nonclustered index point to the corresponding clustered index key. If the underlying table does not have a clustered index, the leaf node pages in the nonclustered index point to the corresponding row in the heap.

View Indexes

When a view is queried, the resulting data is materialized at runtime. Depending on the amount of data returned, a high cost can be associated with the materialization process. To reduce the cost of using complex views, you can create an index for the view.

> **Note**
>
> The query optimizer may select a view index automatically, even if the view is not explicitly named in the FROM clause.

The data that would normally be materialized during runtime is stored in a b-tree structure, similar to a nonclustered index. When the underlying data is changed, the related indexed views are automatically maintained just as clustered and nonclustered indexes are maintained.

XML Indexes

XML indexes can be created on XML table columns and should be considered when working with XML data types. The XML columns in a table are stored as binary large objects (BLOBs). Normally, when XML columns are queried, the data is shredded during runtime and placed into a relational table. The cost associated with this operation can be very high, depending on the size of the XML column. An XML index shreds the data when the index is created, eliminating the cost of this operation during runtime.

A single primary index and three different types of secondary indexes can exist on each XML column in a table for a total of 249 different XML indexes. Unlike traditional indexes, XML indexes cannot be created on views.

Exploring General Index Characteristics

Whereas pages in a heap are not linked or related to each other, index pages are linked; this link type is typically referred to as a *doubly linked list*. This means one link points to the previous page, and one points to the next page. The doubly linked list effectively allows the Database Engine to quickly locate specific data or the starting and ending points of the range by moving through the index structure.

Both clustered and nonclustered indexes are stored as a b-tree structure. The b-tree structure logically sorts pages with the intention of reducing the amount of time needed to search for data. For example, when you're querying a heap, the entire table must be scanned because the data is not sorted. However, when you're querying a b-tree, the logical and physical organization of data allows the correct rows to be located quickly.

When creating an index, you must select one or more key columns. The index key can be any column with the exception of the varchar(max), nvarchar(max), varbinary(max), ntext, text, image, and XML data types. The combined length of the selected key column cannot exceed 900 bytes.

The effectiveness of an index is based on the key columns, so choosing the correct key columns is an important part of the clustered index design.

How Column Constraints Affect Indexes

Constraints can be defined on columns to ensure data integrity. For example, a constraint can be configured on a column that contains phone numbers to make sure that only valid phone numbers are entered in the correct format with the correct number of digits.

When the primary key constraint is applied to a column, a unique clustered index is automatically created. If a clustered index already exists for the table, a nonclustered index is created.

How Computed Columns Affect Indexes

A computed column uses an expression to generate its value. Unless the computed column is marked as PERSISTED, the value of the computed column is not stored in the table like other columns; it is calculated when the data is queried.

Indexes can be created that include these columns. However, because of the complexity associated with computed columns, specific prerequisites must be met. Following are the prerequisites for indexes on computed columns:

- **Determinism**—The computed column expression must be deterministic. For example, the computed column expression can't use the SUM,AVG or GETDATE functions because the result may change. On the other hand, the DATEADD and DATEDIFF functions are considered deterministic as they will always produce the same result based on the dates being calculated.

- **Precision**—The computed column expression must use precise data types. For example, the computed column expression can't normally use the float or real data types because the returned value may change slightly between queries. However, the float and real data types can be used if the column is also marked as PERSISTED because the imprecise data is calculated and stored in the table.

- **Data Type**—The computed column expression cannot evaluate to the text, ntext, or image data types. However, these columns can be included as nonkey columns in a nonclustered index.

- **Ownership**—The table and all functions referenced by the computed column must have the same owner.

- **Set Options**—The ANSI_NULLS option must be ON when using the CREATE TABLE and ALTER TABLE statements. When you're using the INSERT, UPDATE, and DELETE statements, the NUMERIC_ROUNDABORT option must be set to OFF, and the ANSI_NULLS, ANSI_PADDING, ANSI_WARNINGS, ARITHABORT, CONCAT_NULL_YIELDS_NULL, and QUOTED_IDENTIFIER options must be set to ON.

Exploring Clustered Index Characteristics

When a clustered index is created, the data in the table is actually sorted into the leaf nodes of a b-tree, essentially making the data in the table part of the index. Each table can contain only one clustered index because the data can be physically sorted only one time.

Exploring Nonclustered Index Characteristics

When a nonclustered index is created, the data in the table is not modified. Instead, the leaf nodes of the b-tree contain a pointer to the original data. This pointer can either reference a row of data in a heap or a clustered index key, depending on the structure of the underlying table. For example, if the underlying table has a clustered and nonclustered index defined, the leaf nodes of the nonclustered index point to the key location in the clustered index. Conversely, if the underlying table is a heap, because it does not have a clustered index defined, the nonclustered index simply points to rows in the heap to locate the queried data.

Exploring Nonclustered Index Include Columns

Just as with clustered indexes, the combined length of the selected key columns cannot exceed 900 bytes. However, nonclustered indexes are able to "include" columns in the index that are not counted as part of the key. This feature is important because it allows indexes designed to cover all columns used by queries while maintaining a key length below the 900-byte limit.

Also like clustered indexes, the index key can be any column with the exception of the ntext, text, image, varchar(max), nvarchar(max), varbinary(max), and XML data types. However, the varchar(max), nvarchar(max), varbinary(max), and XML data types can be selected as included columns.

Exploring XML Index Characteristics

An XML index should be used when dealing with XML column types. The first index on the XML column must be the primary index. The primary

XML index shreds the XML data, allowing faster access to the data because the shredding operation does not need to be performed at runtime.

After a primary XML index is created, up to three secondary XML indexes can be created. Each secondary index is a different type and serves a different purpose. The different secondary indexes can be based on the path, value, or properties of the XML data.

Traditional indexes can be stored in different filegroups separate from the associated table. However, XML indexes are always stored in the same filegroup as the underlying table.

Index Design and Strategy

Data in a SQL Server 2005 database can be accessed and managed through a variety of methods depending on how the database application was developed. This can make the index design process relatively complicated because the correct indexes must be created for the correct scenario. The following sections provide guidance and strategy for the index design process.

Using Clustered Indexes

You should select the smallest number of key columns within the 900-byte limit. The selected key column or columns should provide uniqueness that allows the data to be searched quickly.

It is recommended to avoid making clustered indexes on columns with few unique values because the query optimizer often skips the index and resorts to a table scan. This means the index is not used, yet the index still needs to be maintained by the Database Engine, causing unnecessary overhead. Following are some general guidelines and best practices for creating clustered indexes:

- A clustered index is often used when large amounts of data or a range of data is queried, such as the data spanning a single month from a table that contains data for an entire year.

- Queries that use the ORDER BY or GROUP BY clauses generally benefit from a clustered query because the data is already sorted and doesn't need to be re-sorted.

- A clustered index is effective when the data is accessed sequentially, the data is searched frequently, or the data would have to be sorted.

The data in the table is sorted as the clustered index is built. From this point, the index is automatically maintained. A downside of a clustered index is the potential cost of index maintenance. Specific operations such as frequent inserts into the middle of the table or many delete operations cause the entire table to shift because the order of the data is automatically maintained. These types of operations also cause nonclustered queries to be updated because the nonclustered index relies on the location of index data within the clustered index.

Using Nonclustered Indexes

Nonclustered indexes cover costly queries with the fewest number of key and included columns. Each nonclustered index introduces additional cost associated with maintaining the index; for this reason, it is important to select the key and include columns carefully. Following are some general guidelines and best practices for creating clustered indexes:

- A nonclustered index is often used when smaller data sets or exact matches are returned because the data page can be located quickly, and additional nonkey columns can be included to avoid exceeding the 900-byte key length limit.

- Nonclustered indexes should also be used to cover additional query scenarios the clustered index does not cover. As many as 249 nonclustered indexes can be created per table.

When the underlying table has a clustered index defined, all nonclustered indexes on that table depend on the clustered index. If the clustered index is disabled, the nonclustered indexes are also automatically disabled.

Using Unique Indexes and the Uniqueifier Column

When creating new indexes or altering existing indexes, you can enable the unique option to force unique values across the key column rows. If the unique option is not selected, the SQL Server Database Engine appends a 4-byte *uniqueifier column* to the index key. This column is used to ensure uniqueness when nonunique data is included in the key. This column is maintained internally and cannot be changed.

Calculating Disk Space Requirements

When index creation and maintenance operations are performed, enough temporary space must exist in the filegroup the index will be created in; otherwise, the operation will fail.

When the index operation is performed, the sorting is done either in the same filegroup as the table or the filegroup where the index is located. However, the sort operation can also be done in the tempdb to potentially improve performance at the expense of temporary disk space. For additional information on how to use the tempdb with indexes, see the section "Sorting Indexes in the tempdb" later in this chapter.

The sum of space needed for both the old and new structure is the starting point to determine the approximate amount of free space needed to perform the index operation. For example, if a heap has 64,000 rows and each row is 1000 bytes, approximately 61MB of free space is required for the source data. This can be calculated with the following formula:

Current Number of Rows * Average Row Length in bytes = Source structure size

Or

64000 * 1000 bytes = 61.0351562 megabytes

The size estimate should be rounded up for the calculation. In this case, the 61MB heap size is rounded to 70MB. To create a clustered index on this heap, you need a total of 70MB free space. When the new index has been created, the space used by the old structure is reclaimed.

When a new index is created or an existing index is rebuilt, a fill factor can be defined. The target structure requires additional space if the fill factor setting is configured.

Note

The fill factor index option allocates additional space in each index page to anticipate growth. This reduces the chance of page splits and fragmentation as data is changed but reduces the performance of the index as the index becomes larger.

For example, if an 80% fill factor is specified, the 70MB heap requires approximately 88MB free space because 20% additional space is allocated for each page. You can use the following calculation to determine additional space needed due to the fill factor:

Source structure size / Fill Factor Percentage

Or

70 MB / 80% = 87.5 megabytes

Existing nonclustered indexes also have to be worked into the formula. When a new clustered index is created, existing nonclustered indexes must be rebuilt because the leaf nodes must now use the clustered key instead of the heap row indicator to find data.

For example, if an existing nonclustered index has 64,000 rows and each row is 100 bytes, approximately 8MB is used for the existing nonclustered index. The following formula can be used to calculate the size of the existing nonclustered index:

> Rows in Index * Average Row Length in bytes / Current Fill Factor Percentage

Or

> (64000 * 100 bytes) / (80%) = 7.62939453 megabytes

The expected size of the nonclustered key can be estimated by adding the new clustered key size to the existing row length and then subtracting the existing 8-byte row indicator. For example, if the new clustered key size is 36 bytes, the expected space needed for the rebuilt nonclustered index is about 10MB. You can then use the following calculation to estimate the size of the new nonclustered index:

> Rows in Index * (Average Row Length in bytes – 8 + Clustered Key Size in bytes) / Fill Factor Percentage

Or

> (64000 * ((100 bytes) – (8 bytes) + (36 bytes))) / (80%) = 9.765625 megabytes

The total source structure would then be 78MB (70MB heap + 8MB nonclustered index) and the total destination structure would be 98MB (88MB cluster + 10MB nonclustered index). A total of 98MB free space is required to complete the index operation with 78MB space reclaimed after the operation has completed.

If the option to sort the index in the tempdb is enabled, the tempdb must have enough space to hold the equivalent of the source table. In this example, the source table is about 70MB. The sort in tempdb option is ignored if the sort operation can be performed in memory.

Administering Indexes

The administration of SQL Server 2005 indexes can be performed through the SQL Server Management Studio interface or through Transact-SQL

(TSQL) code. When you are performing administration of SQL Server indexes, it is important to understand the different options available in the different versions of SQL Server.

The code examples provided in the following sections can be executed through the SQL Server Management Studio. Follow these steps to establish a connection to INSTANCE01 on the server SQL01 to execute the code provided here:

1. Choose Start, All Programs, Microsoft SQL Server 2005, SQL Server Management Studio.

2. Type **SQL01\INSTANCE01** in the Server Name field, select Windows Authentication from the Authentication drop-down menu, and then click the Connect button.

3. Select the New Query button from the toolbar. Type the code from one of the examples in the following sections in the query window; then click the Execute button.

Transact-SQL Index Syntax

Transact-SQL code can be used to manage indexes on tables in a SQL Server database. The CREATE INDEX statement can be used to create new indexes, the modification of existing indexes can be performed through the ALTER INDEX statement, and the removal of indexes can be performed through the DROP INDEX statement. Examples that use each of these index-related TSQL statements are provided throughout this chapter.

Creating Indexes

The following code shows the complete syntax of the CREATE INDEX TSQL statement. You can use the CREATE INDEX statement to create a relational index on a table or view, or an XML index on an XML column.

```
CREATE [ UNIQUE ] [ CLUSTERED | NONCLUSTERED ] INDEX index_name
    ON <object> ( column [ ASC | DESC ] [ ,...n ] )
    [ INCLUDE ( column_name [ ,...n ] ) ]
    [ WITH ( <relational_index_option> [ ,...n ] ) ]
    [ ON { partition_scheme_name ( column_name )
        | filegroup_name
        | default
        }
    ]
[ ; ]
```

```
<object> ::=
{
    [ database_name. [ schema_name ] . | schema_name. ]
        table_or_view_name
}

<relational_index_option> ::=
{
    PAD_INDEX  = { ON | OFF }
  | FILLFACTOR = fillfactor
  | SORT_IN_TEMPDB = { ON | OFF }
  | IGNORE_DUP_KEY = { ON | OFF }
  | STATISTICS_NORECOMPUTE = { ON | OFF }
  | DROP_EXISTING = { ON | OFF }
  | ONLINE = { ON | OFF }
  | ALLOW_ROW_LOCKS = { ON | OFF }
  | ALLOW_PAGE_LOCKS = { ON | OFF }
  | MAXDOP = max_degree_of_parallelism
}
```

The following code shows the complete syntax used to create an index on an XML column:

```
CREATE [ PRIMARY ] XML INDEX index_name
    ON <object> ( xml_column_name )
    [ USING XML INDEX xml_index_name
        [ FOR { VALUE | PATH | PROPERTY } ] ]
    [ WITH ( <xml_index_option> [ ,...n ] ) ]
[ ; ]

<object> ::=
{
    [ database_name. [ schema_name ] . | schema_name. ]
        table_name
}

<xml_index_option> ::=
{
    PAD_INDEX  = { ON | OFF }
  | FILLFACTOR = fillfactor
  | SORT_IN_TEMPDB = { ON | OFF }
```

```
    | STATISTICS_NORECOMPUTE = { ON | OFF }
    | DROP_EXISTING = { ON | OFF }
    | ALLOW_ROW_LOCKS = { ON | OFF }
    | ALLOW_PAGE_LOCKS = { ON | OFF }
    | MAXDOP = max_degree_of_parallelism
}
```

The following code shows the CREATE INDEX options used in previous versions of SQL Server. Backward compatibility is provided to allow easier transition to SQL Server 2005 from previous versions of SQL Server. You should not use these options when developing new code.

```
CREATE [ UNIQUE ] [ CLUSTERED | NONCLUSTERED ] INDEX index_name
    ON <object> ( column_name [ ASC | DESC ] [ ,...n ] )
    [ WITH <backward_compatible_index_option> [ ,...n ] ]
    [ ON { filegroup_name | "default" } ]

<object> ::=
{
    [ database_name. [ owner_name ] . | owner_name. ]
        table_or_view_name
}

<backward_compatible_index_option> ::=
{
    PAD_INDEX
  | FILLFACTOR = fillfactor
  | SORT_IN_TEMPDB
  | IGNORE_DUP_KEY
  | STATISTICS_NORECOMPUTE
  | DROP_EXISTING
}
```

Modifying Indexes

The following shows the complete syntax of the ALTER INDEX TSQL statement. You can use this code to rebuild indexes, disable indexes, reorganize indexes, or modify or set options on existing indexes.

```
ALTER INDEX { index_name | ALL }
    ON <object>
    { REBUILD
```

```
        [ [ WITH ( <rebuild_index_option> [ ,...n ] ) ]
        | [ PARTITION = partition_number
             [ WITH ( <single_partition_rebuild_index_option>
                    [ ,...n ] )
             ]
          ]
       ]
   | DISABLE
   | REORGANIZE
       [ PARTITION = partition_number ]
       [ WITH ( LOB_COMPACTION = { ON | OFF } ) ]
   | SET ( <set_index_option> [ ,...n ] )
   }
[ ; ]

<object> ::=
{
    [ database_name. [ schema_name ] . | schema_name. ]
        table_or_view_name
}

<rebuild_index_option > ::=
{
    PAD_INDEX  = { ON | OFF }
  | FILLFACTOR = fillfactor
  | SORT_IN_TEMPDB = { ON | OFF }
  | IGNORE_DUP_KEY = { ON | OFF }
  | STATISTICS_NORECOMPUTE = { ON | OFF }
  | ONLINE = { ON | OFF }
  | ALLOW_ROW_LOCKS = { ON | OFF }
  | ALLOW_PAGE_LOCKS = { ON | OFF }
  | MAXDOP = max_degree_of_parallelism
}

<single_partition_rebuild_index_option> ::=
{
    SORT_IN_TEMPDB = { ON | OFF }
  | MAXDOP = max_degree_of_parallelism
}

<set_index_option>::=
```

```
{
    ALLOW_ROW_LOCKS= { ON | OFF }
    | ALLOW_PAGE_LOCKS = { ON | OFF }
    | IGNORE_DUP_KEY = { ON | OFF }
    | STATISTICS_NORECOMPUTE = { ON | OFF }
}
```

Deleting Indexes

The following shows the complete syntax of the DROP INDEX TSQL statement. You can use this code to remove a relational or XML index.

```
DROP INDEX
{ <drop_relational_or_xml_index> [ ,...n ]
| <drop_backward_compatible_index> [ ,...n ]
}

<drop_relational_or_xml_index> ::=
        index_name ON <object>
    [ WITH ( <drop_clustered_index_option> [ ,...n ] ) ]

<drop_backward_compatible_index> ::=
    [ owner_name. ] table_or_view_name.index_name

<object> ::=
{
    [ database_name. [ schema_name ] . | schema_name. ]
        table_or_view_name
}

<drop_clustered_index_option> ::=
{
    MAXDOP = max_degree_of_parallelism
    | ONLINE = { ON | OFF }
   | MOVE TO { partition_scheme_name ( column_name )
            | filegroup_name
            | "default"
            }
}
```

Creating Clustered Indexes

The following procedure demonstrates the creation of a clustered index and shows the effect of creating a clustered index on a table. To begin the demonstration, run the following code with the SQL Server Management Studio. This code creates a table called AllItems in the AdventureWorks database. If an existing table called AllItems already exists, it is dropped. When the table is created, three rows of three columns of data are inserted.

Follow these steps to create the AllItems table in the AdventureWorks database:

1. Choose Start, All Programs, Microsoft SQL Server 2005, SQL Server Management Studio.

2. Type **SQL01\INSTANCE01** in the Server Name field, select Windows Authentication from the Authentication drop-down menu, and then click the Connect button.

3. Select the New Query button from the toolbar. Type the following code in the query window and then click the Execute button.

```
USE AdventureWorks
IF object_id('AllItems') is not null
   DROP TABLE AllItems
CREATE TABLE AllItems([ID] INT, [Item] INT, [Value] INT)
INSERT INTO AllItems VALUES (4, 23, 66)
INSERT INTO AllItems VALUES (2, 27, 28)
INSERT INTO AllItems VALUES (3, 28, 93)
SELECT * FROM AllItems
```

When the code is executed, the results pane located below the query windows displays the following data:

```
ID    Item    Value
4     23      66
2     27      28
3     28      93
```

When a clustered index is added to the table, the data is sorted into the clustered index b-tree. Follow these steps to add a clustered index to the AllItems table:

1. From within SQL Server Management Studio, expand SQL01\INSTANCE01, Databases, AdventureWorks, and then Tables. Expand the dbo.AllItems table, which should be located near the top of the list. If the AllItems table is not displayed, click F5 to refresh the table list.

2. Right-click the Indexes folder located beneath the AllItems table and select New Index from the menu. The New Index Properties dialog box opens.

3. In the Index Name field, type **IX_ID**. In the Index Type field, select Clustered from the drop-down menu. Click the Add button, select the ID column, and then click OK. Click OK to create the index.

4. Select the New Query button from the toolbar. Type the following code in the query window and then click the Execute button.

```
SELECT * FROM AllItems
```

When the code is executed, the results pane located below the query windows displays the following data:

```
ID    Item    Value
2     27      28
3     28      93
4     23      66
```

The results show the data has been sorted based on the ID column in the table. The data has been sorted into a b-tree structure. The index nodes contain the ID, and the leaf nodes contain the Item and Value columns.

You can easily create a clustered index through the CREATE INDEX statement. The following code looks for an existing index called IX_ID, and if the index is found, it is dropped with the DROP INDEX statement. A new clustered index using the ID column as the index key is then created.

```
USE AdventureWorks
IF EXISTS (SELECT name FROM sys.indexes WHERE name = 'IX_ID')
   DROP INDEX [IX_ID] ON [dbo].[AllItems]
USE [AdventureWorks]
GO
CREATE CLUSTERED INDEX [IX_ID] ON [dbo].[AllItems]
(
    [ID] ASC
) ON [PRIMARY]
GO
```

Creating Nonclustered Indexes

The following procedure can be used to add a nonclustered index to the table. This index includes the ID column as the key. The Item column is included in the index as a nonkey column.

Follow these steps to create this index:

1. From within SQL Server Management Studio, expand SQL01\INSTANCE01, Databases, AdventureWorks, and then Tables. Expand the dbo.AllItems table, which should be located near the top of the list.

2. Right-click the Indexes folder located beneath the AllItems table and select New Index from the menu. The New Index Properties dialog box opens.

3. In the Index Name field, type NX_ID_Item. In the Index Type field, select Nonclustered from the drop-down menu. Click the Add button, select the ID column, and then click OK.

4. Select the Included Columns page. Click the Add button, select the Item column, and then click OK. Click OK to create the index.

When you create a clustered index and include the Item column as a nonkey column, SQL Server can locate all the data required to support queries that include only the ID and Item columns. This can reduce the cost of executing queries that include these columns because all the data necessary to satisfy the query can be found in the index.

Disabling and Deleting Indexes

When a clustered index is disabled, the underlying data in the table is inaccessible. In addition, nonclustered indexes on the table are also disabled because nonclustered indexes rely on the clustered index key data to locate data in the table.

Follow these steps to disable the clustered index on the Person.Address table located in the AdventureWorks database:

1. From within SQL Server Management Studio, expand SQL01\INSTANCE01, Databases, AdventureWorks, and then Tables. Expand the Person.Address table.

2. Expand the Indexes folder located beneath the Person.Address table. Right-click the PK_Address_AddressID index and select Disable.

3. When the Disable Index window opens, verify that the correct index is listed and then click OK.

4. The Disable Index information dialog box is displayed as a reminder that disabling the index prevents access to the underlying table. Click Yes.

When the clustered index has been disabled, data in the table cannot be accessed. The following code demonstrates using the ALTER INDEX statement to disable the index:

```
USE [AdventureWorks]
GO
ALTER INDEX [PK_Address_AddressID] ON [Person].[Address] DISABLE
GO
```

Use the following code to query the table. The results pane should state, "The query processor is unable to produce a plan because the index 'PK_Address_AddressID' on table or view 'Address' is disabled." This shows the table is inaccessible when the index is disabled.

```
USE [AdventureWorks]
SELECT *
FROM [Person].[Address]
GO
```

Disabling nonclustered indexes and indexed views does not prevent access to the underlying data. Disabling this type of index simply prevents the query optimizer from potentially selecting the index as part of the execution plan.

With nonclustered and view indexes, the b-tree structure is physically deleted when the index is disabled; only the index metadata is kept. You can use the same procedure used to disable a clustered index to disable a nonclustered index.

If the all indexes on a table will be deleted, remove the clustered index last. If the clustered index is removed before nonclustered indexes, the nonclustered indexes have to be maintained when the clustered index is removed.

Enabling and Rebuilding Indexes

When an index is disabled, you can enable it by either rebuilding the index or re-creating the index. When a clustered index is disabled, nonclustered indexes for the table are automatically disabled, too. When the clustered index is rebuilt or re-created, the nonclustered indexes are not automatically enabled unless the option to rebuild all indexes is used.

Follow these steps to enable the clustered index on the Person.Address table located in the AdventureWorks database:

1. From within SQL Server Management Studio, expand SQL01\INSTANCE01, Databases, AdventureWorks, and then Tables. Expand the Person.Address table.

2. Expand the Indexes folder located beneath the Person.Address table. Right-click the PK_Address_AddressID index and select Rebuild.

3. When the Rebuild Index window opens, verify that the correct index is listed and then click OK.

When the clustered index has been rebuilt, the data can once again be queried. However, the nonclustered indexes cannot be selected by the query optimizer because they need to be enabled individually. You can use the same procedure to enable each nonclustered index.

Alternatively, you can use the following code to rebuild all indexes on the table, effectively enabling each index as the rebuild is complete:

```
USE [AdventureWorks]
GO
ALTER INDEX ALL ON [Person].[Address] REBUILD
GO
```

Implementing Index Maintenance and Maintenance Plans

A SQL Server 2005 maintenance plan allows different maintenance tasks to be performed automatically based on a customizable schedule. These tasks help reduce the administrative effort needed to keep the database healthy because the tasks are scheduled and executed automatically.

You can access maintenance plans through the SQL Server Management Studio by navigating to the Management\Maintenance Plans folder in the Object Explorer pane. You can create a new maintenance plan by right-clicking the Maintenance Plans folder and selecting New Maintenance Plan. You also can access a Maintenance Plan Wizard by right-clicking the Maintenance Plans folder and selecting Maintenance Plan Wizard.

When attempting to launch the Maintenance Plan Wizard, an Agent XPs component error might be displayed, depending on how your environment was setup. By default the Agent XPs component is disabled unless the Agent service was selected to start automatically during the SQL Server 2005 installation, or the Surface Area Configuration Tool was used to start the SQL Agent service after installation.

Use the following code to enable the Agent XPs component:

```
sp_configure 'show advanced options', 1;
GO
RECONFIGURE;
GO
sp_configure 'Agent XPs', 1;
GO
RECONFIGURE
GO
```

When a maintenance plan is created either manually or through the Maintenance Plan Wizard, several tasks are available to maintain indexes. Following are the index-related maintenance plan options:

- **Check Database Integrity**—This task performs consistency checks on one or more databases. When you're configuring this task, an option is available to include the indexes in the integrity verification process.

- **Rebuild Index**—This task can be used to rebuild a specific index or all indexes in a database. This task can specify the fill factor and can sort the index results in tempdb to improve efficiency. This task can also use the online indexing option available in the SQL Server 2005 Enterprise and Developer Editions.

- **Reorganize Index**—This task can be used to reorganize a specific index or all indexes in a database. This task can also compact large objects during the reorganize process.

For additional information on how to administer SQL Server 2005 maintenance plans, see Chapter 8, "SQL Server 2005 Maintenance Practices."

SQL Server 2005 also provides the ability to back up indexes. For more information, see Chapter 17, "Backing Up and Restoring the SQL Server 2005 Environment" (online).

Configuring Indexes for Maximum Performance

When you are administering indexes, several options are available and should be considered to improve the overall performance of the indexes and index management operations.

Configuring Index Statistics

When an index is created, the option to recompute statistics is enabled by default. The query optimizer uses these statistics to determine the best method of accessing the data. Inaccurate statistics may cause the query optimizer to select a less than optimal execution plan.

The Database Engine periodically updates the statistics by testing them for accuracy. If necessary, the maintenance of statistics can be disabled. You can use the ALTER INDEX statement to disable collection of statistics. The following code demonstrates using the ALTER INDEX statement to disable statistics on the PK_Address_AddressID index on the Person.Address table:

```
USE [AdventureWorks]
GO
ALTER INDEX PK_Address_AddressID ON [Person].[Address]
SET(STATISTICS_NORECOMPUTE=ON);
GO
```

During the creation of an index through the SQL Server Management Studio, you can disable the collection of index statistics by deselecting the Automatically Recomputed Statistics option on the Option page.

Exploring Fragmentation Considerations

When a row is added to a full index page, a page split occurs, and about half the rows are moved to a new page. This is a costly operation because additional I/O operations are necessary to move the data. Additional I/O operations are then needed each time the data is accessed because the data is no longer continuous. When an index is created or altered, the fill factor option can be used to address fragmentation issues. This option can reduce the amount of fragmentation as the index grows by preallocating free space in the index data pages.

Follow these steps to determine the amount of fragmentation for an index:

1. From within SQL Server Management Studio, expand SQL01\INSTANCE01, Databases, AdventureWorks, and then Tables. Expand the Person.Address table.

2. Expand the Indexes folder located beneath the Person.Address table. Right-click the PK_Address_AddressID index and select Properties.

3. When the Index Properties dialog box opens, select the Fragmentation page to view the total fragmentation percentage for the index.

The DBCC SHOWCONTIG command can also be used to determine index fragmentation. The following code shows how to use DBCC to show the fragmentation of all indexes in the Person.Address table:

```
DBCC SHOWCONTIG ('Person.Address')
WITH ALL_INDEXES, FAST;
GO
```

The results are

```
DBCC SHOWCONTIG scanning 'Address' table...
Table: 'Address' (53575229); index ID: 1, database ID: 7
TABLE level scan performed.
- Pages Scanned...............................: 278
- Extent Switches............................: 34
- Scan Density [Best Count:Actual Count].......: 100.00% [35:35]
- Logical Scan Fragmentation .................: 0.00%
DBCC SHOWCONTIG scanning 'Address' table...
Table: 'Address' (53575229); index ID: 2, database ID: 7
LEAF level scan performed.
- Pages Scanned...............................: 56
- Extent Switches............................: 6
- Scan Density [Best Count:Actual Count].......: 100.00% [7:7]
- Logical Scan Fragmentation .................: 0.00%
DBCC SHOWCONTIG scanning 'Address' table...
Table: 'Address' (53575229); index ID: 3, database ID: 7
LEAF level scan performed.
- Pages Scanned...............................: 211
- Extent Switches............................: 26
- Scan Density [Best Count:Actual Count].......: 100.00% [27:27]
- Logical Scan Fragmentation .................: 0.00%
DBCC SHOWCONTIG scanning 'Address' table...
Table: 'Address' (53575229); index ID: 4, database ID: 7
LEAF level scan performed.
- Pages Scanned...............................: 27
- Extent Switches............................: 4
- Scan Density [Best Count:Actual Count].......: 80.00% [4:5]
- Logical Scan Fragmentation .................: 7.41%
DBCC execution completed.
If DBCC printed error messages,
  contact your system administrator.
```

The DBCC command is deprecated and will be removed from future versions of SQL Server. It is recommended to use the management function sys.dm_db_index_physical_stats to replace the DBCC SHOWCONTIG command when checking index fragmentation.

You also can use the following code to show the fragmentation. When this code is executed, the percentage of fragmentation for all indexes in the Person.Address table is returned.

```
USE AdventureWorks;
GO
SELECT
  a.index_id,
  b.name,
  a.avg_fragmentation_in_percent
FROM sys.dm_db_index_physical_stats (DB_ID(),
 OBJECT_ID(N'Person.Address'), NULL, NULL, NULL) AS a
  JOIN sys.indexes AS b
    ON a.object_id = b.object_id
      AND a.index_id = b.index_id;
GO
```

The result is

```
1    PK_Address_AddressID    0
2    AK_Address_rowguid    0
3    IX_Address_AddressLine1_AddressLine2_City_StateProvinceID_
➥PostalCode    0
4    IX_Address_StateProvinceID    7.40740740740741
```

Implementing Fill Factor Administration

The fill factor can be configured so that each page in the leaf level allocates extra space for new rows. By default, the fill factor is set to 0, allowing only one additional row to be added to the page before a split operation is necessary. If the pages in the leaf level are expected to grow, you can use the fill factor setting to allocate extra space in each page. For example, set the fill factor setting to 80% to leave 20% room in each page for growth. The fill factor can be configured only when an index is created or rebuilt.

Note

Increasing the amount of free space in each page results in a larger index. A larger index increases the I/O cost when accessing the data and degrades performance.

You can use the ALTER INDEX statement to set an 80% fill factor on the PK_Address_AddressID index located on the Person.Address table in the AdventureWorks database:

```
USE [AdventureWorks]
GO
ALTER INDEX PK_Address_AddressID ON [Person].[Address]
REBUILD WITH(FILLFACTOR=80);
GO
```

The fill factor can also be configured through the SQL Server Management Studio. For example, to set the fill factor, create a new index by right-clicking the Indexes folder located beneath the Person.Address table and select New Index. In the New Index window, select the Options page and set the fill factor to the desired level.

Figure 9.3 shows the Set Fill Factor option set to 80%, allowing 20% free space within the leaf node of the index. The Pad Index option can also be configured to provide the intermediate level with additional free space.

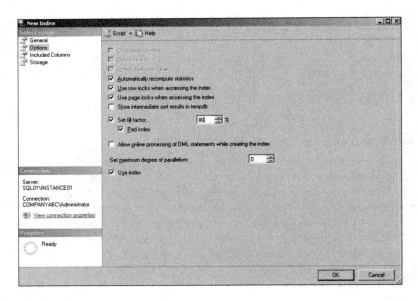

FIGURE 9.3
Fill factor options.

> **Note**
>
> The free space allocated by the fill factor setting is not maintained; the space is allocated once. When the additional space is filled, a split operation occurs. To reallocate the space again, you must rebuild the index.

To view the fill factor value of one or more indexes, use the sys.indexes catalog view. You can use the following code to determine the fill factor on the PK_Address_AddressID index. The fill factor number is located in the fill_factor column.

```
USE AdventureWorks
SELECT fill_factor FROM sys.indexes
WHERE name = 'PK_Address_AddressID'
```

Determining When to Rebuild or Reorganize an Index

When a split operation occurs, the data pages can become fragmented, and fragmentation can lead to performance-related issues. Two different options exist for dealing with fragmentation: The first is to reorganize the index, and the second is to rebuild the index.

When the level of fragmentation is greater than 5% but less than 30%, the reorganize option is recommended. When an index has 30% or greater fragmentation, a rebuild is recommended.

The reorganize process physically reorganizes the leaf nodes of the index, allowing more efficient access. The reorganize is much lighter on the server and doesn't block queries or updates, essentially minimizing the impact on people using the database. The rebuild process actually drops the existing index and re-creates it with the specified settings, such as fill factor. This option is more thorough but also uses more server resources, and if the ONLINE option is not selected, the index is unavailable during the rebuild process.

Sorting Indexes in the tempdb

Normally, when an index is created, the sorting of the index data is done within the same filegroup as the table or the filegroup where the index is stored. However, when you are rebuilding existing indexes or creating new indexes, you can sort the data in the tempdb.

If the tempdb is physically located on a different set of disks, performance improvement can be achieved because the reading of data from one set of disks can be separated from the writing of data to the tempdb.

> **Note**
>
> To increase processing effectiveness, one tempdb file should be created per CPU.

You can use the `ALTER INDEX` statement to rebuild all indexes located on the Person.Address table in the AdventureWorks database, using the tempdb to sort the data:

```
USE AdventureWorks;
GO
ALTER INDEX ALL ON Person.Address
REBUILD WITH (SORT_IN_TEMPDB = ON);
```

Using the Database Engine Tuning Advisor

The Database Engine Tuning Advisor is an effective tool to analyze and report the indexing potential. This tool allows the selection of a single table, single database, or multiple databases for analysis. This is one of the key tools that you should use when attempting to determine the appropriate indexes and the effect of indexes.

This tool works by placing a load on the selected objects. The results of this load are evaluated, and a recommendation is provided, along with a potential improvement percentage. The recommended changes can then be implemented directly from within the tool.

This demonstration creates a sample workload file and then runs it against the Production.Product table in the AdventureWorks database. Before you start, the existing clustered indexes on the table are dropped using the `DROP INDEX` statement. To drop the nonclustered indexes on the Production.Product table, run the following code:

```
USE [AdventureWorks]
GO
DROP INDEX [AK_Product_Name] ON [Production].[Product],
[AK_Product_ProductNumber]ON [Production].[Product],
[AK_Product_rowguid] ON [Production].[Product]
GO
```

After the nonclustered indexes have been deleted, the table can be more effectively analyzed for possible indexes. The next step is to create a workload file; this is SQL code that will be used in the analysis process of the table. Follow these steps to create the workload file:

1. Choose Start, All Programs, Microsoft SQL Server 2005, SQL Server Management Studio.

2. Type SQL01\INSTANCE01 in the Server Name field, select Windows Authentication from the Authentication drop-down menu, and then click the Connect button.

3. Select the New Query button from the toolbar. Then type the following code in the query window:

```
USE [AdventureWorks]
SELECT [Name],
    [ProductNumber],
    [StandardCost],
    [ListPrice]
FROM Production.Product
WHERE [ListPrice] - [StandardCost] > 50
```

4. Select File, Save SQLQuery1.sql As. Then type **Workload.sql** in the File Name field and select a path to save the file.

After the workload file has been created, follow these steps to analyze a table for indexing purposes:

1. Choose Start, All Programs, Microsoft SQL Server 2005, Performance Tools, Database Engine Tuning Advisor.

2. Type **SQL01\INSTANCE01** in the Server Name field, select Windows Authentication from the Authentication drop-down menu, and then click the Connect button.

3. On the General tab, select the File option and then browse for the Workload.SQL file created in the previous steps. Select AdventureWorks from the Workload Analysis drop-down menu.

4. Click the down arrow next to the AdventureWorks database and select the Product table from the list, as shown in Figure 9.4.

5. Select the Tuning Options tab and review the available options. Options include the ability to analyze different types of indexes and partitioning strategies. Click the Advanced button to specify space and online processing restrictions. The default options are acceptable for this demonstration.

6. The default options evaluate the table for nonclustered index potential and disable partitioning recommendations. Click the Start Analysis button.

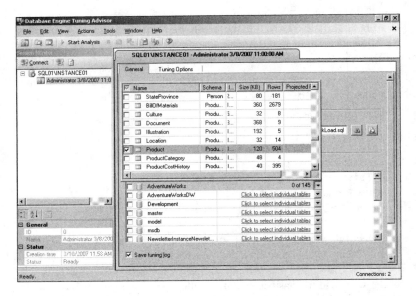

FIGURE 9.4
AdventureWorks table selection.

The analysis of the table is performed. The results, shown in Figure 9.5, show a nonclustered index with ListPrice and StandardCost as key columns, and ProductNumber as an included nonkey column that would improve performance by 46%.

From within the Recommendation tab of the Database Engine Tuning Advisor, click the blue text in the Definition column to see the code necessary to create the recommended indexes. To apply all the recommendations, choose Actions, Apply Recommendation from the menu. The Apply Recommendations dialog box is displayed, allowing you to apply the recommendations immediately or schedule them for later.

This demonstration used a simple workload file to place a load on the database. This is often not appropriate or practical for large complex databases. As an alternative, you can use the information captured from the SQL Server profiler utility to place a more real-world load on the database.

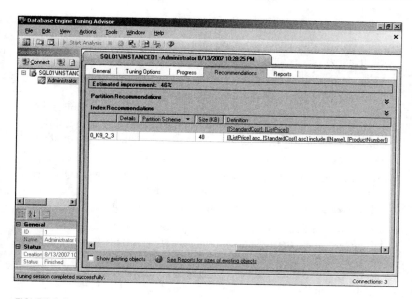

FIGURE 9.5
Database tuning recommendations.

Exploring Additional Indexing Options

When you're creating new indexes or altering existing indexes, additional options are available. These options are listed on the General and Options pages found within the Index Properties dialog box. Follow these steps to access the Properties dialog box for the PK_Address_AddressID index on the Person.Address table in the AdventureWorks database:

1. From within SQL Server Management Studio, expand SQL01\ INSTANCE01, Databases, AdventureWorks, and then Tables. Expand the Person.Address table.

2. Expand the Indexes folder located beneath the Person.Address table. Right-click the PK_Address_AddressID index and select Properties.

The Index Properties dialog box opens. The General page contains the Unique option, and the Options page contains the other options available:

■ **Unique**—When creating new indexes or altering existing indexes, you can enable the Unique option to force unique values across the key columns. When defined, this option forces uniqueness across all columns. For example, if a unique index is created and multiple columns are selected as index key columns, each column can have duplicate values as long as the entire row is unique.

- **Ignore Duplicate Values**—When the Unique option is selected on the General page, Ignore Duplicate Values on the Options page is available. This option changes how SQL Server reacts when a duplicate key is inserted into a unique column. When this option is disabled, the entire transaction fails; when this option is enabled, only the duplicate insert part of the transaction fails.

- **Automatically Recompute Statistics**—This option allows SQL Server to track statistics on indexes. This is important because the query optimizer uses statistics to calculate the best execution plan.

- **Use Row and Page Locks**—This option allows the SQL Server granular control when altering and building indexes. A table lock is often necessary when the index is created or altered; however, this option allows single rows or individual pages to be locked, effectively reducing the possibility of blocking users. The result is that the index operation will take longer.

Enterprise Indexing Features

The Enterprise Edition of SQL Server 2005 offers additional features not available in the Standard Edition. Note that these features are also available in the Developer Edition of SQL Server 2005.

Partitioning Indexes

The table that holds data and the index pages, along with standalone index structures, can be partitioned. This physically divides the data into partitions that can reside in different filegroups across different physical disks. This feature allows large tables and indexes to be physically managed as smaller sets of data while maintaining one logical table.

When you create an index through the SQL Server Management Studio or through TSQL statements, you can set the partition scheme of the index. However, the partition scheme must already exist before the index can be configured to use the partition scheme.

If you create the index on a table that is already partitioned, the index automatically uses the same partition scheme as the parent table. Because of this, it is often easier to create the partition scheme for the underlying table first before creating the index. In this scenario, the table and index are "aligned" because they are using the same partition scheme.

However, if the index is stored away from the table in a different filegroup, the index partition scheme is not inherited from the underlying table and must be specified if necessary. In this scenario, the table and index can be "unaligned."

Online Indexing

When an index is created or rebuilt, the operation can be performed online. This allows the underlying table to be accessed during the operation. Use the following command to rebuild each of the indexes on the Person.Address table while keeping the data online:

```
USE [AdventureWorks]
GO
ALTER INDEX ALL ON [Person].[Address]
REBUILD WITH(ONLINE = ON);
GO
```

You also can access the online indexing option through the SQL Server Management Studio as follows:

1. From within SQL Server Management Studio, expand SQL01\INSTANCE01, Databases, AdventureWorks, and then Tables. Expand the Production.Product table.

2. Right-click the Indexes folder located beneath this table and select new Index.

3. In the Name field, type **IX_SellStartDate_SellEndDate**, and in the Index Type field, select Nonclustered from the drop-down menu. Click the Add button and choose the SellStartDate and SellEndDate columns. Then click the OK button.

4. Click the Option page. Enable the option Allow Online Processing of DML Statements While Creating the Index option. Then click OK.

The index is then created online because the Allow Online Processing of DML Statements While Creating the Index option was selected.

Parallel Indexing

When an index is created, altered, or dropped, the number of processors used can be limited. Use the following command to rebuild each of the indexes on the Person.Address table in the AdventureWorks database, specifying the maximum number of processors to use is four:

```
USE [AdventureWorks]
GO
ALTER INDEX ALL ON [Person].[Address]
REBUILD WITH(MAXDOP=4);
GO
```

By default, the MAXDOP is set to 0, allowing the Database Engine to configure the number of processors based on how busy the server is. When the MAXDOP option is used, additional memory is used on the server.

Summary

Index design needs to be tested because different indexes are used for different situations. Creating indexes on the correct key columns and including appropriate nonkey data can significantly improve the efficiency of database operations. Creating the wrong types of indexes, too many indexes, or even setting the wrong indexing options can increase the overhead of the index along with the associated maintenance cost, resulting in decreased database performance. For this reason, it is important to understand the characteristics of each type of index along with the limitations and advantages of each.

In addition, it is also important to understand how to use the different SQL Server 2005 tools available to assist with the index design and maintenance process.

Best Practices

The following best practices were demonstrated and discussed in this chapter:

- Managing and optimizing indexes is an ongoing process because performance can suffer both with the lack of indexes and poorly implemented and managed indexes.

- Nonclustered indexes are dependent on the clustered index. Be careful when disabling a clustered index because the nonclustered indexes are also automatically disabled.

- A table can have only one clustered index. Take care to ensure the key length of the clustered index doesn't exceed 900 bytes.

- Use nonclustered indexes to cover frequent or costly queries that are not covered by the clustered index. As many as 249 nonclustered indexes can be created on a table.

- Take care to ensure the key length of the nonclustered index doesn't exceed 900 bytes. Add columns as nonkey included columns to place additional data into the index.

- If the tempdb is stored in a different filegroup or on a different set of physical disks, use the option to sort the index in the tempdb for a performance improvement.

- When deleting all indexes on a table, remember to remove the clustered index last. If the clustered index is removed first, any nonclustered indexes are unnecessarily maintained as part of the removal process.

CHAPTER 10

Managing Full-Text Catalogs

As the amount of digital data in an organization continues to grow, so does the demand for a cost-effective solution to make the data easily searchable and available to the people who need it most. Organizations have realized that having too much data that isn't organized can't help them make business decisions.

By developing applications based on SQL Server 2005, an organization can quickly and effectively implement a full-text indexing and searching solution that can successfully scale from a single-server environment to the most demanding enterprise.

This chapter focuses on the management and administration of full-text catalogs in the environment to help ensure the overall performance and accuracy of the full-text solution.

What's New for Full-Text Catalogs in Service Pack 2

Not many things have changed for full-text search in SQL Server 2005 Service Pack 2. However, small improvements have been made when configuring full-text schedules. For example, the Properties dialog box for the full-text catalog allows you to create the index using a schedule for named SQL Server database instances.

Full-Text Search

The Microsoft full-text engine provides both full-text indexing and querying support for data found within a SQL Server 2005 database. The indexing function takes the data found in the table and populates the index, while the querying function is responsible for interpreting words submitted in the query.

The structure of full-text indexes is significantly different from standard indexes. Whereas standard indexes are based on a b-tree structure, full-text indexes are inverted, stacked, compressed structures based on tokens. A *token* is simply a word identified by the full-text engine.

> **Note**
>
> In previous versions of SQL Server, a single instance of the MSSearch service was implemented for all SQL Server instances to share. Needless to say, this did not scale well. With SQL Server 2005, each SQL Server instance has an independent, dedicated full-text search service.

Full-Text Search Terminology

The following components work together to provide the functionality found in the SQL Server 2005 full-text search:

- **Statistics and Ranking**—When an index is built, statistics are created based on the indexed data. For example, the number of occurrences of a word in each document is counted and recorded. Statistics can then be used to rank the query results.

- **iFilters**—The full-text search engine uses iFilters to index columns of the varbinary(max) or image data types. These columns can hold documents created in MS Word and Adobe PDF formats. The iFilter can distinguish between relevant words found in the document from the document's metadata.

- **Word Breakers and Stemmers**—The full-text search engine implements word breakers and stemmers to analyze submitted queries. These components can perform linguistic analysis on the words in the query. Twenty-three word breakers are included with SQL Server.

- **Thesaurus**—The full-text search engine can perform substitution on words in the query. The thesaurus must be manually populated and is commonly used to catch spelling mistakes or provide common substitutions for abbreviations that may otherwise be excluded from the query results.

- **Noise Words**—Each registered language contains a list of noise words. Noise words are excluded from queries by default because they are found to have no useful effect on the search. The words *can*, *so*, and *if* can be found in the U.S. English version of the noise words file.

What's New for Full-Text Search in SQL Server 2005

SQL Server 2005 introduces several key enhancements to the full-text search and indexing components. Besides the significant improvement in indexing and search performance, SQL Server 2005 now provides the capability to include XML columns in the full-text index. The contents of the XML values are indexes, but the XML markup is ignored.

Note

XML attribute values are treated as part of the XML markup and are also excluded from the full-text index.

The Full-Text Search component of SQL Server 2005 is now fully cluster aware. When a failover cluster is created, the SQL Server Full-Text Resource is automatically added as a cluster service.

Finally, full-text queries are fully exposed to the SQL Server Profiler tool. This allows advanced performance analysis and diagnostics of the full-text search with the SQL Server Profiler.

Reviewing the Full-Text Data Definition Language

The full-text data definition language (DDL) is provided as a reference. Each of the following code samples is demonstrated throughout the section "Managing Full-Text Catalogs and Indexes" later in this chapter.

The CREATE FULLTEXT CATALOG command is used to define a new full-text catalog for a database. It is a best practice to place catalogs into different file-groups, separate from the data and log files. Following is the syntax of this command:

```
CREATE FULLTEXT CATALOG catalog_name
    [ON FILEGROUP filegroup ]
    [IN PATH 'rootpath']
    [WITH <catalog_option>]
    [AS DEFAULT]
    [AUTHORIZATION owner_name ]

<catalog_option>::=
    ACCENT_SENSITIVITY = {ON|OFF}
```

The CREATE FULLTEXT INDEX command is used to define a new full-text index on a table. Following is the syntax of this command:

```
CREATE FULLTEXT INDEX ON table_name
    [(column_name [TYPE COLUMN type_column_name]
        [LANGUAGE language_term] [,...n])]
    KEY INDEX index_name
        [ON fulltext_catalog_name]
    [WITH
        {CHANGE_TRACKING {MANUAL | AUTO | OFF
➡[, NO POPULATION]}}
    ]
```

The ALTER FULLTEXT CATALOG command can be used to manage existing full-text catalogs; this includes the capability to rebuild and reorganize the data in the catalog. Data in the catalog is commonly rebuilt and reorganized to improve query performance and improve the ranking accuracy. The following code shows the syntax of this command:

```
ALTER FULLTEXT CATALOG catalog_name
{ REBUILD [ WITH ACCENT_SENSITIVITY = { ON | OFF } ]
| REORGANIZE
| AS DEFAULT
}
```

The ALTER FULLTEXT INDEX command is used to manage existing full-text catalogs; this includes the capability to modify the configuration of the index and execute the different levels of population. Following is the syntax of this command:

```
ALTER FULLTEXT INDEX ON table_name
    { ENABLE
    | DISABLE
    | SET CHANGE_TRACKING { MANUAL | AUTO | OFF }
    | ADD ( column_name
        [ TYPE COLUMN type_column_name ]
        [ LANGUAGE language_term ] [,...n] )
        [ WITH NO POPULATION ]
    | DROP ( column_name [,...n] )
        [WITH NO POPULATION ]
    | START { FULL | INCREMENTAL | UPDATE } POPULATION
    | { STOP | PAUSE | RESUME } POPULATION
    }
```

The DROP FULLTEXT INDEX and DROP FULLTEXT CATALOG commands can be used to remove existing catalogs and indexes from a database:

```
DROP FULLTEXT CATALOG catalog_name
DROP FULLTEXT INDEX ON table_name
```

Managing Full-Text Catalogs and Indexes

Part of your role as database administrator is to manage and maintain full-text indexes. The management of full-text catalogs and indexes includes tasks such as creating and deleting catalogs and indexes, as well as updating the properties and scheduling and performing maintenance on catalogs and indexes.

Subsequent sections within this chapter look into and demonstrate common procedures used to manage full-text catalogs and indexes in the environment.

Creating Full-Text Catalogs

The full-text catalog provides the base structure for one or more full-text indexes. Before defining a full-text index, you need an understanding of how much data will be indexed and how the data will be updated and accessed because these factors determine how the catalogs are designed and where they are stored. For example, it is common to group indexes with similar update properties in the same catalog. Grouping indexes this way maintains indexing ranking consistency because the ranking statistics can change depending on whether intermediate indexes have been merged.

Defining a Full-Text Filegroup

For improved performance in a large-scale environment, you should place full-text catalogs into different filegroups. This allows you to perform backup and restore operations of full-text catalogs independently of the data and log files. Secondary file groups also allow restoring of online full-text catalogs.

The following procedure demonstrates the placement of a new full-text catalog for the AdventureWorks database into a new filegroup. To begin the procedure, you add an additional filegroup to the AdventureWorks database. The full-text catalog is ultimately associated with this filegroup.

Follow these steps to create an additional filegroup on the AdventureWorks database:

1. From the test server (SQL01), choose Start, All Programs, Microsoft SQL Server 2005, SQL Server Management Studio.

2. Select Database Engine from the Server Type drop-down; then enter the server and instance name (**SQL01\INSTANCE01**).

3. Select Windows Authentication from the Authentication drop-down menu and then click the Connect button.

4. A connection to the database engine is made. If the Object Explorer pane is not visible, press the F8 button.

5. From within the Object Explorer pane, expand Databases. The AdventureWorks database should be listed.

6. Right-click the AdventureWorks database and select Properties. The Database Properties window opens.

7. Select the Filegroups page and click the Add button. Then type **DOCUMENTS FTS** in the Name column. Figure 10.1 shows the Filegroups Properties page with the new DOCUMENTS FTS filegroup.

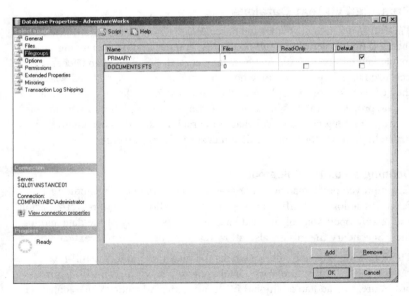

FIGURE 10.1
AdventureWorks filegroups.

Now you can create a database file and associate it with the new filegroup. Follow these steps to create the database file and associate it with the DOCUMENTS FTS filegroup:

1. From within the Database Properties window, select the Files page and click the Add button.

2. In the Logical Name field, type **AdventureWorks_FTS**.

3. Select DOCUMENTS FTS from the Filegroup drop-down menu.

4. Set the initial size of the database to 16MB. Figure 10.2 shows how the Files configuration page should look.

5. Click OK to create the data file and complete the configuration changes.

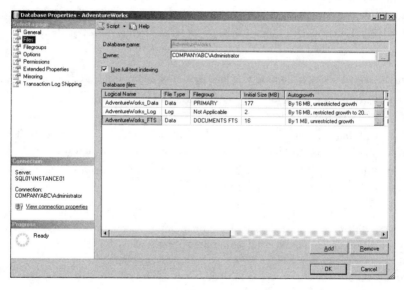

FIGURE 10.2
AdventureWorks files.

Creating the Full-Text Catalog

After creating the filegroup, you can define the full-text catalog and add it to the new filegroup. Follow these steps to create a full-text catalog and associate it with the DOCUMENTS FTS filegroup:

1. From the test server (SQL01), choose Start, All Programs, Microsoft SQL Server 2005, SQL Server Management Studio.

2. Select Database Engine from the Server Type drop-down; then enter the server and instance name (**SQL01\INSTANCE01**).

3. Select Windows Authentication from the Authentication drop-down menu and then click the Connect button.

4. A connection to the database engine is made. If the Object Explorer pane is not visible, press the F8 button.

5. From within the Object Explorer pane, expand Databases, AdventureWorks, and Storage.

6. Select the Full Text Catalogs folder. This folder lists existing full-text catalogs for the AdventureWorks database.

7. Right-click the Full Text Catalogs folder and select New Full Text Catalog. The New Full-Text Catalog window opens.

On the New Full-Text Catalog window, the following options are available:

- **Catalog Name**—This name is used to identify the catalog; it cannot exceed 120 characters.

- **Catalog Location**—This is the physical path to the full-text catalog. If this option is left blank, the catalog is created in the default location.

- **File Group**—This option allows the selection of the filegroup that the full-text catalog is associated with.

- **Owner**—This option specifies the owner of the full-text catalog.

- **Additional Options**—The Additional Options section allows specification of the default catalog and the accent sensitivity.

Follow these steps to define the full-text catalog. The catalog will be associated with the DOCUMENTS FTS filegroup.

1. Enter **Documents Catalog** in the Full-Text Catalog Name field.

2. Leave the Catalog Location field blank to create the catalog in the default location.

3. Select DOCUMENTS FTS from the Filegroup drop-down menu to associate the catalog with the newly created filegroup.

4. Enable the Set as Default Catalog option and accept the default Accent Sensitive option. Then click OK. A new catalog for the AdventureWorks database is created.

Because the path of the catalog is not specified, the catalog is created in the default location. The default location for catalogs is the FTData folder located beneath the MSSQL instance folder. For example, the full-text catalog for instance INSTANCE01 on the server SQL01 is D:\Program Files\Microsoft SQL Server\MSSQL.1\MSSQL\FTData\Documents Catalog. The Documents Catalog folder contains the actual catalog data. After a full-text catalog for the database has been established, full-text indexes can be added.

Creating the Full-Text Catalog with DDL

The same process of defining the full-text catalog can be performed through the full-text data definition language (DDL). Use the following code to create a full-text catalog using the same options from the previous example:

```
USE AdventureWorks
GO
CREATE FULLTEXT CATALOG [Documents Catalog]
    ON FILEGROUP [DOCUMENTS FTS]
    WITH ACCENT_SENSITIVITY = ON
    AS DEFAULT
GO
```

You can check the current status of the catalog through the SQL Server Management Studio by right-clicking the catalog and selecting Properties. Figure 10.3 shows what the properties look like.

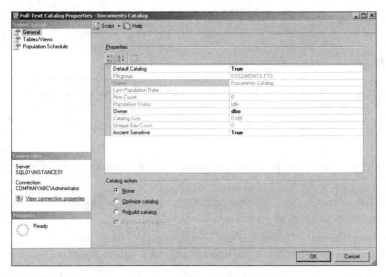

FIGURE 10.3
Documents catalog status.

The Full-Text Catalog Properties window shows several important pieces of information. The following key fields can be used to identify what the catalog is currently doing and how much data is in the catalog:

- **Last Population Data**—This field shows the last time the catalog was populated.

- **Item Count**—This field shows the number of items that have been indexed.

- **Population Status**—This field shows the current status of the catalog. For a complete list of status codes, see Table 10.2 in the section "Accessing Full-Text Properties" later in this chapter.

- **Catalog Size**—This field shows the current size of the catalog in megabytes.

- **Unique Key Count**—This field shows the number of unique words in the catalog.

Additional catalog actions are also available from within the Full-Text Catalog Properties window. These administrative actions are described in the section "Advanced Management of Full-Text Catalogs" later in this chapter.

Creating Full-Text Indexes

This section demonstrates the creation of full-text indexes through the SQL Server Management Studio and through the full-text DDL.

Note

If the underlying table is very large, it may be beneficial to place all indexes into unique catalogs. Each catalog can then be placed on a different set of disks, ultimately reducing possibility of the disk subsystem being a bottleneck.

The following options need to be considered when you are creating a full-text index:

- **Table Name**—This option specifies the name of the table that contains columns to be included in the full-text index.

- **Index Name**—This option specifies the name of the unique, single-key, non-nullable index that the full-text index will be based on.

- **Column Name**—This option specifies the names of the columns to include in the full-text index.

- **Language**—This option specifies the language of each column included in the full-text index. A different language can be specified for each column.

- **Change Tracking**—This option specifies how the full-text index will be maintained and populated.

Running the Full-Text Indexing Wizard

The following procedure creates a full-text index for the Production.Document table located in the AdventureWorks database. To begin the process, establish a connection to INSTANCE01 on the SQL01 server and locate the Production.Document table. Then do the following:

1. From the test server (SQL01), choose Start, All Programs, Microsoft SQL Server 2005, SQL Server Management Studio.

2. Select Database Engine from the Server Type drop-down; then enter the server and instance name (**SQL01\INSTANCE01**).

3. Select Windows Authentication from the Authentication drop-down menu and then click the Connect button.

4. A connection to the database engine is made. If the Object Explorer pane is not visible, press the F8 button.

5. From within the Object Explorer pane, expand Databases, AdventureWorks, and Tables.

6. Locate the Production.Document table in the list.

After locating the table, you can launch the Full-Text Indexing Wizard. The Full-Text Indexing Wizard provides a simple and effective method to manage indexes. Follow these steps to start the wizard on the Production.Document table:

1. Right-click the Production.Document table and then select Full-Text Index, Define Full-Text Index.

2. When the Full-Text Indexing Wizard opens, click Next on the Welcome page to start the process.

3. Select PK_Document_DocumentID from the Unique Index drop-down menu. Click Next.

In the preceding steps, you must select a valid index. Valid indexes consist of a single key column that is unique and non-nullable.

> **Note**
>
> When choosing a unique index, you often achieve a performance gain when you select a clustered index. However, the key size of the unique index is even more important when attempting to achieve maximum performance. An index key based on the INT data type is considered the best performing unique keys for a full-text index. While the maximum key size is 900 bytes, it is recommended never to exceed a unique key size of 100 bytes.

Next, you must select the columns to include in the index. Full-text indexes can be created on columns defined as char, varchar, nchar, nvarchar, text, ntext, image, XML, and varbinary data type. Follow these steps to define the indexed columns to use in the full-text index:

1. Enable the Document column. This includes the Word data found inside the stored documents in the index.

2. Select FileExtension from the Type Column drop-down menu so the index knows what iFilter to use on each document in the Document column.

3. Enable the Title column to include the title of the document in the index. Figure 10.4 shows how the column selection page should look.

4. Click the Next button.

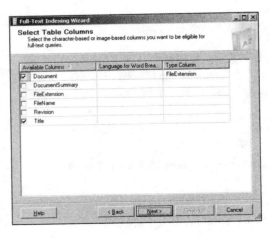

FIGURE 10.4
Production.Document indexed columns.

The Document column is of the binary data type; this column contains actual MS Word documents that have been uploaded into the database. When a binary column is selected, the Type column must also be populated. The Type column specifies the name of a column that contains the document extension. The FileExtension column in the Production.Document table simply contains .doc for each document in the table.

Defining Full-Text Index Change Tracking Options

The next steps in the process are used to configure how the full-text engine (MSFTSQL process) populates and maintains the index. The following options are available:

- **Automatically**—When this option is selected, changes are tracked as they occur, and the index is maintained and updated in the background. This often results in indexes that contain the latest data and thus provides more accurate searches.

- **Manually**—When this option is selected, changes are still tracked. However, the index is not automatically maintained. The indexes can be updated programmatically through a SQL Server Agent job, or you can update them manually.

- **Do Not Track Changes**—When this option is selected, changes are not tracked and cannot be used to update the index. The indexes can still be updated programmatically through a SQL Server Agent job, or you can update them manually.

Follow these steps to configure the change tracking options for the full-text index:

1. Select Do Not Track Changes from the list of available change tracking options.

2. The option to start a full population is now available. This option is applicable only when the Do Not Track Changes option is selected.

3. Uncheck the Start Full Population When Index Is Created option to prevent the index from being populated when the wizard is finished.

4. Click the Next button to continue the wizard process.

Only when the Do Not Track Changes option is selected can the immediate full population of the index be disabled by clearing the Start Full Population When Index Is Created option. Depending on the size of the index and the available server resources, the initial population can be resource intensive, so it is often better to defer the population.

The full population of the index can then be scheduled for a more appropriate time. The change tracking functionality, along with auto and manual updates, can also be enabled after the full population is started.

Defining Full-Text Population Schedules

In the final steps of the process, the index is associated with a catalog, and any optional population schedules can be defined. Follow these steps to configure the associated catalog and schedule the full population for a future date:

1. Select Documents Catalog from the Full-Text Catalogs drop-down menu; then click Next.

2. On the Population Schedules page, click the New Table Schedule button.

3. Type **Documents FTS Full Population** in the Name field.

4. Set a default one-time schedule to run at some point in the future; then click OK.

5. Click Next, review the actions summary, and then click Finish to complete the Full-Text Indexing Wizard.

In the preceding steps, you can place the new index in an existing full-text catalog or define a new catalog. For simplicity, the index was placed in the existing catalog created in the section "Creating Full-Text Catalogs."

Note

If you want to improve the efficiency of the index update processes, it is recommended to group indexes with similar update properties into the same catalog. In a large-scale environment, you can often achieve a performance gain by having each index in a different catalog. Each catalog should also be located on different physical disks to further reduce the possibility of the disk contention.

The preceding steps defined the full-text index and delayed the initial population of the catalog until a more appropriate time.

Caution

At the time of this writing, a bug has been experienced with the Full-Text Indexing Wizard. When an index is created through the Full-Text Indexing Wizard, the option to prevent population of the index is ignored, and the full population starts regardless of the options selected.

This is not the case when you use the full-text DDL code to create the index with the NO POPULATE option enabled. To successfully work around the bug, create the index using the full-text DDL.

You can easily check the status of the index through the SQL Server Management Studio by right-clicking the table where the index was created (Production.Document) and then selecting Full-Text Index, Properties. Figure 10.5 shows what the properties look like.

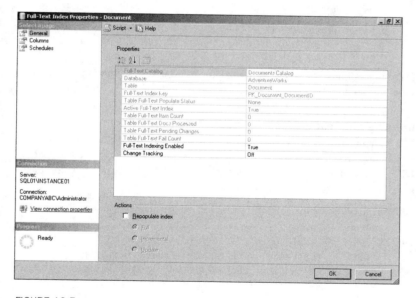

FIGURE 10.5
Production.Document index status.

The Full-Text Index Properties window shows several important pieces of information. The following key fields can be used to help manage the index and identify the current index status:

- **Table Full-Text Populate Status**—This field displays the status of the index population. Table 10.3 later in this chapter shows possible status codes.

- **Active Full-Text Index**—This field displays True if the index is currently enabled and False if the index is currently disabled.

- **Table Full-Text Item Count**—This field displays the number of rows that have been successfully indexed.

- **Table Full-Text Docs Processed**—The field displays the number of rows processed since the indexing began.

- **Table Full-Text Pending Changes**—When change tracking is enabled, this field displays the number of outstanding changes that have to be applied to the index.

- **Table Full-Text Fail Count**—This field displays the number of failures encountered by the index.

- **Change Tracking**—This field displays the current status of the change tracking option.

If the preceding steps were successful, the current status of the index should show the population was successfully deferred.

Creating Full-Text Indexes with DDL

The same steps used to define the full-text index on the Production.Document table can be quickly performed through the full-text DDL. You can use the following code to create the full-text index using the same options as in the previous example:

```
USE AdventureWorks
GO
CREATE FULLTEXT INDEX ON Production.[Document]
    ([Title], [Document] TYPE COLUMN [FileExtension])
    KEY INDEX PK_Document_DocumentID
        ON [Documents Catalog]
    WITH
        CHANGE_TRACKING OFF, NO POPULATION
GO
```

The full population schedule is not available using the CREATE FULLTEXT statement. However, the schedule can be created through standard SQL

Agent job stored procedures. The SQL Agent job actually runs the following full-text DDL statement to initiate the full population:

```
ALTER FULLTEXT INDEX ON [Production].[Document]
➥START FULL POPULATION
```

Populating Full-Text Catalogs

In the section "Creating Full-Text Indexes," you defined a full-text index and scheduled a full population for sometime in the future. This section demonstrates the options available to manage the population schedule and manually initiate the population of the index.

When the population of the catalog is started, the columns in the table are scanned and the index is built. You can schedule the population for a future date or execute it manually. When a full or incremental population is performed on a single full-text index, only the columns associated with the selected index are scanned.

Identifying Full-Text Population Jobs

The following procedure demonstrates how to locate existing population jobs and manually execute the population process. This demonstration uses the full-text index created in the section "Creating Full-Text Indexes" earlier in this chapter.

When the population occurs, the full-text catalog is built. To begin the procedure, establish a connection to INSTANCE01 on the SQL01 server. Then do the following:

1. From the test server (SQL01), choose Start, All Programs, Microsoft SQL Server 2005, SQL Server Management Studio.

2. Select Database Engine from the Server Type drop-down; then enter the server and instance name (**SQL01\INSTANCE01**).

3. Select Windows Authentication from the Authentication drop-down menu and then click the Connect button.

4. A connection to the database engine is made. If the Object Explorer pane is not visible, press the F8 button.

5. From within the Object Explorer pane, expand SQL Server Agents and select Jobs.

The job used to initiate the full-text index population should be listed. If the job is not listed, be sure to run through the procedures in the section

"Creating Full-Text Indexes." This job can be manually executed independent of the schedule by right-clicking the job and selecting Start Job at Step. The properties of the job can also be modified by double-clicking the job. The job properties allow changes, such as when the job is executed and if the job should reoccur or run only once.

Manually Populating Full-Text Indexes

Alternatively, the full-text indexes can be manually populated through actions found on the context menu of a table. Follow these steps to initiate the full-text population from the table object:

1. From the test server (SQL01), choose Start, All Programs, Microsoft SQL Server 2005, SQL Server Management Studio.

2. Select Database Engine from the Server Type drop-down; then enter the server and instance name (**SQL01\INSTANCE01**).

3. Select Windows Authentication from the Authentication drop-down menu and then click the Connect button.

4. A connection to the database engine is made. If the Object Explorer pane is not visible, press the F8 button.

5. From within the Object Explorer pane, expand Databases, AdventureWorks, and Tables.

6. Right-click the Production.Document table and then select Full-Text Index, Start Full Population.

Populating Indexes with DDL

Finally, you can initiate the full population with the full-text DDL. The following code demonstrates how to initiate a full-text population on the Production.Document table in the AdventureWorks database:

```
USE AdventureWorks;
GO
ALTER FULLTEXT INDEX ON Production.Document
START FULL POPULATION
GO
```

You can quickly verify the status of the update through the SQL Server Management Studio by right-clicking Documents Catalog and selecting Properties.

Then you can locate the Documents Catalog from within the Object Explorer pane by expanding Databases, AdventureWorks, and Storage and then selecting the Full Text Catalogs folder. An example of the Documents Catalog properties during the population is shown in Figure 10.6.

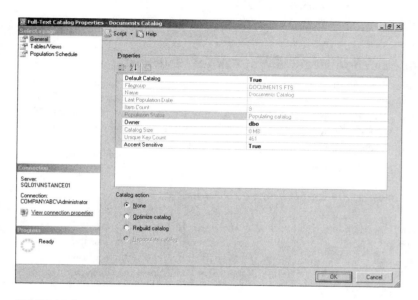

FIGURE 10.6
Populated Production.Document catalog status.

Programmatically Accessing Index Statuses

The population status of a full-text catalog can be accessed through the following command. Status codes are shown in Table 10.2 in the section "Accessing Full-Text Properties" later in this chapter.

```
USE AdventureWorks
GO
SELECT FULLTEXTCATALOGPROPERTY (N'Documents Catalog' ,
➥'PopulateStatus');
GO
```

The population status of a full-text index can be accessed through the following command. Status codes are shown in Table 10.3 in the section "Accessing Full-Text Properties" later in this chapter.

```
USE AdventureWorks
GO
SELECT OBJECTPROPERTYEX
  (OBJECT_ID(N'AdventureWorks.Production.Document'),
   'TableFulltextPopulateStatus')
GO
```

Advanced Management of Full-Text Indexes

After creating the full-text index, you can modify the properties of the index both with the SQL Server Management Studio and the full-text DDL. Run the sp_help_fulltext_tables stored procedure to obtain a list of tables associated with a specific catalog. For example, the following command returns a list of tables in the catalog named Documents Catalog:

```
USE AdventureWorks
GO
EXEC sp_help_fulltext_tables [Documents Catalog]
```

An important change should be made on the full-text index created in the section "Creating Full-Text Indexes" earlier in this chapter. The index was originally created with change tracking disabled, and in the section "Populating Full-Text Catalogs," the full population of the index was initiated.

Now that the full population of the index has been initiated, the properties of the index can be changed to allow change tracking and automatic updates. This allows the index to be updated in the background as the underlying data is changed.

By right-clicking on a table, you can access the Full-Text context menu. This menu provides access to actions that can be performed on the full-text index associated with the table. Following are some of the more advanced management actions found on this menu:

- **Enable Full-Text Index**—Provides the ability to enable a full-text index that is currently disabled.

- **Disable Full-Text Index**—Provides the ability to disable a full-text index that is currently enabled.

- **Delete Full-Text Index**—Provides the ability to delete an existing full-text index.

- **Start Full Population**—Executes a full population of the underlying table data.

- **Start Incremental Population**—Starts an incremental population for the underlying table data.

- **Stop Population**—Stops an existing population.

- **Track Changes Manually**—Enables change tracking. The changes must be manually or programmatically applied to the full text catalog.

- **Track Changes Automatically**—Enables change tracking and enables background updates of the full text catalog.

- **Disable Change Tracking**—Disables the change tracking feature for an index.

- **Apply Tracked Changes**—Updates the catalog with the current set of tracked changes.

Each of these index management actions can also be accessed through the full-text DDL. The following code shows the syntax of the ALTER FULLTEXT INDEX statement:

```
ALTER FULLTEXT INDEX ON table_name
  { ENABLE
  | DISABLE
  | SET CHANGE_TRACKING { MANUAL | AUTO | OFF }
  | ADD ( column_name
    [ TYPE COLUMN type_column_name ]
    [ LANGUAGE language_term ] [,...n] )
    [ WITH NO POPULATION ]
  | DROP ( column_name [,...n] )
    [WITH NO POPULATION ]
  | START { FULL | INCREMENTAL | UPDATE } POPULATION
  | { STOP | PAUSE | RESUME } POPULATION
  }
```

Follow these steps to enable automatic change tracking on the Production.Document table:

1. From the test server (SQL01), choose Start, All Programs, Microsoft SQL Server 2005, SQL Server Management Studio.

2. Select Database Engine from the Server Type drop-down; then enter the server and instance name (**SQL01\INSTANCE01**).

3. Select Windows Authentication from the Authentication drop-down menu and then click the Connect button.

4. A connection to the database engine is made. If the Object Explorer pane is not visible, press the F8 button.

5. From within the Object Explorer pane, expand Databases, AdventureWorks, and Tables.

6. Locate the Production.Document table in the list.

7. Right-click the Production.Document table and then select Full-Text Index, Track Changes Automatically.

Alternatively, you can use the following code to enable automatic change tracking on the Production.Document full-text index:

```
USE AdventureWorks;
GO
ALTER FULLTEXT INDEX ON Production.Document
SET CHANGE_TRACKING AUTO
GO
```

Advanced Management of Full-Text Catalogs

After creating the full-text catalog, you can change the properties through both the SQL Server Management Studio and the full-text DDL. To obtain a list of catalogs associated with a database, use the following command:

```
USE AdventureWorks
GO
SELECT name
FROM sys.fulltext_catalogs;
GO
```

By right-clicking on a catalog and selecting properties, you can access more advanced management options. Following are some of the more advanced management actions found on this menu:

- **Optimize Catalog**—This option reorganizes the data in the catalog, subsequently improving query speed and search result relevance ranking.

- **Rebuild Catalog**—This option deletes and then rebuilds the full-text catalog. The catalog must be rebuilt in certain situations, such as when the accent sensitivity is changed.

- **Repopulate Catalog**—This option updates the catalog with recent changes.

- **Tables/Views**—This configuration page allows tables and views to be added or removed from the catalog. This page also provides the capability to manage the change tracking functionality of an index.

- **Population Schedule**—This configuration page allows the scheduling of the catalog rebuilding process.

> **Note**
>
> Only the full crawl is designed to maximize hardware resources for maximum speed. Incremental, manual, and auto change tracking are not designed to maximize hardware usage.

Many of the catalog management actions can also be accessed through the full-text DDL. The following code shows the syntax of the ALTER FULLTEXT CATALOG statement:

```
ALTER FULLTEXT CATALOG catalog_name
{ REBUILD [ WITH ACCENT_SENSITIVITY = { ON | OFF } ]
| REORGANIZE
| AS DEFAULT
}
```

Accessing Full-Text Properties

Table 10.1 lists Transact-SQL (TSQL) functions that can be used to access the properties of the full-text search components.

Table 10.1   **Full-Text Properties**

Function	Property
COLUMNPROPERTY	IsFullTextIndexed
COLUMNPROPERTY	FullTextTypeColumn
SERVERPROPERTY	IsFullTextInstalled
DATABASEPROPERTYEX	IsFullTextEnabled
INDEXPROPERTY	IsFullTextKey
OBJECTPROPERTYEX	TableFullTextBackgroundUpdateIndexOn
OBJECTPROPERTYEX	TableFullTextCatalogId
OBJECTPROPERTYEX	TableFullTextChangeTrackingOn
OBJECTPROPERTYEX	TableFullTextDocsProcessed

Table 10.1 **continued**

Function	Property
OBJECTPROPERTYEX	TableFullTextFailCount
OBJECTPROPERTYEX	TableFullTextItemCount
OBJECTPROPERTYEX	TableFullTextKeyColumn
OBJECTPROPERTYEX	TableFullTextPendingChanges
OBJECTPROPERTYEX	TableFullTextPopulateStatus
OBJECTPROPERTYEX	TableHasActiveFullTextIndex
FULLTEXTCATALOGPROPERTY	AccentSensitivity
FULLTEXTCATALOGPROPERTY	IndexSize
FULLTEXTCATALOGPROPERTY	ItemCount
FULLTEXTCATALOGPROPERTY	LogSize
FULLTEXTCATALOGPROPERTY	MergeStatus
FULLTEXTCATALOGPROPERTY	PopulateCompletionAge
FULLTEXTCATALOGPROPERTY	PopulateStatus
FULLTEXTCATALOGPROPERTY	UniqueKeyCount
FULLTEXTSERVICEPROPERTY	ResourceUsage
FULLTEXTSERVICEPROPERTY	ConnectTimeout
FULLTEXTSERVICEPROPERTY	IsFullTextInstalled
FULLTEXTSERVICEPROPERTY	DataTimeout
FULLTEXTSERVICEPROPERTY	LoadOSResources
FULLTEXTSERVICEPROPERTY	VerifySignature

You can use the following example to access the PopulateStatus property associated with the FULLTEXTCATALOGPROPERTY function:

```
USE AdventureWorks
GO
SELECT FULLTEXTCATALOGPROPERTY (N'Documents Catalog' ,
➥'PopulateStatus');
GO
```

Table 10.2 shows the possible codes returned by the command and the meaning associated with each code.

Table 10.2 **Full-Text Catalog Population Status Codes**

Code	Name
0	Idle
1	Full population in progress
2	Paused
3	Throttled
4	Recovering
5	Shutdown
6	Incremental population in progress
7	Building index
8	Disk is full; Paused
9	Change tracking

You can use the following example to access the
TableFulltextPopulateStatus property associated with the
OBJECTPROPERTYEX function:

```
USE AdventureWorks
GO
SELECT OBJECTPROPERTYEX
  (OBJECT_ID(N'AdventureWorks.Production.Document'),
    'TableFulltextPopulateStatus')
GO
```

Table 10.3 shows the possible codes returned by the command and the
meaning associated with each code.

Table 10.3 **Full-Text Index Population Status Codes**

Code	Name
0	Idle
1	Full population in progress
2	Incremental population in progress
3	Propagation of tracked changes in progress
4	Background update index in progress
5	Full-text indexing is throttled or paused

For additional information on the specific syntax required by each function and the different return codes associated with each property, review the following MSDN link:

http://msdn2.microsoft.com/en-us/library/ms142579.aspx

Removing Full-Text Catalog and Indexes

Full-text catalogs and indexes can be removed from the database through the SQL Server Management Studio as well as full-text DDL.

You can use the following command to remove the full-text index on the Production.Document table:

```
USE AdventureWorks
GO
DROP FULLTEXT INDEX ON Production.Document
GO
```

To remove the Documents Catalog from the AdventureWorks database, you can use the following command:

```
USE AdventureWorks
GO
DROP FULLTEXT CATALOG [Documents Catalog]
GO
```

Administering the Full-Text Search

Part of your role is to administer the server running the full-text search. The administration of full-text search includes adding iFilters and word breakers, backing up and restoring the catalog, and configuring the Full-Text Service account.

Subsequent sections within this chapter look into and demonstrate common procedures used to administer a full-text search environment.

Administering iFilters

iFilters are used to extract key words from documents stored as binary and image data types. This can include MS Word, MS Excel, Adobe PDF, and TIFF images.

Use the sys.fulltext_document_types catalog view to obtain a list of currently installed iFilters. The following code demonstrates the syntax of the catalog view:

```
select document_type, path from sys.fulltext_document_types
```

If an iFilter is not included by default, it must be manually added to prevent the full-text search engine from logging errors when attempting to index data. One of the most common iFilters is provided by Adobe; this iFilter allows extraction of key words from Adobe PDF files stored in columns of the varbinary(max) and image data types.

Follow these steps to add the Adobe PDF iFilter to the SQL Server, but before beginning the process, download the iFilter from

http://www.adobe.com/support/downloads/detail.jsp?ftpID=2611

1. Launch the PDF iFilter setup program.
2. On the Welcome page, click the Next button.
3. On the License page, click the Accept button.
4. On the Destination Location page, accept the default path and click the Next button.
5. When prompted, click OK to finish the installation.

After the iFilter has been installed, execute the following command to register the operating system iFilters with SQL server; this includes the newly installed PDF iFilter.

```
exec sp_fulltext_service 'load_os_resources',1
```

Now restart SQL Server.

When the server restarts, the sys.fulltext_document_types catalog view should now list the .pdf type.

Administering Word Breakers

SQL Server 2005 comes with word breakers for 23 different languages; however, not all of them are installed by default. Only 17 of the 23 available languages are available when you're creating full-text indexes. Use the following command to retrieve a complete list of registered word breakers:

```
select * from sys.fulltext_languages
```

Following are the languages that are not installed by default and the three-letter keys that SQL Server uses to identify these languages. The three-letter key is used in the following demonstration.

- Danish (dan)
- Polish (plk)
- Portuguese-Brazilian (ptb)
- Portuguese-Iberian (pts)
- Russian (rus)
- Turkish (trk)

The following procedure demonstrates how to add the Polish language word breaker and stemmer to the SQL Server instance. The location for the noise and stemmer files used when adding language support is in the FTData folder located beneath the MSSQL instance folder. For example, the file path for INSTANCE01 on the server SQL01 is D:\Program Files\Microsoft SQL Server\MSSQL.1\MSSQL\FTData\.

First, follow these steps to add the Polish stemmer class to the list of CLSIDs located under the MSSearch\CLSID Registry key:

1. To open the Registry Editor, click Start, Run; type **Regedit** in the Run field, and then click OK.

2. Navigate to the HKLM\SOFTWARE\Microsoft\Microsoft SQL Server\MSSQL.1\MSSearch\CLSID key.

3. Select Edit, New, Key and type **{B8713269-2D9D-4BF5-BF40-2615D75723D8}** as the key name.

4. Right-click the Default Registry value, click Modify, type **lrpolish.dll** in the Value data field, and click OK.

Next, follow these steps to add the Polish word breaker class to the list of CLSIDs located under the MSSearch\CLSID Registry key:

1. To open the Registry Editor, click Start, Run; type **Regedit** in the Run field, and then click OK.

2. Navigate to the HKLM\SOFTWARE\Microsoft\Microsoft SQL Server\MSSQL.1\MSSearch\CLSID key.

3. Select Edit, New, Key and type **{CA665B09-4642-4C84-A9B7-9B8F3CD7C3F6}** as the key name.

4. Right-click the Default Registry value, click Modify, type **lrpolish.dll** in the Value data field, and click OK.

Finally, follow these steps to add the Polish language details to the list of Languages located under the MSSearch\ Language Registry key:

1. To open the Registry Editor, click Start, Run; type Regedit in the Run field, and then click OK.

2. Navigate to the HKLM\SOFTWARE\Microsoft\Microsoft SQL Server\MSSQL.1\MSSearch\Language key.

3. Select Edit, New, Key and type **plk** as the key name.

4. Under the plk key, add the values listed in Table 10.4. The <path> represents the full path to the NoiseFile and TsaurusFile files.

Table 10.4   **Polish Language Support Details**

Type	Name	Value
String	NoiseFile	<path>\noisePLK.txt
String	TsaurusFile	<path>\tsPLK.xml
DWORD (HEX)	Locale	00000415
String	WBreakerClass	{CA665B09-4642-4C84-A9B7-9B8F3CD7C3F6}
String	StemmerClass	{B8713269-2D9D-4BF5-BF40-2615D75723D8}

Figure 10.7 shows what the plk key should look like after each of the Polish language values from Table 10.4 has been entered.

After entering the required information, run the command EXEC sp_fulltext_service 'update_languages' and then restart SQL Server. Follow these steps to execute the necessary command before restarting the SQL Server:

1. From the test server (SQL01), choose Start, All Programs, Microsoft SQL Server 2005, SQL Server Management Studio.

2. Select Database Engine from the Server Type drop-down; then enter the server and instance name (**SQL01\INSTANCE01**).

3. Select Windows Authentication from the Authentication drop-down menu and then click the Connect button.

4. A connection to the database engine is made. If the Object Explorer pane is not visible, press the F8 button.

5. Click the New Query button, type EXEC **sp_fulltext_service 'update_languages'**, and then click the Execute button.

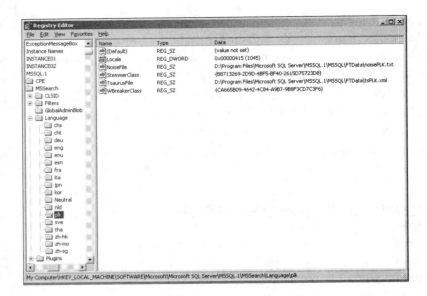

FIGURE 10.7
Polish language details.

The command should complete successfully. Now restart SQL Server to complete the configuration change. After the server restarts, run the following command, and the Polish language should be listed:

```
select * from sys.fulltext_languages
```

Information for the additional languages not registered by default is shown in Table 10.5 through Table 10.9.

Table 10.5   **Danish Language Support Details**

Type	Name	Value
String	NoiseFile	`<path>`\noiseDAN.txt
String	TsaurusFile	`<path>`\noiseDAN.txt
DWORD (HEX)	Locale	00000406
String	WBreakerClass	{16BC5CE4-2C78-4CB9-80D5-386A68CC2B2D}
String	StemmerClass	{83BC7EF7-D27B-4950-A743-0F8E5CA928F8}

Table 10.6   **Portuguese-Brazilian Language Support Details**

Type	Name	Value
String	NoiseFile	`<path>\noisePTB.txt`
String	TsaurusFile	`<path>\tsPTB.xml`
DWORD (HEX)	Locale	`00000416`
String	WBreakerClass	`{25B7FD48-5404-4BEB-9D80-B6982AF404FD}`
String	StemmerClass	`{D5FCDD7E-DBFF-473F-BCCD-3AFD1890EA85}`

Table 10.7   **Portuguese-Iberian Language Support Details**

Type	Name	Value
String	NoiseFile	`<path>\noisePTS.txt`
String	TsaurusFile	`<path>\tsPTS.xml`
DWORD (HEX)	Locale	`00000816`
String	WBreakerClass	`{5D5F3A69-620C-4952-B067-4D0126BB6086}`
String	StemmerClass	`{D4171BC4-90BE-4F70-8610-DAB1C17F063C}`

Table 10.8   **Russian Language Support Details**

Type	Name	Value
String	NoiseFile	`<path>\noiseRUS.txt`
String	TsaurusFile	`<path>\tsRUS.xml`
DWORD (HEX)	Locale	`00000419`
String	WBreakerClass	`{20036404-F1AF-11D2-A57F-006052076F32}`
String	StemmerClass	`{20036414-F1AF-11D2-A57F-006052076F32}`

Table 10.9   **Turkish Language Support Details**

Type	Name	Value
String	NoiseFile	`<path>\noiseTRK.txt`
String	TsaurusFile	`<path>\tsTRK.xml`
DWORD (HEX)	Locale	`0000041f`

Table 10.9   **continued**

Type	Name	Value
String	WBreakerClass	{8DF412D1-62C7-4667-BBEC-38756576C21B}
String	StemmerClass	{23A9C1C3-3C7A-4D2C-B894-4F286459DAD6}

Backing Up and Restoring Full-Text Catalogs

This version of SQL Server enables you to back up and restore full-text catalogs independently of the database that holds the indexed data. This functionality is new to SQL Server 2005 and provides numerous advantages:

- **Backup Time**—The backup time is reduced because the full-text catalogs do not have to be backed up with the entire database.

- **Recovery Time**—In the event a catalog becomes corrupt or otherwise unusable, the recovery time is improved because the entire database doesn't need to be restored just to recover the full-text catalog.

- **Repopulation Requirements**—Restoring a full-text catalog, along with attaching and detaching the catalog, no longer requires a full population.

- **Management**—Full-text catalogs can be backed up and restored essentially the same way database files are managed. This includes advanced features such as differential backups and reliability options.

For additional information on backup and restore best practices for SQL Server and full-text catalogs, see Chapter 17, "Backing Up and Restoring the SQL Server 2005 Environment" (online).

Configuring the Full-Text Service Account

If you want to ensure a secure environment, it is highly recommended to use a low-privileged domain user account to run the Full-Text Search service. Likewise, do not use LOCAL SYSTEM, LOCAL SERVICE, or NETWORK SERVICE because these accounts could provide an elevation of privileges for the Full-Text Search service.

Note

As a security best practice, it is highly recommended to change the Full-Text Service account after installation of SQL Server.

Use the following procedure to configure the Full-Text Service account on SQL Server:

1. From the test server (SQL01), choose Start, All Programs, Microsoft SQL Server 2005, Configuration Tools, SQL Server Configuration Manager.

2. Select the SQL Server 2005 Services menu item to display all the SQL-related services on the server.

3. Right-click SQL Server FullText Search (<*instance name*>) and then click Properties.

4. On the Log On tab, enter the low privileged user account and password in the fields provided.

5. Click the Restart button to restart the Full-Text Search service and complete the change.

Summary

By developing applications that use SQL Server 2005, an organization can immediately benefit from the enterprise class full-text search functionality. Full-Text Search provides robust and highly scalable indexing and querying components that allow a large amount of unstructured data to be tamed.

As with other aspects of SQL Server, the management and maintenance of the full-text components play an important factor in keeping the Full-Text Search component functioning correctly and running smoothly.

Best Practices

Following are best practices that can be taken from this chapter:

- Group indexes with similar updated properties in the same catalog to help maintain indexing ranking consistency because the ranking statistics can change depending on whether intermediate indexes have been merged.

- If the underlying table is very large, place the index into its own catalogs. Each catalog can then be placed on a different set of disks.

- When choosing a unique index, you often achieve a performance gain when you select a clustered index.

- The key size of the unique index is very important when attempting to achieve maximum performance. An index key based on the INT data type is considered the best-performing unique key for a full-text index.

- Although the maximum key size is 900 bytes, it is recommended to never exceed a unique key size of 100 bytes.

- Regularly defragment indexes and rebuild catalogs to improve query performance and ranking.

- Change the Full-Text Service account after installation of SQL Server.

CHAPTER 11

Creating Packages and Transferring Data

Packages allow you to control not only the transfer of data in and out of the SQL Server 2005 server (commonly referred to as extraction, transformation, and loading, or ETL for short), but also to automate a variety of maintenance and administrative functions. This can all be done through a graphical development environment that provides debugging and troubleshooting support.

The types of tasks you are likely to want to automate include the following:

- Transfer data
- Maintain databases
- Run commands

The packages model gives you access to intensive script-like control and power, but in an easy-to-use and modular interface. Similar capabilities exist in scripting, batch files, or programming languages such as Visual Basic. However, Integration Services packages bring those capabilities to a model that is built around the database architecture, the tool set, and has predefined tasks that are database oriented and geared toward a database administrator (DBA).

Throughout this chapter, the optional SQL Server 2005 sample files will be used. This allows you to do the procedures shown in the chapter with the same data and follow the steps exactly. The procedures for installing the sample files are found in the appendix of this book (online).

> **Note**
>
> The SQL Server 2005 Integration Services provide a complex and rich set of development tools for integrating and processing information. These tools allow sophisticated programmatic solutions to be developed to meet complex business needs.
>
> However, the administration and maintenance requirements of DBAs are usually more straightforward, simple, and require less development effort. The SQL Server 2005 Integration Services tools also simplify the process of developing administration and maintenance solutions. This chapter focuses on the needs of the DBAs rather than those of a developer.

Packages

Packages consist of control flows and control elements, data flows and data elements, connections, and various supporting structures such as event handlers. Although each package is self-contained, packages are organized into projects for ease of development and distribution.

Understanding how these various pieces fit together is key to being able to use packages to automate administrative and maintenance tasks.

Projects and Solutions

Packages are organized into projects and solutions. Projects are containers for packages. Each project can contain multiple packages. In addition to the packages, a project contains the definitions for data sources and data source views that are used by the packages.

A solution is a container for organizing projects that are related or that compose a business solution. When a project is created, the Business Intelligence Development Studio automatically creates a solution for the project if one does not already exist.

DBAs rarely use solutions or projects, because most packages used by DBAs are standalone packages.

Tasks and Elements

Tasks are the individual units of work in a package. You can use tasks to do such things as execute a SQL statement, import data, copy a database, send mail, or initiate a data flow. Each task will have a variety of configuration parameters contained within it.

For ETL within the data flows, the individual units of work are known as components. These come in three types: sources, transformations, and destinations. These control where data comes from, how it is changed, and where it goes to, respectively.

A multitude of different task and component types gives you a rich set of tools to automate work. The full list of task types is given in the "Control Flow" and "Data Flow" sections.

Tasks are connected into a flow, which specifies the execution order for the tasks. Each package contains a control flow and one or more data flows.

Control Flow

The control flow is the organizing element of the package. This is the flow of tasks that control what the package will do, including multiple data flows, if needed. The control flow can contain nested control flows in what are known as containers.

Table 11.1 shows different control flow tasks.

Table 11.1   **Control Flow Tasks**

Task Type	Description	Task
Data Flow Task	The task that runs data flows to extract data, apply column level transformations, and load data	Data Flow Task
Data Preparation Tasks	The tasks that copy files and directories, download files and data, execute web methods, and apply operations to XML documents	File System Task FTP Task Web Service Task XML Task
Workflow Tasks	The tasks that communicate with other processes to run packages, run programs or batch files, send and receive messages between packages, send email messages, read Windows Management Instrumentation (WMI) data, and watch for WMI events	Execute Package Task Execute DTS 2000 Package Task Execute Process Task Message Queue Task Send Mail Task WMI Data Reader Task WMI Event Watcher Task

Table 11.1   **continued**

Task Type	Description	Task
SQL Server Tasks	The tasks that access, copy, insert, delete, and modify SQL Server objects and data	Bulk Insert Task Execute SQL Task Transfer Database Task Transfer Error Messages Task Transfer Jobs Task Transfer Logins Task Transfer Master Stored Procedures Task Transfer SQL Server Objects Task
Scripting Tasks	The tasks that extend package functionality by using scripts	ActiveX Script Task Script Task
Analysis Services Tasks	The tasks that create, modify, delete, and process Analysis Services objects	Analysis Services Processing Task Analysis Services Execute DDL Task Data Mining Query Task

Additional information about each of the tasks can be found in the SQL Server 2005 Books Online.

Containers are the building blocks of the packages. They allow package developers to organize tasks and set up repeating tasks, such as conditional loops. Containers can contain tasks and other containers, allowing for sophisticated logic.

The different types of containers are list in Table 11.2.

Table 11.2   **Container Types**

Container	Description
Foreach Loop	The control flow in the container is repeated using a counter.
For Loop	The control flow in the container is repeated until a test condition is reached.
Sequence	This container is used to sequence and isolate a package into smaller control flows that run in order.
Task Host	This container is used to isolate a single task, which is useful for extending variable and event handling to the task level.

Data Flow

The data flow determines how data is moved, which is ultimately the main goal of the package. This is the nuts and bolts of the extraction, transformation, and loading of the data. Data flows are organized into sources, transformations, and destinations.

The data flows consist of connected components. Each components output is connected to the input of the next component, which allows for the transfer of data as columns.

A variety of sources are available to you in the data flow elements. The sources and destinations are listed in Table 11.3 and Table 11.4.

Table 11.3 **Source Types**

Source	Description
DataReader Source	Consumes data from a .NET Framework data provider
Excel Source	Extracts data from an Excel file
Flat File Source	Extracts data from a flat file
OLE DB Source	Consumes data from an OLE DB provider
Raw File Source	Extracts raw data from a file
XML Source	Extracts data from an XML file

Table 11.4 **Destination Types**

Destination	Description
Data Mining Model Training Destination	Trains data mining models. This allows the data flow to send its output to SQL Server 2005 Analysis Services model.
DataReader Destination	Exposes the data in a data flow by using the ADO.NET DataReader interface.
Dimension Processing Destination	Loads and processes to a SQL Server 2005 Analysis Services (SSAS) dimension.
Excel Destination	Writes data to an Excel Workbook.
Flat File Destination	Writes data to a flat file.
OLE DB Destination	Loads data using an OLE DB provider.
Partition Processing Destination	Loads and processes an Analysis Services partition.
Raw File Destination	Writes raw data to a file.
Recordset Destination	Creates an ADO recordset.

Table 11.4   continued

Destination	Description
SQL Server Mobile Destination	Inserts rows into a SQL Server Mobile database.
SQL Server Destination	Bulk inserts data into a SQL Server 2005 table or view.

The possible transformations are where the data flow really shows its versatility. There are transformations that operate on individual rows and on sets of rows. There are transformations that can join rows, split rows, or even do lookups into another table for references. This gives you a multitude of options for what to do with the data being moved between a source and a destination.

The transformation can also be executed sequentially to allow more than one transformation to be done on the data, and different flow paths can be taken dependent on the data as well, allowing decisions to be made at the data level.

Table 11.5 lists the data flow elements that can clean data and run data mining transformations.

Table 11.5   Business Intelligence Transformation Types

Transformation	Description
Fuzzy Grouping Transformation	The transformation that standardizes values in column data
Fuzzy Lookup Transformation	The transformation that looks up values in a reference table using a fuzzy match
Term Extraction Transformation	The transformation that extracts terms from text
Term Lookup Transformation	The transformation that looks up terms in a reference table and counts terms extracted from text
Data Mining Query Transformation	The transformation that runs data mining prediction queries

Row transformations (listed in Table 11.6) are the most commonly used data flow transformation elements. They can transform the column values or create new columns. Typical uses are to change the data type of a column, manipulate text, such as splitting a name field into first and last names, or create a copy of a column for future manipulation.

Table 11.6   **Row Transformation Types**

Transformation	Description
Character Map Transformation	The transformation that applies string functions to character data
Copy Column Transformation	The transformation that adds copies of input columns to the transformation output
Data Conversion Transformation	The transformation that converts the data type of a column to a different data type
Derived Column Transformation	The transformation that populates columns with the results of expressions
Script Component	The transformation that uses script to extract, transform, or load data
OLE DB Command Transformation	The transformation that runs SQL commands for each row in a data flow

The rowset transformations (listed in Table 11.7) perform operations on an entire set of rows. Examples of typical uses include sorting a rowset or averaging columns in a rowset.

Table 11.7   **Rowset Transformation Types**

Transformation	Description
Aggregate Transformation	The transformation that performs aggregations such as AVERAGE, SUM, and COUNT
Sort Transformation	The transformation that sorts data
Percentage Sampling Transformation	The transformation that creates a sample data set using a percentage to specify the sample size
Row Sampling Transformation	The transformation that creates a sample data set by specifying the number of rows in the sample
Pivot Transformation	The transformation that creates a less normalized version of a normalized table
Unpivot Transformation	The transformation that creates a more normalized version of a non-normalized table

The various data flow transformations show in Table 11.8 allow data to be split, joined, or used as a lookup reference. Frequently, rowsets must be split into separate groups, such as when cleaning a set of data where rows meeting a certain condition must be separated. For example, maybe a table of customers is being cleaned to remove those below a certain age. The conditional split would be used to separate the data on the basis of that condition.

Table 11.8   **Lookup, Split and Join Transformation Types**

Transformation	Description
Conditional Split Transformation	The transformation that routes data rows to different outputs
Multicast Transformation	The transformation that distributes data sets to multiple outputs
Union All Transformation	The transformation that merges multiple data sets
Merge Transformation	The transformation that merges two sorted data sets
Merge Join Transformation	The transformation that joins two data sets using a FULL, LEFT, or INNER join
Lookup Transformation	The transformation that looks up values in a reference table using an exact match

The miscellaneous transformations shown in Table 11.9 allow for information to flow into and out of the data flow stream. For example, the import and export transformations allow data to be brought into and out of the data flow via files. The audit transformation allows data from the running environment to be brought into the data flow, for example, by allowing the login name of the user to be put into a column.

Table 11.9   **Miscellaneous Transformation Types**

Transformation	Description
Export Column Transformation	The transformation that inserts data from a data flow into a file
Import Column Transformation	The transformation that reads data from a file and adds it to a data flow
Audit Transformation	The transformation that makes information about the environment available to the data flow in a package
Row Count Transformation	The transformation that counts rows as they move through it and stores the final count in a variable
Slowly Changing Dimension Transformation	The transformation that configures the updating of a slowly changing dimension

Connections

Connections allow the package to connect to a variety of sources, destinations, and services. These include databases, flat files, email services, FTP services, and others. Table 11.10 contains a list of the various connection types.

Table 11.10   **Connection Types**

Connection Managers	Description
ADO Connection Manager	For connecting to relational data sources by using ADO
ADO.NET Connection Manager	For connecting to relational data sources by using ADO.NET
Microsoft .NET Data Provider for mySAP Business Suite	The Microsoft .NET Data Provider for mySAP Business Suite, for accessing SAP data
Analysis Services Connection Manager	For connecting to an instance of Analysis Services or an Analysis Services project
Excel Connection Manager	For connecting to Excel workbooks
File Connection Manager	For connecting to a single file or folder
Flat File Connection Manager	For accessing data in a single flat file
FTP Connection Manager	For connecting to an FTP server
HTTP Connection Manager	For connecting to a web service or website
MSMQ Connection Manager	For connecting to a Message Queuing (also known as MSMQ) message queue
Multiple Files Connection Manager	For connecting to multiple files and folders
Multiple Flat Files Connection Manager	For accessing data in multiple flat files
ODBC Connection Manager	For connecting to data sources by using ODBC
OLE DB Connection Manager	For connecting to data sources by using OLE DB
SMO Connection Manager	For connecting to SQL Server Management Objects (SMO)
SMTP Connection Manager	For connecting to SMTP servers
SQL Server Compact Edition Connection Manager	For connecting to SQL Server Compact Edition databases
WMI Connection Manager	For connecting to a Windows Management Instrumentation (WMI) server and specifying a server namespace

Connections are instantiated with connection managers, which are logical representations of the connections. The connection managers contain all the properties needed for the connection. There can be more than one connection manager of the same type, such as when connections to multiple flat files are needed. The connection managers can also be shared, such as for a single SMTP mail server.

Event Handlers

Event handlers trigger when the package raises events. These events are raised when significant conditions occur, including errors (OnError), warnings (OnWarning), information messages (OnInformation), or when the package completes (OnPostExecute).

Table 11.11 lists the various event handler types. The most commonly used ones are OnError, OnWarning, and OnPostExecute.

Table 11.11   **Event Handler Types**

Event Handler	Trigger Event
OnError	The event handler for the OnError event. This event is raised by an executable when an error occurs.
OnWarning	The event handler for the OnWarning event. This event is raised by an executable when a warning occurs.
OnPostExecute	The event handler for the OnPostExecute event. This event is raised by an executable immediately after it has finished running.
OnExecStatusChanged	The event handler for the OnExecStatusChanged event. This event is raised by an executable when its execution status changes.
OnInformation	The event handler for the OnInformation event. This event is raised during the validation and execution of an executable to report information. This event conveys information only, no errors or warnings.
OnPostValidate	The event handler for the OnPostValidate event. This event is raised by an executable when its validation is finished.
OnPreExecute	The event handler for the OnPreExecute event. This event is raised by an executable immediately before it runs.
OnPreValidate	The event handler for the OnPreValidate event. This event is raised by an executable when its validation starts.

Table 11.11   **continued**

Event Handler	Trigger Event
OnProgress	The event handler for the OnProgress event. This event is raised by an executable when measurable progress is made by the executable.
OnQueryCancel	The event handler for the OnQueryCancel event. This event is raised by an executable to determine whether it should stop running.
OnTaskFailed	The event handler for the OnTaskFailed event. This event is raised by a task when it fails.
OnVariableValueChanged	The event handler for the OnVariableValueChanged event. This event is raised by an executable when the value of a variable changes.

Event handlers launch control flows, which can include all the same tasks as the package control flow. In effect, the event handlers are containers with control and data flows that execute only when their trigger condition is encountered.

Log Providers and Logging

When packages execute, detailed information is generated about the execution of the package. This information is very useful for troubleshooting and auditing the package. By default, this information is displayed in the console but not stored anywhere. This information can be captured for later review and analysis into logs.

The package can log to a variety of providers, including a text file, the Windows Event Log, or SQL Server. Table 11.12 shows the different log provider types. Custom log providers can be created as well.

Table 11.12   **Log Provider Types**

Log Provider	Description
Text File	The Text File log provider, which writes log entries to ASCII text files in a comma-separated value (CSV) format. The default file name extension for this provider is .log.
SQL Server Profiler	The SQL Server Profiler log provider, which writes traces that you can view using SQL Server Profiler. The default file name extension for this provider is .trc.

Table 11.12   **continued**

Log Provider	Description
SQL Server	The SQL Server log provider, which writes log entries to the sysdtslog90 table in a SQL Server 2005 database.
Windows Event Log	The Windows Event log provider, which writes entries to the Application log in the Windows Event log on the local computer.
XML File	The XML File log provider, which writes log files to an XML file. The default file name extension for this provider is .xml.

The package can log to more than one provider at a time—for example, to both the Windows Event Log and to the SQL Server.

Creating Packages

As stated earlier, packages are the core of the Integration Services. Packages are developed in the Business Intelligence Development Studio, which is a sophisticated development environment with extensive development and debugging features. The specific tool is the SSIS Designer, which is the graphical tool to develop and maintain the SSIS packages. The SSIS Designer allows you to

- Build control and data flows
- Configure event handlers
- Execute and debug packages
- Graphically follow the package execution

This section will cover using the Designer in creating a package, reviewing the package, and finally running the package.

Create a Project

To start, a project needs to be created to contain the packages. This project can contain multiple packages that are related for ease of maintenance and organization.

To create a project, follow these steps:

1. Launch SQL Server Business Intelligence Development Studio.

2. Select File, New, Project.

3. Select the Integration Services Project template.

4. Change the name—in this case, **Customer Project**.

5. Select a location to store the project, such as c:\projects\.

6. Leave the Solution Name as is—in this case, Customer Project. A directory will be created for the new solution.

7. Click OK.

The project will be opened with a default package name Package.dtsx.

Create a Package

Create a simple package, as was done in Chapter 5, "Administering SQL Server 2005 Integration Services." This package will import the Customers.txt sample file, which contains customer records for more than 2,000 customers. The data contains name, birth date, yearly income, occupation, and other key data.

To create the import package, follow these steps:

1. Launch the SQL Server Business Intelligence Development Studio.

2. Open the Customer Project created in the previous section.

3. Click Project, SSIS Import and Export Wizard.

4. Click Next.

5. In the Data Source pull-down, select Flat File Source.

6. In the File Name field, click Browse to browse for the file to import.

7. Navigate to C:\Program Files\Microsoft SQL Server\90\ Samples\Integration Services\Package Samples\ ExecuteSQLStatementsInLoop Sample\Data Files\.

8. Select the Customers.txt file and click Open.

9. Check the box Column names in the first data row.

10. Click Next.

11. Review the columns the wizard will import.

12. Click Next.

13. Click New to create a new database for the data import.

14. Enter the name for the database—in this case, **Customer**.

15. In the Data file size section, change the Initial size to **20** megabytes.

16. In the Log file size section, change the Initial size to **4** megabytes.

17. Click OK to create the database.

18. Click Next.

19. Click Preview to review the columns. Click Close to close the preview window.

20. Click Next.

21. Review the summary. Note that the location that the package will be saved to and that the package will not be run.

22. Click Finish to build and save the package. A new package name, Package1.dtsx, will be created.

23. Click Close to exit the wizard.

24. Select File, Save All to save the project.

The project now has a package that will import the Customers.txt source file into a Customers table in the Customer database.

Walkthrough of a Package

To better familiarize you with the Business Intelligence Development Studio SSIS Designer package development user interface, this section will explore the interface by using the newly created customer import package.

The Solution Explorer shows the view of the Customer project with the packages, as can be seen in Figure 11.1. This view is located in the SSIS Designer in the upper-right pane. The package that was created in the previous section can be seen.

Selecting the Package1.dtsx package will show the properties of the package in the Properties window in the lower-right pane. This is true of the interface in general; selecting an object will show its properties.

The name of the package can be changed here to something more appropriate, such as Import Customers. To do this

1. Select the Package1.dtsx package in the Solution Explorer.

2. In the Properties pane, change the filename to **CustomerImport.dtsx**.

3. The interface asks whether the package object name should be changed as well. Click Yes to accept the change.

4. Select File, Save All to save the changes.

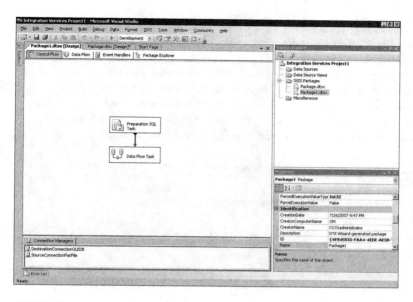

FIGURE 11.1
The Customer project.

The SSIS Packages folder in the Solution Explorer will show the updated name. The default package Package.dtsx can be deleted in the Solution Explorer window as well by right-clicking the package and selecting Delete. After the changes, only one package, named CustomerImport.dtsx, should be in the Solution Explorer.

The Error List window is located below the Connection Managers window and shows any errors, warnings, or messages that the package generates. This is active and will show messages as soon as they are detected by the interface during the design of the package.

Walkthrough the Control Flow

In the Control Flow window in the left pane, the control steps of the CustomerImport package can be seen. These steps are called *tasks* or *components*. There are only two tasks in this particular package, the Preparation SQL Task and the Data Flow Task. Clicking the Preparation SQL Task will change the focus of the Properties pane and show the properties of the task. These properties are somewhat cryptic.

A better method of reviewing the configuration of a task is to use the edit function. This can be accessed by selecting the task in the designer pane and right-clicking to select Edit. Doing this for the CustomerImport package Preparation SQL Task shows the configuration shown in Figure 11.2. The figure shows that the task is an Execute SQL Task type, and the SQL Statement parameters can be seen in the SQLStatement field, although the statement scrolls off the field. This task essentially creates the Customers table in the Customer database in preparation for the import.

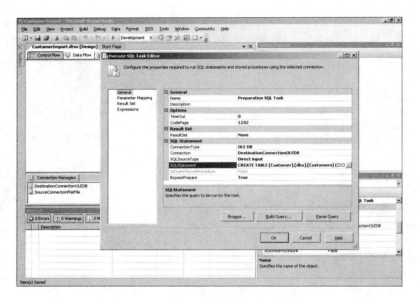

FIGURE 11.2
The Task Editor window.

The Task Editor will change depending on the specific task being edited. On the left side of the interface is a vertical toolbox tab. Clicking this pulls out the Toolbox window that shows all the control flow tasks that are available. These range from the Execute SQL Task to Send Mail Task to maintenance tasks such as Back Up Database Task. In the Control Flow designer window, the toolbox window will show only control flow tasks. See the "Control Flow" section earlier in this chapter for a list of all the control flow tasks.

Walkthrough the Data Flow

The Data Flow Task shown in the Control Flow designer window is expanded in the Data Flow designer window, which can be accessed by editing the Data Flow Task or by clicking the Data Flow tab in the Designer window. The steps in the data flow are called *items,* or also more generically as components, especially when referring to control flow tasks and data flow items at the same time. The Data Flow designer window for the CustomerImport package shows three items:

- Source—Customers_txt
- Data Conversion 1
- Destination—Customers

These three items are shown in Figure 11.3. The overall architecture of the data flow is to take data from a source, transform it in some manner, and finally put the transformed data into a destination.

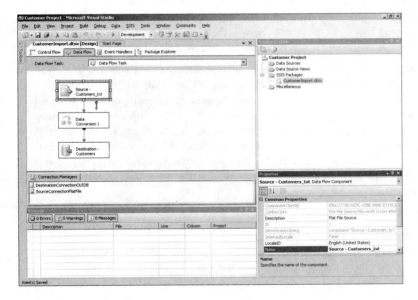

FIGURE 11.3
The Data Flow designer.

Right-clicking the Source—Customers_txt item and selecting Edit shows the configuration of the source. The item in this case is a Flat File Source, as indicated by the title of the window. Clicking the Connection Managers option shows the name of the connection manager, which will be examined a bit later in this section. Clicking the Preview button shows a preview of the first 200 rows that will be imported from the source. Selecting the Columns option on the right shows the columns that are available from the source and also how the columns are mapped into the output. Columns can easily be renamed in this area, for example, by changing EmailAddress to SMTP in the Output Column. Finally, selecting the Error Output option allows you to indicate what to do, on a column-by-column basis, in response to errors. In the case of either errors in or truncation of the column data, the choices are to either fail the component (the default behavior), ignore the failure, or to redirect the row. Clicking OK saves the changes to the item.

Right-clicking the Data Conversion 1 item and selecting Edit shows the configuration of the transformation. The Data Conversion Transformation window shows the input columns, which are derived from the output of the previous step. This can be verified by noting that one of the available input columns is SMTP, which was changed in the source item. Again, in this step you can change the name of the column and specify the data type to be output. The data types can be any of the supported SQL data types. Other conversion attributes can be specified here as well.

Right-clicking the Destination—Customers item and selecting Edit shows the configuration properties of the OLE DB Destination. Selecting the Connection Managers option shows the destination configuration. The OLE DB connection manager setting specifies the destination connection manager, which will be discussed in the next section, "Walkthrough the Connection Managers." The Data access mode shows how the data will be inserted into the destination, and the table or view within the database can be selected as well. Various other options exist on this screen, as well, such as whether to lock the table when inserting.

> **Note**
>
> Because the table has not yet been created, an error is generated indicating that the Customers table does not exist in the Customer database.
>
> Click OK to clear the error and then click the New button next to the Name of the table or the view field. Then click OK to create the table.

Selecting the Mappings options in the OLE DB Destination Editor shows the mappings of the columns. This can be adjusted here if needed. Finally, the

Error Output option shows what will be done if errors occur during the insertion of the data.

Much like the control flow, the Data Flow designer pane has an associated toolbox that can be accessed via the vertical tab on the left pane. The toolbox is organized by sources, transformations, and destinations. See the "Data Flow" section earlier in this chapter for a description of all the item types in the data flow designer.

In both the control and data flow diagrams, notice that the tasks and items have arrows connecting the boxes. These arrows indicate the direction of the logic and the flow of the steps within the package. The output of one item leads directly to the input of the next item.

Walkthrough the Connection Managers

The Connection Managers window, located below the designer window, shows the source and destination connections—that is, where data is coming from and going to. The source connection will be looked at first and then the destination connection.

Right-click the SourceConnectionFlatFile connection manager and select Edit to see the properties of the source. In the General options, the filename and the format of the file are specified. In the Columns options window, the columns of the source are shown with the first 100 rows for verification. In the Advanced options window, you can adjust the details for each column, including the data type, the name of the column, and the length. You can click the Suggest Types button to scan the data and adjust the data type. Finally, use the Preview option window to preview the first 200 rows to ensure that the data is being read properly.

Editing the DestinationConnectionOLEDB connection shows the configuration setting of the destination. In this case, under the Connection options, the provider is shown as Native OLE DB\SQL Native Client. The server name is specified, as well as the form of authentication to use and the database to connect to. A Test Connection button lets you know whether the connection succeeded. The All options window allows you to set the configuration at a very detailed level, such as encryption or timeouts.

Interestingly, the specific table within the database is not specified in the destination connection manager. The connection is to the database rather than the table. The table to insert data to is specified at the item level in the data flow.

Running a Package

One of the nice features of the Business Intelligence Developer Interface is the capability to run the package in the UI. This allows you to test and debug packages in a controlled environment before unleashing them on production.

The Control Flow and Data Flow tabs of the package show the graphical view of the tasks in the package. In the graphical view of the flows, the status of the box is reflected in the color of the box:

- Green—Task Successful
- Yellow—Task in Progress
- Red—Task Failed

The Progress tab of the package shows the detailed progress, including useful information such as phase start and end, the percentage complete, and key diagnostic information. Within this window, it is easy to copy any message to paste it into a search or documentation.

Caution

The shortcut for running the debugger is the F5 key. This key conflicts with the standard Refresh key, which is also F5. This means if you attempt to refresh the screen using the standard shortcut screen, the package may unexpectedly execute.

Be careful when refreshing in the Business Intelligence Development Studio.

The package in the designer runs in debugging mode. To start debugging the package, follow these steps:

1. Launch the Business Intelligence Development Studio.

2. Open the Customer Project created earlier.

3. Click the CustomerImport.dtsx in the Solution Explorer.

4. Select Debug, Start Debugging to run the package.

5. The CustomerImport package control flow Preparation SQL Task will change to yellow and then to red, indicating a problem in the execution of the package.

6. Review the messages in the Output window in the lower-right corner. In particular, note the message "There is already an object named 'Customers' in the database."

7. Select the Data Flow tab and note that the data flow items have not executed, as they are still white (rather than yellow, green, or red).

8. Select the Debug, Stop Debugging menu option to halt the execution.

The problem is that the Customers table was already created earlier. This table could be manually deleted, but maybe it should be dropped as part of the package execution on a normal basis. To do this, the control flow of the CustomerImport package will be adjusted to drop the Customers table. To add this task to the control flow, follow these steps:

1. With the CustomerImport package Control Flow tab selected, click the Toolbox tab.

2. Select the Execute SQL Task control flow item and drag it to the Control Flow window. Position the task above the Preparation SQL Task.

Note

Two errors will come up immediately in the Error List, which are validation errors. One indicated that no connection manager is specified, and the other indicated that validation errors exist.

These errors are normal and will be resolved as the task is configured.

---

3. Edit the newly created task by right-clicking it and selecting Edit.

4. In the Name field, enter **Drop Customers Table SQL Task**. Enter this same text into the Description field.

5. In the Connection drop–down list, select the DestinationConnectionOLEDB connection manager.

6. In the SQLStatement field, click the button to expand the field and enter the text:

```
drop table [Customer].[dbo].[Customers]
GO
```

7. Click OK to close the SQLStatement window.

8. Click OK to close the Task Editor.

9. On the Drop Customers Table SQL Task there is a green arrow. Click the arrow and drag it to the top of the Preparation SQL Task. Click to attach the arrow.

10. Save the project.

The control flow for the package should now look like the flow in Figure 11.4. Notice that the errors have been resolved and there should be no errors in the Error List.

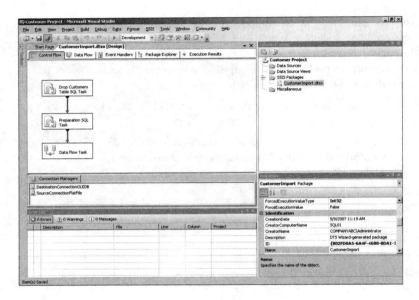

FIGURE 11.4
The CustomerImport package with Drop Customers Table SQL Task.

Now the CustomerImport package can be run again using the menu commands Debug, Start Debugging. The control flow steps will change from white to yellow as they execute, then from yellow to green as they complete successfully. This also applies to the data flow steps. This color coordination helps identify where the package is in its execution, which is much more useful in large or complex packages. This status can be viewed while the package is executing by selecting the appropriate tab in the design window.

Another useful tab is the Progress tab in the design window. The Progress tab show the detailed progress of each task in the control and data flows. It includes start and stop times, as well as detailed activities and percentages of completion. In the case of the Drop Customers Table SQL Task that was added to the package, the actual SQL query can be seen.

The package should execute successfully. This can be verified by reviewing the Output window, which gives a more concise view of the package status than the Progress window. The window should show a series of messages (the first and last two messages are shown) similar to the following:

```
SSIS package "CustomerImport.dtsx" starting.
....
Information: 0x4004300B at Data Flow Task,
     DTS.Pipeline: "component "Destination - Customers" (94)"
➡wrote 2058 rows.
SSIS package "CustomerImport.dtsx" finished: Success.
```

The last line indicates that the package completed successfully. The line above that indicates that 2,058 rows were written to the destination, in this case the Customers table in the Customer database.

After the execution has been verified, select Debug, Stop Debugging to return to design mode. Even after exiting the debugging mode, the previous package execution results can be reviewed in the Execution Results tab of the design window.

Note

Even though the package executed in the SSIS Designer in debugging mode, the changes to the data were real. The data was read from the customers.txt file, the Customers table in the Customer database was deleted, and a new table was created with the data from customers.txt. Any data in the original Customers table is lost.

When developing packages and projects, it is important to use a development database server to ensure there is no impact to production data.

Now that the package has been run, the next step is to save it where it can be used in production. Rarely will a package be executed in the Business Intelligence Development Studio for production use. See Chapter 5 for ways to import and export, store, and execute packages that are created in the designer.

Transforming Data

In the CustomerImport package, the data was transferred without any transformation. In this section, we'll look at how the data can be transformed while being transferred.

Suppose you get a request to import the Customer data into the Customer database, but the data owner wants the customers partitioned into two separate tables. One table (HighIncomeCustomers) will contain the customers with a yearly income of $100,000 or more and the other table (ModerateIncomeCustomers) will contain customers with less than a yearly income of $100,000.

The CustomerImport package will need to be modified to support this. This requires a conditional split, which is essentially a case statement based on the yearly income.

The first step is to adjust the control flow. In the control flow designer of the CustomerImport package, do the following:

1. Copy and paste the Drop Customers Table SQL Task.

2. Edit first the Drop Customers Table SQL Task, changing the Name and Description to **Drop HighIncomeCustomers Table SQL Task.**

3. Edit the SQLStatement to change the [Customer].[dbo].[Customers] to **[Customer].[dbo].[HighIncomeCustomers].**

4. Edit the second Drop Customers Table SQL Task, changing the Name and Description to **Drop ModerateIncomeCustomers Table SQL Task.**

5. Edit the SQLStatement to change the [Customer].[dbo].[Customers] to **[Customer].[dbo].[ModerateIncomeCustomers].**

6. Copy and paste the Preparation SQL Task.

7. Edit the first Preparation SQL Task, changing the Name and Description to **HighIncomeCustomers Preparation SQL Task.**

8. Edit the SQLStatement to change the [Customer].[dbo].[Customers] to **[Customer].[dbo].[HighIncomeCustomers].**

9. Edit the second Preparation SQL Task 1, changing the Name and Description to **ModerateIncomeCustomers Preparation SQL Task.**

10. Edit the SQLStatement to change the [Customer].[dbo].[Customers] to **[Customer].[dbo].[ModerateIncomeCustomers].**

11. Remove the existing arrows between the tasks by highlighting them and pressing Delete.

12. Drag the tasks into order with the drop tasks first, the preparation tasks next, and finally the Data Flow Task.

13. Select each task starting at the top and then drag the green arrow on the task to make them sequential.

14. Save the package as **CustomerImportr2.dtsx.**

The control flow should now look like the control flow in Figure 11.5. The boxes in the figure have been adjusted to improve the readability.

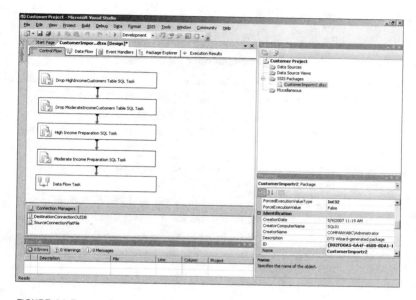

FIGURE 11.5
Conditional CustomerImport package control flow.

The next adjustment to the package is to change the data flow. This is where the actual work of splitting the customers takes place.

In the data flow designer of the CustomerImportr2 package, do the following to set up the conditional split:

1. Drag the Conditional Split item from the Toolbox.

2. Rename the Conditional Split to **Conditional Split on Yearly Income**.

3. Remove the existing arrows between the Data Conversion 1 and the destination by highlighting them and pressing Delete.

4. Select the Data Conversion 1 item and then click the green arrow. Drag the arrow to the Conditional Split item.

5. Edit the Data Conversion 1 item and change the YearlyIncome Data Type to numeric. This will allow a comparison in the conditional split item.

6. Edit the Conditional Split item.

7. Expand the Columns folder and drag the Data Conversion 1.Yearly Income column to the first Condition Field. The Output Name will be labeled Case 1.

8. Expand the Operators folder and drag the Greater Than or Equal To operator to the end of the condition for Case 1.

9. Enter **100000** after the >= operator. The line should now be black, indicating that it parsed correctly and that the data types match.

10. Expand the Columns folder and drag the Data Conversion 1.Yearly Income column to the second Condition Field. The Output Name will be labeled Case 2.

11. Expand the Operators folder and drag the Less Than operator to the end of the condition for Case 2.

12. Enter **100000** after the < operator. The line should now be black, indicating that it parsed correctly and that the data types match.

13. Change the Output Name Case 1 to **High Income** and the Case 2 to **Moderate Income**. Click OK to save the changes.

The Conditional Split item is now ready to split the customers between high income and moderate income. The next step is to set up the destinations and link them to the conditional split to complete the flow.

To set up the destinations, follow these steps:

1. Copy and paste the Destination—Customers item to create a second one.

2. Rename the first Destination—Customers to Destination—**High Income Customers**.

3. Edit the Destination—High Income Customers. If you get an error, select the Delete invalid column reference from the Column mapping option for selected rows dropdown.

4. Click the New button next to the Name of the table or view the pull–down list.

5. On the first line, change the text [Destination—High Income Customers] to **[HighIncomeCustomers]** and click OK.

6. Click OK to save the item.

7. Rename the second Destination—Customers 1 to **Destination-- Moderate Income Customers**.

8. Edit the Destination—Moderate Income Customers.

9. Click the New button next to the Name of the table or view the pull–down list.

10. On the first line, change the text [Destination—Moderate Income Customers] to **[ModerateIncomeCustomers]** and click OK.

11. Click OK to save the item.

12. Drag the tasks into order with the Source—Customers_txt item first, followed by the Data Conversion 1 item, the Conditional Split next, and finally, the two Destinations next to each other on the same line.

13. Select the Conditional Split item.

14. Drag the green arrow to the Destination—High Income Customers item. Select High Income from the Output pull-down list and click OK.

15. Drag the green arrow to the Destination—Moderate Income Customers item. Select the Moderate Income from the Output pull–down list and click OK.

16. Save the package.

The data flow should now look like the flow in Figure 11.6. Again, the boxes have been adjusted to improve the readability of the flow.

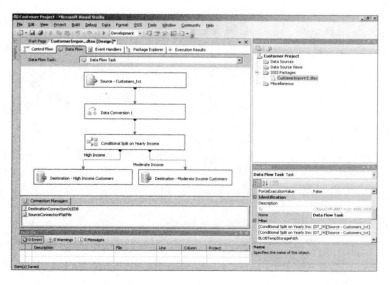

FIGURE 11.6
Conditional CustomerImport package data flow.

The CustomerImportr2 is now ready to execute. Clicking Debug, Start Debugging executes the package. The package executes and shows the following messages in the Output window.

```
SSIS package "CustomerImportr2.dtsx" starting.
....
Information: 0x4004300B at Data Flow Task,
    DTS.Pipeline: "component "Destination - Moderate Income
➡Customers" (252)" wrote 1848 rows.
Information: 0x4004300B at Data Flow Task,
    DTS.Pipeline: "component "Destination - High Income
➡Customers" (94)" wrote 210 rows.
SSIS package "CustomerImportr2.dtsx" finished: Success.
```

The results of the execution can also be viewed graphically in the Data Flow design window when you are debugging the package in the Business Intelligence Development Studio. This view, shown in Figure 11.7, is a color-coded representation of the data flow, as discussed before. In this instance, the graphic also shows the count of rows output at each step. In the figure, the number of row in each of the transitions is 2,058 until the conditional split. At the output of the conditional split, 210 rows went to the high income table and 1,848 rows went to the moderate income table. This information matches the results in the Output window.

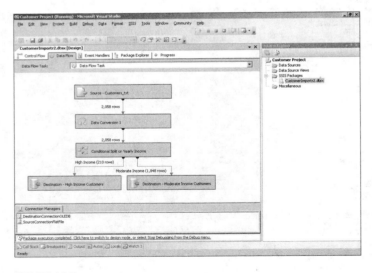

FIGURE 11.7
Graphical view of package execution.

This example illustrates how easy it is to transform and manipulate the data during the data flow. A multitude of different data flow transformations exist, which are discussed in the "Data Flow" section at the beginning of the chapter.

Instrumenting Packages

Instrumenting a package refers to adding the controls to ensure that the package execution can be monitored and controlled. This includes logging, error checking, checkpoints, and notifications.

Add Logging

During the execution of the package, it might be important to log the activities package. Logging can be enabled for an entire package or for a single container.

To add logging to the CustomerImportr2 package, follow these steps:

1. Select the menu SSIS, Logging.

2. Check off the top level package in the Containers window, in this case the CustomerImportr2.

3. Select the Provider type for the log. In this case, use the default SSIS log provider for Text files.

4. Click Add.

5. In the window, click Configuration and use the pull-down list to select New Connection.

6. In the File Connection Manager Editor, from the Usage type pull-down list select Create File.

7. Enter the File, in this case `C:\data\CustomerImportr2.txt`.

8. Click OK.

9. Click the Details tab to select the events to log.

10. Select the check box next to the Events column to select all the events.

11. Click Save to save the logging details settings. Enter the name of the XML file to create and click Save.

12. Click OK to save the logging configuration.

13. Save the package.

To test the logging, debug the package. After the package has executed, review the log file `CustomerImportr2.txt`. It should be 302KB long with lots of details.

Sending Email

Another useful method of instrumenting a package is to have the package notify when the package completes. For example, you might want to get an email message when the CustomerImportr2 package completes.

Follow these steps:

1. Select the Control Flow tab in the Designer window of the CustomerImportr2 package.

2. Drag the Send Mail Task from the Toolbox to the Control Flow Designer window.

3. Select the Data Flow Task.

4. Select the green arrow and drag it to the Send Mail Task.

5. Edit the Send Mail Task.

6. Select the Mail options.

7. From the SmtpConnection pull–down list, select New Connection.

8. In the SMTP Server field, enter the fully qualified domain name (FQDN) of the SMTP server, such as smtphost.companyabc.com.

9. Click OK.

10. In the From field, enter the from email address.

11. In the To field, enter the destination email address.

12. In the Subject field, enter a subject, such as **CustomerImportr2 Completed**.

13. In the MessageSource, enter a message body.

14. Click OK to save the settings.

15. Save the package.

The modified CustomerImportr2 will now look like the package shown in Figure 11.8. The package will send an email after the Data Flow Task completes. Notice in the Connection Manager window that there is a new SMTP Connection Manager.

The feature could be used to send an email when the control flow starts, ends, or even in intermediate stages as required.

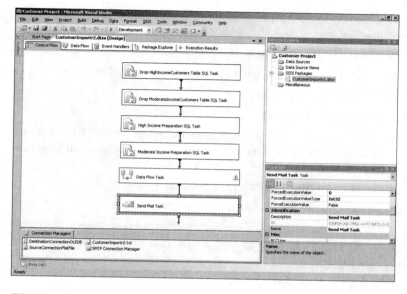

FIGURE 11.8
Adding a Send Mail Task.

Adding Error Handling

In spite of the best-laid plans, errors will occur during the execution of packages. You can control what happens when errors occur through the use of event handlers.

To notify if the CustomerImportr2 package experiences an error, execute the following steps:

1. Launch the Business Intelligence Development Studio and open the Customer Project created earlier.

2. Select the CustomerImportr2 package.

3. Select the Event Handler tab.

4. The CustomerImportr2 executable (package) and the OnError event handler are selected by default. In the drop–down list, you can see the other event handler types.

5. Click the link in the middle of the pane, which reads "Click here to create an 'OnError' event handler for executable 'CustomerImportr2'."

6. Drag the Send Mail Task from the Toolbox to the Control Flow window.

7. Select the Data Flow Task.

8. Select the green arrow and drag it to the Send Mail Task.

9. Edit the Send Mail Task.

10. Select the Mail options.

11. From the SmtpConnection pull-down list, select the SMTP Connection Manager. This is the same one created previously, which will be reused for this task.

12. In the From field, enter the from email address.

13. In the To field, enter the destination email address.

14. In the Subject field, enter a subject, such as `CustomerImportr2 Error`.

15. In the MessageSource, enter a message body. Figure 11.9 shows the Send Mail Task.

16. Click OK to save the settings.

17. Save the package.

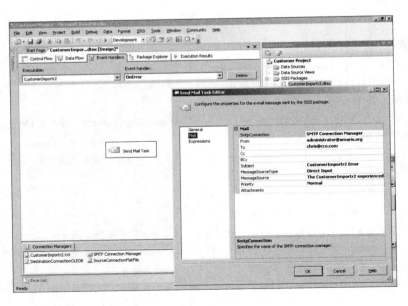

FIGURE 11.9
Error event handling Send Mail Task details.

To introduce an error to test the error handling, rename the source file Customers.txt in the directory C:\Program Files\Microsoft SQL Server\90\Samples\Integration Services\Package Samples\ ExecuteSQLStatementsInLoop Sample\Data Files\ to **Customers.tst**. This will cause an error when the package attempts to import the data.

After renaming the source data file, running the package will cause an error and the OnError event handler will trigger and execute the Send Mail Task. Interestingly, the task color will show the execution status as with any other task. If no errors exist, the event handler tasks remain white. If an error occurs, the event handler tasks will change color to reflect the execution (yellow) and their completion (green).

Restore the original filename for the source data file Customers.txt to run the package. The package should now generate the successful completion email message and not the error email message.

Although this example is a single simple task, more complex control and data flows can be created to handle error events in a more sophisticated fashion. All the tasks that are available in the control and data flow toolboxes are available in the event handler.

Maintenance Tasks

Packages are not just for ETL (extraction, transformation, and loading). Packages are very useful in the maintenance of SQL Server 2005. You can execute maintenance tasks such as backing up a database, rebuilding indexes, or shrinking a database. These tasks can be executed in a series and include conditional elements to control the execution.

The various maintenance tasks are listed in Table 11.13.

Table 11.13 **Maintenance Tasks Types**

Maintenance Task	Description
Back Up Database Task	Performs different types of SQL Server database backups.
Check Database Integrity Task	Checks the allocation and structural integrity of database objects and indexes.
Execute SQL Server Agent Job Task	Runs SQL Server Agent jobs.
Execute TSQL Statement Task	Runs Transact-SQL statements.
History Cleanup Task	Deletes entries in the history tables in the SQL Server msdb database.

Table 11.13 **continued**

Maintenance Task	Description
Maintenance Cleanup Task	Removes files related to maintenance plans, including reports created by maintenance plans and database backup files.
Notify Operator Task	Sends notification messages to SQL Server Agent operators.
Rebuild Index Task	Rebuilds indexes in SQL Server database tables and views.
Reorganize Index Task	Reorganizes indexes in SQL Server database tables and views.
Shrink Database Task	Reduces the size of SQL Server database data and log files.
Update Statistics Task	Updates information about the distribution of key values for one or more sets of statistics on the specified table or view.

Suppose that after looking at the CustomerImportr2 package, you decide that it would be good to back up the Customer database before overwriting the data. Because the imported data might be significantly smaller than the old data, you also want to shrink the database at the end of the package execution.

To add a backup task and a shrink database task to the package, execute the following steps:

1. Open the CustomerImportr2 package and select the Control Flow tab.
2. Drag the Back Up Database Task from the Toolbox.
3. Select the Back Up Database Task.
4. Select the green arrow and drag it to the first component in the control flow, which should be the Drop HighIncomeCustomers Table SQL Task.
5. Edit the Back Up Database Task.
6. Click the New button next to the Connection.
7. Enter a Connection name, such as **Customer**.
8. Enter or select the SQL Server name, such as **SQL01**. Verify the authentication information as well.
9. Click OK.
10. In the pull–down list for Database(s), select the Customer database.

11. Click OK to close the task. The Back Up Database Task is now configured to back up the Customer database.

12. Drag the Shrink Database Task from the Toolbox.

13. Select the green arrow that connects the Data Flow Task and the Send Mail Task.

14. Delete the green arrow.

15. Select the Data Flow Task and then select the green arrow at the bottom of the task.

16. Connect the arrow to the Shrink Database Task.

17. Select the Shrink Database Task and then select the green arrow at the bottom of the task.

18. Connect the arrow to the Send Mail Task.

19. Edit the Shrink Database Task.

20. The Connection should be defaulted to Customer.

21. Select the Customer database from the Database pull-down list.

22. Click OK to leave the default parameters, which are to shrink the database when larger than 50MB and to leave 10% free space.

23. Click OK to save the Shrink Database Task.

24. Save the package.

The package control flow should now look something like that shown in Figure 11.10.

Tip

Laying out the tasks in a presentable manner can be a time-consuming process. However, the Format menu can be used to automatically lay out the tasks. Then align the tasks by selecting one or more tasks and then selecting the Format, Align menu. Adjust the task size to be the same by selecting one or more tasks and then using the Format, Make Same Size menu.

View the results by using the View menu. You can set the view to show all tasks by selecting View, Zoom, To Fit. To get more screen space, select the View, Full Screen menu.

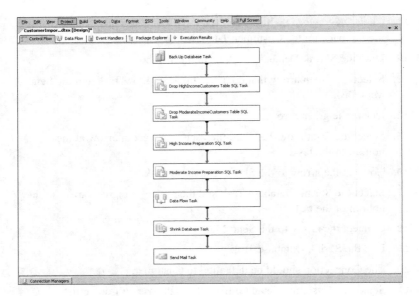

FIGURE 11.10
Package control flow with maintenance tasks.

The package should now back up the Customer database before dropping the tables and then shrink the database after the data import from Customers.txt. To test, first increase the size of the Customer database to something greater than 50MB to ensure that the Shrink Database Task threshold of 50MB is crossed. To increase the database size, perform the following steps:

1. Launch the SQL Server Management Studio.

2. Connect to the database server.

3. Expand the Databases folder and select the Properties of the Customer database.

4. Select the Files options page.

5. Set the Initial Size (MB) of the Data file to 200MB.

6. Click OK to save the changes.

Start debugging the package in the Business Intelligence Development Studio and verify that the email confirming the successful completion of the package is received. Then check the default SQL backup directory (C:\Program Files\Microsoft SQL Server\MSSQL.1\MSSQL\Backup) to verify that the backup file was created. In the SQL Server Management Studio, select the

Properties of the Customer database and verify that the size was reduced to approximately 24MB.

> **Note**
>
> Many of the maintenance tasks can be executed in a Maintenance Plan in SQL Server Management Studio. This provides a rich wizard-driven interface to create and modify maintenance plans to back up, reindex, shrink, and perform all the other maintenance tasks. This is the preferred method of running maintenance in SQL Server 2005.
>
> However, when specific maintenance tasks need to be executed in line with control flows in a pack or in response to errors in a package, the maintenance tasks in SSIS are well suited to that use.

Deploying Integration Services Packages

After a package is designed and tested, the package will need to be deployed to an instance of SQL Server Integration Services. You can run the packages from the SSIS Designer, but they will not perform as quickly and can't be scheduled from that interface. See Chapter 5 for the advantages of running packages in the SSIS and procedures for scheduling and administering packages.

Packages can be deployed primarily in two ways:

- Manually
- Packaged

Each has its advantages and disadvantages. Manual deployment requires little preparation, but does not scale well if deploying to many servers. Packaged deployments are very customizable and can adapt to different server configurations, but require effort to create the packages.

Manual Deployment

Manual deployment is straightforward and consists of importing the package into the SSIS, either to the File System storage or the SQL Server storage (MSDB).

To import a package in SQL Server Management Studio, follow these steps:

1. Open SQL Server Management Studio.
2. Select Integration Services from the Server Type drop-down list.

3. Click Connect.

4. Expand the Stored Packages folder.

5. Right-click the File System folder.

6. Select Import Package.

7. Select the location of the package, in this case File System.

8. Enter the path and filename for the package. Alternatively, click the button next to the Package path field to browse for a package. Browse to the locations of the CustomerImportr2 package, which is `C:\Projects\Customer Projects\Customer Project\` and select the CustomerImportr2.dtsx.

9. Click Open.

10. Click in the Package name field. The package name CustomerImportr2 will be filled in automatically, but can be changed if needed.

11. Click OK to save the package.

The package will be displayed in the File System folder and can now be run or scheduled from there.

Configuring a Package

Many of the configuration settings in packages are static, meaning they don't change. But the servers to which the package will be deployed may have different configurations and settings, which can cause the package to fail. A different package could be created with different settings for each server, but this would become a maintenance headache. Package configurations allow you to create a package with dynamic settings, allowing the package to flex the local conditions.

Package configurations can come from the following sources:

- Environment variables
- Registry entries
- SQL Server
- Parent package variables
- XML configuration file

For the DBA, the most common sources will be either environmental variables or registry entries.

An example of a static setting is the CustomerImportr2 logging to the log file on C: (that is, `C:\data\CustomerImportr2.txt`) on the SQL Server 2005 server SQL01. For another SQL Server 2005 Integration server SQL02, the log files need to be created in the data directory in a different directory (that is, `C:\custdata\CustomerImport.txt`). To address this problem, you decide to store the data directory in an environment variable called LOGFILE and then use Package configurations to adjust the setting in the package. This allows the package to be deployed to different servers easily without having to customize the package for each server.

The steps needed to accomplish this are as follows:

1. Create Environment Variables

2. Create the Package configuration

The environment variable LOGFILE will store the folder for the data directory on each local computer. This will need to be created on each of the target servers, in this case the SQL Server 2005 servers with Integration Services. To create the environment variable, execute the following steps:

1. On the first server SQL01, open Start, Control Panel, System.

2. Select the Advanced tab.

3. Click the Environment Variables button.

4. In the System variables window, click the New button.

5. Enter **LOGFILE** for the Variable name and the path **C:\data\ CustomerImportr2.txt** for the log file in the Variable value.

6. Click OK to save the settings.

7. Click OK to close the System applet.

8. Restart the server.

Note

The reason that the server needs to be restarted is to allow the environment variable to show in the list of variables later in the process. If restarting is not an option at the time, the environment variable name can be typed directly into the dialog box.

---

9. On the second server SQL02, open Start, Control Panel, System.

10. Select the Advanced tab.

11. Click the Environment Variables button.

12. In the System variables window, click the New button.

13. Enter **LOGFILE** for the Variable name and the path **C:\custdata\CustomerImport.txt** for the log file in the Variable value.

14. Click OK to save the settings.

15. Click OK to close the System applet.

16. Restart the server.

The steps to set up an environment variable would be complete on each server where the package will be deployed.

The environment variables are now set up to allow the package to automatically adjust the configuration of the logging file. The next step is to create the package configuration.

Follow these steps to set up the package configuration:

1. Launch the SSIS Designer and open the Customer project.

2. Open the CustomerImportr2 package.

3. Select SSIS, Package Configurations.

4. Check the Enable Package Configurations check box.

5. Click the Add button. Click Next.

6. From the Configuration type pull-down menu, select the Environment variable type.

7. From the Environment variable pull-down menu, select the LOGFILE variable.

Note

If the server was not rebooted after creating the LOGFILE Environment variable, type **LOGFILE** into the Environment variable field.

---

8. Click Next.

9. In the Objects window, expand the CustomerImport2.txt connection manager in the Connection Managers folder.

10. Expand the Properties folder.

11. Select the ConnectionString property.

12. Click Next.

13. Enter **Logging Connection Configuration** for the Configuration name. The result should look like the screen in Figure 11.11.

14. Click Finish.

15. Click Close to close the Package Configurations Organizer.

16. Save the project.

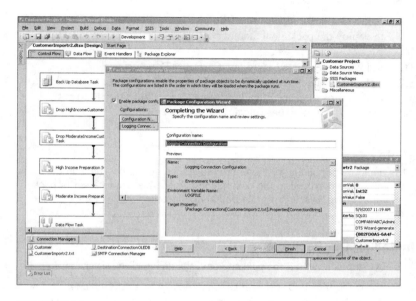

FIGURE 11.11
Package configuration.

The package configuration will now in effect dynamically replace the logging location with the contents of the LOGFILE environment variable at runtime.

Before deploying the package, it is important to test that the package works in the SSIS Designer by running it and verifying that the log was updated.

Building a Package Deployment Utility

Deploying the package requires that a deployment utility be built. This utility is the executable that will install the package on a target server.

To build the deployment utility, execute the following steps:

1. Select the Properties of the Customer Project in the Solution Explorer window.

2. Select the Deployment Utility option page.

3. Change the CreateDeploymentUtility to True.

4. Note the DeploymentOutputPath option. This is the location to which the utility will be built underneath the project directory structure.

5. Click OK to save.

6. Select Build, Build Customer Project. This will create the files needed to deploy the package to another server.

The build will have created two files: Customer Project. SSISDeploymentManifest and CustomerImportr2.dtsx. These will be located in the project directory, specifically `C:\Projects\Customer Project\ Customer Project\bin\Deployment\`.

> **Note**
>
> The deployment build is for the entire project, so all the packages in the project will be deployed to the destination server. This allows a set of packages that deliver a solution to be bound and installed together as a unit.

Installing the Package

The next step is to install the package onto the destination server.

1. Copy the files in `C:\Projects\Customer Project\Customer Project\bin\Deployment\` to the destination server, in this case SQL02.

2. On the destination server, in this case SQL02, double-click the Customer Project.SSISDeploymentManifest file. This launches the Package Installation Wizard.

3. Click Next.

4. Leave the default File system deployment and click Next.

5. Click Next to accept the default Folder.

6. Click Next to install the package.

7. Click Finish to close the Summary window.

The package installation can be verified by launching the SQL Server Management Studio. The Customer Project and the CustomerImportr2 package should be visible in Stored Packages, File System.

The package can now be run or scheduled as described in Chapter 5. Now that the package has been deployed, it is important to test that the package functions properly.

On testing, there should be an error generated indicating that no Customer database exists on SQL02. The package fails to drop or create the tables for the customers.

The Customer database could be transferred manually or you could create a package that will accomplish the same task, as shown in the next section.

Transferring a Database

In this section, a package will be added to the Customer Project to transfer the Customer database from the source server (SQL01) to the current destination server. This will require leveraging the package configurations again to dynamically set the destination server name. Luckily, a COMPUTERNAME environment variable already exists that can be used for this.

To add a package to the Customer Project that will transfer the Customer database, execute the following steps:

1. On the development server, in this case SQL01, open the Customer Project.

2. Add a new package to the project named TransferCustDB.

3. In the Control Flow tab, drag the Transfer Database Task from the Toolbox.

4. Edit the Transfer Database Task.

5. Select the Databases options.

6. Change the Method to DatabaseOnline.

7. In the SourceConnection, enter the name of the source database server. In this case, the server name is SQL01.

8. In the DestinationConnection, enter the name of the destination server. In this case, the server name is SQL02. However, this name will be adjusted with a Package Configuration later.

9. Select the Customer database as the SourceDatabaseName. This will automatically populate the DestinationDatabaseName.

10. Select the defaults as the SourceDatabaseFiles.

11. Select the DestinationDatabaseFiles option button. This will automatically populate the DestinationDatabaseFiles.

12. Change the DestinationOverwrite to True.

13. Click OK to save the changes.

14. Add a Package Configuration.

15. Use the Environment variable type and set the variable to
COMPUTERNAME.

16. For the Target Property, select the Connection Managers, Destination, Properties, SqlServerName.

17. Save the configuration as Destination Server.

18. Save the project.

19. Build the project again, using the Build, Build Customer Project.

20. Copy the resulting files from the Deployment directory to the destination server, in this case SQL02. Note that there is an additional file for the TransferCustomerDB package.

21. On the destination server, in this case SQL02, double-click the Customer Project.SSISDeploymentManifest file. This launches the Package Installation Wizard.

22. Click Next.

23. Leave the default File system deployment and click Next.

24. Click Next to accept the default Folder.

25. Click Next to install the package.

26. Click Finish to close the Summary window.

There will now be two packages on the destination server in the Customer Project folder. To transfer the Customer database from the source SQL01 database to the current server, execute the TransferCustomerDB package.

Now executing the CustomerImportr2 on the SQL02 server should complete successfully.

Copy Database Wizard

In addition to the Transfer Database Task within a package, a database can be copied using the SQL Server Management Studio Wizard. This process is useful if the database will be copied only once and does not need to be integrated within a package.

Follow these steps to copy the customer database from SQL01 to SQL02 using the Copy Database Wizard:

1. Launch SQL Server Management Studio.

2. Connect to the source database server, in this case SQL01.

3. Expand the Databases folder.

4. Right-click the Customer database and select Tasks, Copy Database.

5. Click Next.

6. Select the Source server, which should be the SQL01 server.

7. Click Next.

8. Select the Destination server, which should be the SQL02 server.

9. Click Next.

10. The default Transfer Method is to use the detach and attach method, which will bring the source database offline. Because this would be disruptive, select Use the SQL Management Object method. This will keep the source database online.

11. Click Next.

12. Verify that the Customer database is selected.

13. Click Next.

14. Change the option to drop the destination database if it already exists, which is the Drop Any Database option. This forces an overwrite of the database on the destination server.

15. Click Next.

16. Don't select any additional objects to transfer.

17. Click Next.

18. Click Next to leave the package defaults.

19. Click Next to run immediately.

20. Review the choices and click Finish to execute the transfer.

This method is easy to use for a one-time copy of a database. Note that the wizard actually creates a package in the MSDB storage of the destination server, which can be seen by connecting to the SSIS on the destination server.

Note

There is also the Bulk Copy utility (bcp.exe) to manually import data from a table. The bcp utility bulk copies data from a data file to an existing table in a database.

The bulk copy utility is less convenient than the wizards because it requires that the table be created in advance, and the command options are relatively obscure.

Summary

Packages and the Business Intelligence Development Studio provide a rich environment for creating packages for automating and controlling the movement of data. Packages are very useful, not only to import or export data but also to automate maintenance activities. The SSIS Designer is a graphical development interface that makes it easy for even the beginning DBA to create, test, and deploy packages.

Best Practices

Some important best practices from the chapter include the following:

- Monitor progress of the package in the Business Intelligence Development Studio.
- Don't use the F5 shortcut key to try to refresh the screen, because it executes the current package instead.
- Log the package execution.
- Add error event handlers to packages.
- Use manual package deployments for few servers.
- Use packaged deployments for larger numbers of servers.
- Use package configurations to dynamically adjust the settings of packages.
- Use maintenance plans to set up maintenance for databases, rather than packages.
- Use package tasks to include specific maintenance tasks within packages.
- Use the Copy Database Wizard for one-time database transfers.

PART III

Securing the SQL Server Implementation

IN THIS PART

CHAPTER 12

Hardening a SQL Server 2005 Environment

SQL Server is regularly targeted by hackers because it is a repository of sensitive data for organizations. If the server is breached, hackers can gain access to confidential information, including credit card numbers, Social Security numbers, or marketing information.

To prevent cybercrime or, at the very least, reduce it, Microsoft has been working very hard since 2002 in bringing the community more secured products with the Microsoft Trustworthy Computing Initiative. Although Microsoft products are being transformed and are more secure by default and design due to Trustworthy Computing, the company is not delusional about where things stand today. Microsoft knows it still has much work to do to bolster security. This is important for all database administrators to understand because it means that you should take additional steps to further harden your SQL Server environment until you can rely fully on Trustworthy Computing.

This chapter shows how important it is to harden the SQL Server environment when the SQL Server installation is complete. The chapter explains how to manage a secure SQL Server implementation based on industry best practices so that vulnerabilities and security breaches are minimized. The following security topics are covered to harden a SQL Server environment: using SQL Server configuration tools to minimize attack surface, deciding which authentication method to use, enforcing strong passwords, using SQL Server security logs, verifying security with Microsoft Baseline Security Analyzer, and installing Windows and SQL Server Service Packs.

What's New for Hardening a SQL Server 2005 Environment with Service Pack 2?

Microsoft SQL Server 2005 Service Pack 2 improves the SQL Server product by delivering improved features and functionality. Service Pack 2 does not provide any new tools to harden a SQL Server environment; however, the service pack itself is a major release that addresses the issues that can compromise a SQL Server environment, such as bugs and vulnerabilities. By directly focusing on and resolving existing issues, Service Pack 2 ultimately improves overall security.

> **Note**
>
> To see a full list of the bugs addressed and fixed with SQL Server 2005 Service Pack 2, review the Knowledgebase (KB) article 921896. You can find it at http://support.microsoft.com/default.aspx ?scid=kb;en-us; 921896.

Windows and SQL Server Authentication

Authentication is commonly identified as a security measure designed to establish the validity of a user or application based on criteria such as an account, password, security token, or certificate. After a user or an application's validity is verified, authorization to the desired object is granted.

At present, SQL Server 2005 continues to support two modes for validating connections and authenticating access to database resources: "Windows Authentication mode" and "SQL Server and Windows Authentication mode." Both of these authentication methods provide access to SQL Server and its resources.

> **Note**
>
> During installation, the default authentication mode is Windows. The authentication mode can be changed after the installation, however.

Windows Authentication Mode

Windows Authentication mode is the default and recommended authentication mode. It leverages Local accounts, Active Directory user accounts or groups when granting access to SQL Server. In this mode, you, as the database administrator, are given the opportunity to grant domain or local server users access to the database server without creating and managing a separate SQL Server account.

When Windows Authentication mode is used, user accounts are subject to enterprisewide policies enforced by the Active Directory domain such as complex passwords, password history, account lockouts, minimum password length, maximum password length, and the Kerberos protocol. These enhanced and well-defined policies are always a plus to have in place.

SQL Server and Windows Authentication (Mixed) Mode

SQL Server and Windows Authentication mode, which is regularly referred to as mixed mode authentication, uses either Active Directory user accounts or SQL Server accounts when validating access to SQL Server. SQL Server 2005 has introduced a means to enforce password and lockout policies for SQL Server login accounts when using SQL Server authentication. The new SQL Server polices that can be enforced include password complexity, password expiration, and account lockouts. This functionality was not available in SQL Server 2000 and was a major security concern for most organizations and database administrators. Essentially, this security concern played a role in helping define Windows authentication as the recommended practice for managing authentication in the past. Today, SQL Server and Windows Authentication mode may be able to successfully compete with Windows Authentication mode.

Which Mode Should Be Used to Harden Authentication?

When you are aware of the authentication methods, the next step is choosing one to manage SQL Server security. Although SQL Server 2005 now can enforce policies, Windows Authentication mode is still the recommended alternative for controlling access to SQL Server because this mode carries added advantages; Active Directory provides an additional level of protection with the Kerberos protocol. As a result, the authentication mechanism is more mature and robust; therefore, administration can be reduced by leveraging Active Directory groups for role-based access to SQL Server.

Nonetheless, this mode is not practical for everything out there. Mixed authentication is still required if there is a need to support legacy applications or clients coming in from platforms other than Windows and there exists a need for separation of duties. It is common to find organizations where the SQL Server and Windows teams do not trust one another. Therefore, a clear separation of duties is required because SQL Server accounts are not managed via Active Directory.

Using Windows authentication is a more secure choice. However, if mixed mode authentication is required, you must make sure to leverage complex passwords and the new SQL Server 2005 password and lockout policies to further bolster security.

> **Note**
>
> The ability for SQL Server authentication in SQL Server 2005 to manage both password and lockout properties is available only if SQL Server is installed on Windows Server 2003.

Configuring SQL Server 2005 Authentication Modes

To select or change the server authentication mode, follow these steps:

1. In SQL Server Management, right-click on a desired SQL Server and then click Properties.

2. On the Security page, as shown in Figure 12.1, select the desired server authentication mode under Server Authentication and then click OK.

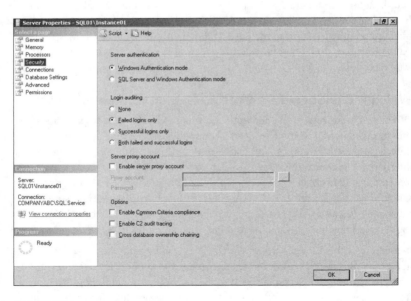

FIGURE 12.1
Configuring SQL Server 2005 authentication modes.

3. In the SQL Server Management Studio dialog box, click OK to acknowledge the need to restart SQL Server.

4. In Object Explorer, right-click on a desired server and then click Restart. If the SQL Server Agent is running, it requires a restart also.

Note

If Windows Authentication mode is selected during installation, the SA login is disabled by default. If the authentication mode is switched to SQL Server mixed mode after the installation, the SA account is still disabled and must be manually enabled. It is a best practice to reset the password when the mode is switched.

Security Ramifications of the SA Account

If SQL Server Authentication mode is used, a strong SA password should also be used. By default, the SA account has full administrative privileges over a SQL Server installation; therefore, in the event this account is compromised, the intruder will have full access to SQL Server and all databases.

In the past, it was common to find production SQL Server installations with a weak or blank SA password, which naturally increased the risk of security vulnerabilities and compromises. Microsoft introduced the idea of checking for blank SA passwords during the installation of Service Pack 4 on SQL Server 2000. Database administrators were further informed of the security vulnerabilities associated with maintaining a blank password; however, they were not forced to enter a password, which once again left the account and server in a vulnerable state.

This situation is no longer an issue in SQL Server 2005. If you use SQL Server authentication, you must enter a strong SA password; otherwise, you cannot continue with the SQL Server 2005 installation. A strong password for SQL Server must contain at least six characters and satisfy at least three of the following four criteria:

- The password must contain uppercase letters.

- The password must contain lowercase letters.

- The password must contain numbers.

- The password must contain nonalphanumeric characters such as #, %, or ^.

In addition, a strong password cannot use typical or commonplace words that everyone in the IT field is accustomed to, such as *Password*, *Admin*, *Administrator*, *SA*, or *Sysadmin*, and cannot use either the name of the user logged on to the computer or the computer name. These are all considered weak passwords.

Not allowing a weak or blank password reinforces the fact that Microsoft is serious about its ongoing Trustworthy Computing Initiative. In the past few years, Microsoft has invested significant time and resources to enhance the security of each of its products, including SQL Server 2005.

> **Tip**
>
> It is a best practice not to use the SA account for day-to-day administration, logging on to the server remotely, or having applications use it to connect to SQL.

Enforcing or Changing a Strong Password

To change or assign a strong SA password, do the following:

1. In Object Explorer, first expand the Security folder and then the Logon folder. Right-click on the SA account and then click Properties.

2. On the General page in the Login Properties dialog box, as shown in Figure 12.2, enter a new complex SA password, confirm it, and then click OK.

3. Restart Microsoft SQL Server Services, including SQL Server Agent.

Disabling and Renaming the SA Account

When attackers want to compromise a SQL Server, they don't want to access the system as common users; they want complete control of the server so that they can gain access to all the data within it. Because most hackers already know the SA account exists, this makes hacking one step easier because this account would grant them complete control of the SQL Server if compromised. Similar to the way you use a Windows Administrator account, it is a best practice to rename and disable the SA account in SQL Server 2005 when running in mixed authentication mode. This technique increases security one step further because most hackers are familiar with the SA account and the rights associated with it.

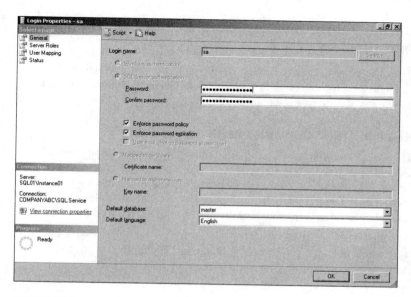

FIGURE 12.2
The SQL Server Login Properties dialog box for the SA account.

The following syntax first disables the SA account and then renames it to something not easily identified. This example uses the name *Ross-Mistry*:

```
USE MASTER
ALTER LOGIN sa DISABLE;
GO
ALTER LOGIN sa WITH NAME = [Ross-Mistry];
GO
```

> **Tip**
>
> Before renaming or disabling the SA account, make sure another account exists with administrator privileges; otherwise, you will not have access to the SQL Server. Also, it is a best practice to rename the account to something that is not related to an administrator, SA, or service, or is easily identifiable so that it's not so obvious that this account was previously SA.

Using Configuration Tools to Harden the Installation

After you've installed SQL Server 2005, you should run the SQL Server Configuration Manager and SQL Server Surface Area Configuration tools to harden the SQL Server installation.

Reducing the SQL Server 2005 Surface Area

The SQL Server Surface Area Configuration tool is a new security-enriched configuration tool in SQL Server 2005. Its primary function is to proactively reduce the system's attackable surface area by disabling unused services, components, features, and remote connections. In particular, this tool can be run to harden local or remote installations of SQL Server 2005.

Although SQL Server and the Trustworthy Computer Initiative have promised to help deliver a secure design, secure installation by default, and a secure deployment, it is never a bad idea for you to run the SQL Server Surface Area Configuration tool after the installation to further bolster security.

If you're launching the Surface Area Configuration tool for the first time, be aware that there are two configuration options:

- **Configuration for Services and Connections**—This option allows you to independently manage services and network connections for each component installed. The Service Startup Type can be set to Automatic, Manual, or Disabled, and the Service Status can be Started, Stopped, or Paused. When you're managing network connections for each component, it is possible to choose Local Connection Only or Local and Remote Connections. The tool can also be leveraged to change the network protocols on which SQL Server listens for incoming client connections. In addition, the tool can be viewed by instance or by component.

- **Surface Area Configuration for Features**—After configuring the services and network settings, you should use the Surface Area Configuration for Features option to further harden the SQL Server installation. This option allows you to either enable or disable specific features based on the components installed. When you're using this tool, it is a best practice to disable unused features to enhance security. Similar to the Surface Area Configuration for Services and Connections option, this tool can be viewed by instance or by component.

> **Tip**
>
> Even though the SQL Server Surface Area Configuration tool can reduce surface area to mitigate attacks, it is a best practice to install only the necessary components required during a SQL Server installation. Far too many times, organizations install every component associated with a SQL Server installation when they need only the Database Engine. This situation only increases surface area, which in turn increases the potential for vulnerabilities and compromises.

Typically, real-world production systems require only the Database Engine, SQL Server Agent, and SQL Server Browser services for a base SQL Server installation. Of course, for more advanced installations, Full-Text Search, Analysis Services, and Reporting Services may be needed. However, the point here is to install only what is necessary for the organization to operate successfully.

Hardening Services and Connections to Reduce Attack Surface

In the event you want to reduce surface attack and disable unneeded services on a SQL Server installation, follow the steps in this section. Note that the following example makes the assumption that all components were selected during the installation of SQL Server 2005. All services with the exception of the Database Engine and SQL Server Agent are disabled in the following steps.

1. Choose Start, All Programs, Microsoft SQL Server 2005, Configuration Tools, SQL Server Surface Area Configuration.

2. On the SQL Server Surface Area Configuration start page, click on the Surface Area Configuration for Services and Connections hyperlink.

3. For the basic SQL Server 2005 installation, on the View by Instance tab, shown in Figure 12.3, change the startup type from Automatic to Disabled on all unnecessary services except for the Database Engine, SQL Server Agent, and SQL Server Browser. Then stop the service, click Apply, and click OK.

Hardening Features to Reduce Attack Surface

As discussed earlier, after all unnecessary services are disabled, it is possible to take security a step further by leveraging the Surface Area Configuration for Features hyperlink in the SQL Server 2005 Surface Area Configuration dialog box. The SQL Server 2005 Surface Area Configuration for Features allows you to further customize security by turning on or off the following individual features on SQL Server 2005.

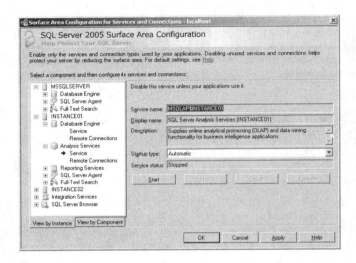

FIGURE 12.3
Managing services and connections and disabling unnecessary SQL services.

Analysis Services Features:

- *Ad hoc Data Mining Queries* allows Analysis Services to use external data sources via OPENROWSET.

- *Anonymous Connections* allows unauthenticated users to connect to Analysis Services.

- *Linked Objects* enables linking dimensions and measures between instances of Analysis Services.

- *User-Defined Functions* allows loading of user-defined functions from COM objects.

Database Engine Features:

- *Ad hoc Remote Queries* allows you to use OPENROWSET and OPENDATASOURCE.

- *CLR Integration* allows you to use stored procedures and other code written using the .NET Common Language Runtime.

- *Database Mail* lets you use the new Database Mail system to send email from SQL Server.

- *HTTP Access* enables HTTP endpoints to allow SQL Server to accept HTTP connections.

- *OLE Automation* enables the OLE automation extended stored procedures.

- *Service Broker* enables Service Broker endpoints.

- *SMO* and *DMO* turn on Server Management Objects and Distributed Management Objects, respectively.

- *SQL Mail* lets you use the older SQL Mail syntax for sending email from SQL Server.

- *Web Assistant* enables the Web Assistant for automatic output to web pages.

- *xp_cmdshell* turns on the xp_cmdshell extended stored procedure.

Reporting Services Features:

- *HTTP and Web Service Requests* allows Reporting Services to deliver reports via HTTP.

- *Scheduled Events and Report Delivery* enables "push" delivery of reports.

Tip

When you're using the SQL Server 2005 Surface Area Configuration tool to configure services, connections, or features, it is best to fully understand what components of SQL Server are needed for the installation. Failure to understand what components are needed will ultimately result in the SQL Server components failing.

Using the SQL Server Configuration Manager Tool to Harden an Installation

The SQL Server Configuration Manager tool is another new SQL Server 2005 configuration tool that you can use when hardening a SQL Server environment. This tool goes above and beyond the capabilities of the SQL Server Surface Area Configuration tool. This tool can not only configure and lock down unwanted services like the SQL Server Surface Area Configuration tool, but can also configure services, network configurations, native client configurations, client protocols, and aliases installed on a server.

To launch this tool, choose Start, All Programs, Microsoft SQL Server 2005, Configuration Tools, SQL Server Configuration Manager. The SQL Server Configuration Manager window is shown in Figure 12.4. The following nodes appear in the tool:

- **SQL Server 2005 Services**—This node enables you to start, stop, pause, resume, or configure services. In addition, you should use the tool when changing service account names and passwords.

- **SQL Server 2005 Network Configuration**—This node is the place where you can configure, enable, or disable SQL Server network protocols for the SQL Server Services installed on a server. In addition, you can configure encryption and expose or hide a SQL Server database instance.

- **SQL Native Client Configuration**—This node enables you to lock down network protocols or make changes to settings associated with ports for client connections. This is the place where you can also create an alias name for a SQL Server instance.

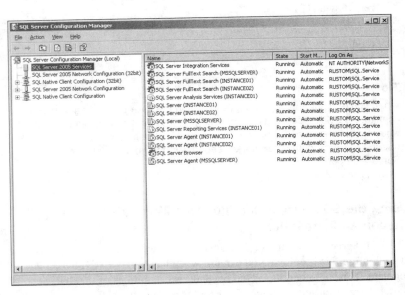

FIGURE 12.4
Managing services, connections, and disabling unnecessary SQL services.

Hardening SQL Server Ports with SQL Configuration Manager

A default installation of SQL Server 2005 uses TCP port 1433 for client requests and communications. These ports are well known in the industry, which makes them a common target for hackers. Therefore, it is a best practice to change the default ports associated with the SQL Server installation to put off hackers from port scanning the default ports of the SQL Server installation. Unfortunately, SQL Server requires an open port for network communications. Therefore, this procedure prolongs the inevitable as the used port will eventually be found.

Note

SQL Server 2005 no longer automatically listens on port UDP 1434. The task has been turned over to SQL Server Browser Services, which listens and resolves client connection requests made to the server. It also provides name and port resolution to clients when multiple instances are installed.

Follow these steps to change the default port using SQL Server Manager Configuration tools:

1. Choose Start, All Programs, Microsoft SQL Server 2005, Configuration Tools, SQL Server Configuration Manager.

2. Expand the SQL Server 2005 Network Configuration node and select Protocols for the SQL Server instance to be configured.

3. In the right pane, right-click the protocol name TCP/IP and choose Properties.

4. In the TCP/IP Properties dialog box, select the IP Addresses tab.

5. There is a corresponding entry for every IP address assigned to the server. Clear the values for both the TCP Dynamic Ports and TCP Port for each IP address except for the IP addresses under IPAll.

6. In the IPAll section for each instance, enter a new port that you want SQL Server 2005 to listen on, as shown in Figure 12.5.

7. Click Apply and restart the SQL Server Services.

Hiding a SQL Server Instance from Broadcasting Information

It is possible for SQL Server clients to browse the current infrastructure and retrieve a list of running SQL Server instances. The SQL Server Browser service enumerates SQL Server information on the network. When the SQL

Server is found, the client obtains the server name and can connect to it if it has the appropriate credentials. This can present a large security threat to organizations because sensitive production data can be compromised.

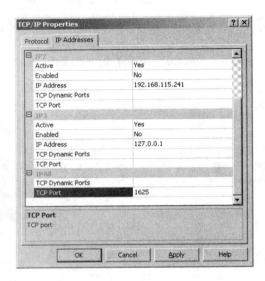

FIGURE 12.5
Changing the default SQL Server ports.

Organizations don't need to worry because there is help for this type of situation. The SQL Server Configuration Manager tool can be used to hide an instance of SQL Server. This is typically a best practice for mission-critical production database servers that host sensitive data because there isn't a need to broadcast this information. Clients and applications still can connect to SQL Server if needed; however, they need to know the SQL Server name, protocol, and which port the instance is using to connect.

To hide a SQL Server instance with SQL Server Configuration Manager, follow these steps:

1. Choose Start, All Programs, Microsoft SQL Server 2005, Configuration Tools, SQL Server Configuration Manager.

2. Expand the SQL Server 2005 Network Configuration node and select Protocols for SQL Server instance to be configured.

3. Right-click Protocols for [Server\Instance Name] and then choose Properties.

4. In the Hide Instance box on the Protocols for [*Server\Instance Name*] Properties page, shown in Figure 12.6, select Yes.

5. Click OK and restart the services for the change to take effect.

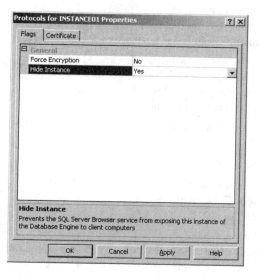

FIGURE 12.6
Hiding a SQL Server instance.

Hardening a Server with the Security Configuration Wizard in Windows Server 2003 Service Pack 1

The most impressive and useful addition to Windows Server 2003 Service Pack 1 has to be the Security Configuration Wizard (SCW). SCW allows you to completely lock down a server, except for the particular services that it requires to perform specific duties. The role-based security policies are predefined and assist you by configuring services, network security, auditing, Registry settings, and more. This way, a WINS server responds only to WINS requests, a DNS server has only DNS enabled, and a SQL Server responds only to SQL requests. This type of functionality was long sought after and is now available.

SCW allows you to build custom role-based templates that can be exported to additional servers, thus streamlining the security process when setting up multiple systems. In addition, current security templates can be imported into SCW so that existing intelligence can be maintained.

The advantages to using the SCW service on SQL Server are immediately identifiable. SQL Server, because it houses sensitive data and is often indirectly exposed to the Internet by web service applications, is vulnerable to attack and therefore should have all unnecessary services and ports shut down. A properly configured firewall normally drops this type of activity, and although the previous section focused on minimizing surface attacks, it is always a good idea to put in an additional layer of security for good measure.

When you're installing Service Pack 1 for Windows Server 2003, the SCW service is installed. If you use Windows Server 2003 R2 edition, SCW is included by default. It is not, however, installed by default and must be set up from the Add or Remove Programs applet in Windows as follows:

1. Log in as a local administrator and choose Start, Control Panel, Add or Remove Programs.

2. Click Add/Remove Windows Components.

3. Scroll down and check Security Configuration Wizard in the list of components. Click Next to Continue.

4. Click Finish when the installation is complete.

When it's installed, the wizard can be run to lock down SQL Server based on a SQL Server role-based template to run only the bare necessities required. This includes SQL access, web and ASP-related web access, and any other access methods required for the server. In addition, network security, port configuration, and Registry settings can be configured. Each SQL Server implementation differs, so it is important to run the wizard on a prototype to determine what settings are right for each individual SQL Server.

Note

For best results, when you're locking down a server with the Security Configuration Wizard, it is a best practice to first harden the SQL Server installation with the configuration tools described in the previous sections and then run this tool.

To launch the Security Configuration Wizard, choose Start, All Programs, Administrative Tools, Security Configuration Wizard. Use the wizard to create a role-based SQL Server security policy that locks down unnecessary services, network security, ports, Registry settings, and audit policies.

Verifying Security Using the Microsoft Baseline Security Analyzer (MBSA)

Like Windows Server 2003, Microsoft SQL Server 2005 also requires the latest service packs and updates to reduce known security vulnerabilities. Microsoft offers an intuitive, free downloadable tool called the *Microsoft Baseline Security Analyzer (MBSA)*. This tool identifies common security vulnerabilities on SQL Servers by identifying incorrect configurations and missing security patches for SQL Server, Windows Server 2003, and Internet Information Services (IIS).

MBSA can not only scan a single SQL Server, but can also scan multiple instances of SQL Server. The MBSA SQL Server scan works by detecting and displaying SQL Server vulnerabilities, including the following: members of the sysadmin role, weak or blank SQL Server local accounts and SA passwords, SQL Server Authentication mode, SQL Server on a domain controller, and missing service packs such as the new SQL Server 2005 Service Pack 2.

> **Note**
>
> Unfortunately, MBSA does not provide all the scanning bells and whistles for SQL Server 2005 administration vulnerabilities as of yet. Microsoft is currently working on upgrading the tool to support SQL Server 2005. In the meantime, the tool still identifies missing security patches and service packs.

Before installing MBSA, you should become acquainted with some specific Microsoft system requirements for the installation. Being familiar with the following list will help you on your way to a successful installation:

- The operating system must be Windows Server 2003, Windows XP, or Windows 2000.

- Internet Explorer must be version 5.01 or higher.

- An XML parser such as the one available with Internet Explorer 5.01 or MSXML version 3.0 SP2 must be available.

Installing MBSA on a Server

Installation of MBSA is predictably straightforward. It can be installed on any workstation or server in the network. To install, complete these steps:

1. Download the latest version of the MBSA from the Microsoft website. The current link is http://www.microsoft.com/mbsa.

2. Double-click the MBSA installation file `mbsasetup-en.msi` to launch the installation.

3. At the Welcome screen, shown in Figure 12.7, click Next to begin installation.

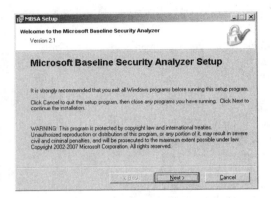

FIGURE 12.7
Microsoft Baseline Security Analyzer Setup welcome screen.

4. Read and accept the license agreement and then click Next.

5. Select the destination folder where the application will be installed. The default destination path is C:\Program Files\Microsoft Security Baseline Analyzer 2.

6. Click Install when ready. The application is installed automatically.

7. Click OK when informed that MBSA is installed correctly.

Scanning for Security Vulnerabilities with MBSA

MBSA can scan a single computer or a range of computers, or all computers in a domain based on an IP address, range of IP addresses, or computer name. The security scanner can identify known security vulnerabilities on several Microsoft technologies such as Windows, IIS, or SQL Server.

To scan SQL Server for known SQL or Windows vulnerabilities, weak passwords, and security updates, follow these steps:

1. Choose Start, All Programs, Microsoft Baseline Security Analyzer.

2. Click on Scan a Computer to pick the system to scan. You can scan more than one computer here by entering either a valid IP address range or domain name.

3. On the next screen, which is Pick a Computer to Scan, enter the computer name or IP address of the desired SQL Server. Select all options you want, as shown in Figure 12.8, and click Start Scan.

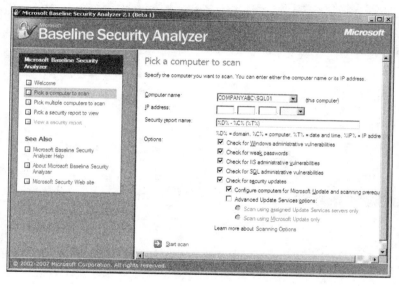

FIGURE 12.8
MBSA computer scan and options screen.

Viewing MBSA Security Reports

A separate security report is generated for the desired SQL Server on completion of the computer scan. This report is generated regardless of whether a local or remote scan is conducted. In addition, scanned reports are stored for future viewing on the same computer where the Microsoft Baseline Security Analyzer is installed.

The information yielded in the MBSA security reports is quite intuitive and addresses each vulnerability detected. For example, if MBSA detects a missing SQL Server service pack, Windows patch, or hot fix, it displays the vulnerability in the Security Update Scan section and provides the location that focuses on the fix.

In the security report example shown in Figure 12.9, note that each section scanned has a score associated with it. An end user or administrator can easily browse each section identifying known security vulnerabilities, verifying what was scanned, checking the results, and analyzing how to correct anomalies that MBSA detected.

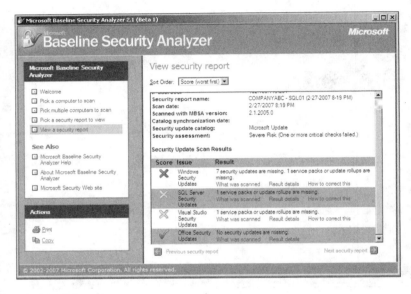

FIGURE 12.9
Viewing a Microsoft Baseline Security Analyzer vulnerability report.

Using the SQL Server 2005 Best Practice Analyzer (BPA) Tool to Harden an Installation

Another tool that is typically a database administrator's best friend is the much-awaited SQL Server 2005 Best Practice Analyzer (BPA) tool. The BPA gathers data from Microsoft Windows and SQL Server configuration settings. The first beta public release was in February 2007. The BPA is a database management tool that uses a predefined list of SQL Server 2005 recommendations and best practices to determine whether there are potential issues in the database environment. The BPA also covers security hardening best practices.

Viewing a BPA Vulnerability and Recommendation Report

The BPA was run against a test server for this book and came back with the following security hardening vulnerability and recommendations on how to resolve the issues:

SQL Server 2005 Vulnerability

SQL Login Password Policy Violation By Login SA on Server SQL01\Instance01

Login [sa] on Server [SQL01\INSTANCE01] has Password Policy set to [True] and Password Expiration set to [False]. We recommend that both Password Policy and Expiration must be enabled for SQL accounts.

This rule checks the password properties of each login to determine the threat level for password exploitation. If SQL Server Authentication is enabled and if the operating system version is earlier than Windows Server 2003, an attacker could repeatedly exploit a known SQL Server login password.

Best Practices Recommendations

We recommend that you upgrade the operating system to Windows Server 2003. If SQL Server Authentication is not required in your environment, use Windows Authentication. Enable "Enforce password policy" and "Password expiration" for all the SQL Server logins. Use ALTER LOGIN (Transact-SQL) to configure the password policy for the SQL Server login.

Note

For more information on the SQL Server 2005 Best Practice Analyzer (BPA) tool, review Chapter 7, "Conducting a SQL Server 2005 Health Check." BPA is covered there in its entirety.

It is a best practice to run the BPA tool after SQL Server has been installed, configured, and hardened to expose any outstanding security vulnerabilities. This tool enhances the hardening process.

Hardening SQL Server Service Accounts

You are prompted to enter a service account during the initial installation of SQL Server. Services can run under domain-based accounts, local service accounts, or built-in accounts such as Local System or Network Service. You can select to use a single service account for all instances and components being installed or customize the installation by entering a dedicated service account for each instance and component.

The following SQL Server service accounts are available:

- **SQL Server Service**—This account provides core database functionality by facilitating storage, processing, and controlled access of data and rapid transaction processing.

- **SQL Agent Service**—This account provides auxiliary functionality by executing jobs, monitoring SQL Server, creating alerts, and automating administrative tasks.

- **Integration Services Service**—This account provides management support for SSIS package storage and execution.

- **Analysis Services Service**—This account provides business intelligence applications by supplying online analytical processing (OLAP) and data mining functionality.

- **SQL Server Reporting Services**—This account acts as a liaison between Reporting Services and SQL Server by managing, executing, rendering, and delivering reports.

- **SQL Server Full-Text Search**—This account manages full-text indexes on content and properties of structured and semistructured data to allow fast linguistic searches on this data.

- **SQL Server Browser**—This account acts as a liaison with client computers by enumerating SQL Server connection information.

- **SQL Server Active Directory Helper**—This account enables integration between SQL Server and Active Directory.

- **SQL Server VSS Writer**—This account provides the interface to back up and restore SQL Server via the Windows Server 2003 Volume Shadow Copy Service (VSS) infrastructure.

There aren't necessarily any hard and fast rules to follow when trying to determine the type of service account to use. The main objective is to understand the limitations and positive offerings of the service account being used. It is equally important to analyze the value of the data residing within SQL Server and the risks and amount of security exposure that would take place if the SQL Server database was compromised. Lastly, when hardening and choosing SQL Server service accounts, you should employ the principle of least privilege and isolation.

The Principle of Least Privilege

It is a best practice to configure a service account based on the principle of least privilege. According to the principle of least privilege, SQL Server service accounts should be granted the least number of rights and permissions to conduct a specific task. Based on this recommendation, you should *not* grant a service account unnecessary elevated privileges such as domain administrator, enterprise administrator, or local administrator privileges. This enhances the protection of data and functionality from faults. Also, you should recognize that these highly elevated privileges are really not required. In fact, gone are the days when the SQL Server service accounts required domain administrator or local administrator privileges.

Service Account Isolation

For isolation purposes, a separate account should be created for each SQL Server instance and component being installed. Therefore, if the service account is compromised, only the one instance or component is breached. For example, say a bank is running 100 SQL Server instances and each instance maintains financial information. If one service account is used for all these instances, all 100 instances would be compromised in the event of a service account breach. This type of situation could be disastrous for a bank, especially with today's laws and regulatory compliances.

The need to create and manage more than one service account definitely increases administration and can be monotonous; however, it is a best practice to isolate each instance or component. One other notable benefit of isolation is witnessed with the amount of control organizations achieve through it. Organizations can grant specific permissions to one service account without elevating permissions to another service account that does not need elevated permissions.

The Types of Service Accounts Available

The following types of service accounts are available to choose from:

- **Local System Account**—This account grants full administrative rights to users on the local computer, which makes it a highly privileged account. As such, its use should be closely monitored. Note that this account does not grant network access rights.

- **Network Service Account**—This built-in account grants users the same level of access as members of the User group. This account allows services to interrelate with other services on the network infrastructure.

- **Domain User Account**—This account is used if the service will interrelate with other services on the network infrastructure.

- **Local Service Account**—Users of this built-in account have the same level of access that is designated to members of the Users group. This limited access protects against service breaches.

Determining Which Type of Account to Use for SQL Server Services

The question that always surfaces regarding service accounts is "Which service account should be used with SQL Server 2005?" The answer depends on your intended use of the service account and the relationship it will have to the server and network.

Services that run as the local service account access network resources with no credentials. As a result, this account should not be used if you want the services to interact with other network resources.

If you are looking for a service account that grants limited privileges like the local service account but also runs services that can interrelate with other services on the network infrastructure, you should consider using a network service account. This account uses the credential of the computer account to gain access to the network. It is not recommended that you use this account for either the SQL Server service or the SQL Server Agent service account.

Consideration should also be given to the domain user account if its services will interact with other services on the network infrastructure. If you also want to perform certain activities including replication, remote procedure calls, or network drive backups, a domain user account is preferred over a network service account because only this account allows server-to-server activity. One point to keep in mind when using a domain account is that it must be authenticated on a domain controller.

The local system account is not recommended for use for the SQL Server service or SQL Server Agent services. The reason is that it is a best practice to configure a service so that it runs effectively with the least number of privileges granted. The local system account is a highly privileged account, which means it should be used very carefully. In addition, it probably has privileges that neither SQL Server Agent services nor SQL Server services actually require.

Changing a SQL Server Service Account with SQL Server Configuration Manager

Typically, server administrators use the Services component included with Windows Server 2003 Administrative tools to make changes to Windows Services. There are serious negative ramifications if SQL Server service accounts are changed using this tool. SQL Server service accounts require special Registry, NTFS file system permissions, and Windows user rights to be set, which the Windows tool does not address, thus causing a SQL Server outage. Fortunately, these additional permission requirements can be updated automatically if you use SQL Server native configuration tools such as the SQL Server Configuration Manager or SQL Server Surface Area Configuration. Therefore, it is a best practice to use the native SQL Server configuration tools when making changes to SQL Server service accounts; changes should not be made using the Windows Server 2003 Services tool.

Follow these steps to change the user account, including credentials for a SQL Server service such as the SQL Server Agent, using the SQL Server Configuration Manager:

1. Choose Start, All Programs, Microsoft SQL Server 2005, Configuration Tools, SQL Server Configuration Manager.

2. Select the SQL Server 2005 Services node.

3. In the right pane, double-click on the SQL Server Agent Service.

4. In the SQL Server Agent box, enter a new service account name and password.

5. Confirm the password by retyping it, as shown in Figure 12.10, and click Apply.

6. Accept the message to restart the services and click OK.

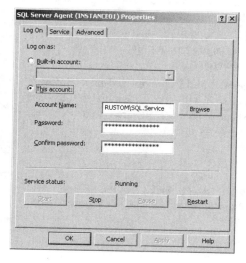

FIGURE 12.10
Changing the service account credentials.

The SQL Server Agent now uses the new service account credentials for authentication. In addition, Registry, NTFS permissions, and Windows rights are updated automatically.

Installing Service Packs and Critical Fixes

SQL Server 2005, like all other Microsoft applications and server products, is subjected to periodic software updates. Interim updates can be downloaded and installed through the Microsoft/Windows Update option on the system or by visiting the Windows Update website (http://update.microsoft.com), which initiates the installer to check for the latest updates for Windows.

Likewise, major updates are essentially bundled as service packs that roll up patches and updates into a single installation. Installation of the latest service pack brings a server up-to-date, which means to the point in time when the service pack was issued. It is also worth noting that the service packs for SQL Server 2005 are cumulative. This means Service Pack 2 includes every update released until it was issued. As such, it contains all the Service Pack 1 updates. The same is true for Windows Server service packs.

You can install a service pack update in one of three ways:

- **Microsoft/Windows Update**—The service pack can be downloaded and automatically installed as part of the normal update process.

- **Download and Install**—The service pack can be downloaded as a file. This file can then be launched to install the update. This is frequently done when a system is not connected to the Internet or when a scheduled installation is desired as opposed to an immediate installation after downloading from the Internet.

- **Automated Patch Management and Deployment Tools**—Software distribution tools can be used to install service pack updates. Systems Management Server (SMS) and Windows Software Update Services (WSUS) are examples of two tools you can use to accomplish the task.

> **Note**
>
> See the "Installing SQL Server 2005 Service Pack 2," in the appendix, "SQL Server 2005 Management and Administration" (online), for information on how to install SQL Server Service Pack 2.

Updating and Patching SQL Server and the Operating System

In addition to the patches that were installed as part of the SQL Server 2005 service pack, security updates and patches are constantly being released by Microsoft. It is advantageous to install these updates made available for SQL Server and the operating system. These patches can be manually downloaded and installed, or they can be automatically applied by using Microsoft Update.

It is a best practice to install critical fixes for both SQL Server and the operating system when they are released. In addition, major service packs and security rollups should be installed in a timely manner. All patches should be tested in a prototype lab before being installed in production, and it is recommended that you conduct a full backup of the system prior to the installation of the patches.

Understanding How SQL Server Security Logs Play a Part in Security

In the previous sections, you learned ways of minimizing security vulnerabilities on SQL Server. Now that SQL Server is hardened, it is beneficial to enable auditing. SQL Server security auditing monitors and tracks activity to log files that can be viewed through Windows application logs or SQL Server Management Studio. SQL Server offers the following four security levels with regards to security auditing:

- **None**—Disables auditing so no events are logged
- **Successful Logins Only**—Audits all successful login attempts
- **Failed Logins Only**—Audits all failed login attempts
- **Both Failed and Successful Logins**—Audits all login attempts

At the very least, security auditing should be set to Failed Logins Only. As a result, failed logins can be saved, viewed, and acted on when necessary. Unless a change is made, security auditing is set, by default, to Failed Logins Only. On the other hand, it is a best practice to configure security auditing to capture Both Failed and Successful Logins. All logins are captured in this situation and can be analyzed when advanced forensics are required.

Configuring SQL Server Security Logs for Auditing

To configure security auditing for both failed and successful logins, follow these steps:

1. In SQL Server Management Studio, right-click on a desired SQL Server and then click Properties.

2. On the Security page, as shown in Figure 12.11, under Login Auditing, select the desired auditing criteria option button and then click OK.

3. Restart the SQL Server Database Engine and SQL Server Agent to make the auditing changes effective.

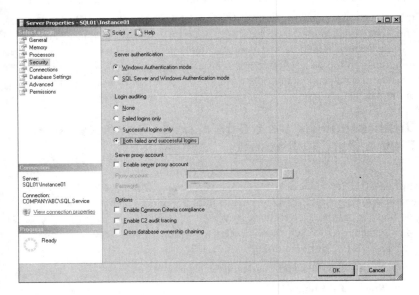

FIGURE 12.11
Configuring security auditing to both failed and successful logins.

Additional SQL Server Hardening Recommendations

The following sections focus on additional hardening techniques to further lock down SQL Server. The items include removing the BUILTIN/ Administrators Windows group, using a firewall to filter out unwanted traffic, and hardening IIS.

Understanding the Need to Remove the BUILTIN/Administrators Windows Group

Many database administrators in the industry are concerned about the BUILTIN/Administrators Windows group having sysadmin privileges by default over a SQL Server instance. Some people believe that this situation is one of the biggest out-of-the-box security flaws for SQL Server. The reason is that all local Windows administrators, including domain administrators, are given full control over SQL Server because they are part of the BUILTIN/ Administrators Windows group. It is a best practice to remove the BUILTIN/Administrators group to address this situation. Doing this hardens the SQL Server installation.

> **Note**
>
> As when you disable the SA account, make sure another administrator account with sysadmin privileges exists before removing this group.

Removing the BUILTIN/Administrators Windows Group with Transact-SQL

The following Transact-SQL (TSQL) syntax removes the BUILTIN/ Administrators Windows Group from a SQL Server instance. If you decide to run this syntax, you should execute it on each SQL Server instance installed in the organization:

```
Use Master
IF EXISTS (SELECT * FROM sys.server_principals
WHERE name = N'BUILTIN\Administrators')
DROP LOGIN [BUILTIN\Administrators]
GO
```

Using a Firewall to Filter Out Unwanted Traffic

Now that the default SQL Server ports have been changed according to the instructions in the previous section, the next step is to enable a firewall that will filter out unwanted traffic and allow connections only to the SQL Server designated from within the organization's infrastructure. The basic Windows firewall included with Windows Server 2003 should be sufficient. However, if more advanced firewall features are sought, a full-fledged hardware-based firewall or software-based firewall should be used, such as ISA Server 2006.

Note

A common problem in the past was that some organizations had their SQL Server reside within the demilitarized zone (DMZ) or configured with a public IP address. This made their SQL Server public-facing and, therefore, accessible from the outside world. As a rule of thumb, when you're implementing SQL Server from within an infrastructure, it should never be Internet-facing, within the DMZ, or publicly accessible.

When configuring the Windows firewall, you can either create an exception for SQL Server based on the instance's port number or by adding the path to the SQL Server program. The default instance of SQL Server uses port 1433; however, ports are assigned dynamically when running more than one instance.

Follow these steps to create a SQL Server exception on the Windows firewall by adding the path of the SQL Server program:

1. Choose Start, Control Panel, Windows Firewall.

Note

A message box will be displayed if the Windows Firewall/Internet Connection Sharing (ICS) service is not running. Click Yes to activate the service and the firewall.

2. On the General tab, as shown in Figure 12.12, either select or verify that the firewall is turned on.

3. On the Exceptions tab, click Add Program.

4. Select the SQL Server instance from the program list. If the program is not available in the list, click Browse to search for it and provide the path for the appropriate SQL Server instance. For example, `D:\Program Files\Microsoft SQL Server\MSSQL.5\MSSQL\Binn\sqlservr.exe`, as illustrated in Figure 12.13. Then click Open.

Note

Microsoft SQL Server provides an instance ID for every SQL Server instance installed on a server. Typically, the ID is incremented by 1 when more than one instance is installed on a server. Use the SQL Server Configuration Manager tool to obtain the instance ID and installation path of a SQL Server instance. To find it, double-click the server name, and the Advanced tab displays the instance ID and installation path to the SQL Server instance.

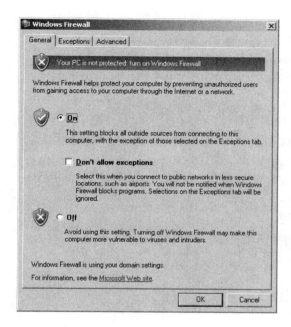

FIGURE 12.12
Setting Windows firewall options.

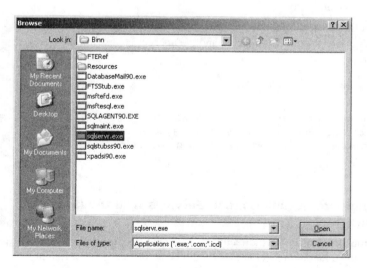

FIGURE 12.13
Setting the Windows firewall exception screen.

5. As an optional step to further tighten who can access this SQL Server, click Change Scope and specify a computer or set of computers that can access this SQL Server based on their IP address or addresses, as shown in Figure 12.14. Then click OK twice.

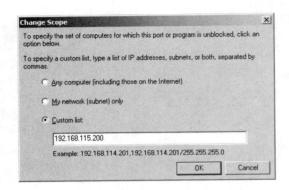

FIGURE 12.14
Specifying custom IP addresses on the Windows firewall.

6. Repeat these steps for every SQL Server instance or SQL component that requires an exception, such as Analysis Services, Integration Services, and so on.

7. Test the connection to the SQL Server from a desired client to validate both that the firewall is enabled and the appropriate exceptions were created.

> **Note**
>
> Create an exception for the SQL Server Browser service if there is a need to broadcast SQL Server information to clients over the network. Otherwise, SQL Server clients must know the names and ports of the clients when connecting.

Hardening Internet Information Services with the IIS Lockdown Tool

The previous sections focused directly on hardening the SQL Server installation. Additional hardening techniques should be employed if IIS is running in conjunction with SQL Server. For example, IIS is needed if the Reporting Services component is installed or if it is common that IIS will be used as a front-end application and SQL Server as the back-end database repository. If this is the case, IIS should be hardened and locked down using the IIS Lockdown tool for both scenarios.

The IIS Lockdown tool provides a template for major Microsoft products. It works similarly to the Security Configuration Wizard included with Windows Server 2003 Service Pack 1 and the Surface Area Configuration tools. It turns off unnecessary features, thereby reducing the amount of attack surface available to attackers. It also includes additional tools that you can use to remove unwanted IIS services and configure URLScans.

The IIS Lockdown Wizard is integrated into IIS 6.0 with Windows Server 2003. If Windows 2000 is being used, the tool must be downloaded from the Microsoft website, installed, and configured.

> **Note**
>
> Hardening IIS is a complicated process because the procedures are customized and differ for each application and installation. For additional information on the IIS Lockdown tool, including configuring the tool and running URLScan, visit the Microsoft website.

Summary

When the SQL Server installation is complete, it is imperative that you harden the SQL Server environment. You should understand all hardening techniques available to determine which hardening strategies work best for your organization.

Additional security strategies such as encrypting SQL Server data and communications and administering SQL Server Security are covered in the next two chapters.

Best Practices

Following is a summary of best practices for hardening a SQL Server environment:

- Once the SQL Server installation is complete, harden the SQL Server environment.

- Install the most recent critical fixes and service packs for both Windows and SQL Server. As of this writing, the current service pack version for SQL Server is SQL Server 2005 Service Pack 2 and for Windows, it is Windows Server 2003 Service Pack 1.

- When you're selecting authentication modes, Windows Authentication is a more secure choice; however, if mixed mode authentication is required, leverage complex passwords and the new SQL Server 2005 password and lockout policies to further bolster security.

- Do *not* use the SA account for day-to-day administration, logging on to the server remotely, or having applications use it to connect to SQL. It is best if the SA account is disabled and renamed.

- Create a role-based security policy with the Security Configuration Wizard tool.

- After SQL Server 2005 is installed, run the SQL Server Configuration Manager and SQL Server Surface Area Configuration tools to disable unnecessary features and services.

- Install only required components when installing SQL Server.

- After the server has been hardened, periodically asses the server's security using the MBSA and SQL Server 2005 BPA.

- Either hide the instance or disable the SQL Server Browser service for production SQL Servers running mission-critical databases.

- Change the default ports associated with the SQL Server installation to put off hackers from port scanning the server.

- Enable a firewall to filter unnecessary and unknown traffic.

- At the very least, set security auditing to failed login attempts; otherwise, both failed and successful logins should be captured and monitored.

- Remove the BUILTIN/Administrators group from the SQL Server Logins.

- Use the IIS Lockdown and URLScan tools to harden IIS.

CHAPTER 13

Administering SQL Server Security

Important changes have been introduced with SQL Server 2005 to allow a much more effective method of design, implementation, and administration of security across resources and services provided by the SQL environment. Security permissions can be defined on a wide range of objects, from network endpoints that facilitate client communication, to execute permissions on a stored procedure, even down to the cell level within a table. Complex security implementations can be efficiently controlled with granular role-based authorization and database security schemas.

Administering SQL security is a key database administrator task that normally begins immediately following the hardening of the system, and understanding the different components related to security is essential to effective SQL security administration. This chapter discusses and demonstrates common administrative security tasks, incorporating best practices and new features introduced with SQL Server 2005.

SQL Server Security

SQL Server 2005 continues to support two modes for validating connections and authenticating access to database resources: *Windows Authentication* mode, along with *SQL Server and Windows Authentication* mode. Both provide the ability for users to authenticate to SQL Server and access resources.

> **Note**
>
> It is important to understand that security can be most effectively managed when the environment has been prepared and hardened. See Chapter 12, "Hardening a SQL Server 2005 Environment," for additional information.

When you're administering SQL Server security, it is important to follow the *principle of least privilege*. This basically means only the necessary permissions should be given to the different user and service accounts needed to accomplish the task. The principle of least privilege ensures that only the required resources are exposed to the client, while other resources are inaccessible and locked down. This improves the environment in multiple ways, including lowering the probability of accidental and intentional damage, increasing system scalability, and simplifying administration and deployment.

SQL Server 2005 facilitates flexible and scalable management of object permissions by allowing database users to be added to roles. Roles can then be given permissions on objects and security schemas, which provide grouping of related objects. Figure 13.1 depicts at a high level how database objects are accessed by clients.

In Figure 13.1 the client communicates to SQL Server through an endpoint. The client provides credentials used for authentication either by explicitly entering them or by passthrough Windows-based authentication. Server logins can be assigned permissions—for instance, scoped securable objects including the SQL Server, endpoints, and other logins.

> **Note**
>
> The login cannot be given permissions for database securable objects directly.
>
> The login must be mapped to a database user; the database user then can be given permissions on database-scoped securable objects either directly or through roles and schemas.

To obtain permissions on database securables, you map the server login to a database user. Permissions for database objects can be applied directly to the database user; however, it is a best practice to add the database user to roles and schemas and then give roles and schemas the correct permissions.

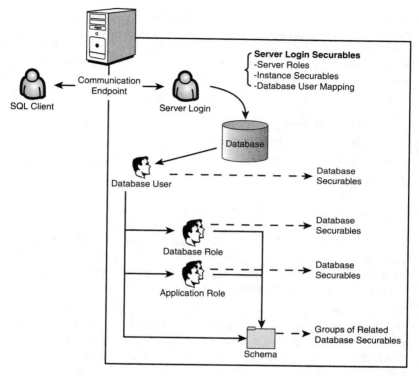

FIGURE 13.1
Overview of SQL Server security.

Endpoints and Communication

To communicate and access resources provided by a SQL Server, you must establish a connection to a tabular data stream (TDS) endpoint. TDS packets sent by the client to the endpoint are encapsulated with a standard network protocol by way of the SQL Server Network Interface (SNI) protocol layer. The SNI layer used for TDS encapsulation is common to both the SQL Server and SQL client.

> **Note**
>
> All communication to the SQL Server is provided by TDS endpoints. This creates an effective method of controlling access to the server, starting with the initial communication.

Endpoints for several default protocols supported by SQL Server are created by default. In addition, an endpoint is created by default for the dedicated administrator connection (DAC); this endpoint can be used only by members of the sysadmin fixed server role to establish an administrative connection to the server. Following are the default endpoints and protocols:

- Dedicated Administrator Connection (TCP)
- TSQL Local Machine (Shared Memory)
- TSQL Named Pipes (Named Pipes)
- TSQL Default TCP (TCP)
- TSQL Default VIA (VIA)

Default system endpoints cannot be dropped or disabled. However, they can be stopped and started, and the permissions for the endpoints can be altered as necessary. For each SQL Server instance, only a single named pipe and shared memory endpoint are supported. User-defined endpoints can have multiple instances per SQL Server instance; the protocol for user-defined endpoints is always HTTP or TCP.

The default system endpoints are all configured for the TSQL payload type. This means they communicate with the endpoint using Transact-SQL. When a user defines an endpoint, the payload type can be configured as TSQL, SOAP, Service Broker, or Database Mirroring. For example, a database that is mirroring communicates with its partners through endpoints configured with the Database Mirroring payload type.

Note

The DAC allows you to connect to a server when the Database Engine does not respond to regular connections. By default, the DAC endpoint cannot be accessed remotely and is available only from the local computer. The SQL Server 2005 Surface Area Configuration tool can be used to enable remote access for the DAC endpoint.

With the exception of HTTP, the protocols for each of the default endpoints are listed and can be configured in the SQL Server Configuration Manager. In addition, the different protocols, including HTTP, can be enabled or disabled through the Surface Area Configuration tool.

When a protocol is disabled, the endpoint that implements the protocol cannot be used, although the endpoint may still be in the started state. In

SQL Server 2005 Enterprise, Standard, and Workgroup Editions, only TCP/IP is enabled by default. In Developer and Evaluation Editions, TCP/IP is disabled by default.

> **Note**
>
> The Named Pipes protocol is enabled by default in all editions of SQL, but only to support local connections.

You can use the `sys.endpoints` catalog view to see the status of all endpoints on the server. The following query returns all the endpoints for the server:

```
USE MASTER
SELECT * FROM sys.endpoints
```

The `sys.http_endpoints`, `sys.soap_endpoints`, and `sys.endpoint_webmethods` catalog views can be used to get additional information about specific types of endpoints.

The `sys.server_permissions` catalog view can be used to see the permissions on server-securable objects, including endpoints. The `sys.server_principals` catalog view can be used to identify the name associated with the principal ID in the `grantee_principal_id` column.

The `grantee_principal_id` column shows the `Server-principal-ID` to which the permissions are granted. For example, the following query returns the grantee permissions and grantee name for all endpoints on a server. Note that each endpoint has a value of 105 in the class column:

```
USE MASTER
SELECT
  p.class_desc,
  p.major_id,
  p.minor_id,
  p.grantee_principal_id,
  sp.name as grantee_name,
  p.permission_name,
  p.state_desc
FROM sys.server_permissions p
  INNER JOIN sys.server_principals sp
    ON p.grantee_principal_id = sp.principal_id
WHERE class = 105
```

The result set of the query shows that the principal public has been granted CONNECT permission on each of the endpoints by default. This essentially allows all logins to connect to any of the default endpoints, if the underlying protocol has also been enabled.

> **Note**
>
> It is a best practice to enable only communication protocols that are necessary and to allow only specific CONNECT permissions on endpoints.

You can administer existing protocols and endpoints through the Surface Area Configuration tool, SQL Server Configuration Manager, and data definition language (DDL). However, you can create new endpoints only through the CREATE ENDPOINT DDL.

Server Logins and Database Users

Server logins and database users are both principals. SQL Server permissions on securable objects are granted to principals.

Table 13.1 shows all the SQL Server principals.

Table 13.1   **SQL Server Principals**

Type	Description
Server	SQL Server login
Server	SQL Server login from Windows login
Server	SQL Server login from certificate
Server	SQL Server login from asymmetric key
Database	Database user
Database	Database role
Database	Database user mapped to Windows user
Database	Database user mapped to Windows group
Database	Database user mapped to certificate
Database	Database user with no login

> **Note**
>
> Principals are also securable objects; for example, users can be granted control permissions on other users, database roles, and so on.

Clients authenticate to the server using a SQL Server login. The authentication used for the login can be either Windows or SQL based. Windows authentication logins are recommended over SQL authentication logins because Windows logins can leverage Active Directory security and native authentication encryption.

When you're using Windows Authentication mode, the account can be a local or domain-based user account or group. When you're using SQL-based authentication, the account information, including the password, is stored on the SQL Server in the database.

Both SQL- and Windows-based logins provide access to server instance objects but not to database objects. The following securable objects can be assigned permissions for server logins:

- Servers
- Endpoints
- Logins

SQL logins are mapped to database users. Database users are then given permissions on securable objects in the database to provide access to the authenticated client. Following are database user securables:

- Databases
- Stored Procedures
- Tables
- Views
- Inline Functions
- Scalar Functions
- Table-Valued Functions
- Aggregate Functions
- Application Roles
- Assemblies
- Asymmetric Keys
- Certificates
- Database Roles
- Full-Text Catalogs
- Schemas
- Symmetric Keys
- Synonyms
- Users
- User-Defined Data Types
- XML Schema Collections

Both SQL logins and users are considered securable objects and can have permissions assigned in the same fashion as any other object in the database.

Role-Based Access

Although database users can be given permissions on objects directly, this is generally considered a bad practice when dealing with complex security permissions. It is much more effective to create roles for each type of user and assign the correct permissions to the role. Role-based access reduces the cost of ongoing security administration because users can be added and removed from roles without your having to re-create complex permissions for each user.

Role-based access can be established at both the SQL level and in Active Directory. It is common to establish role-based access for all network services through Active Directory with the added benefit of organization wide control of data services.

Using Active Directory for role-based access follows the standard of placing user accounts into domain global *role groups* and the role groups into domain local *access groups*. The access groups are then added to the SQL instance as logins and mapped to database users. The database users can then be added to the correct database role and/or security schemas. As a result, users added to role groups in Active Directory automatically obtain the correct permissions. Security management for the environment is transferred from SQL Server into Active Directory, where it can be controlled on a granular level.

For additional information on role-based Active Directory security, see "Introduction to Roles-Based Security" and "Technical Example of the Ring Method to Roles-Based Security in Microsoft Active Directory" at the following site:

http://www.cco.com/technote.htm

Note

Active Directory can be leveraged to establish access and role-based security groups for accessing SQL Server resources. However, a limitation exists using this security model because a default schema cannot be assigned to the user.

This is typically not an issue as long as the security design accounts for this limitation. Role-based access through Active Directory is still highly recommended and effective.

Several server-level roles exist in each SQL Server instance. Table 13.2 lists each server-level role and the permissions associated with each role.

Table 13.2   **Server-Level Roles**

Server Role	Default Permissions
bulkadmin	Granted: ADMINISTER BULK OPERATIONS
dbcreator	Granted: CREATE DATABASE
diskadmin	Granted: ALTER RESOURCES
processadmin	Granted: ALTER ANY CONNECTION, ALTER SERVER STATE
securityadmin	Granted: ALTER ANY LOGIN
serveradmin	Granted: ALTER ANY ENDPOINT, ALTER RESOURCES, ALTER SERVER STATE, ALTER SETTINGS, SHUTDOWN, VIEW SERVER STATE
setupadmin	Granted: ALTER ANY LINKED SERVER
sysadmin	Granted with GRANT option: CONTROL SERVER
public	Granted: VIEW ANY DATABASE

> **Note**
>
> All logins belong to the public server role by default. The public role is granted VIEW ANY DATABASE by default.

Several database-level roles exist in each SQL Server database. Table 13.3 lists each database-level role and the permissions associated with each role.

Table 13.3   **Database-Level Roles**

Database Role	Default Permissions
db_accessadmin	Granted: ALTER ANY USER, CREATE SCHEMA
db_accessadmin	Granted with GRANT option: CONNECT
db_backupoperator	Granted: BACKUP DATABASE, BACKUP LOG, CHECKPOINT
db_datareader	Granted: SELECT
db_datawriter	Granted: DELETE, INSERT, UPDATE
db_ddladmin	Granted: ALTER ANY ASSEMBLY, ALTER ANY ASYMMETRIC KEY, ALTER ANY CERTIFICATE, ALTER ANY CONTRACT, ALTER ANY DATABASE DDL TRIGGER, ALTER ANY DATABASE EVENT NOTIFICATION, ALTER ANY DATASPACE, ALTER ANY FULLTEXT CATALOG, ALTER ANY MESSAGE TYPE, ALTER ANY REMOTE SERVICE BINDING, ALTER ANY ROUTE, ALTER ANY SCHEMA, ALTER ANY SERVICE, ALTER ANY SYMMETRIC KEY, CHECK-POINT, CREATE AGGREGATE, CREATE DEFAULT, CREATE FUNC-TION, CREATE PROCEDURE, CREATE QUEUE, CREATE RULE, CREATE SYNONYM, CREATE TABLE, CREATE TYPE, CREATE VIEW, CREATE XML SCHEMA COLLECTION, REFERENCES

Table 13.3   **continued**

Database Role	Default Permissions
db_denydatareader	Denied: SELECT
db_denydatawriter	Denied: DELETE, INSERT, UPDATE
db_owner	Granted with GRANT option: CONTROL
db_securityadmin	Granted: ALTER ANY APPLICATION ROLE, ALTER ANY ROLE, CREATE SCHEMA, VIEW DEFINITION
public	Granted: SELECT on system views

> **Note**
>
> All database users belong to the public database role by default. It is a best practice to avoid using the public database role when assigning permissions.

Database Schema

The database schema is new in SQL Server 2005 and provides several improvements when compared to previous versions of SQL Server. The schema is a key part of establishing flexible database security administration.

When objects are accessed in SQL Server 2005, they are referenced by a four-part identifier, shown in the following code:

```
[DatabaseServer].[DatabaseName].[DatabaseSchema].[DatabaseObject]
```

For example, the following query can be used to access the Employee table created as part of the HumanResources schema in the AdventureWorks database. The AdventureWorks database is hosted on INSTANCE01 on the server SQL01.

```
SELECT *
FROM
➥[SQL01\INSTANCE01].[AdventureWorks].[HumanResources].[Employee]
```

The database schema is part of the namespace used to reference an object in the database. The schema provides a way to manage security on groups of objects with a granular level of control. As new database objects are defined, they must be associated with a schema and automatically inherit the permissions of the schema.

The principal defined as the schema owner effectively owns all objects in the schema. When the owner of a schema is changed, all objects in the schema are owned by the new principal, with the exception of objects for which an explicit owner is defined.

This is a significant improvement over SQL Server 2000 because the schema takes the place of the user account that owned the database objects, allowing much easier transfer of object ownership.

Password Policies

Domain policies and local security policies provide the password and account lockout configuration that affects users' ability to authenticate and access SQL Server resources.

When Windows Authentication mode is used, these settings govern all users according to the defined policy and cannot be overridden.

When SQL Server authentication is used, the logon can be configured to obey the password and lockout policies of the underlying local security or domain group policy. This functionality is new in SQL Server 2005 and is supported only on the Windows Server 2003 or later operating system.

> **Note**
>
> If SQL authentication is used, it is highly recommended to enable the options to enforce the local security policies and to implement encrypted authentication.

The following password policies can be used to help secure Windows and SQL Server authentication:

- **Enforce Password History**—This security setting determines the number of unique new passwords that have to be associated with a user account before an old password can be reused.

- **Maximum Password Age**—This security setting determines the period of time (in days) that a password can be used before the system requires the user to change it.

- **Minimum Password Age**—This security setting determines the period of time (in days) that a password must be used before the user can change it.

- **Minimum Password Length**—This security setting determines the least number of characters that a password for a user account may contain.

- **Password Must Meet Complexity Requirements**—This security setting determines whether passwords must meet complexity requirements. Complex passwords cannot contain the user's name, must be at least six characters in length, and must contain characters from three of the four available character categories. Character categories include uppercase, lowercase, base 10 digits, and nonalphabetic characters.

- **Store Passwords Using Reversible Encryption**—This security setting determines whether the operating system stores passwords using reversible encryption. This setting affects only Windows authentication and has no effect on SQL Server logons.

> **Note**
>
> There can be only a single password policy for each Active Directory domain. Password policy settings for the domain must be defined in the root node for the domain.
>
> This limitation is expected to be fixed in Windows Server 2008, as password policies will be definable on a per-user basis.

These security policies can be accessed through the Windows Settings\ Security Settings\Account Policies\Password Policies node in the Default Domain Policy. Figure 13.2 shows the default Active Directory password policies.

The following account lockout policies can be used to help secure Windows and SQL Server authentication:

- **Account Lockout Threshold**—This security setting determines the number of minutes a locked-out account remains locked out before automatically becoming unlocked. The available range is from 0 minutes through 99,999 minutes. If you set the account lockout duration to 0, the account is locked out until an administrator explicitly unlocks it.

- **Account Lockout Duration**—This security setting determines the number of failed logon attempts that causes a user account to be locked out. A locked-out account cannot be used until it is reset by an administrator or until the lockout duration for the account has expired. You can set a value between 0 and 999 failed logon attempts. If you set the value to 0, the account is never locked out.

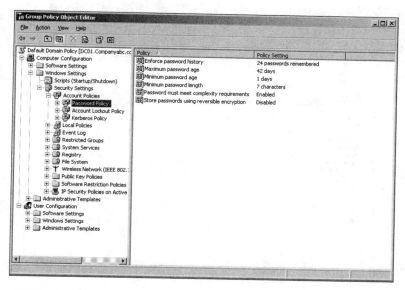

FIGURE 13.2
Windows password policies.

- **Reset Lockout Counter After**—This security setting determines the
  number of minutes that must elapse after a failed logon attempt before
  the failed logon attempt counter is reset to 0 bad logon attempts. The
  available range is 1 minute to 99,999 minutes.

These security policies can be accessed through the Windows
Settings\Security Settings\Account Policies\Account Lockout Policy node in
the Default Domain Policy. Figure 13.3 shows the default Active Directory
account lockout policies.

When these policies are configured, the resulting domain-level group policy
or the local security policy helps secure the environment by preventing low
security passwords.

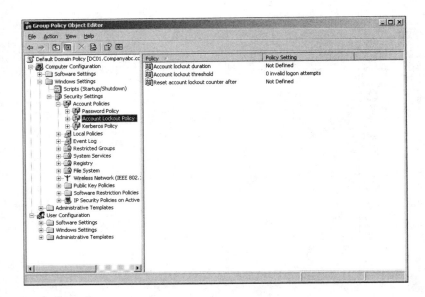

FIGURE 13.3
Windows account lockout policies.

Security Management DDL

The data definition language used to administer SQL Server 2005 security is provided in the following sections as a reference. The Transact-SQL (TSQL) statements shown here are demonstrated in the section "Administering SQL Server Security" later in this chapter.

Managing Logins with DDL

The CREATE LOGIN statement can be used to define new SQL Server logins. The SQL Server login can be a Windows user account, a Windows security group, or a SQL Server account.

```
CREATE LOGIN login_name { WITH <option_list1> | FROM <sources> }

<sources> ::=
    WINDOWS [ WITH <windows_options> [ ,... ] ]
    | CERTIFICATE certname
    | ASYMMETRIC KEY asym_key_name
```

```
<option_list1> ::=
    PASSWORD = 'password' [ HASHED ] [ MUST_CHANGE ]
    [ , <option_list2> [ ,... ] ]

<option_list2> ::=
    SID = sid
    | DEFAULT_DATABASE = database
    | DEFAULT_LANGUAGE = language
    | CHECK_EXPIRATION = { ON | OFF}
    | CHECK_POLICY = { ON | OFF}
    | CREDENTIAL = credential_name

<windows_options> ::=
    DEFAULT_DATABASE = database
    | DEFAULT_LANGUAGE = language
```

The ALTER LOGIN statement can be used to modify existing SQL Server logins. For example, if the password policy of a SQL user causes the account to become locked out, the security administrator can use the ALTER LOGIN statement to unlock the account.

```
ALTER LOGIN login_name
    {
    <status_option>
    | WITH <set_option> [ ,... ]
    }

<status_option> ::=
        ENABLE | DISABLE

<set_option> ::=
    PASSWORD = 'password' [HASHED]
    [
      OLD_PASSWORD = 'oldpassword'
      | <password_option> [ <password_option> ]
    ]
    | DEFAULT_DATABASE = database
    | DEFAULT_LANGUAGE = language
    | NAME = login_name
    | CHECK_POLICY = { ON | OFF }
    | CHECK_EXPIRATION = { ON | OFF }
```

```
| CREDENTIAL = credential_name
| NO CREDENTIAL

<password_option> ::=
    MUST_CHANGE | UNLOCK
```

The DROP LOGIN statement can be used to remove logins from the server:

```
DROP LOGIN login_name
```

The following stored procedures are still available; however, these stored procedures are considered deprecated and should not be used:

- sp_addlogin
- sp_grantlogin
- sp_denylogin
- sp_revokelogin

Managing Users with DDL

The CREATE USER statement can be used to define a new database user. After the SQL Server login is created, the login can be mapped to a database as a user; from this point, permissions for the database can be assigned.

```
CREATE USER user_name
    [ { { FOR | FROM }
      {
        LOGIN login_name
        | CERTIFICATE cert_name
        | ASYMMETRIC KEY asym_key_name
      }
      | WITHOUT LOGIN
    ]
    [ WITH DEFAULT_SCHEMA = schema_name ]
```

The ALTER USER statement can be used to modify existing database users. For example, if you need to update the default schema for a user, you can use this statement.

```
ALTER USER user_name
    WITH <set_item> [ ,...n ]
```

```
<set_item> ::=
    NAME = new_user_name
    | DEFAULT_SCHEMA = schema_name
```

The DROP USER statement can be used to remove a database user from a database. When a login is removed, the mapped database user account is not automatically removed; this step must be done manually to complete the removal.

```
DROP USER user_name
```

Managing Roles with DDL

The CREATE and ALTER ROLE statements can be used to define and modify database roles. Users should be assigned to database roles instead of being assigned to objects directly to get the appropriate permissions.

```
CREATE ROLE role_name [ AUTHORIZATION owner_name ]
ALTER ROLE role_name WITH NAME = new_name
```

The sp_addrolemember statement can be used to add principals to database roles. If a login is specified, a database user is automatically created for the login and added to the role.

```
sp_addrolemember [ @rolename = ] 'role',
    [ @membername = ] 'security_account'
```

The sp_droprolemember statement can be used to remove database users from database roles:

```
sp_droprolemember [ @rolename = ] 'role' ,
        [ @membername = ] 'security_account'
```

The sp_addsrvrolemember statement can be used to add logins to fixed server roles. Note that role membership for SA and Public cannot be changed.

```
sp_addsrvrolemember [ @loginame= ] 'login'
    , [ @rolename = ] 'role'
```

The sp_dropsrvrolemember statement can be used to remove logins from fixed server roles. Note that role membership for SA and Public cannot be changed.

```
sp_dropsrvrolemember [ @loginame = ] 'login' , [ @rolename = ]
➥'role'
```

Managing Schemas with DDL

The CREATE SCHEMA statement can be used to define a new database schema. Database roles and users can be added to the schema to receive permissions on database objects. The schema is used to group database objects together, so permissions don't need to be assigned to individual objects.

```
CREATE SCHEMA schema_name_clause [ <schema_element> [ ...n ] ]

<schema_name_clause> ::=
    {
        schema_name
    | AUTHORIZATION owner_name
    | schema_name AUTHORIZATION owner_name
    }

<schema_element> ::=
    {
        table_definition | view_definition | grant_statement |
        revoke_statement | deny_statement
    }
```

The ALTER SCHEMA statement can be used to transfer ownership to another database user or role. This statement cannot be used to add or remove securable items from the schema. To add or remove securables from the schema, you must modify the securable object directly. For example, to add a table to the schema, you use the ALTER TABLE statement.

```
ALTER SCHEMA schema_name TRANSFER securable_name
```

Managing Permissions with DDL

The statements shown in this section can be used to grant, deny, or revoke permissions on objects to principals. Only the basic syntax is shown; you can find additional object-specific syntax in the SQL Server 2005 Books Online.

Note

Normally, deny permissions take precedence over grant permissions. However, for backward-compatibility, column-level permissions take precedence over object permissions.

The GRANT statement gives principals such as database roles, users, and logins permissions to securable objects such as databases and tables. The WITH GRANT option essentially allows the grantee principal to give other principals the same permissions on the object.

```
GRANT { ALL [ PRIVILEGES ] }
      | permission [ ( column [ ,...n ] ) ] [ ,...n ]
      [ ON [ class :: ] securable ] TO principal [ ,...n ]
      [ WITH GRANT OPTION ] [ AS principal ]
```

The DENY statement prevents principals from accessing objects and inheriting permissions through membership of database roles:

```
DENY { ALL [ PRIVILEGES ] }
     | permission [ ( column [ ,...n ] ) ] [ ,...n ]
     [ ON [ class :: ] securable ] TO principal [ ,...n ]
     [ CASCADE] [ AS principal ]
```

The REVOKE statement essentially removes a GRANT or DENY permission:

```
REVOKE [ GRANT OPTION FOR ]
       {
         [ ALL [ PRIVILEGES ] ]
         |
                 permission [ ( column [ ,...n ] ) ] [ ,...n ]
       }
       [ ON [ class :: ] securable ]
       { TO | FROM } principal [ ,...n ]
       [ CASCADE] [ AS principal ]
```

Administering SQL Server Security

The following sections provide detailed instructions for administering SQL Server permissions and authorizing access to SQL Server resources. The demonstrations are shown using logins configured for either SQL Server or Windows Authentication mode because both can be added to roles and are given permissions the same way.

Note

Using Windows authentication is considered a more secure choice and is recommended over SQL logins because Windows authentication protocols such as NTLM and Kerberos can be leveraged.

Using Windows authentication provides several advantages over SQL Server authentication, including enterprisewide control of access accounts governed by domain security policies. In addition, Windows authentication can leverage Active Directory authentication protocols such as NTLM and Kerberos when SQL Server is located in an Active Directory domain.

If SQL authentication is required, you must make sure to leverage the new SQL Server 2005 password and lockout policies in addition to login encryption to further bolster security.

The section "Password Policies" earlier in this chapter has additional information on how to configure password policies.

Server Login Administration

The SQL login is the basic method of authenticating to the SQL Server. When Windows accounts are used, either NTLM or Kerberos authentication is used to validate the credentials. The user's credentials are also encrypted, making it difficult to discover them as they travel across the network.

When SQL Server logins are used, the passwords are sent over the network using clear text by default. However, new features in SQL Server 2005 allow these credentials to be encrypted, reducing the risk associated with these types of logins. See Chapter 14, "Encrypting SQL Server Data and Communications," for additional information on encrypting SQL authentication-based logins.

Enabling Mixed Mode Authentication

SQL Server can be configured for Windows Authentication mode only or SQL Server and Windows Authentication mode. For simplicity, some of the demonstrations use SQL authentication and require the server to support both authentication modes.

Follow these steps to enable both Windows Authentication mode and SQL Server and Windows Authentication mode:

1. From the test server (SQL01), choose Start, All Programs, Microsoft SQL Server 2005, SQL Server Management Studio.

2. Select Database Engine from the Server Type drop-down; then enter the server and instance name (**SQL01\INSTANCE01**).

3. Select Windows Authentication from the Authentication drop-down menu and then click the Connect button.

4. A connection to the database engine is made. If the Object Explorer pane is not visible, press the F8 button.

5. From within the Object Explorer pane, right-click on a desired SQL Server and then click Properties.

6. On the Security page, under Server Authentication, select SQL Server and Windows Authentication mode and then click OK.

7. In the SQL Server Management Studio dialog box, click OK to acknowledge the need to restart SQL Server.

8. In Object Explorer, right-click on a desired server and then click Restart. If the SQL Server Agent is running, it also requires a restart.

Note

If Windows Authentication mode is selected during installation, the SA login is disabled by default. If the authentication mode is switched to SQL Server mixed mode after the installation, the SA account is still disabled and must be manually enabled. It is a best practice to reset the password when the mode is switched.

Creating SQL Authentication Logins

The Logins node holds all the Windows and SQL logins for the server. From this node, the different server logins can be managed.

The following procedure can be used to create a new SQL login on INSTANCE01 hosted on server SQL01. To start the process, log on to the SQL01 server with an account that has the sysadmin or securityadmin fixed server role. Then do the following:

1. From the server (SQL01), choose Start, All Programs, Microsoft SQL Server 2005, SQL Server Management Studio.

2. Select Database Engine from the Server Type drop-down; then enter the server and instance name (**SQL01\INSTANCE01**).

3. Select Windows Authentication from the Authentication drop-down menu and then click the Connect button.

4. A connection to the database engine is made. If the Object Explorer pane is not visible, press the F8 button.

5. From within the Object Explorer pane, expand Security and select the Logins node.

6. Right-click the Logins node and select New Login. The Login—New window opens.

The following relevant login options are located on the General configuration page:

- **Login Name**—When Windows authentication is used, this is the name of the existing Windows user or Windows security group. When SQL authentication is used, this is the name selected for the login.

- **Windows Authentication**—This option allows the selection of a Windows user account or security group for the logon. The Windows user account or security group can reside in Active Directory or the local server.

- **SQL Server Authentication**—This option allows the creation of an account where the account information including the account password is stored in the SQL database.

The following additional options are available on the General tab when you use SQL Server authentication:

- **Enforce Password Policy**—This option configures the SQL Server to adhere to domain or local server password policies. If SQL Server authentication is used, this option is highly recommended to help improve security.

- **Enforce Password Expiration**—This option configures the SQL Server to adhere to domain or local server password expiration policies. This option should be enabled if the database application provides a way for the user to change the password.

- **User Must Change Password**—When this option is enabled, the user must change the password during the first authentication. This option should be enabled if the database application provides a way for the user to change the password.

Follow these steps to create the SQL Server login and complete the configuration page:

1. Enter `Test.User1` in the Login Name field.
2. Select SQL Server authentication.
3. Enter the password.
4. Confirm the password.
5. Select Enforce Password Policy.
6. Select Enforce Password Expiration.

7. Select User Must Change Password at Next Login.

8. Leave Master as the Default database.

9. Leave <default> as the Default language.

10. Figure 13.4 shows how the Logon Properties window should look. Click OK to complete the page and create the login.

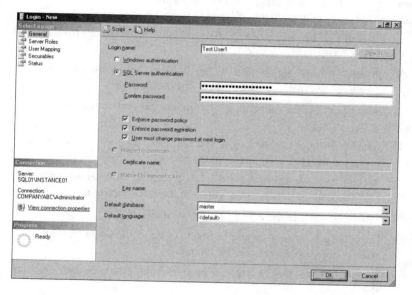

FIGURE 13.4
New SQL authentication logon properties.

The SQL login Test.User1 is created but currently has only a limited set of permissions. By default, all users are members of the default public server role.

You can use the following TSQL code to accomplish the same task. This code creates a user called Test.User2 with `Password!!` set as the default password for the account:

```
USE [master]
GO
CREATE LOGIN [Test.User2] WITH
    PASSWORD=N'Password!!'
    MUST_CHANGE,
```

```
DEFAULT_DATABASE=[master],
CHECK_EXPIRATION=ON,
CHECK_POLICY=ON
GO
```

After the account is created, the next step is to verify the account can authenticate to the server. Configuring permissions for the login is described later in this chapter. To continue, do the following:

1. Launch a new instance of SQL Server Management Studio from the server (SQL01).

2. Select Database Engine from the Server Type drop-down; then enter the server and instance name (**SQL01\INSTANCE01**).

3. Select SQL Server Authentication from the Authentication drop-down menu.

4. Enter **Test.User1** in the Login field and enter the password assigned to the logon. Then click the Connect button.

5. A change password prompt is displayed because the User Must Change Password policy was enabled when the login was defined.

6. Enter and confirm the new password; then click OK.

7. A connection to the database engine is made. If the Object Explorer pane is not visible, press the F8 button.

8. From within the Object Explorer pane, expand Databases and select the AdventureWorks database.

9. An error message is displayed, notifying the login that the database is inaccessible.

Although the account cannot access any of the databases, the authentication should be successful.

Creating Windows Authentication Logins

Creating a Windows login is similar to creating a SQL Server login. Another one of the many advantages to using Windows authentication includes the ability to add domain security groups as the login instead of just the user account.

> **Note**
>
> One of the drawbacks to using Windows security groups for logins is that you cannot assign a default schema.

Before you add a Windows account or security group as a SQL Server login, it must exist in Active Directory or on the local computer. Follow these steps to create a Windows user account in Active Directory:

1. On the test server (SQL01), select Start, Run.

2. Type **DSA.MSC** and then click OK.

3. Create a domain user account called **Test.Domain1**.

After creating the Active Directory user account, you can add the account as a login. Follow these steps to add the Test.Domain1 domain user as a login on INSTANCE01 hosted on SQL01:

1. From within SQL Server Management Studio, expand the Security node.

2. Right-click the Logins node and select New Login.

3. Click the Search button.

4. Click Locations and select Entire Directory, and then click OK.

5. Type **Test.Domain1** in the Object field.

6. Click the Check Name button to confirm the account name.

7. Click OK to return to the Login Properties window.

8. Select Master as the Default database.

9. Select <default> as the Default language.

10. Figure 13.5 shows how the Logon Properties window should look. Click OK to complete the page and create the login.

The user account is listed in the Logins folder. Perform the following steps to verify the account can authenticate to the server. The SQL Server Management Studio can be executed as a different user account through the Run As command.

1. From the server (SQL01), choose Start, All Programs, Microsoft SQL Server 2005. Then right-click on SQL Server Management Studio and select Run As.

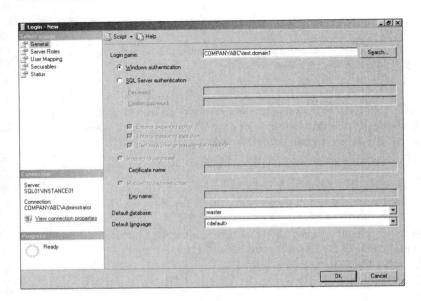

FIGURE 13.5
New Windows authentication logon properties.

2. In the Run As window, enter **COMPANYABC\Test.Domain1** in the User Name field.

3. Enter the associated account password and click OK. The SQL Server Management Studio opens under the Test.Domain1 account.

4. Select Database Engine from the Server Type drop-down; then enter the server and instance name (**SQL01\INSTANCE01**).

5. Select Windows Authentication from the Authentication drop-down menu and then click the Connect button.

6. A connection to the database engine is made. If the Object Explorer pane is not visible, press the F8 button.

7. From within the Object Explorer pane, expand Databases and select the AdventureWorks database.

8. An error message is displayed, notifying the login that the database is inaccessible.

The authentication should be successful because the default database was set to Master and the login is a member of the public server role. The public role has limited access to the master database. If you set the default database to something else, such as AdventureWorks, the authentication would fail because the public role does not have access to this database by default.

You can use the following TSQL code to add the Test.Domain1 user as a SQL login:

```
USE [master]
GO
CREATE LOGIN [COMPANYABC\Test.Domain1] FROM WINDOWS WITH
➥DEFAULT_DATABASE=[master]
GO
```

Database User Administration

After adding a login to the server, you can create a database user. The database user is essentially mapped back to the original login; this means the login is normally required before access to database resources can be authorized.

> **Note**
>
> A new SQL Server 2005 feature allows the creation of a database user without creating a login. This can be done with the WITHOUT LOGIN option, part of the CREATE USER DDL. These users can be assigned to securables and invoked with the EXECUTE AS statement.

Follow these steps to manage database users. This procedure adds the login Test.User1 to the AdventureWorks database in INSTANCE01 on server SQL01.

1. From within SQL Server Management Studio, expand AdventureWorks, Security, and select Users.
2. Right-click Users and select New User.
3. Click the ellipses button next to the Login Name field.
4. On the Select Login page, click Browse.
5. Select Test.User1 and then click OK.
6. Click OK to return to the Database User page.
7. Enter **Test.User1** in the User Name field.
8. Click the ellipses button next to the Default Schema field.
9. On the Select Schema window, click Browse.

10. Select Human Resources and then click OK.

11. Click OK to return to the Database User properties window.

12. The Database User properties window should look similar to Figure 13.6. Click OK to create the database user.

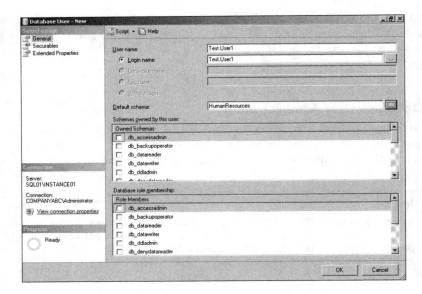

FIGURE 13.6
New database user properties.

A user called Test.User1 is added to the database. You can use the following TSQL code to add a login and an associated database user:

```
USE [AdventureWorks]
CREATE LOGIN [Test.User2]
  WITH PASSWORD=N'Password!'
  MUST_CHANGE,
  DEFAULT_DATABASE=[master],
  CHECK_EXPIRATION=ON, CHECK_POLICY=ON
GO
CREATE USER [Test.User2]
  FOR LOGIN [Test.User2]
  WITH DEFAULT_SCHEMA=[HumanResources]
GO
```

Now that you've added the login to the database, you can assign the correct permissions. Although permissions to objects can be assigned directly to users, it is recommended to create roles and security schemas to control access to database objects.

Windows-based logins can be mapped to database users using the exact same method. Database mapping for logins can also be configured within the Mapping options page of the Login Properties window.

Database Role Administration

For efficient and effective management of data, users should be added to database roles. Each database role can be assigned permissions on a different object found in SQL Server.

The following procedure creates a new database role called Human Resources Reporting, the Test.User1 database user is added to this new role, and the role is given SELECT permissions to the HumanResources schema. Just follow these steps:

1. From within SQL Server Management Studio, expand AdventureWorks, Security, Roles, and select Database Roles.

2. Right-click Database Roles and select New Database Role.

3. Type **Human Resources Reporting** in the Name field.

4. Click the Add button.

5. On the Select Database User or Role page, click Browse.

6. Select Test.User1 and click OK.

7. Click OK to return to the Database Role properties window.

8. Select the Securables properties page.

9. Click the Add button.

10. Select All Objects of Type and then click OK.

11. Select Schemas and click OK.

12. From the Securables list, select HumanResources.

13. In the Explicit Permissions list, enable Grant on the Select permission.

14. Click OK to complete the new role.

You can use the following TSQL code to create and configure the Human Resources Reporting database role in the AdventureWorks database:

```
USE [AdventureWorks]
GO
CREATE ROLE [Human Resources Reporting]
GO
USE [AdventureWorks]
GO
EXEC sp_addrolemember N'Human Resources Reporting', N'Test.User1'
GO
use [AdventureWorks]
GO
GRANT SELECT ON SCHEMA::[HumanResources] TO [Human Resources
Reporting]
GO
```

The code example first creates the database role and then adds the user
Test.User1 to the role. Finally, the role is given permissions to the schema
object named HumanResources.

The sys.database_role_members and sys.database_principals catalog
views can be used to display database roles.

Security Schema Administration

The security schema for a database essentially provides a container for a
group of objects in the database. Besides the default schemas found in all
databases, the AdventureWorks database has several different schemas
defined, including HumanResources, Person, Production, Purchasing,
and Sales.

Follow these steps to establish a new schema called Test Schema for the
AdventureWorks database:

1. From within SQL Server Management Studio, expand
   AdventureWorks, Security, and select Schemas.

2. Expand the Schemas node. Each of the default schemas for the
   AdventureWorks database is listed.

3. Right-click the Schemas node and select New Schema. The new
   Schema Properties window opens.

4. In the Schema Name field, type **Test Schema**.

5. Click the Search button.

6. Click the Browse button.

7. Select Test.User1 and click OK.

8. Click OK to return to the Schema properties page.

On the Permissions page of the schema, you can define the permissions for each database user and role. These permissions can also be defined on the Database User or Role Property pages.

The permissions configured on the schema are applied to each object created in the schema for each principal given rights on the schema. This is very important when managing security because new objects can now inherit the correct permissions automatically.

Managing Application Roles

An application role is another type of principal that can be created in a SQL Server database. Like the database role, the application role is given permissions to database objects, can be added to other roles, and is given permissions through schemas. However, unlike the database role, the application role does not contain database users. The application role is designed to allow applications to obtain permissions on database objects.

When a user runs a database application, the application executes a specific stored procedure designed to activate the application role. The database application must be configured to provide the correct username and password. If the authentication is successful, the user's permissions change exclusively to the permissions obtained through the application role. The user's permissions can be reverted to the original context only by executing another stored procedure. The following syntax is used to define a new application role:

```
CREATE APPLICATION ROLE application_role_name
    WITH PASSWORD = 'password' [ , DEFAULT_SCHEMA = schema_name ]
```

You can also configure application roles through the SQL Server Management studio by selecting the Application Roles node in the Security\Roles node of a database.

The sp_setapprole stored procedure must be executed by the application to activate the application role. Here's the syntax of the stored procedure:

```
sp_setapprole [ @rolename = ] 'role',
    [ @password = ] { encrypt N'password' }
    |
    'password' [ , [ @encrypt = ] { 'none' | 'odbc' } ]
    [ , [ @fCreateCookie = ] true | false ]
  [ , [ @cookie = ] @cookie OUTPUT ]
```

The `sp_unsetapprole` stored procedure must be executed by the application to change the user's context back to the original settings. Following is the syntax of this stored procedure. Note, the cookie option must be used in the `sp_setapprole` for this stored procedure to work.

```
sp_unsetapprole @cookie
```

As an alternative to application roles, database users can be created without explicit logins. Applications can then be configured to execute as this database user instead of the application role.

Server Endpoint Administration

Server endpoints allow communication with the SQL Server through one or more of the supported protocols. All endpoints for a SQL Server instance can be viewed through the SQL Server Management Studio. Follow these steps to view endpoints for the instance INSTANCE01 on the server SQL01:

1. From the test server (SQL01), choose Start, All Programs, Microsoft SQL Server 2005, SQL Server Management Studio.

2. Select Database Engine from the Server Type drop-down; then enter the server and instance name (**SQL01\INSTANCE01**).

3. Select Windows Authentication from the Authentication drop-down menu and then click the Connect button.

4. A connection to the database engine is made. If the Object Explorer pane is not visible, press the F8 button.

5. From within the Object Explorer pane, expand Server Objects, Endpoints, Systems Endpoints, TSQL.

6. The default TSQL endpoints are listed.

If database mirroring or SOAP web services user-defined endpoints have been created, they are listed under the corresponding nodes within the Endpoints node.

The SQL Server Management Studio offers limited management of endpoints, allowing only the administration of permissions for endpoints and providing the ability to drop user-defined endpoints.

Note

System default endpoints cannot be dropped. However, you can start and stop these endpoints and change the permission on system default endpoints.

Endpoint security is important because it controls the different aspects of the endpoint, such as who can connect and who can administer an endpoint for a specific instance or application.

Follow these steps to change the permissions on the default system TSQL Local Machine endpoint:

1. From the server (SQL01), choose Start, All Programs, Microsoft SQL Server 2005, SQL Server Management Studio.

2. Select Database Engine from the Server Type drop-down; then enter the server and instance name (**SQL01\INSTANCE01**).

3. Select Windows Authentication from the Authentication drop-down menu and then click the Connect button.

4. A connection to the database engine is made. If the Object Explorer pane is not visible, press the F8 button.

5. From within the Object Explorer pane, expand Security and select the Logins node.

6. Double-click the Test.User1 login created previously in the section "Creating SQL Authentication Logins."

7. Select the Securables page; then click the Add button.

8. Select All Objects of the Type; then click OK.

9. Enable Endpoints and then click OK.

10. Select TSQL Local Machine from the Securables list.

11. Select the Deny column for the Connect permission.

12. Figure 13.7 shows how the Securables option page should look for the login. Click OK to change the permissions.

Open another instance of the SQL Server Management Studio from the test server SQL01 and attempt to authenticate as Test.User1. Because of the deny permission created, an attempt to authenticate as Test.User1 should fail even though the login is active.

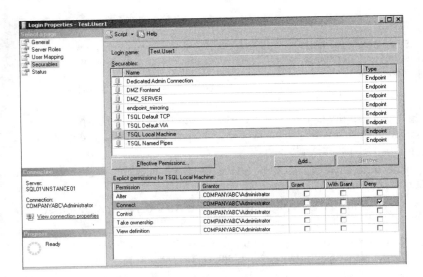

FIGURE 13.7
Login endpoint permissions.

> **Note**
>
> Endpoint permissions are associated with the actual name of the endpoint. This can be a problem when an endpoint is configured for dynamic ports because the name changes when the port changes. As a result, the security associated with the endpoint is lost.
>
> As a best practice, avoid using endpoints with dynamic ports, specifically when endpoint permissions are used.

You can create a new endpoint only through TSQL statements. The CREATE, ALTER, and DROP ENDPOINT statements have many options; for additional information, see the SQL Server 2005 Books Online.

The following code shows how to create a TCP endpoint called DMZ Frontend that listens on port 48620:

```
CREATE ENDPOINT [DMZ Frontend]
AS TCP (LISTENER_PORT=48620) FOR TSQL()
GO
```

The following warning message is displayed when the endpoint is created:

```
Creation of a TSQL endpoint will result in the revocation
of any 'Public' connect permissions on the 'TSQL Default
TCP' endpoint. If 'Public' access is desired on this
endpoint, reapply this permission using 'GRANT CONNECT ON
ENDPOINT::[TSQL Default TCP] to [public]'.
```

If necessary, you must add the public role to the default endpoint by running the command identified in the warning message.

You can use the following TSQL statement to allow the user Test.User1 to connect to the newly created endpoint:

```
USE MASTER
GRANT CONNECT ON ENDPOINT::[DMZ Frontend] to [Test.User1]
GO
```

Securing Other SQL Server Components

It is considered best practice to run SQL Server component services in the security context of an account that has the fewest possible rights. For flexibility and ease of management, this account should be a limited domain user when possible.

The following sections provide an overview of the security administration that should be considered for the different components.

Administering Analysis Services Security

Analysis Services is a component of SQL Server 2005 that provides a foundation for business intelligence applications through online analytical processing (OLAP) and data mining functionality. Similar to the Database Engine component, Analysis Services security management is tightly integrated with Windows authentication. Therefore, users or groups can be granted authorization at a macro or micro level.

From a security perspective, it is a best practice to first harden an Analysis Services installation and then grant access to the server and database objects using a role-based strategy. Hardening concepts for Analysis Services, such as using the configuration tools, are covered in Chapter 12.

When you are connected to the Analysis Services, several new security administrative elements are exposed, including a set of roles with Analysis Services specific permission used to control access to Analysis Services securable objects. These granular permissions can then be set on the Analysis Services Database, Data Sources, Cubes, Cells, Dimensions, Attributes, Mining Structures, and Mining Model levels.

See Chapter 2, "Administering SQL Server 2005 Analysis Services," for additional in-depth information on working with Analysis Services security.

Administering Reporting Services Security

SQL Server 2005 Reporting Services (SSRS) provides an enterprise class reporting infrastructure by exposing multiple extensible components through numerous user and programmatic interfaces. SSRS uses these components to retrieve data from a variety of different sources, turn the data into a readable report, and deliver the data to specified targets. Targets can include a web browser for interactive reporting or an email account when report subscriptions are configured.

SSRS provides access to the site through predefined noncustomizable tasks; each task is assigned to a customizable role. The role can be classified as either an item-level role or a system-level role. For example, an item-level role called Browser is available by default. This role can view reports, view resources, view folders, manage personal subscriptions, and view models. A user or group assigned to this role is subsequently able to perform each of these tasks. Although the tasks cannot be modified, the roles and the application of roles on SSRS objects can be adjusted to secure the environment.

Caution

When you add a user to a group that is already part of a role assignment, you must reset Internet Information Services (IIS) for the new role assignment to take effect for that user. This can be accomplished with the IISRESET command.

The difference between item and system roles is the tasks available for the roles. System roles can be assigned only tasks that relate to systemwide function, whereas item roles can be assigned only tasks that can be performed on items, such as reports and data sources.

See Chapter 3, "Administering SQL Server 2005 Reporting Services," for additional in-depth information on working with Reporting Services security.

Administering Notification Services Security

SQL Server 2005 Notification Services provides a framework for creating notification applications. A notification application can generate and send immediate or scheduled messages to intended targets based on customizable subscription criteria.

Notification Services provides developers with the ability to configure components to run on different servers or to host components within other applications. It is important to communicate with the developers to determine what service accounts are being used for each component to ensure the correct permissions are assigned.

Notification Services uses a role-based security model to help ensure only the required amount of access is granted to each component used in the Notification Services solution.

See Chapter 4, "Administering SQL Server 2005 Notification Services," for additional in-depth information on working with Notification Services security.

Administering SQL Server 2005 Integration Services

The SQL Server 2005 Integration Services (SSIS) component provides services for the extraction, transformation, and loading of data. The SSIS supports a number of security features designed to protect the packages from unauthorized execution, modification, sensitive information, and even the entire contents of the packages.

The SSIS has three database roles for controlling access to packages. They roughly fall into the categories of administrator, user, and operator. If more granularity is needed in the rights assignment, user-defined roles can be created.

Protection levels are set on packages when they are created in the Business Intelligence Development Studio or the wizards. These protection levels prevent the unauthorized execution or modification of packages. Protection levels can be updated on packages when they are imported into the SSIS Package Store.

See Chapter 5, "Administering SQL Server 2005 Integration Services," for additional in-depth information on working with Analysis Services security.

Summary

Administering SQL Server security is a key task bestowed upon database administrators. Understanding and leveraging the different security features associated with the SQL Server 2005 database engine and the different SQL Server 2005 components is essential to ensuring the integrity of the environment.

A properly implemented and well-maintained security model helps reduce the likelihood of sensitive data exposure, while increasing the overall scalability and reliability of the environment.

Best Practices

The following best practices can be taken from this chapter:

- To most effectively manage security, prepare and harden the environment. See Chapter 12 for additional information.

- When administering SQL Server security, follow the principle of least privilege. This basically means giving only the necessary permissions to the different user and service accounts needed to accomplish the task.

- Enable only communication protocols that are necessary and allow only specific CONNECT permissions on endpoints.

- Leverage Active Directory to establish access and role-based security groups for accessing SQL Server resources.

- When you are using Active Directory for role-based access, you cannot assign a default schema to the user accounts. Ensure the security model accounts for this limitation.

- All database users belong to the public database role by default. Avoid using the public database role when assigning permissions unless absolutely necessary.

- The schema provides a way to manage security on groups of objects with a granular level of control. Use the schema to group related objects together—that is, objects that can have the same permissions given to the same principals.

- If possible, always use Windows Authentication mode to leverage Windows authentication protocols, such as NTLM and Kerberos, along with domain-level password policies.

- If you use SQL authentication, enable the options to enforce the local security policies and implement encrypted authentication.

- Create database users without logins in SQL Server 2005. This approach can be used as an alternative to application roles in the database.

- Endpoint permissions are associated with the actual name of the endpoint. This can be a problem when an endpoint is configured for dynamic ports because the name changes when the port changes. As a result, the security associated with the endpoint is lost. Avoid using endpoints with dynamic ports, specifically when endpoint permissions are used.

CHAPTER 14

Encrypting SQL Server Data and Communications

The data stored in Microsoft SQL Server 2005 can be both valuable and confidential. The information stored in databases in SQL Server could be medical histories, incomes, or company trade secrets. This information needs to be protected against unauthorized access.

Many of the controls presented in this book have been *access* controls—that is, controls that determine who has authorization to access what. A determined hacker can circumvent these controls through various means, such as sniffing network traffic, going dumpster diving for backup tapes, or making inference attacks.

A more sophisticated approach to control is to use an in-depth defense strategy, wherein there are multiple layers of defense. If a hacker breaches one layer, other layers underneath provide protection. In addition to the access-based controls, encryption provides another layer of protection.

This chapter shows how to encrypt data both in the database and over the wire to prevent a hacker from seeing valuable data.

Encryption in SQL

The confidentiality of data in your SQL Server system can be compromised. A hacker, as shown in Figure 14.1, can eavesdrop on communications between the client and server. The hacker might also obtain a database export or a backup tape of the database.

FIGURE 14.1
Unprotected client/server traffic.

To protect against these potential attacks, SQL Server 2005 allows you, as database administrator, to encrypt the data in the database and the network communications. Encryption allows you to protect the confidentiality of data during storage and transmission, as shown in Figure 14.2.

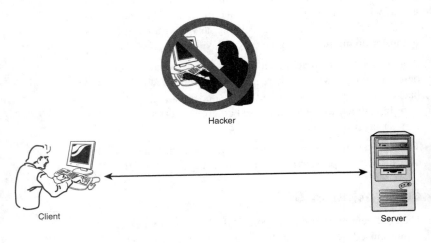

FIGURE 14.2
Encrypted client/server traffic.

Encryption does not prevent an attacker from capturing the data. Rather, it prevents the attacker from understanding what that data means. For example, if confidential salary information is stored in a database, it is open to potential discovery by a hacker. If the hacker can capture the value 100000, it is reasonably clear what the salary is. Suppose, instead, the hacker captures this value:

```
0x00057978740EBC4882D182DE0BC8943401000000B0D27479031
02AD4696BC980217970DAD5B4C38314DB45D065079C9B43F922D0
A04517C38EC8CA9B5CD19702DEE0A042
```

This character string makes it much more difficult to understand what the salary figure is. In this case, it is the encrypted version of the value 100000.

This chapter shows how to encrypt data both while in storage in the database and while in transit over the network between the client and server.

Encryption Hierarchy

SQL Server 2005 has an encryption hierarchy to secure the data. The various levels are

- **Windows Level**—The highest level of the hierarchy is the Windows operating system. This level uses Windows DP API to encrypt and protect the next level.

- **SQL Server Level**—This level contains the *service master key*, which is protected by the Windows Level. The service master key is used to protect the next level.

- **Database Level**—This level contains the *database master key* and the remaining keys. The database master key encrypts and protects the certificates, symmetric keys, and asymmetric keys within the database.

The encryption hierarchy provides a scalable and granular mechanism for protecting the data within the server and databases. It allows for multiple database owners to coexist on the same server without compromising the other databases.

Service Master Key

The service master key is the root of all encryption within SQL Server 2005. This key is generated the first time it is needed by the server. This typically occurs when it is needed to encrypt another key.

This key is accessible only by the Windows service account.

Database Master Key

The database master key is used to secure the keys and certificates used to encrypt data. This key is manually created for each database.

If you don't want a database master key, you can encrypt the keys and certificates with a password rather than the database master key. This can be a useful alternative to prevent the owner of a database from gaining access to encrypted data in highly secure environments.

Keys and Certificates

Asymmetric and symmetric keys are used to encrypt keys, certificates, and data. Each has its own specific uses and pros and cons.

Symmetric keys are relatively straightforward. The keys are used to both encrypt and decrypt. The encryption is relatively fast, so symmetric keys are useful for encrypting large quantities of data. However, symmetric keys need to be shared, and this can make them difficult to use.

Asymmetric keys are composed of a public and private key pair. These pairs of keys are used to both encrypt and decrypt, but with a twist. Each key can decrypt what the other key encrypted, but not its own. Asymmetric encryption is resource intensive, so it is not suitable for encrypting large volumes of data. However, it is uniquely suited to encrypting symmetric keys and sharing them.

Certificates are used to vouch for the identity of an entity presenting a public key. In effect, a *certificate authority (CA)* issues a certificate that presents a public key and an identity that a third party can trust. Certificates can be issued by well-known third-party CAs such as VeriSign, by private CAs on Windows Server 2003 servers, or they can be self-signed certificates issued by SQL Server instances.

Third-party certificates are typically expensive, private certificates require additional configuration, and self-signed certificates are not as secure.

Encryption Algorithms

SQL Server 2005 supports a variety of encryption algorithms. These algorithms are used to secure the data, keys, and certificates.

The algorithms supported by SQL Server 2005 are

- DES
- Triple DES
- RC2
- RC4
- 128-bit RC4
- DESX
- 128-bit AES
- 192-bit AES
- 256-bit AES

The AES families of algorithms are not supported by Windows XP or Windows 2000.

Choosing an algorithm can be a complex undertaking because it requires balancing the strength of the algorithms, the resources required to use the algorithms, and the potential weaknesses of the algorithms.

Although these are all very valid considerations for choosing an algorithm, most organizations are, in reality, not encrypting data at all. Thus, using any of the preceding algorithms is a tremendous improvement in the level of security. Which particular algorithm is chosen matters less than just using one.

In the examples in this book, we used the tried-and-true Triple DES algorithm. It provides a good balance between performance and security.

Securing the Data Storage

While data is in the database, it is vulnerable to being read by a hacker who can elevate his privileges or gain access to backup tapes. To secure the data that is stored in the database, you can encrypt the values to provide an additional layer of security.

Creating a Database for Testing

To facilitate your running the same exercises, these exercises use data from the SQL samples. See the appendix for instructions on installing the samples. Before starting, you need to create the database and import the data.

> **Note**
>
> If the Customer database already exists from previous exercises, delete the database prior to completing the exercises in this chapter.

To create the database, follow these steps:

1. Open SQL Server Management Studio.
2. Connect to the Database Engine of the SQL Server.
3. Expand the Databases folder in the Object Explorer.
4. In the SQL Server Management Studio, create a new database named **Customer**.
5. Right-click the Customer database and select Tasks, Import Data.
6. Click Next.

7. Select the Flat File Source as the data source.

8. Click the Browse button and select the Customers.txt file in
   C:\Program Files\Microsoft SQL Server\90\Samples\Integration
   Services\Package Samples\ExecuteSQLStatementsInLoop Sample\
   Data Files\.

9. Click Open.

10. Check the Column names in the first data row check box.

11. Click Next.

12. Click Next to accept tables and views.

13. Select the Customer database if not selected already and click Next.

14. Click Next.

15. Click Next to Execute immediately and not save the package.

15. Click Finish to run the import.

16. Click Close.

The basic database is now ready for the encryption exercises in this chapter.

Setting Up for Encryption

When the database is created, there is no database master key initially. You
need to create this key for each database.

To create a database master key, open a query window and execute the
following query:

```
USE Customer;
GO
CREATE MASTER KEY ENCRYPTION BY
       PASSWORD = 'The secret password.';
GO
```

This query prepares the database for encrypting the data. Clearly, the secret
password could use some additional complexity.

Note

As stated earlier, the service master key is created when the SQL Server
instance is installed, so you do not need to create it manually.

Create the Encryption Certificate

Now you need to create a certificate to protect the keys that will actually be used to encrypt the data itself.

To create the certificate, execute the following query:

```
USE Customer;
GO
CREATE CERTIFICATE Customer01
      WITH SUBJECT = 'Customer';
GO
```

After creating the certificate, you can create and protect the symmetric key. This key will be used to encrypt the data. Using a symmetric key allows the data to be encrypted rapidly, whereas encrypting it with a certificate provides strong protection.

To create the symmetric key, execute the following query:

```
USE Customer;
Go
CREATE SYMMETRIC KEY YearlyIncome_Key_01
      WITH ALGORITHM = TRIPLE_DES
      ENCRYPTION BY CERTIFICATE Customer01;
GO
```

We chose the Triple DES algorithm due to its security and compatibility.

Encrypting the Data

With the database now prepared, the next step is to encrypt a column of data. In this case, the data to be protected is the YearlyIncome column.

To encrypt the YearlyIncome column, execute the following query:

```
USE [Customer];
GO


ALTER TABLE dbo.Customers
      ADD EncryptedYearlyIncome varbinary(128);
GO


OPEN SYMMETRIC KEY YearlyIncome_Key_01
      DECRYPTION BY CERTIFICATE Customer01;
UPDATE dbo.Customers SET EncryptedYearlyIncome =
```

```
        EncryptByKey(Key_GUID('YearlyIncome_Key_01'),
⮕YearlyIncome);
GO
```

Note that the query adds a new column named EncryptedYearlyIncome of type varbinary to hold the encrypted values.

> **Note**
>
> The Customers table still retains the original column named YearlyIncome with the unencrypted data. In a real-world situation, you would need to drop the column to protect the data. The query to do this is ALTER TABLE Customer.dbo.Customers DROP COLUMN YearlyIncome; GO.
>
> We did not drop this column in the examples to allow comparisons and to allow the column to be re-encrypted.

Using Encrypted Data

The encrypted data is protected but can't be used directly. To select the data with no decryption, execute the following query:

```
SELECT EncryptedYearlyIncome
        FROM Customer.dbo.Customers;
GO
```

Rather than a nice set of Yearly Income numbers, the SELECT query returns a list of hexadecimal characters, as shown in Figure 14.3.

This result is good because it means that a hacker would not be able to discern the customer's yearly incomes. However, valid users need a way to see the actual values and cannot use the column of data directly. To actually use the data, you must decrypt it when selecting it.

To select the data with decryption, execute the following query:

```
OPEN SYMMETRIC KEY YearlyIncome_Key_01
        DECRYPTION BY CERTIFICATE Customer01;
GO
SELECT CONVERT(nvarchar, DecryptByKey(EncryptedYearlyIncome))
        AS 'Decrypted Yearly Income' FROM Customer.dbo.Customers;
GO
```

This query shows the actual values of the Yearly Income in unencrypted form, as shown in Figure 14.4.

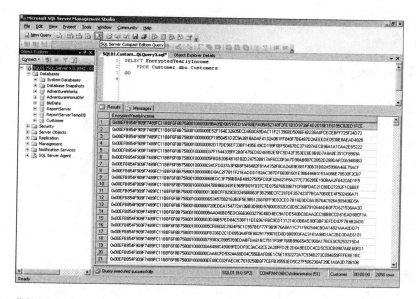

FIGURE 14.3
Encrypted data.

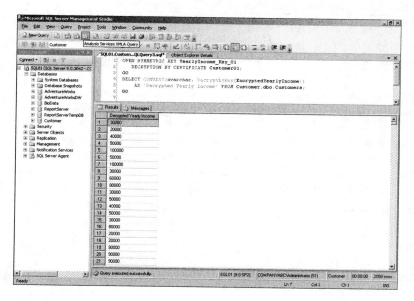

FIGURE 14.4
Decrypted data.

The data is now secured while stored in the database and would be protected in backups.

Attacking the Encryption

Although the data is protected against being viewed, a hacker might be able to subvert the control of the data. One way to accomplish this is to replace the encrypted value with another encrypted value. This is referred to as an *inference attack*.

Consider the two rows in the Customer database shown in Table 14.1.

Table 14.1   **View of Two Customer Records**

Name	Occupation	Yearly Income
Craig Dominguez	Management	100,000
Meghan Gomez	Manual	10,000

The Yearly Income values are encrypted, so a hacker who subverts the access controls might be able to gather the information about the rows shown in Table 14.2.

Table 14.2   **Compromised View of Two Customer Records**

Name	Occupation	Yearly Income
Craig Dominguez	Management	Encrypted Value 1
Meghan Gomez	Manual	Encrypted Value 2

Although the hacker cannot determine the yearly income of either, he can make some assumptions based on the occupations of the two. Without any prior knowledge, a hacker could safely assume that Mr. Dominguez earns more than Ms. Gomez. Using that basic assumption, the hacker can elevate the yearly income of Ms. Gomez simply by moving the encrypted value from Mr. Dominguez without ever needing to know what the value is. In effect, the hacker can elevate the yearly income to $100,000.

To demonstrate this hack, execute the following query to hack the database:

```
USE Customer;
GO


UPDATE Customer.dbo.Customers
SET EncryptedYearlyIncome =
        (SELECT EncryptedYearlyIncome FROM Customer.dbo.Customers
```

```
            WHERE EmailAddress = 'cdominguez@fabrikam.com')
            WHERE EmailAddress = 'mgomez@fabrikam.com';
GO
```

This query copies the Encrypted Value 1 in Table 14.2 over Encrypted Value 2 in the table, in effect replacing Ms. Gomez's income with Mr. Dominguez's income. To verify that the hack was successful, execute the following query:

```
USE Customer;
Go
OPEN SYMMETRIC KEY YearlyIncome_Key_01
     DECRYPTION BY CERTIFICATE Customer01;
GO
SELECT CONVERT(nvarchar, DecryptByKey(EncryptedYearlyIncome))
          AS 'Decrypted Yearly Income'
          FROM dbo.Customers where EmailAddress =
'mgomez@fabrikam.com';
GO
```

The result returned is 100000, indicating that the yearly income for Ms. Gomez was elevated to management-level pay. Good for Ms. Gomez, but bad for the company!

You can foil these types of attacks by using an authenticator when encrypting and decrypting the data.

Using an Authenticator

An *authenticator*, also known as a "salt value" in cryptography, is another column value that is unique to the row that is used in conjunction with the key to secure the data being encrypted. This prevents a hacker from moving an encrypted value between rows.

To encrypt the YearlyIncome column with an authenticator (in this case, the EmailAddress), execute the following query:

```
USE Customer;
GO
OPEN SYMMETRIC KEY YearlyIncome_Key_01
     DECRYPTION BY CERTIFICATE Customer01;
UPDATE dbo.Customers
     SET EncryptedYearlyIncome = EncryptByKey(Key_GUID
          ('YearlyIncome_Key_01'),
          YearlyIncome, 1, convert (varbinary, EmailAddress));
GO
```

Note that the preceding query overwrites the data in the EncryptedYearlyIncome column with freshly encrypted data from the YearlyIncome column.

Verify that the EncryptedYearlyIncome column is still encrypted. To view the results, execute the following query:

```
USE Customer;
GO
SELECT EncryptedYearlyIncome AS 'Encrypted Yearly Income'
       FROM dbo.Customers;
GO
```

The values should be displayed as long hexadecimal numbers, similar to those shown in Figure 14.3. The next step is to see whether the hacker substitution will succeed. Execute the hack again using the following query:

```
USE Customer;
GO

UPDATE Customer.dbo.Customers
SET EncryptedYearlyIncome =
       (SELECT EncryptedYearlyIncome FROM Customer.dbo.Customers
       WHERE EmailAddress = 'cdominguez@fabrikam.com')
       WHERE EmailAddress = 'mgomez@fabrikam.com';
GO
```

The preceding query is the same query that was executed before and successfully hacked the database. Note that the value is still replaced. The question is whether the value will be accepted by the application or the hack will be foiled.

To verify that the hacker was foiled, execute the following query:

```
USE Customer;
Go
OPEN SYMMETRIC KEY YearlyIncome_Key_01
     DECRYPTION BY CERTIFICATE Customer01;
GO
SELECT CONVERT(nvarchar, DecryptByKey(EncryptedYearlyIncome))
       AS 'Decrypted Yearly Income'
       FROM dbo.Customers where EmailAddress =
➥'mgomez@fabrikam.com';
GO
```

Now the decrypted Yearly Income value displays NULL, indicating that the decryption failed and the hacker was not successful in replacing Ms. Gomez's yearly income.

To verify that an authorized user can still access the data correctly, execute the following query:

```
USE Customer;
GO
OPEN SYMMETRIC KEY YearlyIncome_Key_01
     DECRYPTION BY CERTIFICATE Customer01;
GO
SELECT CONVERT(nvarchar, DecryptByKey(EncryptedYearlyIncome, 1,
       convert (varbinary, EmailAddress)))
       AS 'Decrypted Yearly Income'
       FROM dbo.Customers;
GO
```

The Yearly Income values should be displayed for all but Ms. Gomez.

Backing Up the Keys

The service master keys and database keys are critical values that need to be preserved. Losing these keys can result in the loss of any data that is encrypted. Backing up the service master and database master keys allows you to recover the data in case of problems.

To back up the service master key, execute the following query:

```
BACKUP SERVICE MASTER KEY TO FILE =
➥'c:\ServiceMasterKeyBackup.dat'
       ENCRYPTION BY PASSWORD = 'SecretPassword';
GO
```

To back up the database master key, execute the following query for the Customer database:

```
USE Customer;
GO
BACKUP MASTER KEY TO FILE =
➥'c:\CustomerDatabaseMasterKeyBackup.dat'
       ENCRYPTION BY PASSWORD = 'SecretPassword';
GO
```

You repeat this query for each database master key that you need to back up.

You should store both key backup files offsite in case of server problems. In the event of a problem with the keys, the service master key and database master key can be restored from the files.

Securing the Transmissions

Note that the data is encrypted while in the database. However, when the client selects the data, it is unencrypted. The data needs to be protected while being transmitted as well as stored.

SQL Server 2005 can use SSL certificate-based encryption to encrypt all communications between the client and server.

Hacking the Transmission

To understand the problem, you can use the Network Monitor tools for this example to view the contents of the network traffic between the SQL Server and client. This tool is available in Windows Server 2003 Add/Remove Windows Components and can be installed on SQL Server. The examples in this section assume that the SQL Server Workstation Components are installed on the client.

Start the Network Monitor on the server and then execute the following query from the SQL Server Management Studio on the client:

```
USE Customer;
Go
OPEN SYMMETRIC KEY YearlyIncome_Key_01
     DECRYPTION BY CERTIFICATE Customer01;
GO
SELECT FirstName, LastName, BirthDate,
       CONVERT(nvarchar, DecryptByKey(EncryptedYearlyIncome, 1,
       convert (varbinary, EmailAddress)))
       AS 'Decrypted Yearly Income'
       FROM dbo.Customers where EmailAddress =
➥'cdominguez@fabrikam.com';
GO
```

The query returns the information shown in Table 14.3.

Table 14.3   **Query Results**

FirstName	LastName	BirthDate	Decrypted Yearly Income
Craig	Dominguez	7/20/1970	100000

This result is clearly confidential information that should be protected from the prying eyes of a hacker. It even includes the yearly income information that was encrypted in the Customer database to prevent unauthorized disclosure.

Figure 14.5 shows the results of the network capture of the preceding query. The highlighted frame in the figure contains the data sent from SQL Server (SQL01) to the client (172.16.2.1). The circled section of the figure shows the information that a hacker was able to capture simply by listening in on the network transmission. The information includes the name, birth date, and yearly income. Although the information is not formatted in a pretty manner, it is all there for the hacker to see.

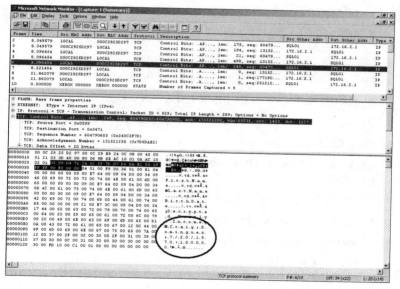

FIGURE 14.5
Hacked data transmission.

Most troubling is the fact that the information that was encrypted in the database is transmitted unencrypted over the wire. The reason is that the query decrypts the information at the server side prior to transmission. The bottom line is that encrypting the columns in the database does nothing to protect the data while it is being transmitted over the network.

To protect data transmissions, you need to encrypt the connections.

Configuring Server-Initiated Encryption

SQL Server 2005 can be configured to require SSL-based encryption. Configuring the ForceEncryption setting of SQL Server to Yes forces all client/server communications to be encrypted. By default, the ForceEncryption setting is set to No, so SQL Server client/server communications are not protected.

> **Note**
>
> The SQL Server 2005 login process is always encrypted, regardless of the ForceEncryption setting of the server. This ensures that login and password combinations are not compromised.

To configure the server to require encrypted connections, follow these steps:

1. Launch the SQL Server Configuration Manager.
2. Expand the SQL Server 2005 Network Configuration.
3. Right-click on Protocols for MSSQLSERVER and select Properties.
4. On the Flags tab, change the ForceEncryption pull-down to Yes.
5. Click OK to save the setting.
6. Click OK on the dialog box indicating the service needs to be restarted.
7. Select the SQL Server 2005 Services folder.
8. Select the SQL Server (MSSQLSERVER) service.
9. Restart the SQL Server service.

The connections to the SQL Server 2005 server are now encrypted.

Hacking the Transmission: The Sequel

Now that the server has been configured to force encryption of the network transmissions, the hacker should not be able to see the contents of the network transmissions.

To verify that the transmissions are protected, start the Network Monitor on the server and then execute the following query from the SQL Server Management Studio on the client:

```
USE Customer;
Go
OPEN SYMMETRIC KEY YearlyIncome_Key_01
        DECRYPTION BY CERTIFICATE Customer01;
GO
SELECT FirstName, LastName, BirthDate,
        CONVERT(nvarchar, DecryptByKey(EncryptedYearlyIncome, 1,
        convert (varbinary, EmailAddress)))
        AS 'Decrypted Yearly Income'
        FROM dbo.Customers where EmailAddress =
➥'cdominguez@fabrikam.com';
GO
```

Figure 14.6 shows the results of the network capture of the preceding query. The highlighted frame in the figure is the frame that contains the data sent from SQL Server (SQL01) to the client (172.16.2.1). The circled section of the figure shows the information that a hacker was able to capture. The information is now a jumble of strange characters and protected from the hacker's prying eyes.

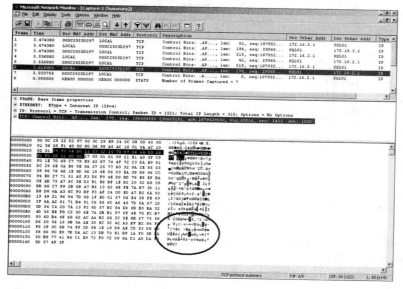

FIGURE 14.6
Encrypted data transmission.

Notice that the frames are a bit different. The encrypted frame length is 270 versus 249 for the unencrypted frame. Encryption carries some overhead both in the size of the frames and in the effort that the server and client have to make in processing the encryption.

Using Certificates

The encryption used until now in the chapter has been based on self-signed certificates. These certificates are generated when SQL Server does not have a certificate provisioned.

Self-signed certificates are vulnerable to certain attacks, most critically man-in-the-middle attacks. This means that without an independent verification of the identity of the SQL Server, there is no way to be sure that the communication is not really between a nefarious third party posing as the server to the client. Note that the communication is encrypted, as shown in Figure 14.7, but the encryption is between the hacker and the client and server.

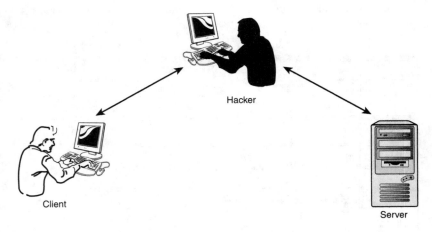

FIGURE 14.7
Man-in-the-middle attack.

Neither the client nor the server detects the ruse because there is no independent third-party certificate authority to confirm that the certificate used to encrypt the transmission is trusted.

This attack is thwarted by using a third-party certificate to verify the identity of the SQL Server. When the hacker attempts to insert himself between the client and server, as shown in Figure 14.8, the attack is detected by both the client and server.

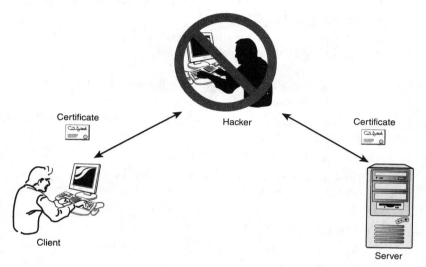

FIGURE 14.8
Third-party certificate protection.

The following sections detail how to provision and configure third-party certificates for SQL Server 2005.

Provisioning a Server Certificate

The first step in protecting the data transmissions with a third-party certificate is to provision the certificate, which entails obtaining and installing the certificate.

If you decide to create a certificate authority and provision certificates in-house (in effect being a third-party CA), you should follow the instructions shown here. These steps assume that the CA has already been installed in the environment and that the web enrollment interface will be used. For steps on how to create a Windows certificate authority, see the appendix of this book (online).

The certificate requirements for SQL Server 2005 SSL encryption include

- The certificate must be in the local computer certificate store or the current user certificate store.

- The current system time must be in the certificate valid range of dates.

- The certificate must be meant for server authentication; that is, the Enhanced Key Usage property of the certificate specifies Server Authentication (1.3.6.1.5.5.7.3.1).

- The common name (CN) must be the same as the fully qualified domain name (FQDN) of the server computer.

If these conditions are not met, the certificate will not be available in the SQL Server 2005 provisioning tool.

To provision (install) a certificate on the server from a Windows certificate authority, follow these steps:

1. On the SQL Server, launch Internet Explorer.

2. Enter the address **http://dc1.companyabc.com/certsrv** to access the Certificate Service Web Request site. This assumes that the certificate services were installed on the dc1.companyabc.com server.

3. Click on the Download a CA Certificate link.

4. Click on the Install This CA Certificate Chain link to configure SQL Server to trust the CA.

5. Click Yes to continue.

6. Click Yes to install the CA certificate.

7. Enter the address **http://dc1.companyabc.com/certsrv** to access the Certificate Service Web Request site again.

8. Click on Request a Certificate to request a certificate for SQL Server to encrypt data transmissions.

9. Click on Advanced Certificate Request.

10. Click on Create and Submit a Request to This CA.

11. Select Web Server from the Certificate Template pull-down.

12. In the Identifying Information section, enter the FQDN of the server in the Name field. In this case, the FQDN of the server is **sql01. companyabc.com**.

Note

It is very important to enter the fully qualified domain name (FQDN) in the Name field. If this name does not match the server FQDN, the certificate will be unavailable to select later in the process.

13. Fill in the other identifying information as appropriate.

14. In the Key Options section, check the Store Certificate in the Local Computer Certificate Store box.

15. Click on the Submit button

16. Click Yes to request the certificate.

17. Click Install This Certificate to install it in the local store.

18. Click Yes to confirm the certificate install.

The Windows CA certificate has been installed and is ready to use.

If the certificate is obtained from a third party such as VeriSign and is delivered as a file, follow these steps to import the certificate into the SQL Server certificate store:

1. Click Start, Run; type MMC; and click OK.

2. In the Microsoft Management Console, on the File menu, click Add/Remove Snap-in.

3. In the Add/Remove Snap-in dialog box, click Add.

4. In the Add Standalone Snap-in dialog box, click Certificates and then click Add.

5. In the Certificates Snap-in dialog box, click Computer Account and then click Finish.

6. In the Add Standalone Snap-in dialog box, click Close.

7. In the Add/Remove Snap-in dialog box, click OK.

8. In the Certificates Snap-in, expand Certificates, expand Personal, right-click Certificates, point to All Tasks, and then click Import.

9. Complete the Certificate Import Wizard to add a certificate to the computer and close the MMC.

The third-party certificate is now installed and ready to use.

Whichever the origin of the certificate, the next step is to configure SQL Server 2005 to use the certificate instead of the self-signed certificate it uses by default.

SQL Server Certificate Configuration

When the certificate is stored in the certificate store, you can configure SQL Server 2005 to use it. You do this with the SQL Server Configuration Manager tool.

The steps to configure SQL Server to use the certificate are

1. Launch the SQL Server Configuration Manager.

2. Expand the SQL Server 2005 Network Configuration.

3. Right-click Protocols for MSSQLSERVER and select Properties.

4. Select the Certificate tab.

5. Select the certificate from the drop-down for the Certificate box.

6. Click OK to save the settings.

7. Click OK to acknowledge that the service needs to be restarted.

8. Restart the SQL Server (MSSQLSERVER) service to use the certificate.

The SQL Server is now protected against man-in-the-middle attacks with the CA certificate. However, the clients need to be configured to use the server certificate and trust the CA if an internal CA was used.

Client Certificate Configuration

The certificate is stored in the SQL Server certificate store and needs to be exported so that it can be shared. To export the server certificate, follow these steps:

1. Click Start, Run; type MMC; and click OK.

2. In the MMC, on the File menu, click Add/Remove Snap-in.

3. In the Add/Remove Snap-in dialog box, click Add.

4. In the Add Standalone Snap-in dialog box, click Certificates and then click Add.

5. In the Certificates Snap-in dialog box, click Computer account and then click Finish.

6. In the Add Standalone Snap-in dialog box, click Close.

7. In the Add/Remove Snap-in dialog box, click OK.

8. From the Certificates MMC snap-in, locate the certificate in the Certificates\Personal folder.

9. Right-click the Certificate, select All Tasks, and click Export.

10. Complete the Certificate Export Wizard, saving the certificate file in a convenient location.

The certificate, stored in the file, is now ready to be used by the client. To import the certificate into the client computer store, follow these steps:

1. Copy the exported certificate file to the client computer.

2. In the Certificates snap-in on the client, expand Certificates.

3. Expand the Personal folder.

4. Right-click on Personal, select All Tasks, and click Import.

5. Complete the Certificate Import Wizard.

The certificate is now ready to use. However, if you used a private CA to issue the certificate, you need to add the CA to the trusted CA list. For a Windows CA, use the following steps to do that:

1. On the client, launch Internet Explorer.

2. Enter the address `http://dc1.companyabc.com/certsrv` to access the Certificate Service Web Request site. This assumes that the certificate services were installed on the dc1.companyabc.com server.

3. Click on the Download a CA Certificate link.

4. Click on the Install This CA Certificate Chain link to configure the SQL Server to trust the CA.

5. Click Yes to continue.

6. Click Yes to install the CA certificate.

The Windows Certificate Authority is now trusted by the client.

Client-Initiated Encryption

In some cases, there might not be the need or the option to configure the server to force encryption for all clients. Perhaps only a few connections need to be encrypted or there is no administrative control over the configuration of SQL Server.

To configure the client to request encrypted connections using the ODBC, follow these steps:

1. Select Start, Control Panel.

2. Double-click on Administrative Tools to open the folder.

3. Double-click on the Data Sources (ODBC) applet.

4. Select the System DSN tab.

5. Click Add to add a new data source.

6. Select either SQL Server or SQL Native Client.

7. Click Finish to launch the configuration of the data source.

8. Enter a name for the data source, in this case `Customer Database`.

9. Enter the name of the SQL Server, in this case `SQL01`.

10. Click Next.

11. Click Next to leave the default authentication.

12. Check the Change the Default Database box.

13. Select the Customer database from the drop-down.

14. Click Next.

15. Check the Use Strong Encryption for Data box to encrypt the client/server traffic.

16. Click Finish.

17. Click Test Data Source to verify the settings.

18. Click OK three times to close out the settings.

The connection now forces itself to use strong encryption regardless of the SQL Server setting. This option does require that a certificate issued by a trusted third-party be used.

SQL Server Management Studio

The SQL Server Management Studio is a potential source of exploits itself. Given the level of communications with data, code, and passwords, a hacker can discover a ton of information from the traffic generated by the SQL Server Management Studio tool. This is the case when the tool is loaded on a client computer rather than the server itself.

Fortunately, the communications from the SQL Server Management Studio on a client to SQL Server can easily be encrypted as well. The steps to do this are

1. On the Object Explorer toolbar, click Connect.

2. Select a service, in this case the Database Engine.

3. Select a server, in this case SQL01.

4. Click on the Options button.

5. Check the Encrypt Connection box.

6. Click Connect to connect.

Now all communications between the SQL Server Management Studio and SQL Server are protected with encryption.

Summary

Confidential data is at risk if not protected by the appropriate measures. Access controls are not enough to secure confidential data, and an in-depth defense strategy is needed. A critical layer in this strategy is encryption.

Encryption is an effective method of protecting Microsoft SQL Server 2005 data, both while in the database and while on the wire. Encrypting data is an easy and straightforward process in SQL Server 2005.

The sections in this chapter illustrate how to encrypt data while in the database and how to encrypt data during transmission. Given the ease with which data can be compromised by a determined hacker, it is important to protect the data with encryption using the methods outlined in this chapter.

Best Practices

Some important best practices from the chapter include

- Encrypt client/server data transmissions.

- Use a third-party certificate to prevent man-in-the-middle attacks.

- Encrypt confidential data in the database to protect the data on disk and in backups.

- Use an authenticator when encrypting data to protect against inference hacking.

- Force the clients to use strong encryption when SQL Server cannot be configured to always require encryption.

- Use self-signed certificates rather than nothing at all to secure data.

- Configure SQL Server Management Studio to use encryption when connecting to servers over the network.

PART IV

SQL Server 2005 Overview

Chapters 15-22 and the appendix (Parts IV-VI) are located online. Go to www.informit.com/title/9780672329562 to register your book and receive this content.

The index that follows this page intentionally begins on page 837 and includes the online chapters.

IN THIS PART

T

W

X–Z